A CENTURY
OF STORIES
NEW HANOVER COUNTY PUBLIC LIBRARY
1906-2006

BUILDING HOUSES OUT OF CHICKEN LEGS

BUILDING
HOUSES
OUT OF
CHICKEN
LEGS

BLACK WOMEN, FOOD, AND POWER

PSYCHE A. WILLIAMS-FORSON

THE UNIVERSITY OF NORTH CAROLINA PRESS Chapel Hill

The paper in this book meets the
guidelines for permanence and durability
of the Committee on Production
Guidelines for Book Longevity of the
Council on Library Resources.

Publication of this work was aided by a
generous grant from the Z. Smith Reynolds
Foundation.

Parts of this book have been reprinted
with permission in revised form from the
following works: "Suckin' the Chicken Bone
Dry: African American Women, History
and Food Culture," in *Cooking Lessons: The
Politics of Gender and Food*, edited by Sherrie
Inness, 200–214 (Lanham, Md.: Rowman
and Littlefield, 2001); and "Chicken and
Chains: Using African American Foodways
to Understand Black Identities," in *African
American Foodways: Explorations of History
and Culture*, edited by Anne Bower, 254–78
(Urbana: University of Illinois Press, 2006).

Library of Congress
Cataloging-in-Publication Data
Williams-Forson, Psyche A.
Building houses out of chicken legs :
Black women, food, and power /
Psyche A. Williams-Forson.
    p. cm.
Includes bibliographical references and
index.
ISBN-13: 978-0-8078-3022-2
(cloth : alk. paper)
ISBN-10: 0-8078-3022-4
(cloth : alk. paper)
ISBN-13: 978-0-8078-5686-4
(pbk. : alk. paper)
ISBN-10: 0-8078-5686-X
(pbk. : alk. paper)
1. Chickens—Social aspects. 2. Meat—
Symbolic aspects. 3. African American
women—Food. 4. African American
women—Social conditions. 5. African
American cookery. 6. Cookery (Chicken).
7. Food habits—United States. 8. Food
preferences—United States. I. Title.
GT2868.5.W55 2006
394.1′2—dc22   2005035088

cloth   10 09 08 07 06   5 4 3 2 1
paper   10 09 08 07 06   5 4 3 2 1

For women building houses out of chicken legs

whose stories we may never hear

CONTENTS

ILLUSTRATIONS

ACKNOWLEDGMENTS

Like many books, this journey began many years ago as part of my own process toward self-definition. There have been many over the years who have helped me to "build my own house."

Thanks to my former colleagues in the English department at McDaniel College for all their support. I am thankful as well to the students, especially the spring 2005 Realism and Naturalism class, who enthusiastically engaged me in discussions on representation, the roles of artists in society, and other issues critical to portions of the manuscript.

The revising process can be arduous and time-consuming, but several people took the time to provide encouragement, comments, and direction. Even before pen was put to paper, Mary Corbin Sies anticipated the richness of this project. She has continued to be there as a sounding board. As a mentor, colleague, and friend, she has always pressed me to reach the highest of standards—and challenged me to exceed them. I appreciate her exceptional scholarly example. The comments and probing questions of Suzanne Lebsock, Martha Katz-Hyman, and Kathryn Dobson helped me to rethink key chapters. Anne Yentsch and Joanne Bowman willingly lent their archaeological expertise by phone and e-mail. Philipia Hillman, Eva George, Belinda Wallace, Ann Denkler, Tammy Sanders, and Carol Gooch read multiple sections and offered pointed comments. Marya McQuirter and Cheryl LaRoche are my intellectual kinfolk and can always be expected to surprise me with an e-mail detailing a new book or pertinent information.

Others I wish to thank include Hasia Diner, who needed a research assistant for her own foodways projects and without whom I might have never considered this subject as a serious field of inquiry, Portia James, Elsa Barkley Brown, Bonnie Thornton Dill, Sharon Harley, Jessica Harris, Sheri Parks, Warren Belasco, Fath Davis Ruffins, Doris Witt, John Caughey, and Lynn Bolles.

Long before this project was completed, Gladys-Marie Fry recognized its potential and enthusiastically recommended me to the University of North Carolina Press. At the press, Elaine Maisner has encouraged me and been very patient as I travel the road of new author.

During the latter stages of writing and preparing the manuscript for publication, when additional research was needed, the staff assistance at the National Agricultural Library Rare Books and Main Reading Rooms was exceptional. Archivists are a treasure. I am especially grateful to the University of

Virginia, Alderman Library, Special Collections Division, and to the Library of Virginia in Richmond.

This project has been financially supported by several institutions during its various stages of completion: the Department of American Studies, University of Maryland, College Park; Winterthur Museum, Garden and Library, Wilmington, Delaware; the Smithsonian Institution's Museum of American History and the Anacostia Museum and the Center for African American History and Life, Washington, D.C.; the National Archives and Records Administration, Still Pictures Division, College Park; and the Virginia Historical Society, Richmond.

Family and friends have always been there in ways too numerous to count. For encouragement I can always rely on Jacquelyn S. Harris, Elena Temple, Kendra Smith-Williams, Deborah Johnson-Ross, Maria Thompson, and Zephia Bryant. I thank my family for undergirding me with prayer. For again providing me with all the love and encouragement any family could offer when sibling and child are undertaking something never seen in the family before, I also thank them. In particular, I want to acknowledge my mother, around whom this study actually centers in many ways. She and her relatives were some of my best sources. The stories of my maternal grandmother, whom I never really knew, and her participation in the underground economies and the fried chicken, biscuits, and succotash breakfasts that she cooked on Sunday mornings inspired and sustained me. This knowledge, coupled with the fact that my mother may never read this book because she does not like to look at chickens, always kept me from taking myself too seriously. Finally, thanks to my husband, Kwame, who married an academic without really knowing exactly what that would mean. His support, encouragement, love, and patience were tested constantly. But I thank him for going all the way with me so that I could put closure to the house I began to build long before we met.

BUILDING HOUSES OUT OF CHICKEN LEGS

INTRODUCTION

My mother paid for this place with chicken legs.
—Isabella "Bella" Winston, Gordonsville, Virginia

When "Bella" Winston uttered the simple but profound statement that her mother purchased their home "with chicken legs," she was
describing the tenacious spirit of the women who served as "waiter carriers"
for many years in Gordonsville, Virginia. Like her mother before her, Bella
Winston learned the trade of selling chicken, hot biscuits, coffee, and other
foodstuffs to hungry train passengers who were eager to purchase their goods
when trains stopped in their rural town. The waiter carriers, like women in
various churches, benevolent associations, and other community institutions who used chicken as a source of fund-raising, valued this object for its
financial, cultural, spiritual, and communal importance.

The women of Gordonsville are all deceased. With them have gone many
of the untold and unknown aspects of their lives in this area of trade. What
remains, however, are the vibrant snatches of this narrative and a lone photograph that captures the women as they lifted food-laden trays to the windows of trains. The life experiences of the waiter carriers—Bella Winston;
her mother, Maria Wallace; Laura Swift; Lucy Washington; Frances Taylor;
Adeline Daniel; and Mary Vest—and countless African American women elsewhere offer narratives about women's uses of chicken that go well beyond
eating.[1]

Building Houses out of Chicken Legs examines the roles that chicken has
played in the lives of black women from the past to the present. It is an inquiry into the ways black women shaped vital aspects of their lives with food.
Some women used chicken for economic freedom and independence; others
used it to show off their cooking skills. Still others used chicken to travel at
times when their own movement was restricted. That is, they metaphorically
traveled by sending packed shoe-box lunches filled with chicken and other
"goodies" when it was impossible for them to go. And still others shunned
chicken completely for one reason or another. Examining chicken makes it
possible for these previously unacknowledged aspects of black women's lives
and creative work to be revealed. It also allows for a stimulating story to un-
fold, a story of feminist consciousness, community building, cultural work,

and personal identity. The aim here is to showcase the voices of black women for whom chicken has served as a tool of self-expression, self-actualization, resistance, even accommodation and power. Revealed in these pages is a virtual cornucopia of narratives that details how chicken has had a central yet complex role in the lives of many African American women.

Black women left a trail of chicken bones—that is, narratives and stories that involve chicken. This trail includes images of black women (and men) cooking in plantation kitchens, selling chicken at railroad stations, cooking for church functions, and fund-raising for industrial schools. There are oral and written forms that recall black women's words and traditions. Sometimes this lore manifests itself in etiquette writing and cookbooks. Other times this writing is found in literature, popular fiction, comedy, and film. The trail also necessarily consists of some materials that were not left by blacks; rather, these artifacts were left for them. Among these are stereotyped visual and material images like postcards, sheet music, greeting cards, and other ephemera illustrating bandanna-wearing women and chicken-stealing men. These visual forms displaying blacks as "chicken lovers" have a long history in American popular culture. This kind of advertising was one of the linchpins with which white racists claimed black inferiority.

Despite the tendency for black people to appear stereotypically with chickens (along with other foods like watermelon) in American popular mediums, this subject has not been a topic for intensive study. Although the relationship between black people and chicken is often referred to in discussions of representation and stereotypes, no exploration has considered the stories that black people have to tell. This book seeks to change that tradition. While it necessarily considers the stereotypes, it does not rest there. To look at black people's lives solely through this preformulated lens limits the discussion. Instead, this book considers the interdisciplinary trail of evidence—the vast array of "bones"—in order to add to the spaces wherein black people's, and in particular black women's, agency emerges.

African American literature has been the one place where black people have been able to define themselves with and against the order of the day. As a result, literature provides one of the best sites to locate African American food traditions.[2] Though largely acts of imagination, these are also spaces of revelation. The signs of cultural hegemony, food politics, and delineations of power are omnipresent. The fact that these signs are often hidden and embedded in the language (consciously and unconsciously) that describes food relations makes literature a fruitful site in which to find black women's acts of self-definition. Various forms of literature have been peppered with the mention of food, and specifically with the presence of foods considered "black" or "African American."[3] African American folktales and slave narratives provide an abundantly rich source, as expected, given the circumstances of enslavement. One of the most notable examples is Booker T. Washington's account of his mother having walked for miles with a stolen chicken in order to feed her children. Although this focus shifted in the immediate aftermath of slavery, novelists nonetheless ventured to discuss foods of all kinds. Nineteenth-century African American novelist Pauline Hopkins is daring for her inclusion of the possum dinner circumscribed by the class-inflected church fair competition.

In addition to literature, oral history narratives are an abundant source. I come from a long line of black women who have worked with chicken, evidence of which is spattered throughout this study. These women cooked chicken in their own homes, in the homes of others as domestic workers, and in restaurants. One of my cousins explicitly refused to cook chicken in her capacity as a domestic worker because she said it was "too much handling." I did not completely understand then, but I know now that handling chicken is intimate work. And it is intimate work that appears here as well. The women in this study have entrusted me with their thoughts, their life histories, and their experiences. Although some are now dead, a large number of them are very much alive and serving in black churches.[4] As a "preacher's kid," chicken was a central part of my black church experience as it is for many African Americans, so it was natural that black church women would inform this project.[5] Not only did I witness my mother and other black women cooking chicken every Sunday for dinner but also I learned early the value of social action and the role that chicken plays in activism—especially in the church setting.

It was necessary to cull my information from these bodies of knowledge because when I first began researching, there was very little literature available on the meanings associated with African American food consumption.[6] Available materials, with limited exceptions, comprised histories of southern food and drink and introductory histories to African American cookbooks.[7]

Cookbooks represent cultural sites where food and memory intersect. Primarily using anecdotal references to discuss African American food history and in some cases to illustrate the inextricable link to the African Diaspora, these cultural documents shed some light on African American people and how food factors into the process of identity formation.[8] Not to be dismissed, some of these cookbooks place African American culinary habits within a political and social history context, sharing the lived experiences and realities of African American women who have long since passed away. In some instances, these cookbooks are the last remaining cultural artifacts of their kind.

Along with representations in cookbooks, history, and anthropology are those found in archaeology. Because most of the formal studies of African American food originated in archaeology, there are few actual voices left to share their experiences. But more important, in most of the extant literature the ways in which black women participated in the production of these foods has been overlooked or marginalized.[9]

Since work began on this project over ten years ago, African American food studies has been enriched by the emergence of other studies. Building upon the scholarship mentioned above—and in many ways departing from it, particularly in methodology, scope, and focus—are the more recent contributions by historians and literary theorists.[10] All of these studies provided interesting starting points and reference points from which to talk about African American food traditions. However, my research has always sought to ask different questions. Since we now know what people ate historically, how do we find out what these foods meant beyond nourishment? And how have these foods informed and helped to shape modes of black feminist social consciousness and personal identity? None of the studies previously encountered advanced my understanding of these questions. Moreover, I was also concerned to hear the actual voices of black women, an approach heretofore left unexplored. To find out what chicken might have meant and often means today required looking "inside out," that is, reading the silences and hearing what the text does not tell us, hearing and reading the "subtexts." Essentially, this involves bringing a new way of reading to the extant material.

When I asked people to inform this study, the question "Why chicken?" was often raised. The area of food studies is vast and relatively untapped, especially African American foodways. Thus, anyone tackling this subject matter knows that the experience can be daunting. How then does one narrow the field of research? As I was searching for a specific topic, several sad but interesting incidents occurred. In 1997, a New Orleans chapter of a majority white fraternity circulated a flier advertising a party on Martin Luther King Jr. Day with fried chicken from Popeye's, watermelon, and a "forty"-ounce bottle of beer.[11] Also in 1997, Tiger Woods won his first Masters golf tournament. In a follow-up interview, fellow golfer Fuzzy Zoeller remarked, "That little boy is driving well, and he's putting well. He's doing everything it takes to win. So, you know what you guys do when he gets in here? You pat him on the back and say congratulations and enjoy it and tell him not to serve fried chicken next year. Got it?" Zoeller added as an afterthought, "Or collard greens or whatever the hell they serve."[12]

Another incident occurred in 1999. KFC (formerly Kentucky Fried Chicken) launched a new advertising campaign to offer a more up-to-date version of Colonel Sanders. Appealing to the generation of teen and middle-aged consumers, KFC created a new animated version whose voice would resonate in quasi-hip-hop tones. The character was still clad in his familiar goatee, black string tie, and white suit and cane so as not to alienate those consumers who grew up with Sanders, but the overall intention was to make the Colonel "cool."[13]

I was lured to the television commercial by what sounded like the voice of a black man against a backdrop of hip-hop music. What I actually saw was a dancing Colonel, bouncing basketballs, and buckets of fried chicken. The combination of these activities and images struck a chord with me. In that advertisement was the suggestion of age-old stereotypes that linked African American men to playing basketball and eating chicken. Also, seeing the Colonel "hop around" in mock imitation of a dance that happened to be in vogue throughout black communities at one time spoke directly to me about issues of commodification and black minstrelsy.[14] The effect was astounding and surprising. I later learned that the voice actually belonged to Randy Quaid and that KFC acquired an advertising contract with the National Collegiate Athletic Association that enabled them to monopolize the viewing audience's attention during "March Madness"—the height of college basketball season.

Though I have been accused of "reading too much" into the commercial, it nonetheless urged me to consider how far we had come in American society, only to be in relatively the same place. The commercial, coupled with the other incidents, piqued my curiosity about the objects that had been used, when and how they had been used, and their intended audiences. I began to consider how black people think about their relationship to chicken and where black women, and black feminist consciousness, fit into this discussion. The more I listened and talked with people about my proposed topic, the clearer it became that a generation of young people were relatively unaware that any negative associations existed between chicken and black people. Or worse, although aware of the stereotypes, they often saw no sociopolitical correlations between the historical positioning and the current contemporary moment. These variables, and the fact that women's cooking is often overlooked and devalued, made an exploration of black people's relationships with chicken ripe for discussion.

Taken together, all of these issues revealed this topic to be a fertile landscape from which to consider black women's agency. Starting with the latter, women's cooking, I sought to consider how black women saw themselves vis-à-vis the stereotypes and chicken in general. From this standpoint, self-definition and awareness are critical to this project. Writing in the late nineteenth century, Anna Julia Cooper said, "Only the Black Woman can say 'when and where I enter, in the quiet, undisputed dignity of my womanhood, without violence and without suing or special patronage, then and there the whole *Negro race enters with me.*' "[15] One of the messages that Cooper conveys here is black women's undisputed right to speak for and define themselves. Thus, black women are vital in challenging what Patricia Hill Collins says is "the political knowledge-validation process that result[s] in externally defined stereotypical images."[16] By utilizing and identifying symbols commonly affiliated with black expressive culture like chicken, some black women engage in the process of self-definition. They refuse to allow the wider American culture or their own communities to dictate what represents them. But this process of defining one's self is filled with complexities, especially when one person's self-definition collides with another member of the same race, class, region, sexual orientation, and so on. Difficulties certainly may arise when these variables do not coincide.

In this study, I attempt to explore many of these complexities and their feminist implications. All of these interactions illuminate the politics of gender, food, and race and the ways that power works in this discussion. Robert Paynter and Randall H. McGuire argue that objects are often manipulated in power relations and that an analysis of these relations "stresses the interplay between those who use structural asymmetries of resources in exercising power, known as domination, and those who develop social and cultural opposition to this exercise, known as resistance."[17] Power relations are not simply something that the "elite dole out or exercise over an acquiescent subservient." Rather, power is heterogeneous in nature, not limited to a single area of society and thus implicit in the process of sharing cultural norms and values.[18] From this perspective, power can be about defining oneself through exploration—and can be fun!

Black women who "signify" on one another's recipes and cooking styles exercise a form of power through verbal play. This does not always involve "negative critique" but does include "profound intention" in the process of revising and "signifyin'" on one another. Henry Louis Gates Jr. explains it this way in relation to the work of Alice Walker signifying on Zora Neale Hurston:

If Hurston's novel seems to have been designed to declare that indeed, a text could be written in black dialect, then it seems to me that Walker's *The Color Purple* aims to do just that, as a direct revision of Hurston's explicit and implicit strategies of narration. Walker, whose preoccupation with Hurston as a deeply admired antecedent has been the subject of several of her critical comments, revises and echoes Hurston in a number of ways. . . . Walker . . . corresponds to unmotivated Signifyin(g), by which I mean to suggest not the absence of a profound intention but the absence of a negative critique. The relation between parody and pastiche is that between motivated and unmotivated Signifyin(g).[19]

Considering the ways that black women exercise vestiges of power in their everyday lives—verbal, physical, psychological, emotional, or culinary—validates how they construct meaning and give, receive, and even take pleasure on a day-to-day basis. It also expands our understanding of the ways that black women's social relations are laden with power.

This book's topical organization reflects the ways in which black women (and men) have used chicken to express and define themselves over time. Chapters in part 1 look at early African and African American encounters with chicken. Drawing on a body of historical data, they examine how African American women used chicken as a means of gaining a modicum of economic self-sufficiency while black men were simultaneously maligned in the popular culture.[20]

Subsequent chapters in part 1 turn to similar discussions for black women. Whereas black men were considered a major threat to white American society, images of black women as mammies, cooks, and caretakers were perceived as the salve to soothe the burdens caused by a burgeoning new society. Foods like chicken were imbued with class tensions as African Americans struggled for citizenship and acceptance in American society. Consequently, many middle-class members of black society sought to separate migrant communities from their traditional southern mores. Chicken thus functioned—by its presence and its absence—as a tool for working-class and poor black women who struggled to define themselves against the tide.

Against this backdrop of social conflict between and among black and white citizens, chicken is examined for its centrality to African American travel narratives. In the context of this historical examination, chapters in part 2 consider how chicken functions in black women's lives today. Of importance are the ways in which black women in churches use chicken to signify on one another as a means of self-expression. Various forms of verbal and culinary "play" showcase their talents, needs, wants, and desires. More than in any other, chapter 5 turns to the ways in which power is most clearly delineated. Black women use chicken to signify at times by rejecting it during a meal. They also signify by dictating to others where and when public consumption of chicken is appropriate. In this way, tensions around class factor largely in this discussion to show that even though these women share a racial bond, they are steadfastly divided by other variables.

When hegemonic cultures that keep negative images in place are not all white but are formulated by people of varying races and ethnicities, black and male included, definition and representation are surely called into question. This phenomenon is one I call "gender malpractice." My use of this term is borrowed from Tommy Lott's notion of cultural malpractice.[21] His definition of cultural malpractice focuses on perceived misrepresentation. Lott explains that black leaders have levied this charge against various artists because they perpetuate either racism or self-denigration. These leaders believe that the definition of cultural malpractice turns upon almost anything that misrepresents or affects the material image of black people. But ascertaining the exact nature of this misrepresentation is difficult. The goal here is not to foreclose on possibilities of discussion by assigning judgment; rather, it is to lay open these texts to engage the complex questions that correspond to representation.

The concept of gender malpractice is introduced to suggest cases where black women, cooking, and chicken have been signified upon to essentially —but not necessarily intentionally—misrepresent them. As a result, black women's voices have been eclipsed or erased. Comedians, for example, have been accused of perpetuating the stereotype of blacks as "chicken lovers." This humor may be racially subversive, but the performance of this humor is often laden with gender misrepresentations. Film and art also illustrate these misrepresentations. George Tillman Jr.'s *Soul Food* highlights the perceived lives of black women but not necessarily their realities. By neglecting to tackle the issue of black women's health in the film, a clear sense of gender consciousness is lacking. Likewise, the work of African American artist Kara Walker has sparked debate and dialogue around her provocative but visually disturbing imagery of African Americans. In this final discussion, the argument is made that African American women might also commit gender malpractice even in the process of defining themselves.

This book contains several stories within the larger narrative of African American women's lives with chicken. In doing so, it not only signifies on its foremothers—the waiter carriers of Gordonsville, black migrant and church-women—but also hopes to pave the way for future studies of black women's work, particularly those involving foods like chicken.

I

ENCOUNTERS WITH
THE BIRD

WE CALLED OURSELVES WAITER CARRIERS

*Bacon to spare will allow me a preference with the country people
or rather Negroes who are the general chicken merchants.*
—John Mercer

We called ourselves "Waiter Carriers."
—Bella Winston

When Augustus Baldwin Longstreet wrote *Georgia Scenes* in 1835, he included among his characters a rambunctious and offensive native gentleman from Georgia by the name of Ned Brace. Ned was the kind who would wreak havoc wherever he went. Lyman Hall, one of Longstreet's two narrators, accompanies Ned on a three-day venture to Savannah.[1] After a day of playing pranks on everyone from the lodging house hostess to a member of a fancy funeral procession, Ned takes his behavior to the market to "buy something of everybody and some of everything." Being the sort of character who "wanted his articles in such portions and numbers as no one would sell, or upon conditions to which no one would submit," he approaches "an old Negro woman" and explains that his wife is sick and she wants chicken pie. Ned, however, has just enough money to buy half a chicken based upon the seller's asking price. As a result, Ned wants the vending woman to cut the live chicken in half. In her outrage and disbelief, she explains to Ned that this is impossible. She has no place to properly dress the chicken, and she does not want to get feathers all over the other chickens that she has to sell. If this was to happen, she is sure that it would result in her being punished by other white men:

"Do, my good mauma, sell it to me," said he; "My wife is very sick, and is longing for chicken pie, and this is all the money I have" (holding out twelve and a half cents in silver), "and it's just what a half chicken comes to at your own price."

"Ki, massa! how gwine cut live chicken in two?"

"I don't want you to cut it in two alive; kill it, clean it, and then divide it."

"Name o' God! what sort o' chance got to clean chicken in de market-house! Whay de water for scall um and wash um?"

"Don't scald it at all; just pick it, so."

"Ech-ech! Fedder fly all ober de buckera-man meat, he come bang me fo' true. No, massa, I mighty sorry for your wife, but I no cutty chicken open."[2]

Upon the refusal of the woman to sell him the chicken, Ned appears to leave her, ending the scene. The reader is left with no knowledge of whether or not the old woman complied, but one can assume by her closing remarks that she did not. Although I will return to this scene later in this discussion, it is important now for its illustration of at least one level of interaction exchanged between whites and blacks in the New World marketplace. It reveals the boundaries that each established and transversed in his or her desire to consume and obtain goods. Moreover, it lends itself to an examination of how black women left their mark both in kitchens and on the market landscape. It further suggests some of the social, cultural, and economic tensions that were bound to arise in a society marked by patriarchal control and white dominance. The basic goals of this chapter are to discuss two things: some of the various interactions that African and African American people may have had with chicken upon their arrival in the New World and how those relationships have been circumscribed by a discourse of race and capitalism.

Like intricate weavings on a tapestry, so are the stories and the heritages that help to compose the beginnings of African life in America. The accounts that surround the forced migrations of Africans to Brazil, the West Indies, and America have been the source of debate for decades. What remains consistent is that the Atlantic slave trade left an amalgamation of cultures and transformations that permeate every aspect of American life, including its foodways. The historical contexts within which relationships developed between black women and chickens reveal practices that were circumscribed by gender, race, class, and power. Certain boundaries guided the exchange of goods that took place in and around the marketplace. Black people were no freer than their circumstances allowed at that time. But it was the level of market autonomy and relative independence that reveal some of the ways in which black people saw themselves in relationship to certain goods. Far from simply being victims of their circumstances, black women and men were sometimes in positions where they could be enterprising.[3] Chicken may be considered one food with which competency for trade was exercised and meanings were expressed. Chicken may have figured very minutely within the scope of early wide-scale commercial capitalism, but an examination of its role within the marketplace provides a small glimpse of how power, race, and capitalism converged in the American landscape.

When exploring a phenomenon such as the one this study suggests, it is necessary to make some generalizations at the risk of oversimplification and overestimation. Recognizing this pitfall, this chapter will limit its geographic focus mainly to areas of the Maryland and Virginia Chesapeake and the Carolina Lowcountry, even though the marketing activities of slaves and free blacks have been recorded as far north as New England.[4] But, before furthering the discussion on African American relationships to chicken, it seems a brief history of poultry and fowl in American society is necessary.

The history of chicken (*Gallus domesticus*), the common name for what we know today as domestic fowl, is long and complicated primarily due to cultural diffusion as much as anything else. But there seems to be perennial agreement that chickens arrived in the New World from Asia and are descended from the red jungle fowl.[5] The agricultural surplus found in the New World allowed eastern seaboard settlers to be relatively self-sufficient. The areas surrounding the Chesapeake Bay were especially lush with wildlife, fish, plants, nuts, fruits, and other food provisions. Chickens were a part of this surplus and the general exchange of foods, tools, and methods of production between European colonists and Native Americans. Because these birds roamed freely, Native Americans often traded chickens and wild turkeys with the colonists in an effort to obtain more favorable goods like guns and cooking utensils.[6]

Writing in 1634, Captain Thomas Young wrote of a journey to Jamestown, Virginia, wherein he noticed that America was endowed with "very great plenty" of birds, fowl, and other foods: "In so much so that in ordinary planters' houses of the better sort, we found tables furnished with pork, kids, chickens, turkeys, young geese, caponetts and such other fowls as the seas of the year afforded."[7] As Young rightfully observed, goose, duck, and chicken appeared often on the tables of the "better sort." Writing in 1709, William Byrd kept a detailed journal where he secretly recorded the minutiae of his daily life. While many dined on "hash'd or fricasseed" cold remains of turkeys and geese, or "boil'd and roasted" fowl, Byrd broke his fast with boiled milk. Nonetheless, by dinner, boiled beef, blue wing, pigeon, partridge, geese, duck, pork, and boiled or roasted mutton graced his table.[8] And in the latter part of the eighteenth century, German settler Johann Martin Bolzius observed that birds were so plentiful that he could only describe them by their color. He noted that food could not be stored because of worms but added that "chickens are easily kept from which they have eggs regularly, and fresh meat in case of emergency. They usually slaughter in autumn and winter, salt the meat, smoke it, lay it away for preservation."[9]

Wealthy landowners may have dined often on all kinds of fowl, but it was slave men and women who had the primary responsibility of caring for the birds. Landon Carter's diary has several entries wherein the slave Sukey gives him an account of that "which she has been entrusted with."[10] Sukey's "charges" included:

Old geeses	33	
Goslings	78	two geese still to hatch
Old ducks	8	
Young ducks	20	seven hens sitting on duck eggs
Old fowls	32	
Chickens	200	one hen still sitting on her eggs
Old turkey	12	
Young ditto	7	seven turkey hens sitting

Even though the mistress of the house would have had the overall responsibility for supervising the work on the farm, slaves like Sukey would have cared for the livestock.

Although Sukey may have been taught how to care for these animals, this task probably would have been familiar to her ancestors. Almost all West African societies held agriculture as the chief form of subsistence. And usually everyone engaged in the agricultural process. Part of this engagement might have included interaction with the guinea fowl (*Numida meleagris*).[11] The skills held by Africans were not lost on slave traders. For this reason, slaves were taken from certain regions according to their specific knowledge, their dispositions, and their benefits to New World markets. European slave traders like the British took Africans from different coastal regions, including the Bight of Benin, Senegambia, Sierra Leone, West Central Africa, the Gold Coast, and the Bight of Biafra. They were taken to Brazil and the Caribbean to build the sugar industry, to the Carolinas for rice cultivation, and to the Chesapeake colonies for harvesting tobacco, among other crops, cotton being the eventual mainstay of United States economic export.[12]

By the middle of the seventeenth century, trade in Africans had fully taken hold, linking Europe, Brazil, the Caribbean, and North America. The purpose here is not to revisit this discussion but to benefit from it by building on the general consensus that although slaves arrived in America with no material possessions, some were equipped with the sensibilities of marketing and trading foodstuffs and other consumer goods.[13] Using what they or their ancestors knew and that which was acquired in the New World, some slaves were able to better their material lives. Though meager by any comparison, some slaves were able to acquire possessions that would make their lives markedly more improved. This was by no means widespread, and it varied over time and space.[14] The sheer weight of material accumulation by planters necessitated the passing on of goods that were no longer desired. Often times, these possessions fell into the hands of favored slaves. Other slaves acquired goods through barter, trade, recycling, and theft. Archaeological work on slaves' sites throughout the Americas reveals that chicken was one of many food items with which some Africans came into contact and used to gain access to other goods.[15]

Historians point to the economic, social, and cultural importance of African Americans in the profitable capacity of selling foods such as poultry, fowl, and chicken; as hawkers and traders, enslaved and freed blacks entered the early commercial economy.[16] Being able to participate meant a number of things for slaves: it provided the ability to supplement the food and clothing allotted to them by plantation owners, an opportunity to acquire a wider variety of goods, and the ability to exercise a modicum of autonomy and relative economic success on or near the plantation environment. This in no way suggests the beneficence of enslavement; rather, it points to the relative material and economic transactions that could surround plantation life. It also reflects the self-interest of some slave owners who wanted to save money and did so by allowing their slaves to feed themselves.[17]

According to travelers' accounts, it was not an unfamiliar sight to see slave women vending and hawking food items while walking the streets of major towns. Apparently, this scene was so familiar that in 1779 John Mercer was prompted to comment on it to his business agent, Battaile Muse: "I know already that chickens or other fresh meat cant be had but in exchange & bacon to spare will allow me a preference with the country people or rather Negroes who are the general chicken merchants."[18] Mercer realized that in order to trade with blacks for chicken and other goods, he would need to reserve some of his own supply of bacon.

Plantation as well as non-plantation households had to be provisioned from day to day and week to week. To be sure, many of the wealthier plantations like Carter Burwell's Carter's Grove and Thomas Jefferson's Monticello were able to distribute their week's rations from among the many food items grown and tended to by the slaves on the property. However, even some of these plantation owners had to go beyond their own property to stock their household. Also in Virginia, Landon Carter not only "humored" his slaves by purchasing their goods but also saw his own profitability in their ability to trade. Of Nat, a slave, Carter says:

Nat brought me 6 chickens this day; his others not quite big enough. I have been asked why I don't sell my salted Pork. I think I now see a good way of selling it, and perhaps at a great Price than others have got for theirs. My poor slaves raise fowls, and eggs in order to exchange with their master now and then; and, though I don't value the worth of what they bring, yet I enjoy the humanity of refreshing such poor creatures in what they (though perhaps mistakenly) call a blessing. Indeed, I hope this is a good way of selling what I may have to spare out of my own sumptuous fare; and not to inure the small profits which I am content with.[19]

Not all slaves sold chicken, of course; some sold baked goods while other times they marketed foods grown in their gardens or obtained—legally or illegally—from their owners. And while some like Carter's slave Nat had an opportunity to participate in supplemental trade activities, the majority were employed in the production of staple crops like sugar, rice, tobacco, and cotton.

Entry into the slave economy was strictly guarded and regulated on a number of levels. First, slaves who participated did so only with permission from their owners and were limited to a certain traveling distance. Second, even when allowed to trade, they were governed by the constraints of production rhythms and patterns and therefore not relieved of their everyday duties and assignments. And last, they were bound by numerous legal restrictions that dictated the parameters of trade.

Within the diversity and pervasiveness of the slave's participation in the business (mostly informal) of buying and selling, the social, economic, and cultural landscape of black and white, enslaved and master, and rich, poor, and poorer often overlapped and collided. For example, in 1642, the General Assembly of Virginia made it unlawful to "secretly and covertly trade and truck with other mens' servants and apprentices which tended to the great injury of masters of familys, their servants being thereby induced and invited to purloin and imbeasill the goods of their said masters." In neighboring Maryland and other locales, established merchants agitated against itinerant hucksters, intermediaries, and peddlers who would set up their goods and forestall prior to the opening of the markets.[20] Even though many of these laws were ignored because of self-interest, some planters believed it was necessary to press the issue. In 1665, Philip Calvert brought a case to the Provincial Court of Maryland against Thomas and Elizabeth Wynne, who were accused of repeatedly bartering and trading with "ffrank Indian & dyvers others of the slaves of Philip Calvert Esq . . . for Ten poultry or Henns." [21]

To stem the tide of competition by hucksters, peddlers, and other competitors, regulations were established that required traders to be licensed. In 1737, South Carolina passed an act "for licencing Hawkers, pedlars and Petty Chapmen, and to prevent their trading with Indented Servants, Overseers, Negroes, and Other Slaves." Apparently, to the "great prejudice of the store-keepers and shopkeepers" who paid taxes, vagrant traders would travel by land and water to barter and trade rum, sugar, and other goods in exchange for "hogs, fowls, rice, corn and other produce." To prevent this behavior, slaves had to have a "permit" or "ticket in writing" in order to trade, or fines would be levied.[22]

Economic opportunities for blacks were severely limited by eighteenth-century policies. Nonetheless, some, particularly free blacks, continued to exercise their business acumen, drawing upon their knowledge and skills in cooking and preparing foods to open restaurants, inns, and boarding- and catering houses.[23] One of these establishments was Fraunces Tavern in New York City, a frequent haunt of George Washington. Established in the late eighteenth century and owned for twenty-three years by Samuel Fraunces, it catered primarily to northern white elites, including the New York Sons of Liberty who planned many of its major events there. Interestingly, either because of or in order to protect his patronage, Fraunces made it clear that "no black could eat or stay [at his inn]." Because of his daughter Phoebe, Fraunces's establishment is the subject of a legend regarding chickens. Phoebe supposedly thwarted an assassination attempt against Washington by throwing a plate of poisonous peas out the window to the chickens, which ate them and immediately died.[24]

That black people had access to chickens, sometimes in excess, is not altogether surprising. The *Christian Recorder*, *Colored American*, and *National Era* (to name a few) carried a number of articles related to African American chicken husbandry, preachers and their love of chicken and fowl, and concern over accusations of African American chicken stealing. One writer, a southern minister, went so far as to consider himself in "great straits" because his family did not have the same luxuries as one of his parishioners who had plenty of poultry, even though his family had access to bacon and bread.[25] That black people exchanged these goods with one another is also not necessarily hard to believe, because as Michael Gomez has noted, "Exchange and interaction among slaveholding units was extensive, such that an individual's familial, social, and cultural world was by no means confined to the particular unit in which she or he lived." Moreover, if black folks could get to one another "on a regular basis and within a reasonable amount of time," they would, could, and did "re-create a distinctive culture, their pro-pinquity to whites notwithstanding."[26] Part of this "distinctive culture" can perhaps be read in their trade activities. And it can also be said that some of these activities might be at the crux of the stereotypes that evolved around African American associations with and affinity for chicken.

To the extent possible, blacks manipulated the system to their advantage, despite the legal barriers, by procuring, providing, and sometimes prepar-ing goods and commodities to sell and trade. When including foodways in this system, foods like chicken take on a symbolic meaning far greater than mere provisions. Inasmuch as blacks were considered the "primary chicken merchants," they were undoubtedly aware of the modicum of power that this status afforded them.[27] For black women, who by virtue of their reproductive capabilities found their children in perpetual subjugation from birth, activi-ties like participation in the marketplace arena afforded them a measure of resistance in the daily act of going to the place where they could not only sell their wares but also connect with other women and, in some small manner, survive. In the marketplace, slaves could exchange information and merri-ment with other slaves as well as free blacks.

In this regard, the tenor of early marketplaces resonates with Mikhail Bakhtin's concept of carnival in its composition and form: "Carnival is not a spectacle seen by the people; they live in it, and everyone participates be-cause its very idea embraces all the people. While carnival lasts, there is no other life outside it. During carnival time life is subject only to its laws, that is, the laws of its own freedom."[28] It is important to note Bakhtin's caution about carnival as a form—"it is complex and varied, giving rise . . . to diverse variants and nuances depending upon the epoch, the people and the indi-vidual festivity." Unlike carnivals, festivals, and parades, the marketplace did not precede a period of sustained abstinence. Nor was it held in observance of some strict religious ritual. Rather, it was a coming together for economic exchange. Consequently, it was fraught with multiple tensions, horrors, and fears. At the same time, there were multiple levels of cultural performance taking place. The fragile acts of defiance and negotiation might have offered elements of exuberance and rejoicing on the part of blacks, but naturally these acts were tenuous. There was probably less of Bakhtin's public mirth, unrestrained conduct, and rebelliousness and more of a dialectical move-ment from hierarchy to equality and back again in the economy of petty trad-ing between blacks and whites. One's subjugated status notwithstanding, there was no doubt a sense of accomplishment, if not resiliency, garnered by the sale of goods. After all, money accumulated from the sales of chicken and other goods enabled one to have additional provisions and, in some rare instances, the obtainment of freedom for oneself or family members. But, the larger attainments aside, something must be said for psychological triumphs wherein "laughter is not an external but an interior form of truth."[29] When black people were legally trading in the marketplace, concessions were made, large and small, to satisfy the marketplace ritual. This was a very structured time wherein the world of the slave peddler, trader, and seller broke from some elements of official domination, fear, and intimidation.

One important contributor to this victory was laughter—whether internal or external. Writing on the history of laughter in the period of the Renaissance, Bakhtin explains:

> It was the victory of laughter over fear . . . but also a victory over the awe inspired by the forces of nature, and most of all over the oppression and guilt related to all that was consecrated and forbidden. . . . It was the defeat of divine and human power, of authoritarian commandments and prohibitions, of death and punishment after death, hell and all that is more terrifying than the earth itself. Through this victory laughter clarified man's consciousness and gave him a new outlook on life. This truth was ephemeral; it was followed by the fears and oppressions of everyday life, but from these brief moments another unofficial truth emerged, truth about the world and man which prepared the new . . . consciousness.[30]

It was a time, momentary perhaps, when a black person no longer felt completely helpless.

Returning to the account that opened this chapter, we find Ned and the "old Negro woman" engaged in marketplace negotiations about the purchase of half of a chicken. Against the background previously discussed about blacks seeming to have a monopoly over the sale and trade of chickens, this scene is compelling for what it reveals about the interrelationships between gender, race, and power on the landscape of the carnivalesque. At first glance, it seems interesting that Ned does not pursue his desire to obtain the chicken. After the market woman refuses to cut the chicken, he simply walks away. From a racial point of view, white men expected that relations between them and blacks would always be based on servitude and gratitude, and women would always be subordinate to men. However, in the public marketplace, where many whites often relied upon blacks to supply them with foods, market rules required some concessions. These allowances and rules of trade may not have been unfamiliar to the "old Negro woman." By the time this incident was observed (anytime from the late eighteenth to early nineteenth century), she would have been at least two to three generations removed from the direct shores of Africa or the Caribbean. Consequently, she probably would have learned the trade from her ancestors, friends, and relatives. She probably knew that in the marketplace, she had a relatively upper hand. Not surprisingly, she asserts this influence by appealing to Ned's sense of genteel behavior. She calls upon other patriarchal forces to sustain her: "Ech-ech! Fedder fly all ober de buckera-man meat, he come bang me fo' true." Her indication that obliging his request would cause problems for some other "buckera-man" suggests that she plays to the appropriate behavior of a proper southern gentleman. She has no way of knowing, however, that Ned, the native Georgian, is a prankster who had spent the day overturning the codes of behavior that defined his place in high society.[31]

Prior to his antics at the marketplace, Ned offends the residents of his lodging house by exhibiting brutish table manners. He drinks his tea and coffee simultaneously and heaps food upon his plate and mashes it together before eating it. After the guests retire, he innocently and eloquently apologizes for his "eccentricities," appealing to the boardinghouse mistress's sense of maternalism. All of this is done for the sake of Ned's entertainment. Hall, the narrator of the tale, shares this with the reader:

> I had no sooner entered my room than Ned followed me, where we interchanged the particulars which make up the foregoing story. He now expended freely the laughter which he had been collecting during the evening. He stated that his last interview with Mrs. Blank was the result of necessity; that he found he had committed himself in making up and disposing of his odd supper; . . . though he was willing to do penance for one meal in order to purchase the amusement he had enjoyed, he had no idea of tormenting himself three or four days for the same purpose.[32]

The old woman at the market, then, has no way of knowing that Ned never really had an interest in buying a chicken. His real aim was to irritate and confound her, just as he had done to others above and below his level of status.

Ahmed Nimeiri makes the point that an important feature of Longstreet's tales is "its depiction of play—in its two senses of contesting and role playing—as the hallmark of antebellum southern life." Performance and play are both cathartic and affirmative in that they help to "affirm the values of society and educate its members into the significance of these values." For Longstreet, they are key to communal harmony and are the "essence" of life in southern society. He further argues that while Longstreet is aware of the negative aspects of play, which he "perceives in actions without sense or purpose," play is a metaphor. It enables Longstreet "to transcend the limitations of a narrow conservative vision of the antebellum South developed in response to his time and place, to liberating sense of man and human experience."[33]

To some extent, Nimeiri's argument factors into the description of the marketplace as a carnivalesque landscape in that play and performance are at work. But, what seems to be missing from Nimeiri's viewpoint is the infusion of power as a critical element. Although there is some cultural leveling between master and slave, black and white on this social landscape, hierarchy is certainly not overlooked or forgotten. The market woman, for example, is not oblivious to the fact that her liberation is temporal. She is undoubtedly aware that her foodstuffs—chickens, possibly produce, beans, and other foods—though selected from her garden or that of her master, all belong to someone else. Ned is certainly aware of his space as one of power and privilege. The fact that he has a whole day to spend on foolish pranks and antics while others work suggests this awareness.[34] He is used to a prescribed set of expectations that dictate how an exchange between a white man and black woman should proceed, regardless of the marketplace rules. Given all of this and Ned's disinterest in the outcome of his exchange with the "old Negro woman," we can conclude that Ned simply used the opportunity to play with the black woman and secure his assumptions; this being done, Ned could move on. In this respect, his behaviors coincide with Nimeiri's assertion of play as cathartic, affirming, and educating about social values. In reference to a similar scenario, Rhys Isaac says: "One who stands in the significant-other relationship to considerable numbers of persons is thereby endowed with *social power* and enters into transactions on markedly advantageous terms. Typically, the inequalities of interactional exchanges in such cases are formalized into a mode of deference on one side and condescension on the other."[35] And in this liminal space of the black/white landscape of the public marketplace, Ned acted out his condescension secure in his social power.

But we should not leave this scene without acknowledging that the old black woman was not in a mode of deference only but also in one of resistance. By refusing Ned's request both verbally and physically, the black woman's agency offers another reading to Isaac's argument about social power: it can be relative. Ned was secure, indeed, but so was the market woman. She refused to give in, irrespective of his position or the farcical nature of the request. If we see power as contingent upon particular relationships as opposed to reading it only as hierarchical, then it is possible to see various slaves having different kinds of power vis-à-vis food, however small, however ephemeral. And if we consider the concept of internal laughter, then we afford slaves another element of victory.

But, as previously stated, these kinds of victories were short-lived and, more important, relegated to only a few. Blacks who hired out their own time, and therefore were able to produce goods for sale, had a certain kind of audacity that might have been missing from those without these privileges. For women, these minute acts of boldness promoted a sense of survival and innovation that hardly went unnoticed by the competition. According to the *South Carolina Gazette*, one writer complained that almost on a daily basis, black women could be found huckstering and forestalling "poultry, fruit, eggs," and other goods "in and near the Lower Market . . . from morn till night," buying and selling what and how they pleased to obtain money for both their masters and themselves. Oftentimes their prices were exorbitant, and they would use all kinds of marketing strategies to choose which white people to sell to and for how much.[36] Robert Olwell captures this point when he explains: "As slaveholders, Carolina whites felt that slaves should be generally subordinate, but as property holders and capitalists they also had to recognize the legitimacy of the market in which sellers had the right to seek the highest price for their goods." [37] Many whites viewed blacks with "great prejudice" when they sought to engage in the same mode of capitalism. Under slavery's oppression, blacks, regardless of their status, were to be subordinate at all times. Any deviation from this "norm" was a threat to the social order that had been systematically and institutionally constructed over time. Consequently, any element of freedom recognized and enjoyed by black people, and particularly women, was an affront to white social power, as Lawrence T. McDonnell explains:

> The marketplace, economic analysts from Aristotle to Adam Smith to Karl Marx have agreed, is a neutral zone, a threshold between buyer and seller. "The market spells liberation," Fernand Braudel writes, "openness, access to another world." Master and slave confronted each other at the moment of exchange as bearers of commodities, stripped of social dimensions. . . . [This] linked black sellers with white buyers, and hence with white society, not only by assertion of black humanity but through white objectification. Slaves appeared here equally purposeful as whites.[38]

White objectification offered blacks a degree of power, if only briefly. Even more important, it provided blacks with personal access to an ideological freedom. Part of the capitalist charade during slavery was to make black people believe that freedom would never come. Money and a small measure of market power could change that. For planters, some relief may have been gained by attributing black economic gain to theft. Yet, this would also leave many of them in a moral, economic, social, and cultural quagmire. Plantation owners lived by a credo of order and control that they had established. Knowing that their slaves were able to skillfully (at times) pilfer and steal under their roof disturbed this sense of order. By attributing stealing by slaves to an inherent nature rather than a condition of their circumstances, slave owners were able to deflect attention from their own participation in this aspect of slave victimization. Morally, it was much better to believe that slaves were natural thieves than to believe that the institution of enslavement contributed to this condition. So there is some truth to slaves engaging in thievery, but much of this belief is rooted in planter ideology.[39]

There are many possible reasons for the evolution and persistence of these ideologies. By now it has been well established that some blacks kept gardens and livestock like pigs, sheep, goats, and chickens, which were sold in the market on Saturdays when there was surplus. Some women "made do" with the foods they had in order to provide a surplus to use in bartering and exchanging for other goods. Other times, slaves simply traded surplus foods with one another to provision their households. Among other slaves' narratives, Charles Ball's 1837 account details how Nero, the head of the household in which he lived, exchanged corn for the beans that were grown in the garden of Ball's friend Lydia.[40] But this was not altogether as commonplace as it may seem. This type of enterprise took place on many larger plantations where there was economic interaction and exchange between slaves and masters, slaves and freed blacks, and poor whites and other folks. We should not conclude that all slaves were able to engage in this informal economy. For one, even when slaves were given permission to tend to gardens and raise livestock, only those who were able-bodied could do so. Two, it is common knowledge that the diet of most slaves consisted largely of little more than meager rations. Countless slave narratives supported by anthropological and archaeological evidence reflect that most enslaved people survived on meal, molasses, discarded vegetables, and sometimes portions of salted meat. In contrast to one traveler who believed "there are very few [slaves] indeed who are denied the privilege of keeping dunghill fowls, ducks, geese, and turkies," many plantation owners did not provide adequate food for their slaves out of spitefulness and/or economic inability. Friday Jones was a slave in Raleigh, North Carolina, to Bill Jeffries. According to Jones, "His [Jeffries's] niggers should never raise chickens or have any privileges. He never wanted me to eat anything except what he gave me; never wanted me to eat a piece of chicken or buy a pound of butter."[41]

Ball's and Jones's examples provide two rationales for the plausibility of theft: jealousy and hunger. Frederick Douglass provides a third: vindication. He writes that some slaves stole simply because they felt it was their right to do so. And then there is a fourth rationale: theft by blacks was less common than believed but was used as a convenient tool of control. Let us consider this notion of black people's "disposition to theft" in more detail.

From the colonial era onward, many blacks were accused of having stolen the merchandise that they were selling. In 1695, under "An Act Concerning Negroes," the New Jersey General Assembly decreed that

> if any negro, negroes, or other slaves shall steal, or be found stealing, any swine, or other cattle, turkeys, geese, or any other kind of poultry and provisions whatsoever, or any kind of grain, and shall be convicted thereof before two justices of the peace, one whereof being of the quorum, the master or mistress of such negroes, or others slaves, shall within ten days after conviction, pay the value of what he or they have stolen to the party from whom the same is warrant. . . . And the said negro or negroes or other slaves, being so convicted, shall be publickly punished with corporal punishment, not exceeding forty stripes, the master or mistress of such negro, negroes or other slaves, to pay the charge thereof.[42]

Three years after the South Carolina Assembly passed the act preventing trade from occurring with indentured servants, blacks, and other slaves, the legislature passed another act, this time for the "better ordering and governing of Negroes and other slaves." The provision was almost identical to that of 1737 except for its assertion that owners were enticing their slaves to "pilfer and steal, to raise money for their owners, as well as to maintain themselves in drunkenness and evil courses." And in neighboring Virginia on Wednesday, March 29, 1775, Ned, a slave, was tried at a Court of Oyer and Terminer in York County for using "force and arms" to steal two turkeys worth five shillings. Although Ned pled not guilty, he was found guilty and punished with a hand branding. It was a pervasive belief that blacks stole the goods that they sold. To alleviate this crime, laws were enacted in Virginia, South and North Carolina, and Georgia, and had been much earlier in New York, "for the better regulating of the said Markets, for preventing tainted or unwholesome Provisions being sold."[43]

There might have been an element of truth to these accusations, and then again there might not. During the colonial period, most chickens were not kept in henhouses. Chicken and fowl were free to roam, hence the term barn-yard or dunghill fowl. They were often left to find food and shelter wherever possible, an issue that easily lends support to the charge of theft. Exceptions could always be found among the wealthy. When Philip Fithian, tutor to Robert Carter's children at Nomini Hall, toured the grounds with Mrs. Carter, he saw a well-kept lot of "fowls and mutton for the winter."[44] On the other hand, several of Landon Carter's stocks were trampled to death by his sheep because his coop was not completed on time. Inasmuch as there was no widespread formalized system of breeding, it was difficult to distinguish most common fowl from one another, with the exception of certain kinds of partridges, pheasant, and hens. Nonetheless, these truisms did little to hinder the allegations that chickens were disappearing at the hands of black people.

The accusation of theft was levied not only against slaves; free blacks and fugitives were also accused of stealing and other misdemeanors. Newspapers and other information sources often spoke with contempt of poor free blacks in particular: "As they have not the face to apply openly for alms, they rely upon their ingenuity in rascality, and plan an attack upon the poultry, pork, or some other life preserver which the white man has put up for his own use." The writer goes on to note that if free blacks are "too lazy to steal," they will spend the winter in the almshouse awaiting the warmer weather in which to "bask in sunshine, and live another summer in idleness."[45] Fugitives also lived in constant fear of being accused of such petty crimes, which would reveal their identities, resulting in their recapture.

By the 1800s, black men and women had fully come to be associated with chicken stealing. They were often convicted even when the evidence against them was preposterous. In 1876, a black woman from the southeastern corner of Nottoway County, Virginia, was accused of having stolen some chickens that she later went on to sell to Mr. John Powell. Apparently, a female neighbor identified the chickens as belonging to her own lot. When the black woman protested, the mother of the chickens was brought in to see if she would identify them as her own, and after she did so, the black woman received thirty-nine lashes.[46]

Many of these accusations were based on scant evidence. This point aside, there is danger in a line of defense that issues value judgments on one's actions without regard to the circumstances that contributed to this behavior. For example, hunger was a major motivation for theft, despite the obvious risks involved. And the risks surrounding theft were great. According to Annie Burton, during the harvest season planters discovered "cornstalks missing from the ends of the rows." And even though the slaves received their weekly allotment every Monday night of "molasses, meat, corn meal, and a kind of flour called 'dredgings' or 'shorts,'" it was almost always gone before week's end. This left few options for hungry slaves except "to steal hogs and chickens."[47] Charles Ball also provides an example of theft for hunger and its consequences in his narrative: a field foreman once stole a sheep because he was hungry; as a result, slaves were whipped and rubbed with peppered tea.[48] Booker T. Washington wrote of hunger as a similar motivation for theft when he recalled his mother cooking a chicken for him and his siblings. He says, "How or where she got it I do not know. I presume, however, it was procured from our owner's farm. Some people may call this theft. . . . But taking place at the time it did, and for the reason that it did, no one could ever make me believe that my mother was guilty of thieving. She was simply a victim of the system of slavery."[49] Circumstances, then, forced not only desperate measures but also tensions around gaining control over a basic life necessity—food. On this point Alex Lichtenstein notes:

> If theft was a focus of tension on the plantation, that tension is not found in the slaves' attempts to forge a contradictory neutralizing morality, but in the struggle between slaves and masters to define conflicting notions of authority, property and customary rights. . . . In one of the most widespread slave "crimes," the theft of food, we can discern a moral economy rooted, at the least threatening level, as a struggle over the control of the slaves' diet, and at the most threatening level, in conflicting claims of economic rights to agricultural production. For slaves [then], the theft of food was not just a matter of diet. The struggle to control and define the right to sustenance was also a question of power.[50]

This concern with power is evident mostly in the belief that taking and removing foods—whether surplus or not—was a rightful entitlement to the goods that slaves had helped produce. Many black women worked in the kitchens and picked fruit and other vegetables while men fished, hunted, and butchered all day without reaping the benefits of this bounty. For them, stealing was their natural right inasmuch as they needed to eat in order to have strength to perform the tasks demanded of them. Turning again to Ball, he details this point in his account of how he would use the fish he had caught to barter for bacon. In his narrative, he explains that as spring approached, the game became scarce throughout the South Carolina countryside. Ball had to find a new mode "of improving the allowance allotted to [him] by the overseer." The river provided this opportunity. His skills in fishing were acknowledged, and he was assigned to head a fishing party where he had his liberty of "common river fish" like pike, perch, and suckers, which he and his fellow fishermen ate without benefit of salt or frying. Nor were they permitted to eat the shad with which they could have "lived well, if we had been permitted to boil the shad on the coals . . . for a fat shad will dress itself in being broiled, and is very good without any oily substance added to it." After a week of eating boiled fish, bread, and potatoes, they grew bored by the repetitive blandness. When the opportunity came for them to eat the forbidden shad, they "cooked as many as we could all eat; but were careful to carry, far out into the river the scales and entrails of the stolen fish." When on another occasion Ball encountered a white boat master who sought to exchange bacon for the shad, he "felt in [his] conscience that [he] had a better right than any other person" to engage in such a transaction. From Ball's point of view, slaves did not view theft of property in the same way as plantation owners: "I was never acquainted with a slave who believed that he violated any rule of morality by appropriating to himself any thing that belonged to his master, if it was necessary to his comfort. The master might call it theft, and brand it with the name of crime; but the slave reasoned differently, when he took a portion of his master's goods, to satisfy his hunger, to keep himself warm, or to gratify his passion for luxurious enjoyment."[51]

Although few might describe their act of theft as "gratify[ing] their passion for luxurious enjoyment[s]," many might agree with Douglass, who did not like to steal from a moral standpoint but did so out of necessity prompted by hunger. From Douglass's point of view, stealing was "removal" as in "taking his meat out of one tub, and putting it into another; the ownership of the meat was not affected by the transaction. At first, he owned it in the *tub*, and last, he owned it in *me*."[52]

Black people were certainly aware of the fact that white people believed that they were thieves. On some level it seems that the punishment was worth the risk, especially when it meant that one's family would be fed. There is a problem that must be avoided and that is in viewing these acts, and those involved, only from the standpoint of victimization. Doing this almost always denies any agency to the black women and men, bond and freed, who lived and survived the best way they could given their status at that time. We must also avoid this way of thinking because it denies the ingenuity and craftiness —from the act of stealing to the stories that were told to cover the act—employed by some blacks "to outwit ole' massa." One writer called it the "ingenuity of rascality." Others have labeled it chicanery and thievery. Either way, numerous anecdotes detail acts of black men, women, and children pilfering foodstuffs, especially chickens, from the master's coffers in the light of day or under the cover of night.

In his slave narrative, *Sketches of My Life in the South*, Jacob Stroyer tells how he observed Joe, a waiter, outsmart the master's wife, Mrs. King. As he recollects, the Kings were fond of entertaining, and so they always had turkeys and chickens at the ready. One day, Joe killed and dressed a turkey. He put it into the pot, but as he did not cut it up, the "turkey's knees stuck out of the pot." Because Joe could not cover the turkey knees, he threw one of his shirts over the pot to cover his crime. Mrs. King, suspecting that something was amiss, inquired of Joe why he had not responded to her husband's summons. When she went into the kitchen, she asked Joe what was in the pot, to which he replied, "Noffing misses but my shirt, am gwine to wash it." Not believing this story, Mrs. King stuck a fork into the pot, and taking out the shirt she also found the turkey. When she asked Joe how the turkey got in the pot, he feigned innocence but said "he reckoned the turkey got in himself, as the fowls were very fond of going into the kitchen." For his troubles, Joe was punished because "he allowed the turkey to get into the pot."[53]

These examples of African American trickster heroism reflect a kinship to African traditions that viewed this type of behavior as not only morally acceptable but also necessary for survival. Given the widespread disparities between what the slaves produced for enslavers and their own material lives, they saw their behavior, as Frederick Douglass notes, as necessary. John Roberts explains it this way: "Given the desperate and oppressive circumstances under which they lived, enslaved African could not be overly concerned with the masters' definition of 'morality' of behaviors that enhanced their prospects for physical survival and material well-being. The task that they confronted, however, was how to make such individually devised solutions to a collective problem function as a behavior strategy for the group without endangering their adaptability or the physical well-being of members of their community."[54]

In a similar account found in *Weevils in the Wheat*, ex-Virginia slave Charles Grandy tells how many slaves would steal chickens "off de roos." They would steal the chickens, hide them in the hidden trap of the floor, cook them at night, and burn the feathers.[55] In some instances, such as Grandy's, a white accomplice assisted with the theft. This assistance could come in the form of a lookout man, a trader, or the benefactor of the theft. For example, Mr. Norris, an ex-slave residing in Minnesota, shared that many blacks stole at the behest of their overseers and masters: "Talk about the black man stealing; they made us do it. An' after stealing for them if we took out one of them same chickens for ourselves, we'd better burn them feathers, or they'd a burned us."[56]

When whites participated with blacks in crimes like this, they were looked upon as the "worst kind of white man." The *Richmond Daily Dispatch* noted that white men in their "superior adroitness" elude detection of the crime by engaging black men—bond and free—as their "confederates." Most white men could not be prosecuted for their crimes because blacks could not testify against them in southern states. For white men, chicken stealing was considered the "commonest class of misdemeanors." So even if they were prosecuted, they received the lowest sentence or the charge ended in acquittal, except when the crime was considered of a more heinous nature. On the other hand, slave owners would punish blacks with few exceptions.[57]

For all of the accusations of theft by blacks, there were still more who did not acquire their stock in that fashion. Many came to obtain their livestock in the ways previously mentioned, through industry and privilege. Were this not the case, then fewer blacks would have been observed in possession of such flocks. In her mid-nineteenth-century travel observations, Scandinavian novelist and feminist activist Frederika Bremer noted:

Every house has a pigsty, in which there is generally a very fat pig; and many hens and chickens swarm about the garden-plot, in which they grow Indian corn, beans, and different kinds of roots. . . . The slaves sell eggs and chickens, and every Christmas their pig also, and thus obtain a little money to buy treacle, or molasses (of which they are very fond), biscuits, and other eatables. They often lay up money; and I have heard speak of slaves who possess several hundred dollars. This money they generally place out to interest in the hands of their masters.[58]

The travel diaries of landscape architect Frederick Law Olmstead during his yearlong tour of the "back country" from Virginia to Texas in the mid-nineteenth century reveal that he often consumed game (deer and turkeys), which had been "purchased of the Negroes." This was in addition to the "eggs, fowls, and bacon, they frequently sold" or used for their own households.[59] Olmstead's observations were recorded in various newspaper articles prior to the outbreak of the Civil War. Although he did not allude directly to women in Gordonsville, Virginia, his and other observations might be referring to blacks who were precursors to the waiter carriers of this rural Virginia community.

The town of Gordonsville, Virginia, was not incorporated until 1870, but by then a group of black women were well into their entrepreneurial ventures as food vendors or "waiter carriers," as they dubbed themselves. When weary train passengers arrived in town, these black women rushed to offer a combination of foods that included fried chicken, biscuits and breads, hard-boiled eggs, fruit pies, and "their famous hot coffee which was sold in old fashioned pots." [60]

In the post-emancipation South, Gordonsville, like other rural towns, witnessed an influx of people seeking lucrative jobs ushered in by technological advancement. The arrival of the Louisa Railroad in 1840 heavily contributed to the growth and vitality of the small town, and by 1850 the railroad had expanded, offering even more opportunities. African American men were able to obtain employment putting down rails, driving spikes, and servicing the trains when they halted in the town, while women peddled various foods. The women were in fierce competition with trackside taverns and other restaurants that had been given the necessary licenses to sell food to the railroad passengers. Like their ancestors before them, they nonetheless forged ahead with their own marketing plan. According to Isabella Winston, known as "Bella" on the platform, these women sold their dishes "outside" the tracks across from the station platform. This image, captured on film by a turn-of-the-twentieth-century photographer and subsequently converted into a postcard, is one of the only remaining images to reference these women's commercial spirit (figure 1.1).

Bella Winston learned the trade from her mother, Maria Wallace, one of the six waiter carriers pictured in the photograph. In 1970, Winston, at age eighty, contributed to the town's centennial celebration by providing one of the few extant accounts about the entrepreneurial activities of the waiter carriers.[61] In her interview with the *Orange County (Va.) Review*, Winston shared that wings, backs, gizzards, and other innards sold for a nickel, while the more choice pieces of meat—the breasts and legs—sold for a dime. With the proceeds of these sales, the women went on to purchase a better way of life for themselves and their families. As Winston put it, "My mother paid for this place with chicken legs. We first lived in a log cabin but that burned almost 50 years ago and we rebuilt further from the road." Another waiter carrier, Hattie Edwards, went on to establish "Hattie's Inn" in what was described in the article as the "Negro section of Gordonsville." [62]

For Winston, Edwards, their families, and community members, chicken was more than a source of nourishment; it was their livelihood. Most likely, the black people in Gordonsville, like families elsewhere, ate very little of the surplus that provided their families with income. Winston notes in the news article that her own children "never knew there were other parts of the

FIGURE 1.1. Postcard, ca. 1900s, showing waiter carriers on the Gordonsville platform selling their wares to passengers who traveled by train.
Courtesy Orange County Department of Tourism and Visitor's Bureau.

chicken besides wings, backs, and feet until they were big enough to move away."[63] This was not to withhold "the best" from her children; rather, "the best" was reserved for sale so that her children could have even more. Long after Edwards was able to transmit the skill and perseverance of snack vending into a larger commercial enterprise, she lamented the changing conditions around her: "The good old days [when she met the trains] . . . You could make some money then and it meant something after you made it."

But more than serving as a financial resource, cooking and selling chicken was also an example of community cultural work. According to Winston, when there was leftover food, they fed "many a hungry mouth among the neighborhood children who wanted to be fed." And even at the age of seventy-five, Edwards was still catering to her community by providing fried chicken "at the end of each week when the men have some money left from their pay. Early in the week they don't eat fried chicken."[64] This testament to the luxury of dining out as well as enjoying a meal of fried chicken speaks to a time that many of us could not fathom. For many at that time, fried chicken and biscuits was not only a rare treat but also a means to a profitable end.

There are a number of points to be gleaned from this one case study example of early African American female entrepreneurship. In addition to engaging in commercial activity for themselves, these women also participated at times in aspects of cultural work, using food as their source of production. Second, the ways in which Bella Winston and the other waiter carriers used chickens for economic gain, as opposed to solely a food source, illustrate how people make meanings of their material world. Unfortunately, only memory fragments remain of the women who served as carriers. Winston was a second-generation carrier, leaving the material culturalist to raise a number of questions that may or may not ever be answered: Where did the cooking take place, in someone's home or at a nearby facility? If the chickens were cooked at someone's home, how far did the women have to travel to begin a day's work? Did their "workday" begin before they reached the depot? In other words, would they sell to travelers along the way? Did they sell, directly or indirectly, to black people? Were there other people, Native Americans, for example, who lived nearby? Were they customers as well? Did the women work independently or together in the cooking process? How was the money distributed? What were some of the other material attainments acquired from the profits of chicken sales? Were any of the women married or related to the black men who worked on the railroad? If so, might these workers have assisted the women by delaying any of the work that needed to be done on the train? What other occupations did these women assume after ending their stint as a waiter carrier? And how did their communities view this work?[65]

Though there are countless other questions that could be asked, Winston and Edwards provide answers that can be used as a starting point. For example, Winston recalled that health regulators frequently issued citations to the women. The women believed that most of these interventions were in an effort to gain information about their recipes, a practice that often bewildered the waiter carriers. Of one health officer in particular (whose name Winston refused to reveal), she said: "He used to make me so mad that sometimes I would cuss and sometimes I would cry. They would make us wrap our chicken in oil paper and even wanted to see where we cooked it." But health officials were not the only concerns of these women. Gordonsville historian W. L. Davenport, who was called upon not only to "confirm" the existence of the waiter carriers but also to offer insights into their decline, explains that the increased modernization of trains resulted in the gradual elimination of this enterprise. The first indication of decline came with the advent of dining cars, though many travelers still purchased from the vendors. The addition of closed vestibules made access more difficult and proved to be a second hindrance (figure 1.2). Passengers circumvented this blockage, however, by raising their windows rather than disembarking to make their purchases. The women's fate was finally sealed, though, when trains became air-conditioned, permanently closing the windows. Other than the memories detailed here, what remains of the more than fifty-year legacy of the Gordonsville women is a plaque that was erected in 2002 to honor the "first black female entrepreneurs" in the area (figures 1.3 and 1.4).[66]

The foregoing discussion of the Gordonsville waiter carriers further suggests that foods like chicken are filled with multiple complex meanings and interpretations. Being able to touch the product of one's labor from the sale of goods and commodities, especially when those opportunities are few and highly regulated, means that the symbolic representations may be competing and overlapping. For the waiter carriers, selling chickens was critical to their livelihoods as well as to their means of material attainment. That Bella Winston credits her mother with building their home from the food sales and proceeds indicates the degree to which there was an economic imperative to being a waiter carrier. Though we are left devoid of a number of intimate details that would shed more light on their roles as early entrepreneurs, we are made aware of some of the tensions and contestations that surrounded their business practices. To this end we are able to see their economic participation as part of the complex historical circumstances that informed the lives of many black women and men.

Throughout Reconstruction and well into the twentieth century, black women continued to cook as well as sell chickens out of economic necessity. Yet the images resulting from new technologies made a mockery out of one of the few occupations available to black women—domestic work. The life realities, however, of black women—from slavery to freedom—can be seen as a "protest" to the historical conditions that forced them to cook and clean. Ian Hodder suggests that "most material symbols do not work through rules of representation, using a language-like syntax. Rather, they work through the evocation of sets of practices within individual experience. . . . They come to have abstract meaning through association and practice."[67] But the women of Gordonsville, like others before them, suggest an alternative point of view. Objects like chicken are embedded in a set of relations of power and domination that can have very specific meanings.[68]

Food serves more than its intended function to nourish and to satiate. During the market exchange process, poultry and other foodstuffs provided necessities. But, the trading and selling of these foods for commerce also provided relative autonomy, social power, and economic freedom. So much of what was represented in popular culture of the Reconstruction era increased the belief that the legacy of blacks in America was that of an infantile, savage, chicken-loving (in the extreme) people. Constant edification of this ideology sought to keep blacks in mental bondage. It also made the stories of those who achieved monumental strides upon obtaining freedom all the more ex-

FIGURE 1.2.
Photograph of
Gordonsville waiter
carriers, ca. 1900.
Steel trains with
closed vestibules
made it difficult
for passengers to
disembark, so they
raised their windows
to buy food from the
vendors. Courtesy
Orange County
Historical Society.

FIGURE 1.3. Plaque
commemorating the
Gordonsville waiter
carriers, June 15,
2002. Photograph
by author.

FIGURE 1.4.
The plaque
commemorating
the Gordonsville
waiter carriers is
placed in front of the
Exchange Hotel. In
the background are
the railroad tracks,
which run directly
in front of the hotel.
Photograph by
author.

traordinary, perhaps at the expense of those whose day-to-day acts of survival went unnoticed. Focusing on ordinary black women and men lets us consider and recognize survivalisms in a dialectical relationship to the often-static representations of black life that emerged from this period of history. Finding victory within the minutiae of everyday life allows us to recognize the underlying stories of reverse social power that emerged against the discourses circumscribing black peoples' relationships to chicken. This is particularly important as we continue to read black women as historical subjects of change and agency.

This argument is particularly salient to the discussions in the next chapter. In it, I provide a chronological overview of the ways in which blacks were presented in images bearing or related to chicken. For decades, blacks were subjected to racist visual imagery that distorted their physical bodies and social and psychological well-being. Black men, however, were overwhelmingly targeted for this type of visual abuse because they were a perceived threat to the social, cultural, and economic power of white society. These exposés will further illustrate how food can have complex meanings beyond consumption. But more important, these narratives illustrate how black people reverse the tide of denigration imposed by material and visual objects.

"WHO DAT SAY CHICKEN IN DIS CROWD"

BLACK MEN, VISUAL IMAGERY,
AND THE IDEOLOGY OF FEAR

2

"Dat boy jes' live an' breathe chickens!"
—Tom Lea, in Alex Haley, Roots

When the miniseries *Roots*, based on Alex Haley's book, aired on national television in 1977, it provided for many viewers the first glimpse of any aspect of slavery. Despite the challenges to the story's veracity, *Roots* offered a compelling look at many of the probable day-to-day goings-on of enslaved men and women.[1] One aspect of this daily life involved a long-standing element of male social bonding—cockfighting, albeit romanticized. Central to this part of the narrative is the flamboyant characterization of "Chicken George." George is a flashy dresser who could be seen in a "blue stiff-front shirt, red socks, yellow pants and yellow belt-backed suitcoat, and . . . bright orange shoes." George is an even flashier speaker, often using malapropisms. In his fine dress and fancy ways, Chicken George embodies the denigrating caricatured image of "Zip Coon"—a perennial image that has come to be associated with African American men (figure 2.1).[2]

The images of African American men, portrayed in the likeness of Zip Coon in compromising positions with chicken, are perverse and overwhelming. This chapter provides a roughly chronological overview that illustrates and discusses some of the extant imagery that may have helped create the prevailing stereotypes negatively associating African American people with chicken. A study unto itself, this chapter seeks to place the larger focus of this project—black women's agency with regard to chicken—into a racial and economic context. By considering black women in relationship to black men, I argue for the need to read African American lives from the perspective of the people and not from the imagery that tried to define them. Using photographs, sheet music, postcards, greeting cards, and oral history interviews, each section of this discussion will briefly focus upon images or incidents of particular historical periods.

With the ending of the Civil War came freedom for most African Americans. Many began the long journey to other states and regions. People were

FIGURE 2.1.
"Two souls with but a single thought." Postcard, ca. 1910. The man seated would be described as "Zip Coon." Author's collection.

galvanized as most moved north and some westward in search of new beginnings. Inasmuch as there was already a steady but small presence of African American people in the western region during the mid-nineteenth century, racially based economic and political disparities were in effect similar to other locales. Many of these restrictions were already in place prior to the Civil War; as a result, southern legislation ensuring civil rights for blacks was equally consequential to the lives of African Americans outside of that region. Reconstruction, with its steady stream of industrial advancements, did little to diminish antiblack sentiments, which were in existence throughout much of the United States. In many instances, emancipation fueled these emotions. Interestingly, chicken was at the center of some of these emotional battles. Because black men (and women) had been frequently accused of stealing chickens—their "favorite" animal—black men were prime objects for the ideological warfare that was waged upon the psyches of blacks.

The fictional account of Haley's *Roots* puts forth one interpretation of the imagery prevailing at that time that contributes to these ideologies. "Chicken George" is the son of Kizzy and the slave owner, Tom Lea. Kizzy, the daughter of Kunta Kinte and Bell, is sold to Lea's plantation at an early age after it is revealed that she forged a pass for another slave, her beloved Noah. Soon after arriving at the Lea plantation, Kizzy is raped and impregnated by Tom Lea, producing her only son, George. Eventually the reader comes to know George as a cock handler, but when he is first presented, it is in the role of a buffoon.[3] At an early age, George learns to entertain Lea and his friends with his exclamation, "I preaches, Massa!" In one of his first puerile episodes, George mocks a white preacher who frequented the plantation: "If you specks Uncle Pompey done took massa's hog, tell massa! If you sees Miss Malizy takin' missis' flour, tell missis! 'Cause if y'all's dat kin' o good niggers, an' doin' well by you' good massa an missis, den when y'all die, y'all might git into de kitchen of heab'n!"[4] George's presentation lands him a job as Lea's comedian, confirming the prophecy of the plantation soothsayer, Sister Sarah, who declared that George "never gwine be what nobody would call no ordinary nigger! He is always gwine keep gittin' into sump'n new an' different jes' long as he draw breath" (483). The "something new and different" is cock handling.

At the age of twelve, George begins to work as an apprentice to Uncle Mingo, the plantation cock trainer. He learns everything from feeding to fighting cocks, and because of his talent, George is released from working in the fields and becomes the full-time rooster-handler. Lea endeavors to be in the best class of poor whites and achieves this goal. With George's skill, Lea's winning average increases tremendously, greatly improving Lea's financial status among his peers. But unlike the elite men whose wealth is predicated on tobacco, cotton, or land, Lea relies upon gambling, a very tenuous form of material gain. Unequipped with the accoutrements that defined wealth, men like Lea used hackfighting, a bootleg version of cockfighting that usually involved fighting the lesser grade birds, to legitimate their sense of self within their own class.[5]

Among this class of people, Chicken George also builds a modest fortune. After George takes over Mingo's responsibilities as the plantation's cock handler and trainer, he begins to accumulate money. George marries and manages to save almost $6,000 toward the $7,500 needed to buy his family's freedom. But he also squanders a great deal—"twixt three–fo' thousan' dollars"—until he begins to keep company with the free blacks he encounters on his many trips to cockfight tournaments. It is only then that he realizes that the money he is making from fighting could be used to secure not only his freedom but also that of his family.

But along with money, George begins to enjoy a relative amount of fame. He becomes so popular at cockfighting and winning that he is known to "preen and crow like one of his winning roosters" (519). Identified as the "cocky, self-proclaiming" man, he is later dubbed "Chicken George," a name that, in his opinion, "had a certain flair" (521). George would dress the part not only to demonstrate his affinity for his birds but also to be known as the best cockfighter in the region. He begins to embody the rooster's air of cockiness and flair. On his wedding day, he attends partly drunk and oddly attired. He adds to his bizarre combination a green woolen scarf knitted for him by his intended bride, Matilda, and a black derby that is a wedding gift from Mr. Lea (534). There is no doubt that George is flamboyant. And much later in life, his son describes him as a "derby-wearing, bombastic-talking father" (627).

But more than a cause of embarrassment, George's air and behavior was a cause of concern to most white men at that time. Chicken George and others like him put fear in the hearts of southern white men because they posed a threat not only to the social order but also to all that these men had accomplished in trying to maintain a separateness between the races. The success of black men like Chicken George aroused a certain degree of envy among the lesser classes of whites. And with the black men's financial success came freedom and from this generally some form of political involvement, an anathema to white society at that time. A freed black man was a dangerous one who could enlist others to engage in rebellion. Twice in the novel *Roots*, Tom Lea took up arms against his slaves after hearing rumors of rebellion by Nat Turner and then later by Denmark Vesey, prompting at least one slave to observe, "All white folks scairt us niggers sometime gwine organize an' rise up together" (509). As Ira Berlin notes, the black man's desire for liberty and all things equal, his "passion" "exposed the white man's deepest fears." But more than that, Berlin continues, free blacks reminded whites of the inherent contradiction in valuing liberty and freedom while simultaneously owning slaves. This sense of guilt coupled with the fear of insurrection and rebellion was enough to precipitate policies in several southern states that ordered free blacks to leave the state within sixty days or be re-enslaved.[6]

Chicken George found himself in this precarious position. During one particularly eventful cockfight, Tom Lea wagers all that he and Chicken George had accumulated—and loses. Broken and dispirited, Tom is forced to "loan" George to the Englishman whom he owed. He is also forced to sell several of Chicken George's children and most of his own worldly possessions. After six years, George returns from England and obtains his freedom from a broken and alcoholically decrepit Tom Lea. Clad in his green scarf and black derby (and confidently armed with his newly obtained freedom papers), Chicken George and his son Tom venture into town one day for supplies. As was his habit, Chicken George was "stepping about in a cocky manner visually inspecting items of merchandising." His dapper appearance and self-assured attitude raise the ire of the former county sheriff, J. D. Cates. Instantly recognizing the air of an "uppity niggra," Cates orders George's son Tom to "fetch" him a dipper of water. Deciding he is still thirsty, he next turns to Chicken George and thrusts the dipper toward him, remarking, "I'm still thirsty!" In response, George "stood with his head slowly shaking" and then hands Cates his freedom papers (656–57). The next day, the plantation owner who then enslaved George's family gently approaches George. The planter explains that he had been made aware of the law by Cates and that George would have to leave the state or be re-enslaved. This statement is made with the promise that if George chooses to stay, he will be "treated well." Needless to say, Chicken George leaves the plantation in search of a new locale where freedom for him and his family can be found (659).

I have taken pains to elaborate upon the story of Chicken George for two reasons: first, to provide another example of the ways in which some African Americans may have operated within an informal economy using chicken as their source of revenue, and second, to forecast the ways in which food, politics, gender, race, and class can intersect. Chicken George's embodiment of Zip Coon's attributes, including his strut and preen, are significant not only for its literal meaning but also for the metaphorical. Clifford Geertz in his classic ethnographic monograph "Deep Play: Notes on the Balinese Cockfight" found that the word for cock in that country is used metaphorically to mean "hero," "dandy," and "lady-killer," among other male attributes. It is also said to mean "a pompous man whose behavior presumes above his station . . . compared to a tailless cock that struts about as though he had a large spectacular one."[7] It has also been suggested that the cock embodies "the most powerful themes in nature—sexuality, the sun, and . . . resurrection." Cocks were considered sexually potent and virile, and in the ancient world, the chicken keeper was "a person of great importance."[8]

By all accounts, cockfighting is predominantly a male pastime. This was especially the case in the South, where it was favored by generations of men, presidents and working class alike. Well into the middle of the nineteenth century, this carnivalesque landscape permitted men like Tom Lea who started out "dirt poor" to become rich, even if to lose it all in one fell swoop. Because it was also a place where sexuality and chicken fighting were fodder for the same conversation, it is no surprise that race, sexual politics, and gender might intersect. Another example from the life of Chicken George illustrates my point. In the novel, Lea and George are riding to a tournament when Lea strikes up a conversation about sexuality with his slave. Awestruck by this act of familiarity, Chicken George tries to find ways to keep the conversation centered on chicken fighting. A question asked by George leads Lea to reference George's late-night "tomcattin'." In an attempt to avoid a conversation about how his nighttime visits to the plantation of a rival gamecocker has led to Lea being propositioned for George's purchase, George remarks that he has stopped visiting the plantation. Lea, recognizing the attempts at avoidance, remarks: "'Found you another wench somewhere else, huh? . . . Big strapping twenty-year-old buck like you? Boy, don't tell *me* you're not slippin' around nights gettin' plenty of that good hot tail! Hell, I could hire you out

FIGURE 2.2. "Black takes the count, white the victor."
Postcard, ca. 1910. Author's collection.

to stud; bet you'd like that!' The massa's face creased into a half leer. 'Good friend of mine says them black wenches got plenty good hot tail, now tell me the truth, ain't that right, boy? . . . Okay, what about them hot black wenches, boy? How many can you mount in a night?'" (530).

Undoubtedly, comments of this nature were familiar to George. The sexual habits of black men and the exploitation of black women during enslavement is a familiar conversation. But couple the belief of black men as bucks and studs to the symbolic imagery embodied by the cock/rooster (figure 2.2), then apply that imagery to a man like Chicken George—young, black, self-assured, with almost as much money as a poor white like Tom Lea. Taken together, one can surely see how black men (whether or not they had a role as a cock handler) would be perceived as a threat to white men's virility and white women's bodies, a white man's own desires for black and white women's bodies notwithstanding.

But black men were not singled out for portrayals in popular culture images because of their cock-handling skills. Rather, they were singled out because their cocks (literally and figuratively) were often perceived as bigger and better. In this instance, the cock is an object that potentially symbolizes both the sexual prowess and the confidence of some black men. Men like George who were confident, and definitely those who were free and self-assured, intimidated men like Tom Lea and J. D. Cates. For one, these black men were a reminder that some blacks could and did rise above the station permitted them by white society. Two, when measuring their success by these kinds of blacks, men of Lea's ilk were made all the more aware of their own tenuous economic position. By not being part of the southern aristocracy, white men like Lea and Cates were only a cockfight or two away from their beginnings as poor whites.

To overcome these intimidations, Tom Lea constantly remarks on the sexual prowess of black men and women. This is not lost on George, who knows he is the product of his mother's rape. Lea continued to force Kizzy to have sex with him even after George was born; George would often recall with disdain the "grunting of the man who lay there beside him jerking up and down on top of his mammy" (506). Thus, by trying to reduce George to the level of stereotype (a black stud), Lea is able to see Chicken George for what he needs him to be—a slave who knew his place. Though written over a century later, *Roots*, with its characterizations of Chicken George and Tom Lea, offers a compelling literary narrative of the complex dynamics intertwining chicken, gender, and race. In this scenario, chicken is filled with multiple layers of symbolic meaning—for George, for Tom Lea, and for the larger white society. But these examples are not present only in contemporary literature. The June 12, 1864, issue of the *New York Herald* contained the article "Not 'All Quiet Along the Lines.'" The article indicated that rebel soldiers were wasting their ammunition and drummers and that "demoralized negroes" were engaged in coffee boiling and chicken roasting "or some other delightful epicurean occupation denied to the gallant soldiers who front the enemy."[9] So deeply embedded were these assumptions about African Americans and chicken that they were deemed an important point of reference for a Civil War reporter.

The irony here is that while these unfortunate black soldiers were participating in the war to free themselves from enslavement, the condescending rhetoric of this article illustrates the quagmire that daily confronted them, as stereotypes of this nature were inescapable. These kinds of historical references certainly helped to fuel what we understand today to be the stereotypes that distort the perceived relationships that black people have to chicken. Although the exact origins of this stereotype are unknown, narratives from the eighteenth and nineteenth centuries coupled with visual imagery and other ephemera of the twentieth century suggest the beginning of a perennial racial stereotype that continues to persist (figure 2.3).

The post–Civil War era bore witness to the need for white society to subdue black men and, by extension, black people. And what better way to con-

FIGURE 2.3.
"Break Break!"
Postcard, ca. 1905,
depicting the
distorted image of
a black male and a
swan or similar bird
pulling on his penis.
Author's collection.

stantly remind a black man of his rightful place than by using pictures? The image of the happy-go-lucky black man was needed to reassure both northerners and southerners that the South remained "in control." Black people thus became the butt of jokes that offered comic relief to the conscience and fear of white America. Illustrations of "dumb" black men stealing chickens helped to ease this tension (figure 2.4).

Deluded by the false notions of "forty acres and a mule"—and with this the hope of American citizenship—African American ex-slaves nonetheless were resourceful in finding land on which to grow crops, gather nuts, and otherwise engage in enterprises leading to self-sufficiency. Some women hawked their wares—chickens, eggs, vegetables—on the roadside or at the nearest country store in order to feed their loved ones and often to provide food for the ailing or elderly among them. Their material conditions notwithstanding,

A NEW DEVICE.
" Dey say niggahs don't know nuffin.   Well, den let 'em figgah out how dis ol' hoss done got in dat coop and cotched dis pullet."

FIGURE 2.4. "A New Device: Dey say niggahs don't know nuffin.
Well, den let 'em figgah out how dis ol' hoss done got in dat coop
and cotched dis pullet." Cartoon, n.d. Author's collection.

paramount in the minds of black people was progress—familial, social, economic, and political. To this end, black women sought employment wherever
it could be found, and this often thrust them into the homes of white people
in domestic capacities. Black men also inquired of work as blacksmiths and
stewards (particularly out west and in the seaboard areas) but more often
as farmers and planters. Some established their own grocery stores, hostels,
inns, and boardinghouses. In sum, black people were working but making attempts to do so on their own terms. For instance, accounts of African American life during Reconstruction suggest that black women withdrew in large
measure from wage-labor or sought to gain greater control over both their
paid and unpaid labor.[10] When possible, black women "of means" sought to
remain home in an effort not only to engage in a different type of labor (domestic duties and community work) but also to tend to child care and other
family matters. Regardless of their reasons, blacks—both men and women—
were ridiculed for their efforts to try to forge an identity of their own amid

the turbulence of the Reconstruction era. A barrage of images, which sought to wage war upon African American psyches, confronted these measures of autonomy. Most often, these images depicted African American men as lazy, shiftless chicken-stealers while portraying women as loyal, untiring mammies or servants.

The latter part of the nineteenth century has often been referred to as the worst period of race relations because of the intense hatred that was levied against blacks at all levels. General Carl Shurz reported to President Andrew Johnson that everywhere he went, "I hear people talk in such a way as to indicate that they are yet unable to conceive of the Negro possessing any rights at all." He went on to relate how whites would murder, debauch, and rob black people "without feeling a single twinge of their honor." In essence, Shurz remarked, "The people boast that when they get freedmen's affairs in their own hands . . . 'the niggers will catch hell.'"[11]

Much of the disdain that Shurz expressed was due to the loss of power and control that white people previously held over blacks. It was also due to the economic blow meted out to the North as well as the South by the ending of slavery. Animosity toward blacks was not relegated to the South but affected those in the North and the West as well. Many northern whites feared the influx of blacks to their region because they posed a competitive economic danger as a cheap labor source. Blacks were used as strikebreakers (as were European immigrants), which further exacerbated feelings of fear and hatred among white northerners.

Postwar constitutional amendments, which sought to guarantee equal rights to African American people, also fueled the ire of many white Americans. In reaction, legal decisions were made that virtually thrust African American people back into a slave existence. Among these were the Black Codes, which severely limited African American abilities to succeed in most every endeavor: owning land, working certain jobs, and even traveling. Though short-lived, these codes were nonetheless a prelude to several policies that would change the course of African American advancement for years to come. These racist policies were designed to hinder African Americans. Black people were nonetheless able to achieve some measure of progress during this period. For example, politically, African American men were able to acquire leadership roles and marginally participate in other aspects of politics. These acts, however, were not without condemnation. And to some extent, chicken was visually ever-present.

Newly freed African American men in particular, swollen in numbers and having gained the right to vote, provoked fear in the southern political process. D. W. Griffith's *Birth of a Nation* brought this threat to the silver screen and along with it the hint that black men lusted after white women. Adapted from Thomas Dixon's *The Clansman: An Historical Romance of the Ku Klux Klan*, Griffith's film portrays African Americans in government as real-to-life Zip Coons. Silas Lynch, played by white actor George Siegmann (in blackface), is a political aide in the Republican Party. Lynch and other southern blacks in the government are depicted as villains and scoundrels as they participate in the newly formed political arena. During the first legislative session of Reconstruction, the film typecasts blacks as power-hungry but shiftless, lazy, and slothful. Characters are seen stealing money and pushing white people off sidewalks. One character is holding a grotesque chicken or turkey leg, while others are sitting spread-eagled with their bare feet upon office desks. These "black" political aspirants are cast in direct contradiction to those who supposedly long for the Old South where subjugation and loyalty was familiar.

In another scene in the film, a law is passed requiring whites to show equality to blacks by saluting black officers in the streets and consenting to interracial marriage. In the climatic final scenes of the film, the young demure maiden, Flora, jumps to her death rather than allow herself to be touched by Gus, the former slave. Eventually, the film depicts the Ku Klux Klan and other supremacist organizations as successful in quelling "the black threat" to white society's political structure. When they subdue the violent, sexual prowess of black men, America's fears are eliminated, and the "natural southern order" is restored.[12]

The stereotype of the black man as a vicious sexual predator was born out of the gross misperception that all black men had enlarged penises and excessive confidence gained from emancipation. The chicken became a complex symbolic object in this ideological battle. On the one hand, it was considered a relatively insignificant animal in the larger realm of the animal kingdom. On the other, it embodied the symbolic imagery of virility. But it was also a food that black people were considered to love and rumored to steal. The result was a conflation of multiple symbols with black men emerging as societal scapegoats. The thought of the dark savage (black men) "cooking up a meal" of white "meat" (white women) was both racist and sexist for its implications (figure 2.5). And yet, this was one of the many threats that black men posed to white society. From this colonized position, African Americans were made to appear as "brute beasts" unashamedly lusting after white flesh. As Kobena Mercer puts it, "The primal fantasy of the big black penis projects the fear of a threat not only to white womanhood, but to civilization itself, as the anxiety of miscegenation, eugenic pollution and racial degeneration

FIGURE 2.5. "Well, fry mah hide! . . . Ah'm having *chicken* for breakfast!"
Postcard, n.d. Author's collection.

is acted out through white male rituals of racial aggression—the historical lynching of black men in the United States routinely involved the literal castration of the Other's strange fruit."[13] These images suggested a need to control black men, which organizations like the Klan provided. These ideological constructs were necessary salves for the troubled minds of whites who saw their dominance, as they knew it, quickly slipping away. This process of change required that new traditions be invented, and the social ideologies both embedded in these images and reinforced by their constant portrayal in the popular culture of the period provided the necessary conduit.[14] Stereotypical and caricatured modes representing black bodies were useful in helping to instill fear in white people while simultaneously creating some of the most denigrating illusions about blacks that have endured in the American—and more important, African American—minds.

These images and perceptions of chicken, sex, race, and gender speak to how power can be present in even the most mundane objects of our material lives. Chickens were certainly not the sole source of grist for the stereotype mill. But in using a food object to project these cultural stereotypes, whites were able to capitalize on a known truth: that black people raised and sometimes ate chicken. Added to this was a gross oversimplification—black people were chicken stealers. These images did not go unnoticed by scholars and advocates of early civil rights. Writing in 1849, Frederick Douglass observed: "Negroes can never have impartial portraits at the hands of white artists. It seems to us next to impossible for white men to take likenesses of black men, without most grossly exaggerating their distinctive features. And the reason is obvious. Artists, like all other white persons, have developed a theory dissecting the distinctive features of Negro physiognomy."[15] Writing almost a century later, W. E. B. Du Bois questioned: "Can any author [or artist] be criticized for painting the worse [*sic*] or the best characters of a group? Is not the continual portrayal of the sordid, foolish, and criminal among Negroes convincing the world that this and this alone is really and essentially Negroid, and preventing white artists from knowing any other types and preventing black artists from daring to paint them?"[16] Douglass's observations are keen and exact. And Du Bois's questions could be answered in the affirmative.

But Du Bois's questions also illustrate the power of food images to advance the rhetoric of stereotypes. Black people did and do eat chicken. And as the slaves' narratives illustrate, some blacks—feeling wholly justified—stole chickens in order to eat. And while some images capture aspects of black lives, they grossly distort the facts in the process. (Indeed, the embarrassment of these continuous distortions has led many black people to disavow any connections at all to poultry.) But, the images would have viewers believe that all black people are alike. And because society saw black people as a whole as unworthy of citizenship, everyone—gender and class aside—was disenfranchised. Du Bois's questions illustrate some of the complexities that confronted black people, particularly middle- and upper-class blacks who saw themselves as apart from the "folk." Stereotypical food imagery, however, left little, if any, room for distinction.

The image of Zip Coon made a mockery out of blacks who had any kind of aspirations—economic, political, social, or cultural (figures 2.6 and 2.7). The hatred directed toward black men was the result of white racial and class animus. Unable to turn their hostility inward upon themselves, the white community turned their resentment upon black men. One way in which this resentment manifested itself was in the creation of the stereotype of the dandy. Eric Lott explains, "The black dandy literally embodied the amalgamationist threat of abolitionism, and allegorically represented the class threat of those who were advocating it; amalgamation itself, we might even say, was a partial figuration of class aspiration."[17] Zip Coon or "the dandy," as already explained in connection with Chicken George, was considered an overzealous black man. He was the white man's competitor. He was depicted as fashionably dressed, a man intending to make himself better than the other blacks

FIGURE 2.6. "Who's in there?" Postcard, ca. 1905. Author's collection.

and the equal of whites. Regardless of how much he tried, he could never achieve this status because he was considered a buffoon, "a stumbling and stuttering idiot." He was understood to be lazy, unreliable, and an all-around "piece of work."[18] These portrayals relied heavily upon a series of signifiers, signifieds, and linguistic messages to convey these ideologies as natural. But they also sought to reaffirm the notion of blacks on the bottom at a time when war, Reconstruction, and immigration were shuffling the deck and putting the nature of national identity in question. An examination of three photographic images might help to make this point more clear.

Figure 2.8 depicts a man extended through the window of a henhouse attempting to grab a rooster, despite the obvious risk of being pecked on the hand. The first message one sees is fairly clear; a man is trying to grab a chicken and is risking danger to do so. Yet, there is another message that is far more denotative, and that is the linguistic statement that accompanies this image, "I'se Boun' to Hab a Christmas Dinna!"[19] Reading the vernacular reveals an additional signified: that it belongs to someone who is quite possibly illiterate or not well-speaking and perhaps either black or poor. Were it not for the linguistic variables (the caption) that convey a message, one would have to rely on the picture. A man is trying to grab a chicken. However, if the image is analyzed further, the viewer is left with a series of "discontinuous" signs—messages that can be read in any order since linearity is not important. First, there is the simple idea that a man is taking a chicken. Next, the

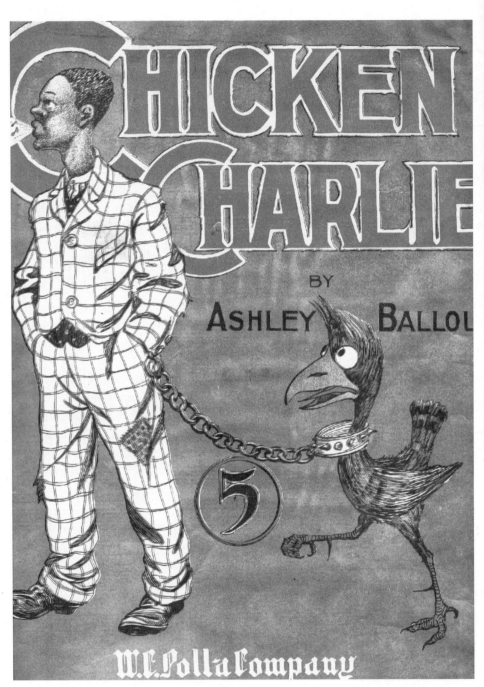

FIGURE 2.7. Sheet music cover for Ashley Ballou,
"Chicken Charlie," 1905. Author's collection.

FIGURE 2.8.
"I'se boun' to hab a
Christmas Dinna!"
Photograph, ca. 1898.
Author's collection.

"signifieds" or the implications are of a chicken and a struggle, since the birds are poised to peck. Yet, the man is hell-bent on taking one of the chickens. He leans through the window while simultaneously grabbing hold of the ledge.

The first sign, that the black man wants a chicken, is grounded in nineteenth-century rhetoric that casts black people as chicken lovers. The second sign is found in the first and that is the ever-present fetishized color of his skin—black—or the "racial epidermal schema," as Franz Fanon calls it. The man's skin color is a key signifier of difference in both the racial and cultural discourse of this time. A number of historical, cultural, and political discourses associated skin color with a range of "common knowledges."[20] This particular sign is reinforced by the redundancies found in the linguistic message, which is based on dialect, and the assumptions about black people, based on cultural stereotypes.

In the image there are two other signs worth noticing. The first is that this image calls to mind an "idyllic" scene of times past when black people were under control and, more important, in need of care by white society. If they would only allow themselves to be led back into slavery, where in their servility they could be cared and provided for, they would not have to steal. These notions were part of the therapeutic salve that was transferred to objects like chicken and black people.[21] Culture here becomes a code that entrusts its

FIGURE 2.9.
"Jes' dis Niggah's fool
luck!—bofe arms full
an' dat rooster a beggin'
to be took along."
Photograph, ca. 1904.
Author's collection.

meanings to material culture objects. The ubiquitous nature of items like chicken makes it a useful, oblique device for representing the various assumptions that were ensconced in the stereotype. Its ubiquity and mundaneness allows these beliefs and ideologies to become part of the natural fabric of everyday life, a point made all the more poignant by the use of photography.

In the new consumer culture, photography was critical for seeing objects and connecting them to their worlds of the real and the imagined. Images such as those shown in figure 2.8, figure 2.9, and figure 2.10—in addition to trade cards, postcards, and other visual ephemera—assisted in helping white people bridge the gap between what was actually happening in their lives and what they would like to have happen in their racialized fantasies.[22] As seen in figure 2.8, photography becomes particularly effective for capturing what people believed to be "the real." But the photograph "gives control over the thing photographed."[23] For example, the Christmas dinner chicken image seems staged. And given that most of these early-twentieth-century stereograph photographs were sold as commercial products, serving primarily to illustrate the text accompanying them, we can assume that they were.[24]

Take for instance figure 2.9. This image appears with different captions (another being " 'Dis Am De Wust Perdickermunt Ob Mah Life' "), though they are suggestive of the same intent.[25] In both the image here and the one used in the article by J. Stanley Lemons, a black man is shown wearing a derby, overcoat, and vest. There is no telling if both photos—this one and Lemons's —were taken in the same area, though it is quite possible, given that they have a similar pastoral background. There is also no particular rationale for roosters being referred to in some photographs while hens are referenced in others. This lends credibility to the fact that the kind of bird or fowl (that is, swan, hen, rooster, duck) was irrelevant; they were all equally useful in getting the point across to the viewer. Once enough of these photos had been circulated throughout popular culture, it did not matter which image or caption was used. The image alone would be suggestive of a crime in progress, even before one considered the intertextual narrative taking place.

The suggestion of staging or the use of props and devices makes this illustration all the more ominous, though not surprising. These types of illustrations were useful for alleviating some of the "nervous prostration" brought on by the rapid social, political, and cultural changes of the time. The sense of "displaced meaning" was pervasive in Victorian America.[26] Goods and commodities were particularly useful for helping individuals contemplate the "possession of an emotional condition, a social circumstance, even an entire lifestyle" by making desires concrete. However, as Grant McCracken suggests, this bridge serves its purpose when the goods are "not yet owned but merely coveted."[27] As commodities of racism, the goods are both owned and coveted in that purchasing one of these photographs or another visual representation enabled the owner not only to own but also to mentally covet the pastoral image that he or she wished to maintain. At the same time, these are staged photos of blacks coveting goods. Consequently, the placement and displacement of desire is duplicitous and overlapping. Although this interpretation is certainly not the only reason that people might have purchased this kind of photo, these images and their owners were complicit in spreading the network of racial power.

The photograph of the man with the two watermelons illustrates how devices could be used to present an image as natural and self-evident. If we return to the notion that all black men/cocks are attracted to white women/ hens, then figure 2.10 supplies that imagery along with signifiers similar to those previously discussed. This image, in addition to the usual suggestion of a crime, also depicts black males starting as early as childhood to acquire their desire for the "white hen." "Dis am de pick ob dat roost" is both a play on having the hen in his possession and a further implication of theft.[28] With this brief caption, the hurried reader can be spared the details in an effort

FIGURE 2.10.
"Dis am de pick ob dat
roost." Photograph,
ca. 1901. Author's
collection.

to get at the main point—even little black boys steal chickens. I noted earlier that images often featured a similar photograph but a different caption. However, the reverse was also true. There are pictures bearing the same caption but with different African American men and boys. This points to their use value as contrived cultural products rather than happenstance moments in African American life.

Not all of the images of blacks and chickens implied that blacks were thieves. There were many illustrations that were used as entertainment. They provided pleasure at seeing the black child, man, or woman in a compromising position or in one that would seem less threatening to white America's already shaken sense of order and hierarchy.[29] Postcards were useful in this purpose, lending themselves as precursors to some of the extant representations found today in popular culture. Here, commodity racism and race fetishism function more as spectacle, a comedy of errors, the carnivalistic and "grotesque realism" that was so much a part of antibourgeois celebrations. Much of the comedic value of these cards can be found in their imagery as well as in the messages on the verso or the back of the card.[30] In some instances, the messages are clearly derogatory, while in others they are either personally representative or merely tools of communication. For example, the message written on the back of the Thanksgiving postcard shown in figure 2.11 was written to wish "Paul" season's greetings and best wishes. There is no

FIGURE 2.11.
"Lost by a Tail."
Postcard, n.d.
Author's
collection.

indication of the author's race, so one cannot make assumptions unless the referent is clearer. The image in figure 2.12 suggests that the reference is to black people. The message on the verso, however, reads, "This is the truth." It is underscored twice and signed simply "Sue." The recipient of the card lived in West Virginia. One might assume, again from the social and cultural contexts, that the sender is white and is making a disparaging remark in her statement, but absent any definitive clarification, the card is ambiguous. The sender could very well have been black and poking fun. But, given that humor seems to be the primary purpose for the card being sent, and the message is underscored, we can assume that mockery was the intended purpose, racial ambiguity and all.

One is led to question how African Americans might have been players in producing their own knowledges and realities amid the proliferation of such images. How did seeing themselves portrayed as criminals manifest itself as personal political action? How did black men and women persist in using the oppositional gaze as a means of resistance? Assuming that induce-ments were given, one might ask about the social value, if any, for blacks who posed for these photographs. Stealing during enslavement certainly was valuable in that it provided food and other non-nutritive functions for black people. Could that same perspective be applied to postslavery periods? What is known is that the creators of these images, whether posed or not, stand in contrast to black photographers who tried to enhance the self-image of African American people by capturing them at their best. Yet "at their best" is a loaded, complex pronouncement because it assumes that black people are only at their best when the depiction is an amiable one. When one reads the actions of those who might have willingly posed for such photographs, it

is all too tempting to remove their agency by declaring them victims of the "chicken-loving darky" stereotype. How instead might their participation be interpreted so as to make them active participants in their own life's performance? Were they "wearing the mask," as Paul Laurence Dunbar would argue, "that grins and lies," smiles laced and mired with "myriad subtleties"? It might be neither of these, and then again, it might be both. These questions are reflective of the more gamboling one posed by Dunbar in his 1898 operetta *Clorindy, the Origin of the Cakewalk*, which he composed with Will Marion Cook and in which Dunbar asked, rhetorically, "Who Dat Say Chicken in Dis Crowd?"[31]

Scholars of black memorabilia refer to the period from the late 1880s to the 1930s as a time of "symbolic slavery" because of the persistence of the Old South imagery.[32] This period, with its sharecropping, lynchings, migrations, wars, and race riots, gave rise in the "Roaring Twenties" to an unprecedented level of racial intolerance. Amid this turmoil, African Americans were witnessing a rebirth and reclamation. It was the era of "the New Negro" with an outpouring of literary and artistic contributions from African American women and men. And though he did not live to see this outpouring in full, Dunbar was a forefather to this period of African American artistic flowering. A close reading of his composition "Who Dat Say Chicken in Dis Crowd" shows that the creators of African American arts and letters were staging overt and subversive political and social action against the myriad assaults they received in popular culture. But it also shows that they were trying to use their work to prepare black people for their rightful places in American society. Black writers used various strategies to encourage this goal. And though he was heavily criticized for writing about the plantation tradition and buying into the "happy darky" motif, it is possible to read Dunbar as using chicken as a cultural weapon in this particular piece of music.

Dunbar's composition has been classified as part of the "coon song" or "Negro song" genre. Generally, this genre boasted a concern with "jamborees," "razors," and the "gastronomical delights of chicken, pork chops and watermelon . . . red-hot 'mammas' and too faithful 'papas.'"[33] Relying on black dialect, this song was one of many that helped to propel *Clorindy*, the first black Broadway play, to fame. The songs were sung by a full black chorus and performed by an all-black cast, including the comedian Ernest Hogan. Even though "Who Dat Say Chicken in Dis Crowd" must be analyzed in the context of *Clorindy* and other "coon songs" like "Darktown Is Out Tonight," it also should be considered for its relevance beyond the standard interpretation.[34] Despite the success of the musical, many, including Cook's mother, were ashamed of the traditional black songs that were performed. Dunbar too is described as being "embarrassed" by the performance because the black performers acted like buffoons.[35]

One of the intentions of Cook and Dunbar in writing this musical was to "remove the minstrel mask" that pervaded the dramatic expressions of African American people since the early nineteenth century.[36] But understanding Dunbar's use of subtle irony opens the song's meaning to more possibilities. It can be read as more than simply a song that proclaimed the opening of the play. And it certainly can fare better than the shame felt by Cook's mother, who declared, "Oh Will! Will! I've sent you all over the world to study and become a great musician and you return such a nigger!"[37] It is possible to read it as a subtle challenge to black people—who dat say chicken in dis crowd?— because it seeks to speak to more than merely the chicken stereotype. Taken together, the panoply of title, visuals, and lyrics yields several interpretations —defiance, compliance, and alliance among them. In a brilliant display of subterfuge and role reversal, Dunbar's title poses a challenge to the black audience attending the play and to larger black communities as well.

At first glance, it seems that the song is specifically about black people wanting to consume chicken. However, the lyrics suggest something more:

> There was once a great assemblage of the cullud population,
>   all the cullud swells was there,
> They had got them-selves together to discuss the situation
>   and rumors in the air.
> There were speakers there from Georgia and some from Tennessee,
>   who were to make feathers fly,
> When a roostah in the bahn-ya'd flew up what folks could see,
>   Then those darkies all did cry.

> Chorus: Who dat say chicken in dis crowd?
> Speak de word agin' and speak it loud—
> Blame de lan' let white folks rule it,
> I'se a looking fu a pullet,
> Who dat say chicken in dis crowd.

Embedded in this stanza is the suggestion of defiance. Black people had come together to "discuss the situation and the rumors in the air." What situation and what rumors? Was the "meeting" about the persistent accusations of white female rape? [38] Was it about an impending lynching? Was it about black men stealing chickens? Might it have been a call to engage in political strategizing? It could be any and all of these, as Dunbar was no stranger to lynching and the political needs of the black community. He often penned poems and fiction encoded in figurative language about lynching, if not other forms of protest.[39] We might read his use of the resulting chorus as a way to mask his intentions for subtle protest.

Whatever it was, "the meeting" apparently garnered quite an audience in Dunbar's mind because speakers were there from Georgia to Tennessee. Could one of the rabble-rousers in the crowd be disguised as the "roostah in the bahn-ya'd"? It is conceivable, given that roosters are adult male fowl and are considered to be cocky and feisty. It is also plausible that Dunbar made this song out to be a fictional meeting about chicken thievery. He evokes the voice of the preacher, one of the most potent spokespersons for the black community, to admonish his "listnin' congregation":

Ef dey want to be respected and become a mighty nation
  to be hones' Fu' a fac'.
Dey mus nebber lie, no nebber, an' mus' not be caught a-stealin'
  any pullets fun de lin' . . .

This reprimand evokes a fierce response from at least one member of the congregation, "an aged deacon" who responds in a voice shaking "wif feelin'":

Who dat say chicken in dis crowd?
Speak de word agin' and speak it loud—
What's de use of all dis talkin',
Let me hyeah a hen a squawkin'
Who dat say chicken in dis crowd.

This response sounds as if more is going on than glorifying chicken eating. Despite the song being relegated to the "coon" genre, Dunbar might indeed have been trying to "slip the minstrel mask."[40] Using the coon genre for his subversive messages was a necessary tactic to reach black audiences while simultaneously appealing to white audiences by using dialect.

Another possible interpretation of the title and the song begs the question, Who will be the first to give in or say chicken? In other words, he asks if black people are going to rise up against their oppressions or simply allow the "situations" to persist and the rumors to "fly." Written during the era of crisis in social welfare institutions, *Plessy v. Ferguson*, and the rise of industrial capitalism, change was inevitable, and racial tensions were high. It was a time when black people were forced to make more hard decisions about their roles (albeit limited) in American society. Under the veneer of the minstrel song, Dunbar seems to be issuing a clarion call to the masses of black people to decide their place.

Various lines in the song suggest that Dunbar was being conciliatory when in fact quite the opposite was true:

Blame de lan' let white folks rule it,
I'se a looking fu a pullet,
Who dat say chicken in dis crowd.

This seems to imply an easygoing nature of black people and to confirm white people's beliefs about chicken. Dunbar believed that black people had to prove themselves "worthy of a place" in American society and had to show they were "civilized" and not "savages." But his writings also note that he believed black people would have to "solve the question [of jobs and education] for [them]selves."[41] However, Dunbar often phrased ideas ambiguously. He also couched his racial consciousness and protest in the ironic tones of his poetry. The poem "We Wear the Mask" is one example. He says, "Why should the world be over-wise, / in counting all our tears and sighs? / Nay, let them only see us, while / we wear the mask."[42] So it is conceivable that behind his declarations that he's "looking fu a pullet" lies something more. Consequently, we can read these lines as a disguise for the intended message. Perhaps, in fact, it was so convincing that even black audiences missed the "slip," which accounts for Dunbar's disappointment during the performance.

Dunbar wrote between separate poles. His work vacillated between humor and pathos, humility and subtle protest. But his work was a reflection of his own position in American society. He was loved and revered by white America for his representations of black dialect. Yet, he was heavily criticized by black America for not waging enough social criticism. He struggled between refuting gross stereotypes that depicted black people as chicken thieves and chicken lovers and celebrating aspects of black culture using black speech and cultural expression.[43] Confronting this struggle at the turn of the twentieth century, when black citizenship relied upon so many variables, would certainly produce ambiguity and anxiety.

Much of Dunbar's later work would reflect this internal warring between compromise and rebellion. It gripped his soul well unto his death. According to one of Dunbar's biographers, Addison Gayle, Dunbar would have been unable to answer the call he issues in the song. Writing about Dunbar's poem "The Haunted Oak," in which a tree relays the story of a lynching, Gayle notes: "His own pain stood in his way. He might sympathize with the hanged man and lash out in anger at those who bore the deaths of such on their consciences, but he would not initiate a sustained, all-out protest against the forces that made reconciliation impossible on a national level. The twentieth century demanded total warfare against racism, not an accommodation with it: and to wage total warfare, one had to be capable of quieting the tumult within his own breast. This Dunbar could not do."[44] It is no wonder then that Dunbar was embarrassed by the portrayal of the song during Clorindy's performance. Perhaps he used "Who Dat Say Chicken in Dis Crowd" as one of many attempts to "stir himself to battle" while using the pen of reconciliation by writing in the minstrel tradition.

Ironically, this battle is visually illustrated on the front cover of the musical score (figure 2.13). Though perhaps not intentional, the cover art suggests that Dunbar's chicken relates to more than mere culinary desire and may, in fact, represent a range of social challenges. Staring down the five black boy-

FIGURE 2.13. Sheet music cover for "Who Dat Say Chicken in Dis Crowd," 1898.
Courtesy The Albert and Shirley Small Special Collections Library, University of Virginia.

like men is a giant rooster. At first glance, it might seem to illustrate the song's refrain of black men preparing to steal a chicken. Yet, a closer look reveals not only the defiant eyes of the chicken but also those of the men registering the oppositional gaze of male rivalry. The pitchfork, musket, and ax belie the sense of fear and shame exhibited by the men in front with their heads slightly bowed. Even though some of the men's heads are lowered, their eyes are, nonetheless, holding an audience with the giant bird. Who, then, is saying chicken in this crowd? The rooster, with its one foot held high, is poised to strike. But will he defeat all five men? Arguably, the rooster is symbolic of the larger social ills confronting black people at that time. He is a representative of the challenges (Ku Klux Klan, Jim Crow, voting intimidation, lynching, rape) that question black people's abilities to rise up or, instead, to cry chicken.

Several other songs in the *Clorindy* performance involve what Marva Griffin Carter has described as "confrontational jabs as verbal weapons aimed at the white audience members."[45] Carter especially points our attention to "Darktown Is Out Tonight," which "celebrate[s] the overall uninhibited pride in black life," and "A Negro Love Song" (or "Jump Back, Honey, Jump Back"). The love song is the result of Dunbar's witnessing a quasi–call and response between busy waiters serving a Chicago hotel during the 1893 World's Fair and those who gathered around the kitchen door recounting their romantic escapades of the previous evening:

Put my ahm around huh weys	(people at the kitchen door)
Jump back, honey, jump back.	(working waiter)
Raised huh lips an' took a tase	(people at the kitchen door)
Jump back, honey, jump back.	(working waiter)

As the "dance" persisted between those who were telling tales and those who were working, Dunbar set the display to rhyme and song. Carter points out the appearance of opposition in the song and says, "The mere fact that blacks were describing a realistic courtship scene in song, rather than a burlesqued, unrealistic encounter, signaled the slipping of the minstrel mask."[46] Black people were able to have wholesome, realistic relationships and lives, exemplified both in "A Negro Love Song" and "Who Dat Say Chicken in Dis Crowd." However, in the attempt to provide white audiences with what they expected, Dunbar found himself in a quandary. He certainly satisfied white society with his dialect. But in doing this, he was unable to successfully slip the yoke of racist imagery that he had hoped to when he portrayed real aspects of black life. Thus, some of his songs were unconvincing in slipping the minstrel mask for either black or white audiences.

The slippage, it seems, occurs not only in relation to the minstrel tradition but also by blacks in society at large. Amid countless innovations ranging from parcel post to mail-order catalogs, the mass influx of Mexican Americans and other ethnic groups into the United States, and Jim Crow laws and Progressive Era politics, most rural African Americans found themselves uneducated, unemployed, and often unable to inveigh against the systems of violence perpetrated against them. Psychologically, blacks were being portrayed in popular culture as worthless figures capable only of menial servitude. Even the black men who adhered to their faith in democracy and joined the war effort were ridiculed. When these veterans returned from the war, they were further derided. In an article to the *Ohio Union*, a writer protests comments like the following that were made against African American soldiers: "Dealers should increase their supplies of pork chops and chickens as the colored troops were returning." The author of the *Union* editorial goes on to explain that given the heroism and suffering of these soldiers, this statement was perhaps out of place. The editorialist attributed the crass statement to "many others of [that] race, which feel that they are violating the very essence of journalistic ethics, when they mention anything that should be creditable to the Negro in aught but a humorous vein." [47]

But as previously stated, these types of comments are complicated by the fact that many African American men and women excelled in capacities where food—namely chicken—was prepared. While black lives were being caricatured using food, men and women were learning valuable skills in cooking and catering. For example, Willie Mae Cartwright worked as a domestic most of her adolescent years and all of her adult life, learning how to cook from her first employer. After she had ruined several dishes, her employer finally asked her if she wanted to be taught to cook. Her inaugural dinner was chicken pie and snap beans, and then "[she] just went on from there." [48] One of my informants for this study shared how her experiences as a domestic provided valuable skills that she applied in her own life. Working for a wealthy family in Washington, D.C., she learned things that had previously been unknown to her. She says: "The experience that I had there was really good to me. Because I got a lot of experience for cooking. I got a lot of experience for cleaning. I got a lot of experience for saving. You know . . . they really believed in saving. They didn't throw anything away. Because you got to start out small and grow up. And so, I got a lot of experience from them. I got

FIGURE 2.14.
Tim and His
City Stinkers.
Courtesy Shipler
Commercial
Photographers
Collection, Utah
State Historical
Society.

a lot of experience because they was neat and clean. I got a lot of experience from Ms. V—— for cooking." [49]

African American men also received a great deal of cooking experience as caterers. Among the more distinguished caterers was the Philadelphia set, led by Thomas Dorsey, "alias Tom Dorsey, alias Dorsey, the prince of caterers." [50] Many black men were employed during World War II in food service capacities. One example is taken from the life of Roy Hawkins, who was a lead waiter at the Coon Chicken Inn. Hawkins is one of several African Americans who migrated to the West during World War II. Many of these migrants came as soldiers and porters. Some, like Hawkins, found employment in the service industry.

Maxon Lester Graham founded the first Coon Chicken Inn restaurant in 1925. The first inn was located in Salt Lake City, Utah, followed by two others: one in Seattle, Washington (1929), and one in Portland, Oregon (1931). [51] With full orchestras and cabarets like "Tim and His City Stinkers" (figure 2.14), along with catering trucks and cars bearing the Coon Chicken Inn trademark, the restaurants were in full swing for almost twenty years (figures 2.15 and 2.16). While there is no extant documentation to explain why the restaurateurs chose to use the logo or the name, Hawkins offered that the logo "was a favorite for children and a big draw for families." It must have been effective because according to Hawkins, "people would be in line for hours and hours" waiting to get that good fried chicken. With a throaty laugh, Hawkins explained to me how to cook "that good ol' chicken" (even though he hinted that he should not reveal his secrets in case he wants to open his own restau-

FIGURE 2.15. Coon Chicken Inn catering menu. Courtesy Shipler Commercial Photographers Collection, Utah State Historical Society.

rant, Hawkeye's Chicken, sometime soon): "I'll tell you how to fry chicken. Use whole hens. You can use fryers if you want, but we used whole hens. Boil it whole. Then, let it cool. Set it in the cooler. Then dip it in whole egg. Don't break it up, leave it whole or you won't get the right taste. Roll it in bread-crumbs and deep-fry it. That's how they fry the chicken. I know how to cook everything they had."[52]

FIGURE 2.16.
Coon Chicken Inn,
unknown location.
Courtesy Curt Teich
Postcard Archives,
Lake County (Ill.)
Discovery Museum.

Despite knowing how to cook "everything," Hawkins was actually the head-waiter. Having gone to the Coon Chicken Inn at the tender age of fourteen, Hawkins had gained a lifetime of experience to prepare him for working at a place that sported a caricatured black face with a doorway of thick red open lips. From his perspective, walking through those doors was relatively minor compared to what he had already lived through:

> See I come from Texas, from a college town . . . Texas A&M. Back then it was all men. They would catch a young black boy and beat him up. I'd hide anytime in the weeds. Who? I get out and hide like a rabbit. See, that's what we had to endure. . . . Yeah so, people ask me how I accepted [working at the Coon Chicken Inn]. Back in those days, coming from every part of the country . . . from southern places and things, it wasn't nothing to see mockery. Black folks was always mocked. You know you would see "Little Daisy" and "Sambo" on the lawn with the water bucket. Those days, we went on to work. Now, I would be upset if somebody call me a Coon.[53]

His patience was tried, even then. In an interview with the *Salt Lake Tribune*, Hawkins explained that one patron to the restaurant insulted him, and in retribution he "'accidentally' spilled a pot of coffee on her mink." Referring to another incident wherein a woman said to her child, "Look, that's a real-live coon," Hawkins stated that he "might do any sort of thing" to retaliate. He elaborated, sardonically adding, "Just don't mess with the people who bring your food."[54] If a customer called him "boy," he would rejoin, "You almost got it right. It's Roy."

Naturally, Hawkins would have had his breaking point. But from his point of view, he was making money and "laughing all the way to the bank." Taking in anywhere from $100 to $200 in tips each night enabled Hawkins to capitalize on the ignorance of his customers: "See, men here, professional men, bricklayers, they were only making $5.00 a day. That's why I say I was laughing all the way to the bank. Why not smile?" By turning the tools of manipulation back upon the offenders, Hawkins exercised his own measure of subversiveness. These measures were not extraordinary, per se, but therein lies the resistance and the agency. Power is not always exercised in grand ways. The everyday acts of surviving help people dispel the denunciation that takes place around them. These daily life acts, usually writ small, are what keep people sane.

Hawkins's life is but one example of this. While the customers at the Coon Chicken Inn valued the restaurant for its menu, Hawkins saw that menu as a source of capital. Here, we see how food demonstrates the various ways that power operates in our lives. Food, as politics, is subtle and unexpected because it is not seen as a tool of opposition but as a necessary substance. Chicken, in the instances that I have discussed here, had the power to be more than sustenance in the lives of black people. And though Hawkins did not work at the restaurant specifically to rebuke the racism that confronted him, the Coon Chicken Inn became a locus for social and political activism almost on a daily basis. He knew this could be the case by the nature of his place of employment. And he was noticeably prepared to fight back, using verbal jabs, quick wit, and anything else he had at his disposal. Thus by studying how food operates in people's lives, and how certain foods have meaning, we begin to appreciate people's connections to those foods. We also grasp how a food as insignificant as chicken holds evidence of the ways black people disrupted the hegemonic cultural assumptions that tried to define them. And we see how ordinary people—perceived as subordinated and subjugated— challenged the dominant ideologies that sought to control them.

Studying a food like chicken also forces us to recognize that black people speak in different voices. Not everyone challenged these normative perceptions in the same way as Hawkins. Some cared little about altering or correcting erroneous perceptions and images. Money was not enough for them to endure some of the behaviors that they encountered. As a headwaiter, Hawkins had several other blacks working for him. In fact, he said that because he had quite a turnover at the restaurant, he would often have to "steal the waiters" from a neighboring hotel. His success was not unusual, given that blacks were always looking for more lucrative positions. But not everyone saw the position as suitable recompense. For one, the restaurant hired black men and women to work "*the dining-room only. The dining-room only*" (Hawkins's emphasis). Once, two black women were hired but soon after quit. Out of the 500 or more black people in Salt Lake City at that time, the restaurant had hired two who could not withstand the offensive attitudes of some patrons. Hawkins explains, "Yeah, they quit because one time some ol' woman came into the restaurant and said to them, 'Oh girls, I seen the cutest little picka-

FIGURE 2.17. Coon Chicken Inn toothpick.
Courtesy Roy Hawkins; author's collection.

ninnies you ever did see' . . . or something like that. See, 'cause at that time, black kids and adults were novelties."[55] And to many white people, novelties they were. Blacks were to others exotic specimens—as were the Japanese and Chinese (not to mention the Mormons). But the same perceptions held true for some blacks. Hawkins first came to Utah as a young boy of thirteen. He had heard that "Mormons had horns and tails," so he was very familiar with how people different from himself could be mocked.[56] But for some employees, understandably, the mockery was too much.

Black people were mimicked on all of the Coon Chicken Inn's entrances, silverware, and paper products (figure 2.17). "It was everywhere," Hawkins reports. Recognizing the richness of that historical moment and its importance today where so much is "slippin', slippin', slippin' . . . compared to how things was twenty-five to thirty years ago," Hawkins has become a purveyor of this history both in oral and material form. When asked why Graham would have used the coon imagery, the response from Hawkins was very matter-of-fact: "Well, you know 'coon' is Southern slang for black folk. Instead of calling us Negroes or whatever, they call 'em coon. . . . And you know, coons steal chickens. . . . So it was things like this surrounding the name. Coons is sneaky. . . . Well, a lot of things make them come up with the name."[57]

The connections between chickens and blacks are obviously not lost on Hawkins. Nor were they lost on the many races and ethnicities living in the West at that time. In fact, some people in those states were subsumed by

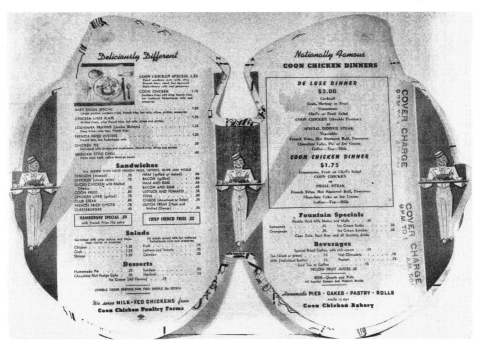

FIGURE 2.18. Coon Chicken Inn menu, 1950. Courtesy Shipler
Commercial Photographers Collection, Utah State Historical Society.

this imagery. As customers, they saw no problem in allowing the big black coon to wholly ingest their bodies as they walked through his lips (which were the doors of the restaurant). In a strange dialectic, they returned the gastronomic "favor" by consuming "deliciously different" foods like the "baby coon special" and "coon chicken dinner" (figure 2.18). When they were done, they carelessly discarded the "Negro" by emptying their waste into the trash. Some white patrons no more saw Hawkins as a man than they saw the images on the wrappings and napkins. Hawkins was nothing more than another item that accompanied their food. In discarding their waste, they also discarded him and any other black man or woman with whom they had come in contact during their culinary journey at the Coon Chicken Inn restaurant. He, in turn, took their tips and laughed his way to a better material existence.

If customers were unaware of the "coon stealin'/chicken stealin' darky" before the Coon Chicken Inn opened, they were by the time the restaurant closed its doors in the 1950s—the dawn of the civil rights era. While Hawkins worked in service at restaurants like the Coon Chicken Inn, his brother, like other black men and women, went off to the military, quite possibly to perform similar tasks. At Craig Field Southeastern Air Training Center in Selma,

Alabama, for example, African American men were photographed preparing and serving "a hearty meal" of fried chicken made from the Farm Security Administration (FSA) chickens supplied by the "Food for Defense" program during World War II (figures 2.19–2.25). The existence of these photographs and the accompanying captions invite a Geertzian approach of peeling away the "thick description" to get at the heart of what is both an interesting and complex cultural interaction.[58] It also invites another close reading of images wherein the focus is again black skin and (white) chicken. Exploring the cultural biography of these chickens permits one to see a range of underlying interactions that far exceed the descriptions often given about food preparation, presentation, and consumption. This illustration provides how objects (and their use at historical moments) can transform material lives, change attitudes, and alter social relationships.[59]

World War II had a great impact on the American home front, especially in the areas of farming and food production, since shortly after the war began, food restrictions became mandatory, complete with ration books. Continuing the World War I theme "Food will win the war . . ." farmers were asked to produce more food and factories more goods to contribute to "growing army and navy men [of] rugged health and courage." As Thomas Parren, M.D., made clear, "Every drop of milk, every egg, every legume, every pound of meat and of fish [that could be produced] for Anglo-American nutrition, plus substantial quantities of animal and vegetable fats, fish liver oils, and certain vitamins [were needed]."[60] Hatcheries in the Delmarva region of the Maryland and Virginia Eastern Shore, along with farms in other poultry areas, helped to satisfy this need.[61] To accomplish this goal at Craig Field, chickens were purchased from the James Drigger Farm, the Josh Smart Farm, and the Enterprise Farm Security Administration Co-op, in Coffee County, Alabama. African Americans were intricately involved in this process to one degree or another. Some worked in the poultry industry, like the farmers in Woodville, Georgia. Others were dressers, pluckers, and handlers in Selma and Enterprise, Alabama. Still others were employed in service capacities by military bases like Craig Field Southeastern Air Training Center. The black men at Craig Field specifically were asked to "do their part" on behalf of the war effort by preparing Sunday feasts of fried chicken. In providing these meals, black men and women were fulfilling the mission of the U.S. Department of Agriculture when it proclaimed "food as the cornerstone upon which lasting goodwill can be created and economic development of needy and new nations of the world can be built."[62]

FIGURE 2.19.
Cadets at Craig Field
Southeastern Air Training
Center, Selma, Alabama,
leave lockers for the field
still smiling over their hearty
meal of fried chicken supplied
through the FSA "Food for
Defense" program, 1941.
Courtesy Library of Congress,
Prints & Photographs
Division, FSA/OWI Collection
(LC-USF34-080265-D);
photograph by John Collier.

FIGURE 2.20.
Employee of the Selma Purity
Ice Plant packs "Food for
Defense" chickens for delivery
to Craig Field, 1941. Courtesy
Library of Congress, Prints &
Photographs Division, FSA/
OWI Collection (LC-USF34-
080309-D); photograph by
John Collier.

The visual narrative of the cooks at Craig Field is an interesting one. It is a part of the larger collection of photographs taken by John Collier Jr. for the FSA/Office of War Information (OWI).[63] Collier, like other FSA photographers, traveled the United States capturing and communicating by film the lives of everyday people. He was one of several government specialists whose mission it was to report what they saw throughout the country. He explains it this way:

FIGURE 2.21.
Private Sykes, assistant
mess sergeant at Craig
Field, says, "I never have
seen such clean birds,"
1941. Courtesy Library
of Congress, Prints &
Photographs Division, FSA/
OWI Collection (LC-USF34-
080310-D); photograph by
John Collier.

FIGURE 2.22.
Craig Field cook says, "They
is so well raised, they fry
themselves—when one's
cooked—they're all cooked,"
1941. Courtesy Library of
Congress, Prints & Photographs
Division, FSA/OWI Collection
(LC-USF34-080311-D);
photograph by John Collier.

FIGURE 2.23.
Craig Field cooks setting out
plates for chicken dinner, 1941.
Courtesy Library of Congress,
Prints & Photographs Division,
FSA/OWI Collection (LC-USF34-
080348-E); photograph by
John Collier.

FIGURE 2.24.
Craig Field flying cadet dressing
for Sunday dinner, 1941. Courtesy
Library of Congress, Prints &
Photographs Division, FSA/OWI
Collection (LC-USF34-080356-E);
photograph by John Collier.

FIGURE 2.25.
Craig Field flying cadet relaxes after a hearty
meal of "Food for Defense" fried chicken,
1941. Courtesy Library of Congress, Prints &
Photographs Division, FSA/OWI Collection (LC-
USF34-080314-D); photograph by John Collier.

[The government] had information specialists of every region in the United States who were feeding into the newspapers, into magazines, into government reports the reality of what was going on. I wouldn't call them propagandists, I think they were more fairly considered historians of what was happening. They were the eyes and ears that fed material into the files and it was very clear what our role was, because whenever we'd get back from any interesting field trip we'd all be shipped across the street to the Department of Agriculture. And we would be pumped dry by specialists who couldn't care less about our photographs. They were interested in our eyewitness experiences.[64]

The narrative of the Craig Field cooks lies buried within the story of farmers who participated in the Food for Defense program. By this I mean that these men were not necessarily the subject of the assignment. But Collier's keen artistic eye and organization provide the viewer a rich experience that might otherwise be overlooked. Two photographers captured experiences from the Food for Defense program—Collier and Jack Delano. By far, Collier's photos tell the more comprehensive story, particularly about the intersection of gender, race, region, food, and power in American society during World War II. It is because Collier offers a visual biography of the Food for Defense chickens that one gets a better understanding of the tensions that existed during that time. As Collier admits, "That much data on one thing is bound to have power, is bound to tell you things about culture you can't get in any other way."[65]

The story begins with Collier's journey to Georgia in August 1941. Following the photographs sequentially, the narrative starts with images of the cadets at the Craig Field training center. They are ready to mount their planes, having been heartily fed chickens from the Food for Defense program.[66] The story then moves to several FSA locations that provide chickens for Craig Field —Enterprise Co-op, Selma Co-op, the Drigger and the Smart farms. Here the viewer is given a sense of the entire process from raising the chickens to packing them in ice to prepare for their arrival at the training center. The viewer first meets the African American cooks as they are loading up platters of fried chicken to serve the cadets. After seeing the cadets enjoy their meal, the viewer is again taken to a series of processing steps, only to arrive back at the cooks. Dispersed throughout the remainder of the narrative are photographs of the chicken frying in vats of hot oil and the cooks gathering and preparing plates and implements and generally "work[ing] all morning preparing a feast of . . . chickens for the Craig Field training center for flying cadets."[67] While these food preparations were being made on their behalf, the cadets dressed for dinner or otherwise busied themselves reading and preparing for flights. "Like real home-cooked chicken," said one Craig Field flying cadet as he heaped pieces of chicken upon his plate. Another exclaimed, "There's hardly room for cake after dinner." All of the cadets agreed that they were "well satisfied" after their "hearty meal." But as the cadets relaxed after their hearty meal and later prepared for departure to defend the country, the story was still incomplete. What was left untold by this photographer was that the tables were cleared and cleaned, the dishes were washed, and the food was either discarded or eaten by those who had worked "all morning" to prepare the feast of Food for Defense chickens.

If we consider that goods are embedded in social processes, then there are several such processes circumscribing this meal. As I emphasized in the first chapter, cooking and preparing foods does not necessarily grant one access. And when access is allowed or given, it is not always equitable. That is, food might be carefully allocated or even have a close watch kept over it. This issue becomes most apparent when foods are connected to situations such as the one illustrated here. Race and gender tensions, food perceptions, and people intertwine in this set of photographs. In this intersecting social relationship, the discussion becomes both paradoxical and complex. On the one hand, whites at that time wanted to argue that black consumption of fried chicken was the norm. On the other hand, they wanted to equate this consumption with something negative. They needed to be able to distinguish black people eating and stealing fried chicken as "normal" from any desire to claim fried chicken as one of the hallmarks of white southern cuisine. Indeed, fried chicken was proclaimed as one of the most recognized foods of the South. The recipe for fried chicken, along with the ability of black women to cook it, had been continuously praised for its taste but seldom for the effort.[68] In the context of Craig Field, the contribution also seems minimized when one reads the caption accompanying one of the photographs that says, "[The chickens] is so well raised, they fry themselves—when one's cooked—they're all cooked."[69]

These images, sometimes overlapping and often contradictory, are part of a gender and race composite. During enslavement, black women dominated the cooking of chicken on many plantations. They were widely credited with lining the "southern groaning boards" with heaping platters of steaming fried chicken. But to share in the consumption of the food, especially in the presence of whites, meant that culinary (and social) boundaries would have to be broken. A cultural demarcation became necessary for symbolically dividing the South. At least one of these demarcations involved food and domestic rituals separating the cook from the consumer. Considering the dinner at Craig Field in this context, the "hearty chicken meal" can be read as a cultural text wherein chicken is part of a social institution shaped by racial and gendered complexities. Craig Field is located in Selma, Alabama, the hotbed of the formal civil rights movement. This chicken dinner, its cooks, and consumers were probably not immune to the popular culture discourse concerning African Americans and chickens. Social segregation, therefore, is represented in the relationships of the period as well as in food.[70] From a semiotic point of view, fried chicken becomes a contested social marker of the "Old South," southern mores, and ways of being.

In the oral history interview conducted by Richard Doud, Collier explains what makes this photographic file collection historically valuable—"photographing between the lines," a viewpoint that countered the expectations of government officials. He argues that these photographers were artists first and foremost. As such, their goal was to capture the subjective while appearing to present the objective point of view. He says, "Some photographers spent all their time . . . photographing culturally between the lines . . . and the richness of the file is the fact that it is very non-objective. . . . You have two levels of important data in the file. Something's . . . going on in America at that time, [and it] usually faced in the other direction from the government project." Collier's point is well-taken. By including the photographs of the African American cooks, he presents that duality—what's going on in plain view and what's going on "between the lines." It is significant, for example, that the African Americans are never seen eating or cleaning up. The focus of these photographs is the Craig Field cadets preparing for war and, more important, the ways in which the Food for Defense program is preparing the cadets for their tasks. As it stands now, the cooks are a sideways glance, a subtext, existing only to advance the discussion about the cadets and the program. The chicken is both important for what it means to the cadets (building strong bodies) and insignificant (for the larger social issues that it reveals about the black cooks). Consequently, it can be argued that food is exemplary in its ability to relate how power is multiple, subtle, and varied in social interactions.

There are multiple stories being told by these photographs. Were we to focus solely on the text given by the images, we would celebrate primarily the contributions of the cadets. We miss the ways in which some black people, albeit subordinated, contributed to the war effort. The considerable amount of work entailed in meals of this kind can be completely overlooked. Though the photographs begin their story long before the cooking process, they serve to tell how Americans farmers, mostly white, did their part to defend their country—the country that black people were not allowed fully to claim as their own. But blacks were expected to do (and did) their part. This, however, is not what the photographs tell us unless we "read around in them" to hear a different narrator.[71] The subtextual story that Collier captures illustrates the ways in which the cooks prepared the meal. Hearing a different voice, we understand that a complex social interaction was taking place, as embodied and symbolized by the chicken. The chicken means different things to everyone involved in this story. For the cadets, it is a hearty meal. For the photographer, it is an opportunity to document diverse Americans working together to "fight the enemy." For the cooks, it is work, maybe hunger, certainly separation, and definitely discrimination. But for these African American men, it may also be emasculation.

Cooking chicken is now and was then really considered "women's work," as I explain in more detail later on in this study (see chapter 6). In order for those men to distinguish their masculinized black bodies from the symbolism of this gendered labor, they have to make it "men's work."[72] Therefore, they have to claim this as a major role in helping the war effort—to do any less further demasculinizes them. Focusing only on the stereotypes associated with this imagery—blacks and chickens go hand in hand—we would overlook the various critical meanings. We would also probably not see the ways in which black men needed to see themselves—visually and psychologically—as (even in small measure) defending their country.

Racial ideologies are powerful in shaping one's worldview. Examining food is useful for analyzing these ideologies and the ways racial and gender politics pervade even the most benign situations, like Sunday dinners. As we turn the focus specifically toward black women, it is helpful to recall the historical and gendered contexts discussed in this chapter and in chapter 1 because the ways in which black women's lives were and continue to be affected by images of chicken cannot be divorced from these discussions. But black women had to contend in some ways very different from their gendered counterpart. As homemakers, reformers, juke joint owners, and artists, black women adopt a number of strategies in literature, travel narratives, cookbooks, and film in dealing with chicken and the definitions emitted by this food.

GNAWING ON A CHICKEN BONE IN MY OWN HOUSE

CULTURAL CONTESTATION, BLACK WOMEN'S WORK, AND CLASS

3

The acquisition of [graces] will go a long way in securing that recognition of ability needed to cope with human society, and will remove some of the commonest objects to our presence in large numbers.
—*Charlotte Hawkins Brown*

"Good manners are better than chicken necks or pork-chop bones."
—*Boyd to Jesse B. Semple, in Langston Hughes, "Bones, Bombs, Chicken Necks"*

Chicken was symbolic of multiple tensions within black communities during the early twentieth century. During the periods following slavery, large numbers of black people migrated to cities, bringing their southern mores with them. In the North, these traditions heavily collided with black class assumptions. The central tenet of the National Association of Colored Women's Clubs was racial uplift, embodied in the motto "Lifting as we climb." This credo called upon educated, upper-class black women to lead poorer black women in the "proper" expressions of morality, decorum, and social grace. Food was a by-product of these larger goals of progressive activism. What poorer black working-class women ate as well as how they obtained their food were often sources of angst for early black feminists. Some women would acquire their food by scrounging and foraging among leftovers at outdoor fruit and vegetable markets. Other working-class women cut corners and saved money by purchasing day-old bread and the lowest cuts of meat. Still others caught carp and other swamp fish or ate chicken remains (feet, neck, back).

The concerns of black reformers are not surprising. Black women's self-concept has, until recently, been highly conditioned by the need for positive representation and imagery. Black women's cooking abilities have always been connected to mammy imagery—sometimes in the process of cooking chicken. So it is not unexpected that these reformers would attempt to divorce *all* black women from this activity, and especially from this food.[1] Chicken therefore becomes interesting for what it represents in the realm of social freedom, manners, morals, culture, refinement, and self-expression. Using oral history, newspaper accounts, and African American fiction, this chapter explores the intersection of chicken, black women's work, and class to consider how these connections formed sites of cultural contestation but also provided spaces from which working- and middle-class women could exhibit self-expression. But first, it is necessary to place the activities of black women in specific historical context vis-à-vis chicken.

As previously discussed, chicken and wild fowl have been a part of the American landscape since or prior to Columbus. It must be stressed, however, that these were the least desirable form of livestock that was brought, primarily as provisions for traders. These birds were left to roam free and therefore intermingled, producing even more wild breeds. Prior to the mid-twentieth century, all fowls except fighting cocks were considered inferior farm animals to be cared for by women and children. Unlike other stock—cattle, sheep, horses—chickens were simply listed as a number or an entry on wills, inventories, and property statements, if listed at all. These birds and their eggs—which by this point were in relative demand—were part of local economies, nothing resembling the modern-day commercial industry. They were a part of a local subsistence economy that was able to flourish despite problems of disease and refrigeration.[2] By the time the Department of the Interior undertook its first poultry inventory, it was estimated that there were approximately 100,000,000 chickens in the United States.

From a scientific standpoint, chickens became all the rage in American society in the early nineteenth century. More professional men in the 1830s and 1840s began to take an interest in the breeding of poultry, a practice that had long been enjoyed in Europe. Suddenly, the largely women-operated system that had provided so much of America's fare was cast aside in favor of more precision. Money was to be made, and the men were not going to be left out. In 1850, physician and breeder John C. Bennett declared: "As a branch of rural economy, the astonishment created by its results has been succeeded by a more careful attention to the matter, as one in which the interests of a large class of men are involved." Bennett was referring to the statistics of 1840 that indicated that the value of poultry in the United States had reached $12,176,170. He stated: "The statistics on this subject are doubtless imperfect, but enough is known not only to excite wonder in the minds of those who have given no attention to it, but to prove beyond doubt that the value of poultry stock in the United States is a very important item of the national wealth."

Bennett was not alone in his exclamations. Several others joined him in publishing books on the state of poultry in American society. In 1843, Caleb Bement, another fancier, took pains to describe the various types of poultry prevalent in the United States at that time in his *American Poultry Book*. It was, for all intents and purposes, a time of "hen fever." [3] It is important to note that these writers were fanciers and breeders. They were not referring to aspects of commercial enterprise—providing eggs and chickens for consumption. So then when Bennett wrote that in the United States, poultry was "universally esteemed a luxury," he was not necessarily referring to eating. Rather, he was arguing that in comparison to the rest of the world, "it seems surprising that information concerning the different breeds, the mode of rearing them, and other matters pertaining to the subject, should not have attracted greater notice." He was lamenting the fact that America had lagged behind in championing the bird from a scientific point of view. [4]

Bennett makes a critical distinction. It has been repeatedly argued that chicken was a "semi-luxury" item, so African Americans could not possibly have had as much interaction with the bird as I suggest throughout this study. But this rebuttal is generally made without regard to region, time, or space. For example, eggs were a luxury in heavily populated areas prior to 1880 because they could not be moved long distances due to the lack of cold storage. Thus, from a large-scale commercial standpoint, it was impractical to transport eggs or chickens. But this was less the case in rural areas where itinerant hucksters provided these items locally on a daily basis. As early as the turn of the twentieth century, specially designed railroad cars were shipping some live poultry. By the time automobiles and trucks became available, access was a nonissue since chickens could easily be moved to local and distant markets. [5]

Throughout their treatises, Bennett and his ilk subtly and not so subtly disparage rural farmwomen when they argue, "It is no longer universally true that fowls are raised without care, or with a perfect indifference as to their kind. The old notion, that fowls are an unprofitable stock to the farmer, is exploded, by force of the demonstrations which have been given that they may be made productive." With only a passing reference, they acknowledge that women made their livelihood and gathered their "pin money" from the sales of surplus poultry and eggs. [6]

Black women were no exception. In 1923, the U.S. Department of Agriculture produced a circular detailing extension service work in black communities. Not surprisingly, the agent found that most farm operators lived in the South and that the livestock on these farms were of a self-supporting nature. Other than swine and dairy cattle, poultry was the area in which most of the agricultural training was done. [7] On Maryland's Eastern Shore, extension work was prevalent, with the first black agent being employed in 1917. Even though southern Maryland's agriculture was built primarily around tobacco, the Eastern Shore could boast of vegetable or crock production. Black families were both tenants and owners. Owners constituted 58 percent of the farm operators; tenants, 27 percent; and croppers, about 15 percent. Nonetheless, farms operated by blacks were small. They produced corn for stock feed and hay and wheat for home use. Some livestock were kept, including chicken and hogs, for home consumption. Horses and mules were kept by 79 percent; 85 percent had hogs; 90.7 percent had chickens; and 59 percent reported cattle. Most of the men were day laborers, bean pickers, or water trade workers. Women were domestics. Even though blacks comprised 17 percent of the overall population in Maryland during the 1940s, in southern Maryland they represented 25 percent and in the lower Eastern Shore, 28 percent. Most of them were rural.[8]

Ruby Baker shared in an interview with me her story of growing up on a tenant farm in rural Virginia in the 1920s and 1930s.[9] Baker said that she grew up in a family that had plenty to eat. Recalling her childhood with fondness, she said, "Back then mama could make some good spoonbread. That's how I learned. We'd eat the spoonbread with poke salad and cress salad. Now cress salad is good too and they easy to make. You just put some onions in them and fry em. Lawd girl, you got a pot. Cook some chicken backs, I love chicken backs, string beans and potatoes and you have a meal."[10] Like many blacks, her parents were tenants on a white farm. Baker remarked that they managed to have a measure of autonomy because her father had a small garden. In addition, her family's stock included chickens, turkeys, hogs, game, and homegrown vegetables. In addition to enjoying chicken backs, they also ate "poke" and "cress" salad, which they could pick from among the fields surrounding their house. She said, "We would go to a field somewhere where the cress salad grow wild and pick it. You pick it just like poke salad. It grows flat to the ground so you have to really clean it. You used to could get it by the sack full. Sometimes people wouldn't tell other people where it was" (presumably because they did not want to share the crop with other families). This history of concealment was made more clear throughout the interview as Baker never revealed—even when asked—any occasion of food sharing.

In contrast to Baker's experience, Onnie Lee Logan was born in Sweet Water, Alabama, in the rural areas of Marengo County, around 1910. Logan's family owned land passed down through the generations. Her family also possessed various kinds of farm animals—goats, cows, turkeys, guineas, ducks, hogs, horses, and mules. As seen in figure 3.1, chicks or "bittys" were a common sight in the yards of some African Americans who resided in rural areas. As Logan indicates in her memoir, *Motherwit*, "We would raise chickens and

FIGURE 3.1. Home supervisor and Farm Security Administration borrower talk over the problem of improper disposal of kitchen waste water, Saint Mary's County, Maryland, 1941. Courtesy Library of Congress, Prints & Photographs Division, FSA/OWI Collection (LC-USF34-080116-E); photograph by John Collier.

little bittys. We have a chicken yard fenced in so they couldn't get out cause there was so many of 'em. I declare I'd walk through there and step on little bittys and kill them a many day. . . . Bout three and fo' hundred in the chicken yard at times, especially in the spring when they hatch out." Despite their relative largesse, or because of it, Logan recalled that her family was not stingy in any way but openly shared all that they had with those less fortunate. She remembered, "Mother didn't give em time to come. She would take em vegetables, she would take em meal, flour, piece of meat, whatever."[11]

Many communities were committed to mutual food sharing in an attempt to stretch resources. Food sharing and networking were ways in which women reached out in collective unity to help themselves and others survive amidst the rapidly changing conditions of their lives. This element of survival is in contrast to the image of the black woman, man, or child whose sole means of obtaining food was turning to criminal activity. This survival mechanism also allows for connections between food and power to be revealed. For example, sometimes sharing with those less fortunate meant that neighbors felt they could freely "borrow" more food.

In Sarah Rice's autobiography, *He Included Me*, food is the vehicle with which black women "made a way out of no way," always providing some type of sustenance for their families and sometimes for their neighbors and friends as well. However, food sharing can also illustrate the sense of selflessness that has sent many black women to an early grave. Rice describes how she and her family "went through so many traumatic times as far as food was concerned."[12] During hog-killing time, they, like many other rural families, had salt pork, smoked ham, sausage, souse, and of course chitlins. Rice's mother often shared food (even with a poor white family) and because of this was often seen as a community caregiver. However, Rice admits that this took a toll on their family. She says, "When times were hard, Mama cried because things weren't going well and she didn't have the things that she wanted for us and for the house, but she always took whatever she had and made the best of it" (36). Making the best of it included making soup from the remains of a bone along with "a few little peas that were left [in the garden] after the harvest, and maybe a last tomato" (36). It also included taking dried corn and grinding it into meal to produce a sweet cornbread. Rice's mother would scold the children about eating the eggs because she needed these along with the chickens and fryers to peddle at the market in order to purchase more household goods. These food management skills did not go unnoticed by those neighbors who would come over to visit and, ultimately, eat: "Mama had a chicken cooking and was trying to cook around until this neighbor left, but the woman said, 'I smell something good. I believe I'm going to spend the night.' So mama gave up and called us in to dinner. That woman ate plenty of chicken, and then said, 'Lord I forgot I done left them children home by themselves. I'd better get on back.' So she got up and left" (36).

The stories shared here involving the lives of Ruby Baker, Onnie Lee Logan, and Sarah Rice's mother are just a few of many that reveal black working-class individuality and black women's heterogeneity. It is true that some black women still "defined the value of the individual as subordinate to the community," but it is also true that some saw themselves very much apart from the community "in opposition to one another."[13] In the post-slavery era when food was sometimes a bit easier to come by, women's work around food provided a new space from which race, gender, and class differences can be read.

Against these real-life examples of individual and collective survival, black women were bombarded by fictional assumptions that sought to relay how they functioned in relationship to food. Within food and domestic imagery, black women were subjected to descriptions of themselves as mammies, either desexualized or exoticized (figure 3.2). Generally portrayed as heavyset, adorned with some kind of head scarf and a large white apron, they are described as "sleek and fat," having grown so "on the steam of her own genius, whose children have the first dip in all the gravies, the exclusive rights to all the livers and gizzards, not to mention breasts of fried chicken."[14] These perceptions speak to the heterogeneous nature of power in even the most mundane objects present in our material lives.[15] In addition to bearing derogatory captions, images such as these share nothing about the real-life concerns of black woman engaged in domestic chores. Figure 3.2, for instance, shares nothing of the pride that this woman might feel knowing that she can cook a fine turkey. The image also tells us nothing of her personal life, if she has siblings or a family whom she might consider feeding with the remains of the turkey. Last, it expresses little about this woman's sense of self and the creative culinary artistry that she might exhibit. But then, that is not the function of this type of image. It did not allow black women to express anything about their self-perceptions. In pictures such as this where the action of the camera acts upon them, viewers are unable to hear a black female voice. Despite what the images reveal, a re-reading of this and other images of black women in the company of chicken affirms that black women's cooking as cultural work can be celebrated.

The image of the mammified black woman turning fried chicken in the Dutch-oven deep fryer, as in figure 3.3, attempted to reinforce multiple stereotypes of black women. In addition to having her embody the characteristics of the mammy, her facial features exhibit no element of femininity or softness. Rather, her body is one of a masculine tower of strength. The only reference to her "femaleness" is her ability to cook chicken. Despite what the image is *meant* to reveal, viewers can read it for what it might have meant to some black women. This image might have given credence to the tradition of competition surrounding the cook of the best fried chicken. Most certainly, when the waiter carriers cooked chicken to deliver at the Gordonsville train station, there was often a measure of competition among them. This is a part of the cooking process. This in no way attempts to pardon these images but offers a way of reading this contested cultural artifact from a position of

FIGURE 3.2. Black cook from Porte Crayon's *Virginia Illustrated*, ca. 1850.
Courtesy The Albert and Shirley Small Special Collections Library, University of Virginia.

value rather than lack. More important, this interpretation lends itself to a consideration of the complexity of black women, and it adds humanity to an otherwise inhumane depiction.

The Snowdrift shortening advertisement found in a 1925 issue of *Ladies' Home Journal* provides another example. "Sarah" is said to have a "repita-

FIGURE 3.3. Dixie Chicken Fryer label, ca. 1930. Author's collection.

shun" for cooking the best fried chicken (figure 3.4). The deliberate misspelling of the word "reputation" is intended to serve as a linguistic signifier to the more visible variable of race. The descriptor of her cooking skills helps to sell the myth that black women are capable of cooking chicken and have a "reputation" for doing so. Here we find black women's character being signified on by their labor, a device commonly used during this time. The meaning of this image relies upon a degree of knowledge, memory, and history that was held in common throughout society at the time of its publication. Race, as the signifier, proposes how one is to read this advertisement: the black woman, the head scarf, the can of Snowdrift, and the chicken all suggest a sufficient rationale—black women not only are among the best in terms of

FIGURE 3.4. Snowdrift shortening advertisement, *Ladies' Home Journal*, ca. 1925. Author's collection.

domestic work but also are by far among the best cooks. The advertisement furthers this suggestion by offering that Mrs. Clark declares that Sarah is a "jewel among cooks." Sarah's reputation is reinforced (and endorsed), and quite possibly her status is heightened as a result.[16]

Two additional signifiers are worth noting here—the knife and Sarah's gaze. Sarah, though a bit thinner and lighter in complexion, is still portrayed as the familiar mammy figure. She wears the necessary clothing and a beaming smile to indicate her "natural happiness" to be in a servile position. While

FIGURE 3.5. "Thanksgiving Greetings." Postcard, n.d. Written on the card is "Imogene, Ula, Me." Author's collection.

the knife she holds is clearly in preparation for cutting the bird in her hand, the utensil curiously lends itself to several additional interpretations, particularly when coupled with the fact that Sarah is looking directly at the camera. At a time when black people were expected to avert their eyes in the presence of whites, it is interesting that Sarah would be posed looking into the faces of her employees brandishing a utensil that could also be used as a weapon. Rather than try and identify the intended purpose of this pose, it seems significant simply to note that these additional signifiers—the knife and the direct gaze—might have been interpreted very differently by those who purchased the magazine and by those employed in the kitchens of the readers.[17]

If the signifiers surrounding Sarah lend themselves to a degree of ambiguity, then the use of the word "me" in the postcard shown in figure 3.5 concretely affirms the agency in the self-reflective act of seeing oneself. More important, it suggests an oppositional stance taken by one black woman in defining herself, despite her clearly subordinate position. This postcard, which was sent to a cousin in Lincoln, Missouri, contains an extensive ink-written message that asks of her family's well-being. She may have been away for some time, because she indicates her wish to see them. She also longs for them to see her "sweet little family," referring to her five-month-old child. She continuously asks her relatives to come and visit her because she "can't go anywhere," perhaps because of domestic and financial obligations. There is no name or farewell greeting on the card. Yet, it is clear from the intimate level of detail that the author and her cousin were fairly close.

The author of this Thanksgiving greeting conveys to anyone who comes into contact with the card that she is pleased according to the details of her life. She communicates this both by writing on the verso and by writing on the front side of the card in the areas made visible by the tablecloth and her apron. On the tablecloth are the names of her charges, "Imogene" and "Ula," and on her apron strap she writes "me." Here, a black woman is issuing an "interrogating" look upon the white world, rejecting the overdetermined representation of black women as merely domestics with no sense of self. By explaining that she has a family and by identifying herself in a positive light despite her subordinate status, she is defining how she wants her family and the world (since this postcard had been mailed) to identify her.

If we read the author of this postcard as a spectator in her own drama, then we do not foreclose on the possibilities of seeing her both as an active agent and as a player in the network of power. She consciously resists being identified as less than a whole being despite being employed in a domestic work capacity. In this way she is a producer of her own self-knowledge and of her own reality, providing illustrative content to the notion that power operates in the smallest of duties in our everyday lives. Producing one's own knowledge of self and community persists at the intersection of race, gender, and class, but here we also see food. An oppositional strategy such as self-definition asserts itself in a variety of ways, and food becomes an important cultural mediator in this process. These kinds of strategies allow black women to practice and preserve the food customs and rituals that are most familiar and comfortable to them in the face of class pressures and racial tensions. In fact, as Jacqueline Bobo so aptly states, "Food is an ideal medium for examining the confluence of social relations, where the values, traditions, mores, and enduring historical linkages of black life are cultivated and preserved."[18] Portraying the range of responses African American women express toward chicken and the ways in which they preserve their cultural traditions reveal the myriad ways that black women have pursued their own self-definition using food.

When black women apply their own reading to the images that have been created to define them, they "reframe the entire dialogue," according to black feminist sociologist Patricia Hill Collins. The conversation then shifts from

protesting the technical accuracy of an image . . . to stressing the power dynamics underlying the very process of definition itself. By insisting on self-definition, Black women question not only what has been said about African-American women but the credibility and the intentions of those possessing the power to define. When Black women define ourselves, we clearly reject the assumption that those in positions granting them the authority to interpret our reality are entitled to do so. Regardless of the actual content of Black women's self-definition, the act of insisting on Black female self-definition validates Black women's power as human subjects.[19]

When the woman in figure 3.5 declared that the picture was "me," she defined herself despite what society was trying to tell her. In a similar way, by providing this type of reading to these images, it is possible then to argue for an exercise of black women's self-definition. Reframing the dialogue denies those who felt they could define black women and what they represented. By rejecting society's impression and their misreading of black women, we open these images to re-readings that allow for self-expression and self-empowerment. This was very important at the turn of the last century and is equally important today.

Mothers, by and large, control and determine the foodways—obtainment, preparation, distribution, and even consumption—within the family. They also monitor the social mores, "which are a microcosm of behaviors and values deemed right and just by society-at-large," and are therefore said to control the "symbolic language of food, determining what foods and meals will say about them, their families, and the world."[20] In their ability to control the "symbolic language of food" and to dictate what foods say about their families, women often negotiate the dialectical relationship between the internal identity formation of their families and the externally influenced medium of popular culture. In this way, they protect their families against social and cultural assault as well as assist in the formation and protection of identity. Migrant women, in their role as primary caregivers and preparers of food, were at the center of mediating these social interactions and power interplays that coalesced around gender, race, class, and region.

Many newcomers to urban landscapes found themselves in tenement dwellings and kitchenettes. In his photographic history, *12 Million Black Voices*, Richard Wright describes the squalor and living conditions that greeted newly arrived African Americans. Farm girls, still in their teens, were often crammed into tight rooms with men who were "restless and stimulated by the noise and lights of the city." Yet, black women did the work that needed to be done to offset some of the devastation that the urban newness brought.

FIGURES 3.6 and 3.7. "Dock Street Market, Philadelphia, PA," August 1938. Courtesy Marketing Research Project, Records of the Bureau of Agricultural Economics, Record Group 83-G, National Archives and Records Administration— Northeast Region (College Park) (photographs 36060 and 36068).

Collecting stale and sometimes rotten food that had been dumped by merchants in the "Black Belts" or left behind and discarded at wholesale markets enabled some of these women to feed their families and purchase property (figures 3.6 and 3.7).[21] Yet, despite this disposition to thrift, black women reformers like Charlotte Hawkins Brown and Nannie Helen Burroughs turned their attentions to mealtimes and the social graces that should accompany those interactions. Using food as one of many platforms, they sought to instill notions of respectability, decorum, and selfhood into the minds of working-class black women. More to the point, they were hoping to impress upon the larger society that black women were indeed "ladies" of decorum and manners, worthy of societal respect, honor, and nationhood. In the quest to be positively perceived by the wider society, some aspects of black cultural expression were avoided. They tirelessly worked against perceptions that suggested that "the Negro problem is primarily a matter of morals and manners and that the real basis of color prejudice in America is the fact that the Negroes as a race are rude and thoughtless in manners and altogether quite hopeless in sexual morals, in regard for property rights and in reverence for truth."[22] Given these kinds of perceptions, racial prejudice, and the enormous burden to represent the race, it is not unexpected that some middle-class black people felt a need to dissociate themselves from foods heavily connected to "the folk." Accordingly, "the thinking Negro[es]" focused their attention upon "the distorted perspective" that rendered black people, and especially working-class black people, as a social problem.[23] This pervasive discourse was present not only in etiquette manuals but also in other media like magazines, newspapers, and novels.

So significant was this emphasis on culture and refinement as a vehicle to full citizenship in American society that by 1940, Brown had republished her directive titled *The Correct Thing to Do, To Say, To Wear*. Her instructional guide follows the premise that "the acquisition of [graces] will go a long way in securing that recognition of ability needed to cope with human society, and will remove some of the commonest objects to our presence in large numbers."[24] This principle was one by which Brown lived and founded her school, Palmer Memorial Institute (PMI).[25] Despite years of varying financial support, which often forced Brown to change her approach and her curriculum, it was always her desire to promote gracious living and refinements. Yet, Brown's message on the "social graces of the Negro" was not a new one but one very much in keeping with some of the concerns held by middle-class northern blacks about migrants who arrived from the South. In some cities, the National Urban League launched campaigns to teach migrants what was perceived to be "proper behavior" in public places, acceptable work habits, and the conventions of good housekeeping. Articles and columns found in African American newspapers like the *Cleveland Journal*, the *Cleveland Advocate*, and the *Chicago Defender* reinforced these admonishments.[26] It was widely believed by the "better classes" of blacks that African American respectability was directly tied to social, political, and economic advancement, including acceptance as full citizens.[27] Modeled in part after the edicts of Emily Post but also garnered from her own New England upbringing amidst white polite society, Brown had a range of principles "upon which charm depends." Many of these "charms" were directly related to food consumption.[28]

Brown admonished that mealtimes are a time for "fitting conversations" in an atmosphere that "appeals to the eye as well as to the taste."[29] Moreover, the setting is to be one of "harmonious social intercourse" and "thorough appreciation of tasty food" (47). This focus was critical in trying to dismantle negative stereotypes and to remove some of the "commonest objects" that she believed plagued black people. While we do not know for certain that chicken (or food like it) was one of the kinds of objects to which she referred, several things can lead us to speculate upon its inclusion. As I have previously discussed, imagery of black women, men, and children in compromising positions with chicken were plentiful during this time. And in her book of manners, Brown provides a question and answer section wherein she includes questions about how to eat foods that have bones or seeds. She instructs the reader on the proper ways to politely remove these foods from the mouth. She also suggests that foods like bacon "when crisp, brittle, and dry may be eaten from the fingers, otherwise it should be cut with the fork" (51). Conceivably, her instructions could also apply to eating chicken, which would clearly fall under the purview of a food with bones but also a food that might be eaten with one's hands.

Suggestive of the fact that chicken was considered a "commonest object" is its notable absence from the text. Chicken, pork chops, or other foods that might in any way be racially associated are nowhere to be found in the menus provided in Brown's book. Instead, the reader is given menus listing "chopped olive sandwiches" and "bonbons" for informal teas, while assorted canapés and frosted cakes are suggested for formal gatherings (54). Buffet meals invite a choice of stuffed tomatoes or cold cuts on a bed of lettuce along with cheese biscuits or "tiny baking powder biscuits" (56). But the reality suggests that these dainties are less food than that actually consumed at formal dinners and teas. According to a program from the Married Ladies Afternoon Club of Xenia, Ohio, oyster soup, sliced turkey, cranberry sauce, and ham were served. And on a dinner program held at Gray's Café in Washington, D.C., to honor Judge Robert H. Terrell (husband of Mary Church Terrell), shad, filet of beef with mushrooms, stewed terrapin, and oysters graced the tables.[30]

One cannot assume to know what most black people of Brown's ilk would eat once they were in the privacy of their own homes. In fact, most African American women at this time kept their private lives very closed. And given the centuries of stereotyping that surrounded black lives and cultural expression, this is hardly shocking. As historian Darlene Clark Hine has noted, African American women engaged in acts of dissembling—they only revealed to the public what they wanted to be seen.[31] But in the absence of these private revelations, advertisements suggest that the offerings were varied and diverse but still included chicken or poultry. Grocery stores, knowing the needs of their community members, advertised "Saturday Only" specials on chicken and beef, appealing to Sunday dinner table familiars. And for those black families who managed to move into better neighborhoods, poultry, fresh pork shoulders, lamb chops, and lamb shoulders were available at the lowest prices.

Migrants valued and needed to maintain their food and meal traditions with which they were accustomed. When migrants went west in the early 1940s, for example, they were unable to find basic dietary staples that they were accustomed to: cornmeal, okra, collard greens, black-eyed peas, and traditional seasonings like filé.[32] Organizations and mutual aid associations such as the Family Welfare Association were enlisted to help them make the necessary adaptations. Regardless of the assimilation processes that these migrants were forced to undergo and the changes that they were encouraged to make, they needed something solidly southern to remain in place.[33] Black women's work in helping to maintain these southern traditions and mores was part of the process of self-definition and self-valuation or respect that was demanded not only from white Americans but also from middle-class African Americans.

Collins notes that self-valuation addresses the ways in which one goes about defining himself or herself. Cooking familiar foods for their families was one of the ways in which lower-class black women negotiated their new surroundings and maintained a sense of self.[34] When middle-class black women sought to denounce these habits and customs, to some extent they devalued and disrespected their working-class sisters. Consequently, working-class black women found their lives fundamentally bound and shaped by the interlocking systems of race, class, and gender with foods like chicken being at the center of this contested dialogue.

But not all clubwomen were as rigid about southern people's culinary affairs. Nannie Helen Burroughs—activist, lecturer, educator, and founder and president of the National Training School for Women and Girls in Washington, D.C.—would proudly announce the "Annual Fellowship Dinner of the Season." The menu basically stayed the same depending upon the year it was held. In 1954, for example, the menu read:

Fried Chicken   Baked Ham

Cream Gravy   Pineapple Sauce

Candied Sweet Potatoes   Fresh Turnip Greens

Rice   Tomato Aspic Salad
Spiced Beets   Hot Rolls and Butter
Fresh Apple Cobbler
Tea   Coffee

Another year the menu advertised:

Vegetables fresh from the garden
Southern Fried Chicken
Premium Ham
Hot Rolls   Spoon Bread
Delicious Dessert

Burroughs's efforts to promote the character and good work being done by her school, and specifically the domestic science department, encouraged her to appeal to both white and black folks' sense of southern food traditions. In fact, the bottom of one announcement read: "Food you like to eat and Folks you like to meet." [35] In another invitation, she calls upon "the language of Dunbar" to entice her guests: "I know 'twill staht a hank'rin' an' yo' mouf'll mence to worter." For two dollars, attendees could be entertained with gifts, programs, and "eats" that promised a "mouf-worterin'" meal.

Was it problematic that Burroughs harkened back to these rural sensibilities in order to tempt the palates of her guests and simultaneously achieve her goal of raising money for a new dormitory or some other necessity for the school? Or, was this simply a method of "saying chicken in the crowd"—that is, distinguishing herself from "the Afro-Americans who refuse to stand up and be counted for his [sic] people"? [36] Was Burroughs the "rebellious" spirit that Dunbar was invoking years ago in his operetta? Perhaps. Most assuredly, however, her conventions and beliefs were at odds with many engaged in the uplift movement who sought to separate newly minted arrivals to the North from their southern mores—including their foods, manners (or lack thereof), customs, and social graces.

Both Burroughs and Charlotte Hawkins Brown were engaged in the cultural work necessary for conveying values and traditions while also preserving historical connections, southern and New England. But in calling upon cultural artifacts like southern food to use as key components in her fundraising efforts, Burroughs was also remarking upon a tradition of women's abilities to use food for collective social action. Early records detail how churchwomen and women's organizations such as the Dorcas Club and the Margaret Murray Washington Club would hold fairs where they displayed their handiwork as well as their "eats," including "eggs, chickens, pork, etc." [37] Proceeds from such events usually went toward the establishment of some entity designed to uplift the race.

The adherence of Burroughs and Brown to particular food patterns and social graces is revealing for their particular class leanings. As scholars have noted, Burroughs, being the daughter of a washerwoman, consistently linked her work and beliefs with those of the black working class. [38] Having a shared knowledge of their cultural forms, it is understandable that she would celebrate with fried chicken, spoon bread, turnip greens, and other foods reflective of black working-class people and the South. Here I want to suggest that her choice of food for the annual fellowship dinner comfortably situated her *within* the community of working-class blacks and particularly southern black folk. Her acknowledgment and use of these foods kept her connected to her people and to their sense of identity. She validated their existence and in turn was an example of the progress that could be made if similar goals were pursued. This model might have done more to recruit young black women to Burroughs's educational program than all the talks and speeches that were given.

If this annual fund-raising event firmly established Burroughs's place among the collective of working-class black people, then Brown used her edict on correct manners and correct foods to comfortably situate herself outside of the folk community. Her comfort was found within the group most likely to offer informal and formal teas, buffets, and suppers on a regular basis. This is not to suggest that black people were solely bifurcated along food lines. Food is a culinary marker of the schism that existed between the classes of black people. In this way, food becomes the signifier of highly coded and necessary symbolic messages of civility and respectability.

It was a new age for black women and men. The period of the "New Negro" and the rebirth and reclamation of African American heritage was upon them. What better way to recognize this florescence than by conveying how black people had taken on a new posture of civility, not just in the arts and letters but at home as well? "Housekeeping" columns found in the popular press such as the *Baltimore Afro-American* and the *Chicago Defender* went far to convey these messages by bombarding southerners with recipes for dishes ranging from Mrs. F. Fletcher's hot cross buns to Swiss steak and chicken croquettes. [39] Under banner headlines that read "Pure Food Builds Better Health," authors appealed to newcomers to consider recipes like creamed cucumber cubes, cucumber-tuna ramekins, stuffed eggplant, ham en casserole, and corn fritters. [40] Undoubtedly, some migrants did their best to "be in vogue," but the majority produced or salvaged their own foodstuffs — chicken, beans, eggs, pork, and cuts of beef. And to further accommodate their desires, restaurants like the Criterion Café continued to ply patrons with breakfasts of "Maryland fried chicken, calf's liver and bacon, ham and eggs, salt water trout, Parker House rolls, Mocha and Java Coffee, and Oolong Teas." Anticipating a longing for the foods of "home," some restaurants offered "Old-Fashioned Country dinners, [with] quick and polite service, and charming waitresses."[41]

Despite the call to participate in the culinary largesse suggested by the local press, most migrants experienced a far more depressing reality. Their inability simply to garner basic food supplies belies the invitation to consider recipes for cucumber sandwiches and other trifles. For all of the admonitions and discussions on trying new foods, maintaining good health, and "avoiding constipation," very little is mentioned in much of the black press about some of the less upbeat aspects of urban living. Poverty, hunger, and despair were pervasive yet unwanted cloaks. More realistic articles would have provided advice on how to survive from day to day. Telling poor people how to sell carp and other swamp fish in order to buy day-old goods at a reduced price would have gone far toward meeting basic needs.[42] It is understandable that the press would prefer to chronicle how black people triumphed over adversity as opposed to reporting on the more bleak aspects of black life. Hearing about the latest advances in the world of the culinary arts probably appealed to middle-class African Americans. But the stories of "Pig Foot Mary's" fried chicken and hog maw sales would have affirmed working-class culinary habits and identities.[43]

For much of the early to mid-nineteenth century, the *Chicago Defender* did its part to "uplift the race" and join in the fight against racial inequality. In addition to sharing the success stories of up-and-coming black professionals, it frequently offered articles about cultural events. On January 15, 1915, the paper announced the grand opening of another "Elite, No. 2" restaurant, which would continue its tradition as the "mecca for high-class amusement." The Elite, No. 2 boasted of the best musical entertainment in the city and "an expert Chinese cook [to] serve fine Chinese and American dishes."[44] Even when the food was not quite up to standard, black people could boast that their palates were savvy enough to identify the blunder. For example, one restaurant "observer" visited an establishment at "Forty-seventh Street and State" and ordered a serving of chicken à la king. The patron was served a "half chicken, fried, on [a] piece of toast and cream gravy poured over [the] chicken." When he inquired about what appeared to be an error with his meal, the waitress informed him "she didn't know . . . she could only serve what the cook gave her."[45]

Observations about food were not relegated solely to the pages of magazines and newspapers. African American literary artists from as early as the late nineteenth century and well into the Harlem Renaissance also encoded their fiction with symbolic messages about food, respect, and self-identity. Though the presence of food in their novels often goes unremarked, it provides broad examples of black people's struggles (usually women, but not always) to negate the stereotypical representations of black people. Pauline Hopkins's novels, among other early fiction, are replete with discussions of social gatherings where "respectable" foods were served.[46] In *Contending Forces*, for example, Saturday gatherings at Ma Smith's boardinghouse always included repasts filled with "good things to eat" like "good homemade cake, sandwiches, hot chocolate," and the occasional ice cream or sherbet.[47] The fiction of black men and women writers such as Langston Hughes, Dorothy West, and Gwendolyn Brooks illustrates how black women sought to define themselves against the negative images of American society. Whereas these images depicted black women as coarse and lacking in manners and decorum or worse—always dark-skinned, heavyset, and sweating over a Dutch fryer—these writers sought a more feminine, refined illustration. Chicken, by its presence and its absence, reflects how food was used in this struggle over the means to define self as female, black, and having class.

When Langston Hughes's Jesse B. Semple sits in his front window gnawing on a pork chop bone, his wife, Joyce, admonishes him, "Do not *please* carry bones to the window."[48] For Simple, a native southerner, the tendency to suck bones is merely a means of "[getting] down to the juicy part" and a way of complimenting his wife on the well-cooked chops and chicken necks (199). And though Joyce cooks the foods he loves—chicken stewed down with dumplings, succotash, sweet potatoes, and beets—she draws the line at after-dinner savoring. For Joyce, gnawing on pork chop or chicken bones is simply just "*not* etiquette." Simple, however, has no use for "white folks' etiquette," stating that it is "wasted" on people who would just as soon "[knock] off their parents," "Jim Cro[w] colored people," and "bomb-burs[t]" than to suck a chicken neck (200). He believes that rule makers who seek to disallow anyone to suck on their *own* chicken bones in their *own* front window are mere hypocrites who "had plenty of time to gnaw [their] bones at the table" since they "were rich." From Simple's perspective, there is no better place to gnaw on his pork bones or to suck on his chicken necks than his own home. Restaurants were clearly off limits both because of segregation laws and because, in the eyes of his wife, Simple lacks proper etiquette.

"Suckin' the chicken bone dry" is a very common after-dinner display, especially for southerners and for those who have no inhibitions about enjoying the marrow found in well-seasoned bones.[49] But the exchange between Simple and Joyce illustrates that as migrants sought to make their way in their new surroundings, they often had to relinquish those cultural exhibitions that were deemed "unbecoming." To this end, they almost always had to learn new ways of "being" when it came to food. Prior to migrating (as in the case of Ruby Baker or Sarah Rice), the presence of certain foods might have identified a person as one of the better classes of poor folk. Now, the presence of those same foods became a cultural marker of one's belonging. Certain foods defined who fit into high society and who did not, who was identifiably southern and who was not. Consequently, migrants learned how power (cultural, social, class, racial) was manifested within the realm of food, around chicken necks and pork chop bones.

Though living in an urban context during wartime America provided lucrative employment options for some blacks, others were still found barely existing. The average black could ill afford such culinary "luxuries" as pork chops but could possibly afford chicken necks. In the case of Simple, having the wherewithal to afford these foods and then being controlled in his ability to enjoy them is undoubtedly an affront to his personal being and psychological welfare. The prescriptions of etiquette communicated by Joyce through the power dynamics of culinary control and containment disrupt Simple's enjoyment of his food. In this way, Simple is dominated not only as a racial and economic subject but also as a cultural one.[50]

Unfamiliar with these new rules of order guiding the ways of life in the city, many migrants turned to drugs, alcohol, excessive religion, violence, and sex as a way of escape. Still others sought the familiarity of cultural rituals and customs, like sucking bones, which could be enjoyed within the sanctity of their homes. But as Simple lounges in his living room window gnawing on a pork chop remain, he soon learns what many women already knew— home was not necessarily a site of refuge but of alienation and displacement. As Carole Boyce Davies reminds us, when black women write about home they may "speak of pain, movement, difficulty, learning and love in complex ways. Thus, the complicated notion of home mirrors the problematizing of community/nation/identity that one finds in Black women's writing from a variety of communities."[51] Simple refuses the connections between community/nation/identity as well as those between cultural artifacts, community, and identity. His frustration over this lack of understanding is evident when he conveys his feelings over the northern rules and regulations to his friend Boyd: "Why should Joyce care if I suck a pork-chop bone in the front window or not? We ain't got no back window. And I do not see why a man can't gnaw a bone and look out in the street at the same time. Nobody is looking up specially to see what I am doing. Nobody in the world cares if I gnaw a bone or not in my window—nobody but Joyce. . . . Manners is sometimes mighty inconvenient" (200–201).

When Simple complains to his friend that manners such as these are "inconvenient," Boyd responds that Joyce's tutelage was to "uphold the tone of the Harlem community." Echoing the pronouncements of "race" women and men like Charlotte Hawkins Brown and W. E. B. Du Bois, Boyd expounds: "One reason why white people don't want Negroes in their neighborhoods is because they say we lower the tone of the community. Eating bones in the window just isn't done in high society" (201). In an exchange of wits and words, Simple rejoins that "white folks might not gnaw bones in windows, but they sure do some awful things." He goes on to explain how they murder their parents, engage in racist practices, and drop bombs on innocent countries (referring to World War II). He quips: "Bone-gnawing, to my mind, is better than bomb-bursting. . . . When I gnaw my bone or suck my chicken neck, I am not hurting a human soul" (201). Continuing the exchange, Boyd remarks that Simple's disregard for the proper rules of etiquette hurts Joyce, and by extension society, because he is being inconsiderate. He concludes with, "Bones and bombs are not unrelated, pal. And certainly good manners are better than chicken necks or pork-chop bones." Simple, being very much aware of the attempts to construct and control his sense of self, rejects this entire palavering by saying, "From whence did you get such wrong information about such good food?" (202). Simple closes the conversation in this way, leaving Boyd frustrated. Yet, it was a way for Simple to exercise agency not only in the conversation but also *over* the conversation and the situation. It was also a way for Simple to transcend the alienation and devaluation that the entire bone-gnawing experience had brought.

Boyd's references to Joyce and society being "hurt" by Simple's desire to gnaw on his bones are well intentioned. Though a fictional character, Joyce embodies the sense of gender and race consciousness inherent in black female reformers of the era. Armed with a sense of "culture" that she inherited from her bricklayer father and educated, Eastern Star mother (who worked for only "fine white folks," never "no poor white trash"), Joyce sees it as part of her wifely duties to transmit the proper cultural values and systems of etiquette to her family (100). And though devoid of the economic resources that would thrust her into the upper echelons, she nonetheless caters to the proper manners and speech that can be ascribed to someone in the upper- or middle-class set. She strives to be accepted by the leading club ladies and is jubilant when issued a compliment: "Darling, you are a clever woman, such as our race needs" (153). The indication that Joyce "had arrived" fortifies her with the courage to further exemplify the strictest of morals and manners credited to one of her station. She does not drink or dance to any excess, at least not publicly, and turns up her nose at the blues, with the exclamation, "You know I never liked the blues. I am from the North." Joyce is seemingly ideologically and culturally different from the working-class and migrant women with whom Simple has had relationships in the past and works hard to maintain this distinction. So strong is this aura that she even looks with disdain upon anyone who acquired their riches from underground economies like "playing the numbers" (132).

But if Joyce reflects the social consciousness of many black clubwomen, she is also imbued with many of their contradictory characteristics. These contradictions on the culinary landscape are revealed when Simple shares with his friend Boyd that Joyce has an affinity for foods associated with the "folk." When Boyd inquires whether or not Joyce likes greens, Simple replies: "Eats them like a horse, when somebody else serve them. The same by chitterlings. Joyce tried to tell me once she did not eat pig ruffles, would not cook them, couldn't bear to clean them, and *loathed* the smell. But when my cousin in the Bronx invited us to a chitterling supper, I could hardly get near the pot for Joyce. I do not believe people should try to pass" (122, original emphasis). These revelations about Joyce's culinary habits and Simple's use of the word "pass" reinforce a point made earlier in this discussion—the disparity between public and private behaviors.

This passage is particularly revealing for its larger commentary on black women and men who tried to regulate the lives of working-class folk by monitoring their eating patterns. Joyce's need to police and control Simple's culinary proclivities is perhaps more indicative of her own temptation to engage in this behavior than it is to transform her husband. In maintaining gastronomic power over Simple, Joyce is struggling over her own place in the black community as well as over a need for self-definition. In policing herself against the behaviors she feels will be rejected by the better classes of blacks and certainly ridiculed by white society, she is trying to come to terms with who she is as a black woman in American society at that time. She is vying for a position from which to express who she is in both the private and public spheres. It is from this interesting space that the ironic nature of food and power relations is made most visible.

The discussion between Joyce and Simple is about more than simply gnawing on a chicken or pork chop bone. It becomes a discussion about class and regional tensions and also about defining and valuing oneself through the prism of food. The home, as one of the primary gendered domains of women, is a space where black women find themselves in "cross-cutting relationships." As black women resist the external white society's definitions, they also struggle against the boundaries posed internally by black communities.[52] Joyce wages a protest against Simple sitting at the window to gnaw on his bones by claiming that the window is also "hers." Far from merely carving out a physical space, she is claiming her place within the body politic of the home. Despite how we might feel about Joyce's insistence upon adhering to Emily Post's and Charlotte Hawkins Brown's rules of etiquette, we must recognize that she is asserting her place not only in the home but also within the realm of her physical body.

For the most part, Joyce seems clear about the level of respect she expects from Simple. However, ensuring these principles is difficult because she is inconsistent in her demands. On the one hand, she defers to her sense of respectability when she admonishes Simple—her boyfriend at this point in the story—about leaving her place in the wee hours of the morning: "When folks see you coming out of my place at two-three-four o'clock in the morning, you know what they think—even if it ain't so" (59). On the other hand, she is dating a married—not yet divorced—man. The struggle here is in Joyce's fictional need to take control of the perceptions and images that circumscribed black women's sexual lives at that time.

Joyce employs a number of strategies to take control over the ways in which both white society and black society seek to objectify her as a black woman. One of these strategies is to distinguish herself from Simple's other girlfriend at the time, Zarita, who Joyce refers to as a "bar stool hussy." By situating herself physically and morally from Zarita, Joyce demands that she be treated with deference.[53] Early in the relationship, Joyce establishes how she is to be treated by Simple. In doing this, Joyce is employing a discourse of feminine control over her space—her body and eventually their home. Joyce refuses to buy into the "loser image" that degrades or otherwise devalues who she believes she is in her own eyes.[54] Regardless of how polite society classifies her relationship to Simple, she refuses to allow Simple to think any less of her. Long before the reader encounters the culinary battle over bone gnawing, Joyce struggles to establish a certain voice of power within the household.

One Christmas, while they are still dating, Simple buys Joyce a "genuine pressure-cooker-roasting-oven to cook chickens" instead of a fur that she had requested. In response to his gift, she gives him the "cold-roll-your-eyes look" and says, "It's just what I wanted—except that I've got too many cooking utensils now to just be rooming—and that cute little fur jacket I showed you last week would've looked so nice on me" (38). She further reacts by buying him a carton of *her* favorite brand of cigarettes. With this act, Joyce reifies her place in Simple's life as a potential mate and as a woman who does not want to be reminded that cooking is a gendered division of labor.

After they eventually marry, Joyce employs a counterdiscourse to convey to Simple how her house will operate—namely, that bones will not be gnawed on while one is sitting in the front window. Joyce's efforts at self-assertion in her home are a necessary part of the daily negotiation to redefine her own subject consciousness as well as her place in society as a black woman of culture. Thus, the conflict of interests over the "proper place" to gnaw on chicken and pork bones takes on more significance when a black feminist dimension is added. In establishing affirming images of herself at home, Joyce is countering the controlling images that link black women with chicken and other objects in anything other than a positive light. Although Joyce recognizes the act of bone gnawing as an important ritual for Simple, her reactions are nonetheless driven by the ways in which the ritual affects her sense of self. With this assertion she illustrates how the intersections of gender, race, class, and food converge to make the home a culinary battleground and a site of female empowerment.

In Dorothy West's *The Living Is Easy*, the home further becomes a contested culinary site and chicken (or its absence) an embattled cultural artifact. Cleo Judson adheres wholeheartedly to shunning the "common ways" of the southern "Negro" in favor of manners associated with northern cities like Boston. But Cleo seeks to straddle this fence by bringing to the North the "easy living" southern feeling. She does this by encouraging/manipulating her three sisters to come to Boston, all the while denying any other connections to the South.[55] Set in early-twentieth-century Boston, *The Living Is Easy* provides a glimpse into the life of Cleo; her husband, Bart; their five-year-old daughter, Judy (who inherited her father's dark skin, much to the chagrin of her mother); and her three sisters, Lily, Charity, and Serena. Cleo's ultimate goal in the novel is to obtain a larger house where she can properly raise her daughter and, more important, take care of her three sisters and their children. She manages the latter by tricking her sisters into coming to Boston and manipulating her husband, "Mr. Nigger" as she calls him, into bankrolling the whole affair.

Cleo wants the idyllic features of the South and the economic prosperity of the North to occupy one home.[56] She "thought, and planned, and lied, and juggled Mr. Judson's money for this sister and that" in order to convince her three sisters to come north for a visit. The visit eventually becomes a long-term stay of four years, resulting in each sister's divorce or separation from her own husband. But the home life of her sisters is of little consequence to Cleo, whose initial intention is to lure them to Boston in hopes that they will remain with her and create a fictional version of their southern past. With the arrival of each sister, she begins this process. She greedily embraces the culinary mores of the South in order to impress and entice her sisters to remain. Using these southern customs as a lure, each morning's breakfast is designed to include foods that would elicit warm memories of the past while affirming the newness of the North: "peaches and cream, butter-soaked muffins, chops, hashed-brown potatoes, broiled bananas, sliced tomatoes and pie for whoever had the capacity" (167). Food is critical to Cleo's sense of identity, and she is surrounded by it. Her husband is a transplanted southerner who managed to make his mark opening a grocery store. He is the product of a plantation, a "shouting Baptist," and a mother whose restaurant and catering business featured fried chicken dinners. Cleo shares none of the pride that Bart feels when he ruminates over his accomplishments. Her only connection to his business is the money it yields and the shrewdness she can employ to obtain it. Despite this disinterest, it would be a mistake to assume that Cleo is unaware of the significance of food and its symbolic value in American society, particularly at that time. Evidence of this is found in a scene that intersects race, gender, class, politics, etiquette, and food.

Over time, as the wife of the "black banana king," Cleo manages to obtain many of the accoutrements of the black elite, including their gallantry. In a scene reminiscent of the parties often given by the literati of the twentieth century, Cleo, having "absorbed like a sponge" the bits and pieces of conversation, protocols, and etiquette of the "well-born," prepares for "the hour which gave her whole life meaning." A dinner party is held at her posh Roxbury home to honor the dean of a southern black college. Cleo has supposedly gathered the black Bostonians in support of the cause for social equality. In reality, however, she holds the party to impress upon her neighbors and friends that she has indeed learned the behaviors and comportment necessary for inclusion in their social set. With true grace and artistry, Cleo decorates the dining room with dainties and other fine cuisine: cracked lobster with "its meat removed and replaced . . . couched on a silver platter edged with lettuce. A grapefruit, dotted all over with toothpicks," and a spiced ham and tongue. Other delights include a decorated cucumber, molded ginger-ale salads, creamed mushrooms, Welsh rarebit, wild duck, and triangle- and diamond-shaped toasted bread with cheese spread and paprika. All of these foods are delightfully arranged to greet the southern gentleman who has come to solicit support against the false imprisonment and possible lynching of a black southern man (251–52).

But from Cleo's point of view, this valiant concern for the southerner is "a major blemish" in what is an otherwise perfect evening. Having succeeded in deftly inviting and then uninviting her sisters to attend the evening (and thus removing any suggestion of Cleo's familiarity with the South), she moves to dismiss her guest of honor's "intrusion" in the same manner. Cleo does this by completely rejecting Dean Galloway's request for assistance from the black northerners. Any initial sympathy offered by the guests for his cause is quickly retracted upon hearing Cleo's rationale:

> Dean Galloway, I am sorry to say I do not see what benefit will be derived from making the name of Robert Jones a household word. He had a reason for killing. But when one colored man commits a crime, the whole race is condemned. Tell Robert Jones's story to the world, and the world will be stirred by the drama and tragedy of the killing. But the rest of the race will be the real martyrs. Wherever white people see them, they will watch them for danger signs. They will be frightened by a dark face, or a slow answer, or a quick step. They will think that all Negroes are armed. (264)

The oxymoronic nature of this affair would not be so plain except for the fact that only a thin veneer of culture separates Cleo from the subject of Dean Galloway's speech—her brother-in-law Robert Jones. The fine line that separates Cleo's southern breakfasts from her gallant dinners is the same one that removes Cleo and other black Bostonians from their southern roots. As Lawrence Rodgers argues: "To be an accepted part of [Boston] society, [Cleo] must outwardly cut all social and psychological ties to her southern roots, 'disclaim' her past, even though she inwardly needs to be fortified by her recollections of its effect on her."[57] And so it is that Cleo continuously exists in this liminal space throughout the novel—neither wholly part of the black bourgeoisie of Boston, nor free of her southern beginnings. Cleo never quite makes it to the top of the social ladder but instead falters somewhere amidst the lies, treachery, and deceit she has used. In her attempts to boost her own sense of self, she ruins the lives of several other people, three of whom are her sisters. By the end of the novel, Cleo's sense of self seems to wane as two of her sisters leave to make their own way and her husband heads to New York, broke and alone.

None of this bothers Cleo too much because one of her sisters remains behind. Charity was once a fine-looking woman who could be "swooped up" in her husband's arms. But her extended stay in Boston forces her husband into the arms of another woman. Surrendering to a broken heart and spirit, Charity turns to food, using it "like a heating pad on her pain" (179). Before sinking into a culinary oblivion, she announces to Cleo, "I'll get me a job soon's I can" (178). Though Cleo resists such a notion, declaring, "You think I want to see my sister slaving in somebody's kitchen?," the reality of past-due rent and the loss of prospective income finds her in need.

Cleo is trying to figure out how to scrape together snatches of money when the owner of the neighborhood bar invites Charity to be his cook. He says, "I see you standing at the window so much I figured you wasn't working. On account of you're colored, I figured you could cook" (311). Cognizant of the excess weight she has gained since her arrival, Charity decides to use it to her advantage by calling upon mammy imagery to assure the visitor of her cooking abilities: "Oh, I can, sir, I can! I can cook plain or fancy. . . . You can see by just looking at me I'll be well at home in a kitchen" (311). Charity then uses her newfound luck to haggle for an old stove that was being discarded from her future employer's house: "She took hold of her courage. Her head went up. She felt proud and capable. 'Mr. Doran, what you going to do with the small stove? Seeing's I'm going to be working, I wish you'd sell it to me and take it out of my wages'" (311–12). After a moment's give-and-take, Mr. Doran departs, having given Charity the stove and the rejoinder that he expects "Mrs. Reid" to arrive at her new job in a few minutes. Despite Cleo's obvious distaste for both Mr. Doran's invitation and her sister's acceptance of the clearly racist proposition, she is in no financial position to argue—she needs the money that Charity will bring in and the stove that she manages to secure.

West illustrates an interesting juxtaposition between Cleo's relationship to southern foods and Charity's reliance upon mammy imagery. Both women use food to define their sense of self in light of their circumstances. Without rendering judgment upon either Cleo's or Charity's decisions, West portrays two black women employing very different strategies to define their sense of self-worth and their ways of gaining respect. The physical (weight gain) and psychological (manipulation) boundaries that these sisters traverse while under the same roof render the home a contested culinary space. Charity, by calling to mind the image of the overweight, asexual black female cook, finds the affirmation of self that was unavailable to her when she was not economically contributing to the household. Accepting the job offered by the neighbor, even if it meant subjecting herself to stereotypes to gain the position, was Charity's way of rejecting her victimized position while putting self-definition to action.

In this novel, the brief appearances of chicken speak to the notion of how black women's work and class intersect as a site of cultural contestation. Cleo's rejection of foods like chicken exemplifies her arrival in polite society. The work that she puts into Dean Galloway's grand evening and the trouble she takes to avoid any connection to the South—culinary or otherwise—illustrate the potency of gender, class, and food to some black women's sense of self. West's mention of the fact that Cleo's mother-in-law actually made her living from selling fried chicken further typifies the sense of regional and cultural separation that Cleo desires. That Cleo would not think twice about having her banquet catered with fried chicken also exemplifies the place that it holds in the hierarchy of foods representing class status.

West's description of the false sense of security and reality often inhabited by black northerners is ironic. So much of the behavior in the novel is based upon a facade of social graces, manners, and mores. West is able to present the inner sanctums of black upper-class life because the narrative portrays her own familiarity with the culture. In the afterword to the novel, Adelaide Cromwell describes West's own upbringing and her familiarity with the intricacies of northern black elites: "Dorothy West, an exception to this insularity, chronicled the secret city. It was a vivid and proud world, not characterized by a search for African roots or survivals or Pentecostal churches. It was as American as apple pie—made of the best apples" (358). In some ways, West answers the call of her predecessor Charlotte Hawkins Brown in her brief depictions of proper decorum, social graces, and manners that defined black polite society. Hers was a society where being a caterer of terrapin soup would classify one as a leader, but being a caterer of fried chicken might simply mean that one had bad taste in food. In this way, both Brown and West can be credited with illustrating some of the finer aspects of African American gastronomy and for expanding the range of African American cuisine—the hidden aspect of expressive culture.

The range of foods consumed by black people who sought respectability through procurement, preparation, and consumption is a portion of black history often left untold. Undoubtedly, this lack of explanation can be attributed to several causes. One, cooking in general (unless haute cuisine) has been slandered in popular culture. This dearth can further be explained by the sole alignment of black women and food with the mammy image, a position often contributed to by many African American scholars. Disregarding black women's cookery as valued cultural work also has greatly hindered the ability to see how food has been used for self-definition and self-valuation. Moreover, lack of attention to African American food has delayed society's ability to see this cuisine as anything other than fried chicken and collard greens. But black women's cookery is important work, and its explorations reveal how ordinary black women have made contributions to African American life and culture. Some of the progressive social action that has long been attributed to middle-class women's activism is notably present in the lives of poor and working-class women. This is particularly revealed when one considers food rituals and customs involving chicken.

Barbara Christian argues that Gwendolyn Brooks was aware of the need to display the "complex existence of the ordinary, dark-skinned woman, who is neither an upper-class matron . . . nor the downtrodden victim." [58] To address this need, Brooks created Maud Martha, a semi-autobiographical portrayal of an ordinary woman. Maud Martha sees herself as having a "little life" within the constructs of her family—especially her husband—her class, her race, and white society. Yet, within this construct, Maud is an artist and a creator of self as she practices the customs and rituals that make her life bearable. One of these rituals is chicken preparation, and even though it involves the drudgery of "dressing," in the end, it is its own reward. [59]

Brooks explains that the vignette in *Maud Martha* titled "Brotherly Love" is based on "my old feelings regarding 'dressing' a chicken, and my continuing feelings that chickens are people . . . people, that is, in the sense that we conceive people to be: things of identity and response." [60] Brooks does not elaborate upon those "old feelings," but something akin to disdain is revealed in the opening sentence: "Maud Martha was fighting with a chicken." [61] She goes on to illustrate some of the labor and "mess" involved in preparing chicken for consumption:

> The nasty, nasty mess. It had been given a bitter slit with the bread knife and the bread knife had been biting in that vomit-looking interior for almost five minutes without being able to detach certain resolute parts from their walls. The bread knife had it all to do, as Maud Martha had no intention of putting her hand in there. Another hack—another hack—STUFF! Splat in her eye. She leaped at the faucet. . . . People could do this! People

could cut a chicken open, take out the mess, with bare hands or a bread knife, pour water in, as in a bag, pour water out, shake the corpse by neck or by legs, free the straggles of water. (293–94)

Maud Martha applauds her ability to find a chicken during wartime because "meat was jewelry and she was practically out of Red Points." Her struggle to create something out of the chicken that she was "lucky to find," despite its being "unsightly and smelly," resolves itself in her final creation: "When the animal was ready for the oven Maud Martha smacked her lips at the thought of her meal."[62]

In "Brotherly Love," the chicken serves multiple roles. It certainly conveys chicken consumption and also represents how people created masterpieces out of foods a bit on the "bad side." But in *Maud Martha*, chicken is also used to portray one black woman's journey to self-definition. In describing herself as having that "little life," Maud Martha is relatively akin to a chicken—one of the lowest animals on the evolutionary food chain. But through small measures of creativity, particularly those involving customs and rituals, she manages to transform that life.[63] When she converts the slightly smelly chicken into a delectable meal worthy of lip-smacking, she is both carrying on the tradition of black women able to makeover "bad" food and illustrating that process as creative work. As Christian points out, "[Maud Martha's] sense of her own integrity is rooted mostly in her own imagination—in her internal language as metaphors derived from women's experiences, metaphors that society usually trivializes but which Brooks presents as the vehicles of insight. Though Maud Martha certainly does not articulate a language (or life) of overt resistance, she does prepare the way for such a language in that she sees the contradiction between her real value as a black woman and how she is valued by those around."[64] In the same way that Brooks used the "ordinariness" around her to create her works of literature, Maud Martha uses food and other objects of daily life to create an aesthetic context for her life and therefore transform it a little in the process.

Ordinary women like Maud Martha used their creative culinary and housekeeping talents to create and reflect change in their lives. This is one of the reasons why the work of black reformers such as Charlotte Hawkins Brown was admirable but troubling. Knowing how black women were portrayed in popular culture at that time, it is understandable that reformers would try to emphasize what they (and white society) denoted as "proper decorum." However, in their quest to present a particular picture of black life, some black social activists often eclipsed the only measures of self-empowerment

FIGURE 3.8.
"Woman with children,"
1935. Courtesy Records
of the Works Progress
Administration, Record
Group 69-N, Box 54,
National Archives
and Records
Administration —
Northeast Region
(College Park)
(photograph 57A).

that many wage-earning black women had at their disposal. Brooks, being aware of these tensions, uses her literature to illustrate how household rituals involving food become a way for black women to mediate the oppression in their lives. This is particularly visible in the images she provides of black women living in the dowdy confines of a kitchenette. As Wright says in *12 Million Black Voices*, "The kitchenette is our prison, our death sentence without a trial, the new form of mob violence that assaults not only the lone individual, but all of us, in its ceaseless attacks" (figure 3.8).[65]

But where Wright is extreme in his presentation of dejection and anguish, recognizing little agency employed by black people, a decade later Brooks is far more hopeful. In her presentation of Sunday meals of chicken and rice or noodles, salad, rye bread, tea, and chocolate chip cookies for dessert, Brooks tries to find a way for Maud Martha to live with the desolation. The residents in Maud Martha's "Kitchenette Building" display rituals that not only belie their material conditions but also try to transcend them. For example, one resident finds contentment in taking daily tea. In this ritual, she spreads a large "stool with a square of lace," adds a "low bowl of artificial flowers, a teacup or teacups," and a pot of tea with sugar, cream, and lemon with sundries. By this example, Brooks allows for humanity to creep in among the "onion fumes," "fried potatoes," and "yesterday's garbage ripening in the hall."[66] The common food objects—chicken, rice, noodles, beans, eggs, bread—that Brown and her contemporaries sought to disassociate from working-class people typify the means by which some black women expressed themselves. These women not only used their homes to feed their families but also used their kitchens to engage in cultural transmission. By practicing certain rituals, customs, and habits, they exhibited a measure of self-definition and instilled in their children and community aspects of socialization.

Poor or wage-earning black women were not the only ones to demonstrate their culinary skills and ingenuity. Black women who engaged in the informal market economy (for whatever reason) of "jookin'" also "kept culture," but in a decidedly different fashion. Using their culinary skills and talents while working in the economic underground, these women carried on a variety of cultural traditions. These practices were most prominent when it involved black people and travel or movement. One wonders how many black women have gone unacknowledged for continuing the custom of packing shoe-box lunches for travelers who made their way across American soils. We are able to consider further the complexities of black women's lives as we turn to narratives of movement and travel.

TRAVELING THE CHICKEN BONE EXPRESS

*We were indeed traveling, but no one knew our destination
nor our arrival date.*
—Maya Angelou, The Heart of a Woman

From the moment that African people reached these shores until well into the period of the Great Migration and then the early civil rights movement, African American people had to measure their freedom of movement by someone else's authority. Once freedom was realized, women, men, and children traveled for days, months, and sometimes years. Some searched for a new existence, while others searched for familiarity in the form of family members and friends. Still others simply searched, not wanting to be confined to any permanent space. One of the most salient components of these black people's travel experiences is food. Yet, more than likely, what early travelers ate, how they obtained their food, and who did the cooking have been lost to the great unknown. Had this information been preserved, we might have a better understanding of the complexities inherent in the experiences of African American travel and movement. We might also have a better sense of how African American travel was complicated or assuaged by the absence or presence of food.

Little has been written about how food factors into individual and collective travel plans.[1] Yet, black women's cookery was central to African American narratives of travel. Black women provisioned travelers with chicken on a regular basis. In addition to being an opportunity for cultural transmission, providing chicken enabled black women to challenge economic and social institutions and ideologies within the wider American society (and within black communities) that sought to relegate cooking to menial female labor. This aspect of the discussion, then, turns on two points—African American travel narratives and how black women's movement within those narratives was constrained by gender issues prohibiting them from taking the same types of journeys as their male counterparts. In considering an example of a black woman who used the underground economy of "jookin'" as a way out of her domestic dilemmas, it can also be argued that black women supplied chicken as a metaphorical way of moving from one domicile to another.

Even before the end of the Civil War, black women were pressing the boundaries of freedom. Journeying near and far with the aid of the Union army, many left plantations carrying all that they had. The journey of one migrant woman was described by a northern white woman in this way: "A huge negress was seen striding along with her hominy pot, in which was a live chicken, poised on her head. . . . One child was on her back . . . and under each arm was a smaller child. . . . A little yellow dog ran by her side, and a half-grown pig trotted on before." [2] Carrying both "chicken and child," this woman made her way into the "promised land." Though this account dates back to the late nineteenth century, few black women have changed their patterns during times of travel. Whether they are moving or provisioning someone else for the move, many black women still carry or send chicken on the journey to the metaphorical "promised lands" of work, upward mobility, pleasure, and survival. [3]

When it was decided that Bernice Reeder would make the move "up North" to perform domestic work, several kinds of provisions had to be made. [4] Getting ready to leave included discussion of "traveling taboos," such as not traveling during certain phases of the moon or during her menstrual cycle. It also included physically and psychologically getting prepared to ride the train. This usually involved a discussion about food. Reeder refers to this very matter-of-fact part of the "getting ready" process by saying: "The next day I was on the train with Brother and Ma-Sis. My mama had give me this big box of fried chicken, which included biscuits, and *two* sweets." [5] Reeder's mother was aware that Jim Crow segregation laws would prevent her daughter from obtaining anything of substance to eat on the train. Providing a box lunch would ensure that Reeder would have something to eat.

Maya Angelou recalls a similar foodways experience in her autobiographical narrative, *I Know Why the Caged Bird Sings*:

When I was three and Bailey four, we had arrived in the musty little town, wearing tags on our wrists, which instructed—"to whom it may concern" —that we were Marguerite and Bailey Johnson, Jr. from Long Beach, California enroute to Stamps, Arkansas, c/o Mrs. Annie Henderson. . . . A porter had been charged with our welfare—he got off the train the next day in Arizona—and our tickets were pinned to my brother's inside coat pocket. I don't remember much of the trip, but after we reached the segregated southern part of the journey, things must have looked up. Negro passengers, who always traveled with loaded lunch boxes, felt sorry for "the poor little motherless darlings" and plied us with cold fried chicken and potato salad.[6]

Travel experiences such as these that involve "shoe-box lunches" are central to African American travel narratives. Though we are often graced with the narrative, seldom are we given the details about the foods that were consumed along the way. Part of the reason for this may be that most people ate the same food when they traveled in those days—chicken.[7]

The legend of the "chicken bone express" has been orally passed along for generations.[8] As the legend goes, during periods of migration when thousands of blacks traveled northward (and westward) in search of education, jobs, and social equality, the routes became known as the "chicken bone express" because most travelers (whether by train, bus, or car) packed a boxed lunch of chicken. After eating, the passengers were said to have tossed their bones from the windows, leaving an "identifiable" trail. These lunches were known as the "shoe-box special" and usually contained these foods in some combination: fried chicken, sweet potato pie or other "sweet" (chocolate cake, coconut cake), biscuits, roast, and sometimes a boiled egg—all foods that were easy to consume when moving about because they "traveled well."

Having food that traveled well was clearly essential given that some journeys could take hours and even days. But what makes the food and travel narratives of African American people most interesting are the Jim Crow policies. Adding issues of race to the terrain of travel necessitates a different reading for black people in general, and women in particular. The experience of freedom brought on by mobility is momentarily disrupted to include an understanding of how many aspects of the American travel landscape—restaurants, rest areas, and gas stations—were harbingers of hostility for black people. This is especially the case for women travelers. When black women decided to "move," great pains had to be taken to properly plan the trip, as I suggested earlier. However, literature provides excellent examples of some of the other dangers black women faced when they traveled during the segregation era.[9]

For example, in Toni Morrison's *Sula*, one of the many dangers that confronted women when traveling is highlighted. Helene Wright, the mother of Sula's best friend, Nel, makes the trip south to visit her dying grandmother. Though she considered the trip with "heavy misgiving," she "decided that she had the best protection: her manner and her bearing, to which she would add a beautiful dress."[10] Knowing in advance that the trip would be a difficult one, Helene decides that her northern airs of refinement and beautiful clothes would be enough to help her escape the treatment accorded to "common folk." Despite her adornments, though, Helene soon realizes that her body becomes the "text on which the narrative of a [racialized] other is written."[11]

As will happen during a long train ride, Helene has a need to use the restroom, so she asks a black woman with four children who had gotten on the train in Alabama, "Is there somewhere we can go to use the restroom? The toilet?" The woman replies, "Yes," explaining that the restroom is just "yonder" in Meridian. She then asks Helene, "Kin you make it?" Disembarking the train in Meridian with her daughter, Helene begins searching for the restroom door that says "Colored Women." She notices, however, that the other woman and her children head off to a field of high grass on the far side of the track.

> Some white men were leaning on the railing in front of the stationhouse. It was not only their tongues curling around toothpicks that kept Helene from asking information of them. She looked around for the other woman and, seeing just the top of her head rag in the grass, slowly realized where "yonder" was. All of them, the fat woman and her four children, three boys and a girl, Helene and her daughter, squatted there in the four o'clock Meridian sun. They did it again in Ellisville, again in Hattiesburg, and by the time they reached Slidell, not too far from Lake Pontchartrain, Helene could not only fold leaves as well as the fat woman, she never felt a stir as she passed the muddy eyes of the men who stood like wrecked Dorics under the station roofs of those towns.[12]

What Morrison presents are the "sacred and profane" aspects of travel for women that often get left out of analyses about the experiences of freedom and mobility. Travel and movement are conceptualized as acts of resistance and "ways of escape," but Morrison's excerpt inserts some of the ways in which the ability to resist and dissent are a necessary part of the female travel experience. Most often, but not always, these abilities include food, which Morrison does not detail.

What the reader is told is that Nel is carrying "a covered basket of food." Given that Helene does not associate with "common folk," it is unlikely that fried chicken rested in the basket. It is more probable that their travel food is comprised of ham slices shaved from the pork that Helene leaves at home for her husband. Given that no mention is made of the foods eaten by the "fat woman" and her four children, the reader can speculate about a couple of things: the woman's economic situation made it impossible for her to feed four children and herself during the trip; and the presence of chicken, during times of African American travel, is assumed and therefore not necessary to reiterate.[13] Furthermore, the pains taken to describe Helene's notions of refinement, coupled with the mention of a "covered basket" (instead of the more recognizable shoe box), leads me to believe that a statement is being made about food—both its absence (chicken) and its suggested presence (ham).

In their memoir cookbook, *Spoonbread and Strawberry Wine*, Norma Jean and Carole Darden do not leave the reader to speculate on the contents of their shoe box. Vividly recalling their traveling experiences and the arrangements that had to be made to accommodate the limitations of segregation, they say:

> We could hardly sleep the night before and would help pack our bags and lunches, which our mother put in shoe boxes with the name of the passenger Scotch-taped to the top so that special requests were not confused. . . . These trips took place during the fifties, and one never knew what dangers or insults would be encouraged along the way. Racist policies loomed like unidentified monsters in our childish imagination and in reality. After the New Jersey Turnpike ended, we would have to be on the alert for the unexpected. So, as we approached that last Howard Johnson's before Delaware, our father would make his inevitable announcement that we had to get out, stretch our legs, and go to the bathroom, whether we wanted to or not. This was a ritualized part of every trip, for, although there would be many restaurants along the route, this was the last one that didn't offer segregated facilities. From this point on, we pulled out our trusty shoe-box lunches.[14]

The contents of the Darden shoe-box lunches included "fried chicken, peanut butter and jelly sandwiches, deviled eggs, carrot and celery sticks, salt and pepper, chocolate layer cake, and lemonade, all neatly wrapped in wax paper, with 'extra treats' like fruit, nuts, raisins, and cheese." When that was gone, the sisters say they would "keep [their] eyes peeled for black-owned establishments, which usually took [them] off the main route."[15] The Darden sisters' experiences and childhood "sense of adventure" belies some of the terrifying travelogues that have accompanied other women's stories of movement. But what it does reveal are the travel networks that were offered by other blacks to humanize the African American travel experience. Black women owned many of these havens.

Ann Denkler details one of these establishments in her work on Luray, Virginia. "Miss Martha's Black Holiday Inn" was a tourist cabin owned by Martha Adams.[16] Located on the outskirts of Luray, the cabin consisted of a living room, kitchen, small bedroom, and various pieces of furniture. According to Denkler, Adams would recall the hordes of people who would arrive at her door ("most often six to ten people at a time") requesting "food and beds." When asked how they had heard of her place, they would reply, "Well, we just asked in town and they told us to come and see you." Unlike many of the well-known motels in the center of town, Miss Martha's did not discriminate. Those who often found their way did so either by word of mouth or by using the *Negro Motorist Green Book*.[17]

Black women like Adams used their domestic skills in the informal market economy to provide goods and services—legal and illegal. Women and men who operated makeshift motels and rooming houses also provided entertainment and liquor to a variety of clientele, not necessarily always black. A plate of chicken and collard greens was as much a part of the income-generating process as the overnight fee of a couple of dollars. Being able to supplement income produced by less profitable positions or even generate income made this type of work all the more appealing. Faced with difficult economic circumstances and seeing a niche in the market, many black women turned to the underground economy for security. Often, larger domestic issues, many of which prevented them from leaving their homes in search of better opportunities, precipitated movement to this arena. A brief reading of Bebe Moore Campbell's *Your Blues Ain't Like Mine* provides an illustration. Black women not only worked the underground but also used it as part of their particular travel narrative and in doing so often were able to make their journey metaphorically while others left literally.

Fiction is one of the sites for the portrayal of black women who work the underground economy.[18] While big cities like Chicago, Los Angeles, and New York tend to provide the setting for these depictions, Campbell chooses rural Mississippi. In what has come to be known as her fictional trademark, Campbell creates black female characters who are shrewd businesswomen despite the social, economic, and political circumstances around them. This is the case of Ida Long in Campbell's novel. In order to understand fully the importance of chicken in Ida's life and its prevalence in the novel, it is necessary to explore the cultural contexts in which chicken, movement, economics, race, class, and power intersect.

Set in the 1950s South, *Your Blues Ain't Like Mine* is embroiled in race, class, gender, and culinary politics, revealing how power roles are reversed and destabilized. The novel reworks the maiming and murder of Emmet Till, a critical episode in American history. The narrative unfolds in a fashion similar to the actual incident. Chicago-born Armstrong Todd is sent to Hopewell, Mississippi, to spend the summer with his grandmother. After whistling at or speaking a few innocent French words to a white woman, Lily Cox, Todd is maimed and killed, changing the lives of many in the rural community. In this narrative where race, social, and cultural politics reside, the roles of the black female characters are particularly noteworthy.

Both Ida Long and Lily Cox are poor and have sons. They enjoy each other's friendship, though they are unable to openly express their amity. The connection between the two women is forged when they incidentally meet at the train depot while each relishes the thought of escaping Hopewell. For these women, the train depot symbolizes not only their mutual desire to escape the dreary life of Hopewell but also a place of sharing courage, dreams, and confidences. On one particular evening while the women are standing in their respective segregated spaces, sharing secrets about their parentage and sexual abuses, Lily confides: "I gotta tell you something. Somebody told my husband that this colored boy was—uh, said something fresh to me today. But he didn't. I told my husband that. And everything's all right now . . ."[19] Hearing this dangerous admission, Ida turns and runs as fast as she can, her own son in tow, to warn Armstrong Todd's grandmother of the fate about to befall her grandson.

The binary juxtaposition of these women poised at the train station, recognizing one another's similarities and differences, foreshadows the remainder of the novel. When Lily explains what happened between her husband, Armstrong, and herself, Floyd Cox becomes the embodiment of all that is ill in Ida's life. An unknown white man fathered Ida. She sells chicken dinners door-to-door to get extra money because white men are threatening to take her property. And now she is running for the life of two black women's sons (hers and Delotha Todd's) in hopes of saving them both before evil strikes at the hands of white men. This enormity of white male power converges at once upon Ida, driving her to run in order to resist—exercising a form of agency in her movement. In contrast to Ida, who from that moment at the train depot is constantly mobile, Lily is presented as a captive of white dominant race and gender ideologies of domesticity. Though Lily and Ida both confront gender, class, and economic limitations, Ida uses the home as a site from which to exercise cultural and economic ingenuity to redefine her circumstances. Lily, on the other hand, seems to lack any consciousness about how to engage in resistance. A discussion of how the Cox family is affected by Armstrong's murder further illustrates the importance of this juxtaposition.

Lily's husband, Floyd, runs the local pool hall and juke joint. After he participates in the murder of Armstrong, Hopewell's black community boycotts his businesses. The sudden realization of the black community's ability to directly affect his material life causes Floyd to question, "What are they trying to do?" To this Lily simply responds, "They're trying to starve us out" (125). Floyd's need to feel like he is "one of the kin" and the false sense of bravado that the murder temporarily provides him is interrupted by the retaliatory power of the black community. This shift in power becomes most apparent around chicken and other foods. Campbell details Lily's observations: "In all her life she'd never conceived of Negroes as having any kind of power that could affect her. Now she was overwhelmed by the realization that the niggers not only could but were going to destroy her family without so much as raising their voices. Lily began to hate colored people with a simmering bitterness she had never known she possessed" (125).

The psychological and economic "destruction" of the Cox family begins when Floyd is unable to provide his family with the foods they are accustomed to having. Prior to the murder, the Coxes would enjoy meals of "neck bones, butter beans, cabbage, rice, gravy, biscuits," and occasionally fried chicken. The strain on their resources, however, forces them to rely upon what they considered to be basic necessities: coffee, eggs, bacon, grits, and cigarettes. When this is gone, they are "reduced" to eating government surplus products while even poor blacks are able to have "fried chicken sandwiches and huge slabs of cake." The fact that Floyd is no longer able to have chicken and desserts for his lunch further reinforces his reduced class and social status. For Floyd, the aromatic smells of the chicken become a powerful metaphor for pain. The presence of "lack" in his life is as fierce and mocking as the eyes of his fellow black laborers that stare at him "full of rage and hatred" (138).

In the exchange of glances between the men, food—and the lack thereof—becomes instrumental in reinforcing how the power relations between poor blacks and poor whites have been reversed. This reversal becomes gendered as well as racial when Floyd seeks employment at the home of a white woman, Mrs. Jameson. Also working at the home is a young black girl who performs domestic tasks. Already resenting that he had to "work like a nigger" digging ditches, these feelings escalate when he is reminded that he and the young girl now share a "missus." Clear about who Floyd is and what he has done, the young girl uses food to exact an ounce of "revenge." In one incident, the girl gives Floyd a lunch meal consisting of red beans, rice, and biscuits. She sets the plate on a little wooden stool on the back porch of the house. When Floyd looks through the window he sees the girl sitting at the kitchen table eating a chicken breast (197).

Chicken becomes the object that further reifies Floyd's demoted class status. Though poor, he always believed that he was better than any black person. However, by boycotting his juke joint and pool hall, as well as by deciding how food is distributed, African Americans demonstrate their economic, social, and cultural power. In these scenes, Campbell captures not only the racial but also the class and gender conflicts that come together around the struggle over food. On the surface, this resentment manifests itself as Floyd's hatred of black people because they have better food to eat and can make the food choices that he cannot.

Underneath, however, are economic and gender tensions. He blames his wife, Lily, because the family now has to eat cheese sandwiches. Picking an argument with her because the government is now supplying the food that he should provide, he thinks, "If it hadn't been for her, he'd still have his business. He wouldn't have to be digging ditches with niggers for two dollars a day. If she'd listened to him and stayed out of the place like he told her to, they wouldn't be eating surplus government food like they was" (139). Floyd blames Lily for compromising the family economics. Had she not been "yearning for excitement" and therefore gone into the store, Floyd believes the status quo would have been maintained. But this is not the case, and despite their son's protestations of "I don't want to eat nigger food," the Cox family is forced to rely upon the government and neighborly blacks who are willing to share. For example, when Lily delivers her daughter at the hands of a black midwife, not only can she not afford to pay the midwife, but also she must turn to her for food. Lily reaches the point where she can take no more and solicits assistance from her church. But when they provide the groceries, they also suggest that she seek welfare.

Ironically, in trying to defeat black people by killing Armstrong Todd, Floyd and his extended family must now rely upon the black community and "their" system of relief for survival. And at the center of this calamity is Lily, totally dependent upon others—her husband, in-laws, black neighbors, and church—for her family's continued existence. Rarely is she seen in a position of personal struggle, gathering the will on her own to go on for herself and her family. Just as Ida and Lily are separated from one another by the racial demarcations at the train depot, these black and white women are again on opposite sides of the divide when it comes to personal and community survival.

Through Ida's character, Campbell draws attention to black females who turn to illegal "free enterprise," using the pleasures and leisure entertainment of black people as the basis for their business. After her stepfather sustains a work-related injury, Ida needs quick money to keep her land. She also wants the money to get her son out of Mississippi — preferably to go north — so he can have a chance at better opportunities. So it takes little coaxing when cousin Louis, with his "conked hair," "flaming red suit, bright yellow patent-leather shoes with little crooked heels, yellow canary hat with a high crown and twirling red feather," shows up at Ida's door and says: "Girl, you need to throw you a rent party."[20] Clearly a "worldly" man, he convinces Ida to use her cooking skills to supplement her meager wages from domestic work. But Ida is no stranger to selling food to supplement her income. Long before she turns her house into a juke joint, she prepares chicken and tamale dinners to sell door-to-door. In this capacity, Ida is a modern-day higgler, hawker, and vendor. Carrying the food in one hand and her son, Sweetbabe, by the other, she goes to rooming houses and other dwellings exchanging chicken dinners for seventy-five cents.

Already using her kitchen to cook more than three meals a day, opening her home to a rent party would prove to be equally, if not more, profitable. At juke joints, buffet flats, rent parties, chitlin struts — whatever they are called — black folks have been "jookin'" in one form or another for a long time.[21] Zora Neale Hurston and her sidekick Big Sweet often visited these "Negro pleasure house[s]." Richard Wright describes it as the way "excluded folk play." Still others indicate that having rent parties was a way to meet the monthly bills and responsibilities. Whether it is expressing sensuality, singing the blues, selling bootleg whiskey and fried chicken to pay the bills, or playing to feel included, jookin' as a form of expressive culture has permeated and surrounded African American lives for over a century.

In the setting of "Ida's place," food takes on multiple meanings. Chicken, ribs, tamales, macaroni and cheese, and greens are culturally familiar to many southerners and certainly to many southern African American people.[22] So while these foods offer nourishment, they simultaneously provide memories, comfort, and security. In this space, where food, memory, and illegal business activities intersect, some social boundaries collapse while others remain intact. For example, when Sheriff Barnes arrives at Ida's to collect his payoff, he often seeks more than money: "Did I ever tell you how much I like me some yella peaches?" The predictable sexual advance by Barnes is illustrative of the sexual and cultural politics that women in Ida's position (selling food, liquor, sensuality, and blues) endured.

As the host of the party, Ida in effect becomes a "blues woman," selling what Hazel Carby suggests is an "alternative form of representation, an oral and musical women's culture that explicitly addresses the contradictions of feminism, sexuality, and power."[23] Though Carby is referring to women like Bessie Smith and Ma Rainey, the appellation is applicable to Ida as well. In addition to selling dinners, she is also selling culture. People come to Ida's to have a good time and to forget their cares amidst the Saturday night sounds of James Brown's "Please! Please! Please!" They come to Ida's to release their old blues and pick up new ones in the form of old and new lovers.

But the burdens of sexual harassment, living in a multigenerational household (her stepfather, her son, and herself), extra cooking on a daily basis, and worrying about future plans overwhelm Ida. Rather than succumb to the pressures, Ida takes control of her life and begins to jog, thus transforming her from merely a "blues woman" to what Angela Y. Davis describes as a "travelin' blues woman."[24] Because blues women like Clara Smith, Ethel Waters, Alberta Hunter, and other black females made it to the "promised land" of the North, the fictional character of Ida has a tradition of hope upon which to build. And she needs this hope to maintain her sanity—especially when her dreams are delayed. Ida's plans to take her son and go to Chicago are halted when she learns that her stepfather is permanently confined to a wheelchair. Recognizing the enormous financial burden associated with this new development, including the effects that this will have on her son's ability to leave, Ida begins to work even harder.

That Ida's desire to migrate to Chicago is thwarted by her father's illness is not surprising. Neither is it surprising that her first decision is to use this disappointment as a catalyst, propelling her to get her son out of Hopewell. These examples typify the restraints often associated with women's mobility. As this scene suggests, mobility and freedom must be articulated among gendered lines because women with children and other household obligations often had to forego freedom (during enslavement) and better opportunities (during various times of migration) in order to sacrifice for their families. But knowing that various blues women made it out and could sing about it encourages Ida to consider, at least mentally, doing the same. Therefore, jogging enables Ida to "migrate" emotionally, psychologically, and physically. For Ida, jogging is a release, a way of cleansing, and a means of escaping the drudgery that faces her in the kitchen and in her life. For instance, at one point in the novel, Ida faces "ten fried-chicken dinners to cook, and nearly as many people [wanting] spareribs." After spending the whole day cutting and seasoning chickens, frying tamales, heaping up plates of potato salad, and slicing tomatoes, she needs to jog. The feeling she gets from this kind of running is freshness and a sense of renewal: "One time [Ida] had spent the night at the home of the colored schoolteacher. The woman had hot and cold water and an indoor bathroom, the first Ida had ever seen; she insisted that Ida take a bath. When Ida was covered with the soapy water, her body felt brand-new. Running was like that for her" (177). The comparison between ablution and running bespeaks a sense of religiosity. The freedom of movement that Ida receives from running is like a resurrection. Though bound by economic and social limitations, Ida—in jogging—is transformed.

Embedded in the novel's illustrations of the ways in which women move are distinctly different gender and race meanings. There is, for instance, the train, which is symbolic of the struggle between black men and women "to define the differing material conditions" of their lives. When the train comes to get Ida's son, Sweetbabe, but leaves her behind, she has an experience familiar to many black women. Women were often left behind while men hopped freight cars in search of better opportunities. For Ida and Lily, both of whom look at the trains with longing and desires of escape, different connections to trains and movement are forged. Ida looks at the depot and hears the voices of blues women encouraging her by "speak[ing] the desires of rural women to migrate." Lily, who is never again mentioned in connection to leaving, may live vicariously through the singing voices of the neighboring share-croppers when they sing with longing of hailing the next train.[25] The train station (and the movements associated with it) becomes a site of disappointment, but also hope. Lily never leaves Hopewell. And though Ida does not physically leave, knowing that her son is getting out is encouraging. More-over, when Sweetbabe leaves, a piece of his mother's aesthetic sensibility goes with him. This is especially true if she prepares a shoe-box lunch filled with chicken and tamales.

The point might seem overly idealistic until one considers how count-less black women "traveled" vicariously through food provisioning. Using the transient shoe-box lunches of their relatives as the vehicle, black women, mentally and emotionally, made it north and other places when their physi-cal bodies could not get there. The relevance of this argument is made clear in the novel when Armstrong's mother is leaving town with his battered body. Delotha Todd waits in the Memphis train station for the railway car to ar-rive to take her son's mutilated body back to Chicago. William, a longtime family friend, gives her some apples and candy bars for the trip. Remarking sadly that this was all he had to offer, he says, "You was moving so fast, 'Dessa didn't have time to fry you up no chicken, did she? I know your mama didn't want to put you on a train without no greasy bag to carry. That ain't natural" (104). William's references to the "naturalness" of black people boarding a train with a "greasy bag" are symbolic for their notions of how chicken is expected during times of travel. It is even more expected at times when comfort and assurance are greatly needed.[26] Mention here of the "greasy bag" bears witness to the historical connections between black women, food, and travel/movement. Both in the novel and in real life, some black women were given an opportunity to embark upon more fulfilling opportunities, and others were not. Thus, in carrying a "greasy bag" or shoe-box lunch prepared by women unable to leave the South (Ida) or those with no desire to leave, people who left symbolically took this journey for them through the foods prepared for them as travelers. In this way, black women were "always on the move," expanding the definitions of domesticity to include psychological female travel experiences.

Using food, the fictional character of Ida, like many black women before her, resists the restrictions imposed upon her by having little money but many needs. Having the good judgment to informally market her cooking, she connects back to the tradition of women who relied upon their skillful hands to provide a margin of economic safety. Furthermore, in seeing the train depot as a sign of hope, Ida signifies upon women like the Gordonsville waiter carriers who used the railroad as a way to make a living. Reading the novel in this way allows one to see how black women have used food preparation, along with mobility, to negotiate the various repressive and chaotic conditions that have functioned as barriers in their lives.

It should be noted that the experiences involving black women, food, and travel are not relegated to fiction or to history. Much of what is illustrated in folklore, fiction, and other sources of African American travel still exists today in the real lives of black people, and especially black women. Interviews and surveys I conducted among female members of various church denominations revealed contemporary thoughts on traveling and chicken.[27]

Psyche: Are there certain occasions when chicken is "a must" in the black community?
Rhonda: Church.
Doris: That's it! Church.
Jackie: Picnics.

Janet: If you go on a trip with your grandchildren.

Doris: School trip, that's it.

Janet: Or just any trip. I mean, just going away, like you're traveling. If you're traveling you're going to have chicken too.

Rhonda: Even when this church, this congregation, is just going a short distance or wherever and we're gonna eat when we get there. That's an hour and a half down the road . . . [but] somebody is gonna unwrap a piece of chicken between here and there. Nine times out of ten it's gonna be Mary (*laughter*).

Mary: You can bet on that!

Psyche: Even for just a short distance?

Janet: Because, it's just the idea that you're going somewhere and you must have a piece of fried chicken.

Doris: When John was 9, I had him to tell me that the eatin' part was the most fun.

Janet: I remember as a child when the church used to go to the beach . . .

Doris: Yes.

Rhonda: We used to eat chicken on the bus before the bus left . . . (*laughter*) before the bus left the church. Before the bus pulled off. It was custom.

Psyche: So it wasn't that you were hungry.

Rhonda: No, we weren't hungry; we had just had breakfast.

When asked at the beginning of the session to indicate what foods they would pack if going on a trip, long or short, every single one of the respondents included chicken. Although they included other foods such as sandwiches, drinks, and fruit, chicken headed the list. The more "health conscious" included chicken as well, along with "raw veggies." The association of chicken with travel for these informants both harkens back to a time when eating in public facilities was restricted and speaks to what one informant regards as "custom" or ritual. Some of these travelers had only shortly before eaten breakfast when they requested a piece of chicken. This suggests that for some black people, movement and mobility—even during short distances—require chicken.[28] From the responses of these women, one can infer that there is more to the traditional clichés "you are what you eat" and "food is a marker of group identity." These women are referring to a continuity and familiarity borne out of historical and cultural circumstances. For a people who have always been on the move—involuntarily and voluntarily, walking, jogging, wandering, and riding—chicken has factored closely in the discourse of mobility. When people settle in fixed locations, it is unlikely that the symbols connected to their history of mobility will evaporate. For black people, these symbols, such as eating chicken when traveling, remain as a psychological, if not visual, reminder of those events. They also articulate how certain foods are integral to the processes of social/cultural affirmation and self-definition.

Social affirmation is critical to the "biological and psychological survival" of humans.[29] In some instances, traveling today with "greasy bags" or other culinary reminders of the past is less about the act of eating and more about reaffirming social and cultural ties.[30] Chicken is not the only food packed for travel, nor do all black people consume chicken. But as I have emphasized throughout this project, black people have particular relationships with chicken that were born out of history but are reflected in contemporary social moments.

The ways in which people define themselves by food has specific class and regional dimensions. As I emphasized in a chapter 3, when people migrate, very rarely do they want to relinquish the cultural behaviors that bring them comfort and familiarity. Though "Gladware" and other plastic carryalls have replaced shoe boxes in most cases, the concept remains. By utilizing and identifying symbols (like foods) that are commonly affiliated with African American cultural heritage, black people refuse to allow the wider American culture to dictate what represents acceptable notions of their expressive culture. Turning to examples taken from my own life experiences, I will illustrate how chicken serves as an overarching symbol of identity in the travel narratives of some African Americans. This discussion will also highlight how family traditions and class values, as well as social activism, can be a part of these narratives.

A group of professional African Americans chartered a bus heading to one of the ski resorts in Pocono, New Jersey. The coordinator of the trip was responsible for obtaining dinner, since the weekend travels began in the evening. After getting settled on the bus, dinner was announced, and boxes of Popeye's chicken began to be passed among the travelers. Initially I was surprised. Do people still eat Popeye's chicken? Because I knew some of the people aboard the bus and their eating habits, Popeye's was not the first thing I thought of when the trip announcement stated, "Dinner will be provided." But what else would feed a busload of people at a reasonably low price? Chicken is quick and cheap, and it "travels well"—not to mention, it is what black people eat when they travel. In fact, as the chicken was being passed, someone said, "Yeahhhhh, Popeye's. I ain't had this in a long time. This is a real bus ride."

What immediately strikes me each time I recall this incident are the multiple levels on which chicken functions in this incident. First, there was the assumption that because we were traveling (especially by bus) and are black, the natural food of choice was chicken. Our trip coordinator, a black woman, could quite obviously have been acting upon her own southern food preferences. Second, and possibly more to the point, she recognized that she had a number of people to feed and wanted to do it at a relatively reasonable cost. She also knew that even though most of us would identify as Black Urban Professionals (buppies), we very well knew that when black people travel, they eat chicken. She operated out of a specific set of cultural beliefs and identity markers. So then, why was I surprised by the appearance of chicken?

The answer to this necessitates an examination of the critical tensions surrounding cultural beliefs and how members of the "in group" are affected when they make the transition to "outsider." I am certainly familiar, from a regional and racial perspective, that chicken is usually the food of choice when traveling. However, I had at that time abandoned eating commercially prepared chicken, primarily for health reasons. Living and working around people who rarely eat this kind of chicken also encouraged this abstention. All of these being personal reasons, it should have occurred to me that within this particular culinary setting, I would be the "outsider." As the outsider, it was incumbent upon me to find other provisions, which I neglected to do. Consequently, my husband and I were basically left hungry. My husband, being Ghanaian, has a preference for free-range chicken (which Popeye's most surely is not). However, with little else left to eat and a five-hour journey ahead of us, he opted for the smallest piece in the box—the wing. I, on the other hand, satisfied myself with the second-best offering in the box—a biscuit. So then, whereas food assumptions might be made on the basis of group identity and cultural belief, they can pose serious dilemmas for those whose preferences have changed, evolved, or been modified. At the same time, when an individual operates outside of specific cultural patterns, like those described here, that individual must take care to consider the consequences that the "outsider" status will have on his or her well-being. Always being prepared to negotiate the contradictions and dilemmas presented by changing traditions helps one to be comfortable on the "outside" while simultaneously being a part of the "in group." [31]

This example illustrates some of the critical tensions inherent when cultural belief systems are changed and/or modified. What this scenario further reveals is the degree to which shared cultural beliefs do not necessarily need to be communicated. However, the lack of communication, especially when the belief would solidify "in-group" identity, can also lead to tension and conflict. A group of African American undergraduates that participated in a focus group for this project exemplified this point.[32] During the discussion, I asked the students, "Do you believe that the setting and/or location is important to your consumption of chicken?" Here are some of their responses:

Nathan: No.

Psyche: Why not?

Nathan: Because you're hungry and you're satisfying your hunger. I don't care. I feel comfortable anywhere.

Angie: I can't eat outside anywhere. I have to eat inside a building.

Tamara: When I'm hungry I eat chicken wings, and I get some fries. If I'm hungry. Especially or if I'm traveling a long way because chicken is like one of the safest foods you can get. I think so.

Kiana: Only on a long trip. We take a lot of bus trips up to Atlantic City. You've got to have your chicken and potato salad. Just keeping it real, you have to have that! Or say if we go up to New York, wherever we're going, and it's a long drive—we're going to cook some chicken.

The last two responses echo the sentiments of the churchwomen when they said, regardless of the distance, if travel was involved, there had to be chicken. None of the others made this connection. I recall watching the last informant as her agitation and frustration seemed to grow. In her response, which resonated with great annoyance, was the challenge to her classmates to stop denying what she believed they should know—black people *need to have* chicken when they travel. This assumption is what prompted her to say, "Just keeping it real, you have to have that!"

Inherent in her declaration is the belief that her classmates were trying to "front" or not be truthful to "their culture" and "their heritage." While her position may be admirable for its intentions to try to get her classmates to think critically about black culture, it is also problematic for its reliance upon her own experiences to inform that of her classmates. The statements "we take a lot of bus trips up to Atlantic City" and "[if] it's a long drive—we're going to cook some chicken" reflect her reliance upon the multigenerational cultural patterns that surround her dietary habits. Because she previously shared that she does not cook on campus, it is further made clear that she is recalling family experiences. However, had she contextualized her experiences by referring to specific periods in time historically when black people's travel options were limited, her argument might be more plausible. What she does not account for in stating her position is that these students are products of a generation of parents who might not practice the "shoe-box lunch" tradition any longer. Even if this was the experience of the other students' relatives, changes in diet, modifications in cultural beliefs, and adherence to newer and "different" class values might have eliminated this cultural tradition from their repertoire. If the practice is maintained, it also might not include chicken any longer. It might include ham sandwiches, like those possibly carried by Helene on her train ride south. More than likely, however, it involves a rest stop for various fast food options.

My own recollections are of family travels from one church event to another where chicken was most certainly on the menu. Each and every time my family traveled, we would pack our "greasy bag" or, in our case, our "greasy" picnic basket full of chicken, bread, fruits, "juicies," and whatever else my mother felt would sustain us along the first leg of our journey. For many African Americans, sharing these memories is part of the social and cultural process of confirming various but also shared identities as black people in U.S. society. The travel experiences of black women tend to be particularly revealing for the ways in which their encounters are specifically gendered, racialized, and often class-based. Black women mediate various experiences with patriarchy, placement, and dislocation in ways that are directly tied to what we choose to remember, forget, reveal, and conceal. Like Ida, who ran and jogged to keep from losing her mind, many black women hold on to generational rituals and practices in order to maintain a sense of identity and sanity. But these decisions are also less dramatic. In some cases, continuing these practices is simply a matter of making familial connections.

For example, during a train ride to St. Louis, I packed food for my husband and me to carry along in order to defray costs and also because I like to carry food when I travel. Since we were riding the train and would be on it for hours, I wanted foods that would "travel well." Naturally, I chose chicken. I cooked "buffalo wings" for my husband and made a veggie pita for myself. Thinking back on this experience months later, I recall feeling a sense of sadness that I had not prepared for my trip in the same way that my mother had often prepared for ours. There existed an interesting sense of loss as I struggled over historical continuity and self-preservation. No longer eating chicken is a very deliberate, health-conscious act. Yet I lamented that this choice, in some small measure, separated me from integral experiences of my childhood.[33]

Childhood experiences, like those had by the Darden sisters, Maya Angelou, and countless other people, have become a filter through which objects, like fried chicken, take on meanings that fashion a collective memory. These are often experiences that validate one's existence. As I think about the comfort foods of my youth, I recognize my own memories as a part of this self-valuation experience. Traveling to Virginia with picnic baskets full of food were fun times for me. I always remember wanting to be the one to stay awake and help my father "watch the road" just in case he "needed" me to help navigate. Staying awake through most of the journey also entitled me to know when we were ready to eat. This way I could assist (and control?) the process of distribution as mommy's helper. When we traveled to the South in the early 1970s, my mother would prepare a big picnic basket with nearly all the foods mentioned by the Darden sisters. This was the economy food basket for a family of five. I was always excited when it was announced that we were going on a trip. I couldn't wait; sleep was elusive. The combination of sightseeing, helping my father watch the road, and considering the contents of the picnic basket always kept me wide awake.

On the morning of our trip, I vividly recall waking to the smells of chicken frying. I would usually be the first one up and in the kitchen, climbing on the stool beside the stove to watch my mother deep-fry chicken and gather foodstuffs for our trip. Sometimes she let me season the chicken (after I washed my hands, of course). At first she used only salt, pepper, and a dash of paprika. Later she began to use garlic powder, an aroma I still love. When the chicken was well floured, she lowered it into the hot and sizzling frying pan or pot filled with Wesson oil. As I got older and began cooking my own fried chicken, I would add my own twist with cayenne to give it an extra spicy taste. These were fun times.

My feelings about these times were slightly hampered, however, when I later learned the reasons we traveled with our own food. In part, it was economics. Feeding a family of five at every stop could be very expensive. The other reason, it turns out, was the late-night eating establishments, some of which were still inhospitable to African Americans, in some of the southern areas in which we were traveling. The 1970s was clearly not far enough removed from the feelings of hostility surrounding the civil rights confrontations. We sought to avoid these encounters, especially in rural Virginia, not wanting to put ourselves in harm's way. Understanding these circumstances and their social and political implications was turned into acts of agency by my parents. In packing our food, they were negotiating the financial aspects of traveling. By explaining racism, they were displaying tactics of resistance. And by allowing us to assist in the process of packing our own boxes, they taught us the meanings of self-support and collective memory.

A great deal of this exposure to acts of agency and activism is directly related to being the daughter of civil rights activists and having a social action minister for a father. Mealtimes were almost always used for discussions and debates on social and political awareness. My mother, a social worker and teacher, came into her own gender consciousness during the 1970s. She made sure my sisters and I understood the dynamics of what it meant to be middle-class black women—burdened with the interlocking systems of oppression—growing up in America. When we came together as a family during mealtime, everyone played a role. My mother would procure, prepare, and present a variety of foods. My father would stress the importance of what we were eating and why ("Eat! There are people starving in the world!"). And, we would consume, absorb, and digest the physical, social, and psychological complexities of life that we learned about during dinner.

Case in point: during the summer of 1974, my sisters and I learned about the nexus of racism, sexism, class, and violence. We also learned how these variables could be connected to dietary exchange. My parents announced that we were driving across town to purchase fried chicken dinners from a group of people raising money for the Joanne Little Defense Fund. Little was accused of first-degree murder for allegedly stabbing to death with an ice pick Clarence Alligood, a corrections officer in Beaufort County, North Carolina, and then trying to escape.[34] To get our dinners, we had to go to the predominantly black section of Buffalo, New York, known as "the Fruitbelt" (because all of the streets were named after fruit). I have a vivid recollection of feeling uncomfortable as my father explained to us something devastating called "rape." And I specifically remember the soothing tones of my mother as she gently helped us (at thirteen, ten, and eight years old) to further process this oppressive phenomenon while we heartily ate our chicken dinners, purchased in the name of self-defense.

Black women's roles are central for the ways in which they prepare travelers both physically and psychologically. Ignoring this and other aspects of black women's cookery leads to overlooking central components of African American travel experiences. And although movement in this discussion is broadly defined, in all, when black women (and sometimes men) provision travelers with various foods, they pass on cultural traditions and in doing so assist others in maintaining and establishing identity. But maintaining identity is not always external—that is, beyond the personal. Ida provides a venue in which all of the variables of the blues can be acted out—singing, dancing, sexuality, eating, and even violence. Though she is anchored to the home because of domestic attachments, when she jogs, she physically and psychologically moves—even if only to return.

Chicken is clearly a central part of African American travel narratives. Further examination of the ways in which black women have used this artifact for cultural transmission, self-definition, and economic sufficiency will illustrate another dimension of black women's work. The next chapter does this by focusing on black churches and the ways in which women use chicken to maintain cultural and social bonds. Using chicken in a variety of church settings, they carry out their personal and community obligations in fashioned responses that communicate gender consciousness and gendered definitions of self.

SAY JESUS AND COME TO ME

SIGNIFYING AND CHURCH FOOD

5

The image of chicken dinners featuring "the gospel bird," is so fixed in the U.S. African American imagination that some see it only as a negative stereotype. Many people will not eat chicken precisely because of the negative dimensions. Yet, the popularity of church dinners featuring chicken, as a source of fund raising and of sociability, remains strong.
—*Jualynne E. Dodson and Cheryl Townsend Gilkes,*
  "There's Nothing Like Church Food"

I heard somebody, a woman's voice "specifying" up this line of houses from where I lived and asked who it was. "Dat's Big Sweet" my landlady told me. "She got her foot up on somebody. Ain't she specifying?"
—*Zora Neale Hurston,* Dust Tracks on a Road

In *Dust Tracks on a Road*, Zora Neale Hurston's landlady defines "specifying" or "putting your foot up," saying:

> If you are sufficiently armed—enough to stand off a panzer division—and know what to do with your weapon after you get 'em, it is all right to go to the house of your enemy, put one foot up on his steps, rest one elbow on your knee and play in the family. That is another way of saying play the dozens, which is also a way of saying lowrate your enemy's ancestors and him, down to the present moment for reference, and then go into his future as far as your imagination leads you. But if you have no faith in your personal courage and confidence in your arsenal, don't try it. *It is a risky pleasure.*[1]

The landlady's warning that "lowrating" and "playing the dozens" is "risky pleasure" if one's arsenal is not full emphasizes the level of seriousness that can surround this type of verbal play. Signifying and playing or "doing" the dozens are rooted in African American oral traditions and cultural expression. Like a modern-day griot, those who enter this area of play do so with "a quickness," without a second thought. They must be able to deflect and respond when the foot has been "put up on them." Similar to the way that rappers (male and female) are expected to "bring it," African American women often "come wit' it" in church kitchens.[2] Borrowing from discussions of ritualized verbal play, specifyin' and signifying, we can see how black women extend their realization of self to the domain of the church kitchen and cooking for church activities. In this signifying context, black women enjoy a relative amount of self-actualization, self-expression, and self-awareness through the camaraderie, celebration, and competition that permeates this form of culinary play.

For ninety-eight years, Workman Memorial AME Zion Church in Hartford, Connecticut, has made the headlines of the local newspaper, the *Hartford Courant*, with news about its annual soul food benefit. With a global mission of helping those less fortunate than themselves, the church has its annual "Soul Food to Go" dinner, selling "southern fried chicken, collard greens, candied yams, macaroni and cheese and corn bread." According to the pastor, Rev. Shelley D. Best, "You don't get soul food in Connecticut. . . . There's something to be said for the food — it's not Kentucky Fried Chicken. . . . Every item is an art form. It's part of American tradition."[3] But Workman Memorial is hardly the only church to sell fried chicken dinners on weekends and Sundays after service. Numerous churches, affiliated or not with black communities, offer chicken cooked any number of ways — fried, barbecued, jerked — to include in their dinner sales.[4] But, it is the "art form" of frying chickens that has had a long-standing tradition among many African American parishioners. Having spent most of the entire day in church (from sunup to sundown), many congregants would not have the time to travel home and back to make it to the late evening service. Because most of the country churches were also devoid of any form of kitchen facilities, women would prepare the meals at home and, during a break in the service, would spread their meals on blankets and other coverings to serve. This allowed worshipers to enjoy not only the fellowship of the spirit but also the fellowship of the members whom they would see only during these occasions.

Many black women seized this opportunity and used the church as a site to display their culinary skills, expand how they identified themselves, and contribute to African American cultural production. Times have changed, however. Many churches no longer necessarily cook their own food; they now hire caterers. Although this is the case, the choices are still relatively similar. They are representative of culinary traditions that have existed within and among black communities for generations. As such, fried chicken has been and still remains a visible part of the culture of African Americans both for nutritive and non-nutritive purposes. Chicken has become so familiar, in fact, that it has been designated "the gospel bird."[5] As seen in the example of Workman Memorial, chicken is not just for eating but is also a useful tool in social action, self-help, and social uplift. It should be noted here that even in the process of shaping cultural identity within the church, cooking is hardly the only activity in which women are engaged. This study does not take the position that this type of church work or any type of cooking is solely "women's work." In fact, a number of men are engaged in church-related cooking events. Further examination of the role of chicken in the process of collective self-help and racial uplift delineates the ways in which chicken has been used to construct parts of cultural identity for women and men.[6] But when women are in the process of cooking for church events, a fair amount of signifying goes on—that is, black women's use of wordplay.

In his well-known study *The Signifying Monkey*, Henry Louis Gates Jr. asserts, "Signifying(s) is so fundamentally black, that is, it is such a familiar rhetorical practice, that one encounters great resistance of inertia when writing about it."[7] Clarence Major's *Dictionary of Afro-American Slang* equates "signifying" with "doing the dozens." In his definition of the "dirty dozens" is the assertion that this game is "traditionally played by black boys." Furthermore, his definition always includes "insult[ing] each other's relatives, especially their mothers."[8] Similarly, Roger Abrahams uses the words "insult," "defend his honor," and "jibes" to describe the process of men playing the dozens. But Abrahams also argues that "signifying" is a "rhetorical strategy that may be characteristic of a number of other designated events."[9] Although Abrahams extends the focus to include a style for doing the dozens, his list is still very male-oriented. It is only Lawrence Levine who, in his notable study of blacks in slavery and freedom, extends this gender-limited ritual exchange to women's participation.[10]

Removing signifying from a specific domain with particular meanings broadens the ways in which this strategy can be used. Therefore, the most useful definition and the one that informs this discussion is taken from linguist Claudia Mitchell-Kernan. According to Mitchell-Kernan, a distinction should be made between "doing the dozens" and signifying. She says that while the dozens involves verbal insult, signifying does not always include this component, although it might. In studying black women, men, and children of all ages from the neighborhood in which she was raised, Mitchell-Kernan determined that

> while the terminological use of signifying to refer to a particular kind of language specialization defines the Black community as a speech community in contrast to non-Black communities, it should be emphasized that further intra-community terminological specialization reflects social structural divisions within the community and related activity specializations. An admirable instance of signifying might well involve a remark

laced with taboo terms for a twelve year old boy. A thirty year old woman or man would not likely utilize the same criterion for judging effectiveness.[11]

In Mitchell-Kernan's framework, when a person signifies on someone or on something (as in "Stop signifying!") in the black community, it can be taken to mean any number of things, covering a range of meanings and events that are not a part of Standard English usage. In this way, signifying is encoded with meanings that distinguish between what is *said* and what is *meant*. For instance, when Rev. Shelley Best of Workman Memorial AME Zion Church made the comment, "It's not Kentucky Fried Chicken," she was clearly referring to the fact that the church's chicken was not from KFC. However, the latent meaning behind her statement was that this is not "white folks' chicken" inasmuch as KFC (despite the number of black franchises) is not a black corporation. Mitchell-Kernan refers to this type of exchange as an allegory because the meaning "must be derived from known symbolic value." In this case, the known symbolic value is the differentiation between KFC and "home cooked" or black women's fried "church" chicken. Several examples of black women signifying on chicken presented themselves during the course of my research, each reifying one of Mitchell-Kernan's definitions.

For example, during a focus group held with members of a self-defined middle-class body of congregants in suburban Maryland (Group A), general questions were asked about African American foods. In response to a question about places where fried chicken should not be consumed, one informant answered, "At my desk at work. Some people do that and that's ghetto![12] Because some people make themselves too much at home in public. And then they start picking their teeth. . . . I'm going to be honest with you, it goes back to the stereotype for me because I'm not going to get but so black at work."

This is a perfect example of what Mitchell-Kernan refers to as "obscuring the addressee." Though this informant was not talking about anyone in particular, she was referring to anyone who eats chicken while at work. Basically, this informant "called people out," but no one in the group issued a formal rebuttal to this respondent. The word "formal" is used here because while no one verbally responded per se, there were a number of replies that were made with "hmmmmm." Neither this answer nor the informant's statement had to be clarified. Everyone in the room knew the meaning of this particular "call-and-response." In fact, many people in the room knew they had been signified on—or "called out."

Defining this type of exchange as "troping," Gates asserts that the "indirect use of words that changes the meaning of a word or words" makes signifying "the black trope for all other tropes." He says it is "the trope of tropes, the figures of figures, Signifyin(g) *is* troping."[13] In this respondent's comment, there is a difference between the Standard English definition of the word "ghetto" and black people's use of the term in today's world of slang. In Standard English, a "ghetto" refers to a section of a city occupied by a minority group because of societal circumstances and/or pressure. However, this definition requires the article "a" and functions as a noun. In the example provided here, however, no clarification is needed because of "known symbolic values." Once you drop the article "a," the word becomes an "adjective" as in a description of a person's action—hence, one of the meanings of "ghetto" in this context is to be "triflin'." From a linguistics point of view, Mitchell-Kernan explains it this way:

> The Black concept of signifying incorporates essentially a folk notion that dictionary entries for words are not always sufficient for interpreting meanings or messages, or that meaning goes beyond such interpretations. Complimentary remarks may be delivered in a left-handed fashion. A particular utterance may be an insult in one context and not another. What pretends to be informative may intend to be persuasive. The hearer is thus constrained to attend to all potential meaning carrying symbolic systems in speech events—the total universe of discourse.[14]

It should be said here that this "total universe of discourse" must be spanned in nanoseconds in order to determine the way in which the remark should be taken. For example, in the last chapter I shared the exchange between another group of informants who were discussing how chicken always gets eaten when their church group travels. At one point in this exchange, an informant literally signifies on another informant named "Mary." The first speaker says: "Even when this church, this congregation, is just going a short distance or wherever and we're gonna eat when we get there. That's an hour and a half down the road . . . [but] somebody is gonna unwrap a piece of chicken between here and there. Nine times out of ten it's gonna be Mary." Mary responds, "You can bet on that!" This form of signifying is explicit and overt in its addressee, but its message is not. Though it appears that the first informant is recognizing Mary for maintaining a ritual familiar to members of the black community, she might also be making fun of this habit. In fact, that is the way that the remark appears to have been received by the audience as there was a great deal of laughter. However, Mary's response (assuming it was Mary and not another informant who confirmed the remark), "You can bet on that," is an indication either that she agrees with the speaker or that she realizes that she has been called out. In this instance, the signifier definitely has encoded her message. The audience is not aware if the speaker has more insidious inside knowledge that she is alluding to or if the comment is to be taken as a compliment.

Signifying is a clever way to make remarks that refer to class status. The statement made about it being "ghetto" to eat chicken at one's desk seems to be one example of this. Or, at the very least it has the appearance of pertaining to class. If we are unsure about the class implications of this statement, there is no mistaking the remarks made by another group of women in Virginia who also informed this study (Group B). In his research on the black working class, early-twentieth-century sociologist Allison Davis states that working-class or lower-class blacks often "accused [an] upper-class person (the 'big shots,' the 'Big Negroes') of snobbishness, color preference, extreme selfishness, disloyalty in caste leadership, ('sellin' out to white folks'), and economic exploitation of their patients and customers."[15] Something akin to this litany of pejorative descriptions was certainly expressed by members of Group B.

The churchwomen in Group B defined themselves as "lower middle-class." The participants worked in a range of jobs from the government to domestic work. The group also included some retired teachers. In searching for consensus between focus groups, I shared the comment about eating chicken at one's workplace being "ghetto." The response of this group was very surprising in its revelations. One respondent vehemently replied: "You . . . was just dealing with a high-class . . . they were just trying to act like they better." Here, this respondent signifies on the originator of the "ghetto" comment. But, she goes further and wholly signifies on the entire set of women in Group A. When this informant said, "They were just trying to act like they better," she decided that the speaker's "ghetto" remark belonged to a group of women, not just one person, who believed themselves to be superior.

It is further interesting to note that those in Group B found a sense of "cultural solidarity" around the act of signifying on class status and chicken. In this process, they distinguished themselves from the other churchwomen (Group A) on the basis of class. This is evidenced both by the choruses of laughter that ensued when a member of their group issued her response and by the call and response among themselves as some words (for example, "ashamed of") were spoken in unison. Group B participants respond:

Karen: I think it's very isolated. I don't really think that many people feel that way [about eating chicken at work]. Because when I was working, every party we had fried chicken. It was at the top of the list. And they ordered it and it was delivered and it was the first thing on that list. Everything else centered around that fried chicken. Everybody ate it. *Everybody.* It didn't matter what color you were or who you were. Everybody had chicken. So, I think that's very isolated.

Rosa: You have a . . . you know you have a complex about who you are and . . . you're worried about what people . . . we have to understand that's who we are . . .

(*lots of different voices*)

Marie: . . . we are a people who utilize everything on the farm to prepare and to feed our . . . families. And I think that's not . . . it shouldn't be a bad thing . . . and it shouldn't be something that we are . . . we've become . . .

Group (*in unison*): . . . ashamed of.

Barbara: Um, that's something that you know, . . . in all reality when you look at it, we need to start getting back to it . . . farming and doing our own farming and . . . living off the land again because of the way things are going.

The examples provided here are significant for what they reveal about the ways in which these two groups of black churchwomen signify on chicken in the context of gender and class. But they are also important for what they relay about race. Major cultural tension is embedded in the idea that it is inappropriate to eat chicken at work. On the one hand, the informant from Group A is struggling with the need to blame black people for living up to the "chicken eating" stereotype. On the other hand, she is grappling with the racism that surrounds the stereotype. Her assertion that she is not going to "get but so black at work" suggests that while at work she engages in culinary subterfuge—that is, she "wears a mask" that portrays her as someone other than who she is. The other implication of her statement is that in the confines of her own home or around friends, she's apt to get "more black" than she would among strangers. Interestingly, this woman is clear that objects and goods are useful in their importance for signifying *on* people (in fact, she employs this technique). But she is even more clear that others wanting to render certain judgments about her can use this particular food. Her decision not to eat chicken while at work and to castigate any black person who does is indicative of this understanding.

Even more, she seems aware that objects are social signs that carry worlds of meaning. Her participation in the game of showing and hiding one's self in public/private is indicative of how objects are used in acts of artifice. She seems to believe that who she is as a person is directly tied to the foods that she consumes. More important, she seems to believe that chicken detracts from how she wants to be perceived at work. These perceptions are tied to unstated notions of power. Will she move up the career ladder if they think that she is "too black"?

These real-life instances exemplify how language and objects are doubly encoded with meaning when used to signify on something or someone. But how does this process of culinary signifying manifest itself in African American literature? Gloria Naylor's *Linden Hills* nicely illustrates how objects, like chicken, can be used in the signifying process—even in the absence of verbal play.

For a black family to live in Linden Hills is to have attained the American Dream. The Tilson family just barely lives in Linden Hills, as they reside in "the smallest house on the street" at the very top. It is a home where son Lester is given a moniker comprised of four multisyllabic names ("Did you know my full name is Lesterfield Walcott Montgomery Tilson, Willie? Or is it Lester *Field*walcott Montgomery Tilson, mom?").[16] His mother had hopes that his "big" name would fit the heights to which he would aspire. But it was not to be. Lester and his friend Willie "White" Mason are street poets, moving around the town performing odd jobs. On one of the many winter days when they are walking through the neighborhood, Lester invites Willie to his home for dinner. The Tilson home is green—jade carpeting, green and white porcelain, and emerald satin balls covering a silver Christmas tree. And it is the home of a slightly fat daughter who eats skimpily on "bits of lettuce and cucumber, dabs of fish and cottage cheese" (53). But Lester's sister, Roxanne, never loses weight because she gorges on chips, Twinkies, and chocolates. The Tilson home has the appearance of "better folks"—a Wellesley education, bleaching creams, hair relaxers, and, of course, a Linden Hills address.

Lester knows that it is proper etiquette in his home to inform his mother when they are having a guest. In an attempt to irritate his mother, and wanting to expose her dislike of his friend, he knowingly breaches the rules of etiquette and invites Willie for dinner. After Mrs. Tilson recovers from the dismay of having Willie in her home to share their evening meal, she condescendingly remarks, "Well, I guess we can always find more. . . ." When Willie apologetically protests she says, "Non-sense. There's always something for company. But we're eating like peasants tonight—just fried chicken. But I'm trying something a bit daring with the potatoes. A cheese and wine sauce I saw in the papers." To this Willie eagerly replies that he loves fried chicken, at which she acknowledges his affirmation with one of her own: "Like I said— common food, but filling" (48).

Mrs. Tilson signifies on Willie with her reference to chicken as "peasant" and "common food." In this remark, she is both confronting and insulting Willie, intentionally. Gates notes that this is the more common form of signifying and that which is usually referred to by linguists in discussing these sorts of exchanges. But Mrs. Tilson is not done with her signifying. She not only verbally insults Willie but then goes on to use objects to continue this insult. She "fronts" (shows off) on Willie by setting her table full of expensive china and stemware, knowing this will make him uncomfortable: "Mrs. Tilson had set the dining room table with china, silverware, and linen napkins in honor of Willie, whom she said she'd always loved, and she emphasized her devotion by sitting beside him and patting his hand. Willie wished she hadn't gone to so much trouble, because the starched linen kept slipping off his lap, and he spent the evening cringing every time his heavy knife hit the thin plate or his teeth clinked against the fragile Norwegian crystal" (54).

In response to this incredible farce put on by his mother, Lester decides to do a bit of signifying on his own. Lester "picked up his chicken with his hand and tore off huge chunks with his teeth. Any juice that dripped on his fingers was wiped off with a slice of bread before he stuffed it into his mouth" (54). When an argument ensues between Lester and Roxanne, he throws down the thighbone he had been sucking and commences to banter with her. Though Mrs. Tilson makes apologies to Willie for her children's behavior, the moment the men are out of the room she mouths something to her daughter behind her hand (56).

Amidst the various instances of signifying in this example is a larger correlation that connects to the notion of being "ghetto." As Lester complains about living in Linden Hills and bemoans the ruses of the people around him, Willie suggests, "Me thinks the nigger doth protest too much." He goes on to explain that what Lester complains about, other people would gladly welcome. Willie admonishes Lester for begrudging his family and others for wanting to make it in life or for distancing themselves from negativity. Wanting to be perceived as "better than" and wanting fine things in life does not make one a "freak." Willie's point notwithstanding, Lester explains that there is a fine line between wanting good things in life and selling your soul to obtain them. He further explains to Willie that his grandmother called it "selling the mirror in your soul." Reflecting upon his grandmother's insights, he says:

You can lose yourself in other people's minds. You can forget what you really want and believe. So you keep that mirror and when it's crazy *outside*, you look inside and you'll always know exactly where you are and what you are. And you call that peace. . . . These people have lost that, Willie. They've lost all touch with what it is to be *them*. Because there's not a damned thing inside anymore to let them know. And if that's what a degree or a five-syllable job title is going to cost you, then you don't want it, believe me, Willie. But you're right, I'm probably not much better than the rest of Linden Hills. I haven't gone all the way, but I've sold myself for a pair of clean socks and a chicken dinner. (59, original emphasis)

Lester's fictional soul-searching response could be applied to the informant who decided that to be "too black" at work is worth more than she is willing to risk. Is she simply doing what she needs to do to survive in a world where she knows she is judged by the presence of the food she consumes? Is she also selling herself for a chicken dinner and a job title? And if not herself, is she selling other people short by denying their consumptive desires? These are rhetorical questions that can be answered only by the informant. However, the relevance of this literary illustration and this discussion point to how signifying on chicken can reveal class and gender tension.

For some black women, the church is a place where these issues collide. It is where food myths can be dispelled and where personal anxiety about eating certain foods can be reassured. Elnora Dean, an informant in Joyce White's biographical cookbook, *Soul Food: Recipes and Reflections from African American Churches*, reinforces this point when she explains: "Food is part of our fellowship. Every Sunday after service we always have food. That way we get to touch and know each other and rub shoulders and socialize; things we don't do during the service."[17] Dean explains what scholars of religion and sociology Jualynne Dodson and Cheryl Townsend Gilkes explore as the connection between food and spirituality. They argue that "traditions surrounding food in African American Christian churches . . . contribute to a distinctive New World African way of 'working the spirit,' which is a process continued by African people in other parts of the Americas."[18]

The tradition of "church food" and particularly the presence of chicken speak to the importance of the food event as central to many black church experiences.[19] This was especially the case when the preacher came by for dinner. In her autobiographical narrative, *You May Plow Here*, Sara Brooks details the process undertaken by her mother in order to prepare a chicken for Sunday dinner. She explains how her mother "would fix a big meal . . . so she sent the kids out to run the chicken down so she'd kill a chicken. . . . My mother would be done fatten the chickens in the coop and cleaned them out. My mother would always put chickens up in the coop, which would be

FIGURE 5.1. Women dressing FSA chickens, ca. 1935–42.
Courtesy Library of Congress, Prints & Photographs Division,
FSA/OWI Collection (LC-USF34-080477-D); photograph by John Collier.

a board box with some planks on top of it. They'd all be sittin around in the yard. And she'd clean the chickens out by givin em cornmeal—wet it and put bakin soda in it—and that would clean the chickens out. We'd put em up about a week or more—we'd always keep chickens on hand cleaned out so that we'd have chickens to eat."[20]

The steps Brooks describes here, known as dressing a chicken, speak to the beginning of the overall process of preparing a meal of fresh chicken (figure 5.1). Cooking chicken, especially when it is fried, is a laborious process from start to finish. (For this reason, some women refused to cook chicken when they worked for white families.) Prior to the commercialization and industrialization of poultry and other foods, cleaning and dressing a chicken involved a number of steps. And the labor was more intensified when one considers the intimacy of handling. To prepare a bird for weeks by cleaning it and then having to chase it down, wring its neck, drain it, and then pluck the feathers is itself enough to cause one unfamiliar with the process to "come undone." Yet, this part of the preparation is merely the beginning. Cutting a chicken (and anyone who has ever attempted this practice knows it is not easy) is even more intimate. Not only does it have to be cut just right so that one gets two legs, two wings, two breasts, two thighs, and a back, but also one has to enter the orifice and extract the liver, gizzard, and neck. This is, of course, assuming a fryer or whole bird has been purchased from the store. If the chicken is fresh from a yard, there will be more to extract in the cleaning—but this work was worth it if the pastor was coming for dinner.

Having the pastor over for dinner was considered an honor (figure 5.2). The opportunity to display the strength of one's cooking skills and thereby solicit praise from the spiritual leader was even more self-satisfying. From this perspective, it is not difficult to understand why Brooks's mother prepared a chicken dinner in eager anticipation of the pastor's arrival. The presence of the pastor was a further manifestation of the overall fellowship of the church body. He or she was the spiritual leader and motivator, and to show gratitude and fondness for the leadership, parishioners would often take turns inviting him (historically the pastor was most likely a male) to their home for Sunday dinner. Brooks captures the excitement of the occasion by her mere use of the words "big meal." This description places the event in a context that demonstrates its importance. Because the pastor holds the position of highest esteem and "cultural power" in the church, and often in the community, it was a privilege to serve him the choicest pieces of chicken. Marvalene H. Hughes indicates, "Whether on the church ground or in the black home, the black preacher is the first to choose his food."[21] Numerous anecdotes and jokes in African American folklore detail stories about the preacher and fried chicken. So powerful is chicken to black communities that it has inspired even some preachers to jest. At one Sunday service, a pastor joked that chicken is one of the four C's that could "bring the preacher down." From his point of view, the C's represent "cash," "chicks," "Cadillacs," and "chicken."[22]

Inherent in this observation, offered by a "man of the cloth," is the second possible meaning behind Brooks's mother's anticipation of the pastor's arrival—the pastor's approval. Though sexuality probably was not a motivating factor in the case of Brooks's mother, it can be an issue for many churchwomen. Sexuality and spirituality are pervasive issues of contestation in some churches. The rumor mill in many black churches has always centered on the sexual liaisons that take place between the pastor and some of the women of the church.[23] It is the manifestation of patriarchy's worst effects and one of the myriad reasons the church can hardly be declared a safe space. In some ways, chicken and other foods provide a vehicle for this abuse. While the literature in black cookbooks often praises women for competing over

D-154

The Darkey Preacher

"Listen Sistern and Bredren,
You must give up your develish way
Give up all your wickedness,
Or de good Lawd'll make you pay.

Stop drinking dat mean corn likker,
Dat makes you crazy to fight,
Stop rolling dose "Galloping
    dominoes"
Dat makes you stay up all night.

Sisters, don't let your tongues wag
    too much,
Stop putting on all dat paint.
And don't use dat bleach and powder,
Dat makes you look white when
    you ain't.

Before we dismiss, we'll jine in prayer
De deacons will now pass the plates
    aroun',
And if you don't help out de
    collection,
St. Peter will mos likely turn you
    down."   Ⓔ

12851-C   (COPYRIGHT BY F. L. HOWE PHOTO CO., ATLANTA, 1905)

FIGURE 5.2. "The Darkey Preacher," ca. 1905. Author's collection.

who can produce the best chicken to please the preacher's palate, left untold is the danger in this game of culinary one-up(wo)manship. Though chicken can be said to "bring the preacher down," it should also be considered as a form of gender oppression. By my own witness, too much acknowledgment and praise of one "sista's" fried chicken over another's can suggest that the pastor is enjoying something at that sista's house other than just the "gospel bird."[24] This can also result in gender conflict that produces ostracism and internal strife among the women known for cooking the best fried chicken. At the same time, strife over who cooks the best bird on Sundays does not always necessarily cultivate negativity. Within the church arena, it can also be a significant indicator of black women's creative culinary achievements. It is in this direction that the remainder of this discussion will now turn to further make clear how black women signify on one another, how black men signify on black women, and how power is exercised while creative energy is being showcased.

Mabel James is a member of a women's group known as the Philathea Club. The club boasts a membership of over thirty women, and though these women are dear friends, they are also highly competitive in the ways of the culinary arts. Accordingly she says, "A member's standing in the group was determined to some degree by how many of the women came out to her house for the meeting."[25] Members often make their decisions on the basis of who prepares the best table. Mrs. James's experience is hardly an isolated one. Numerous women engage in what I call the "culinary dozens" as they compete against one another to prepare the best table whenever the occasion calls. However, given that the dozens almost always involves some element of negative valuation and recitation on mothers, it is better to see this art form as a "subtype" of signifying—"a clever way of conveying messages."[26]

Joyce White's useful collection of recipes and narrative reflections of African Americans in the church provides another excellent example. Martha Hermmans, a member of the Ebenezer Baptist Church in Atlanta, wishes that her church kitchen were bigger because when those sisters get together to prepare for a food event, "there is a lot of bumping into one another." While this example certainly describes the concern over space (or lack thereof), it can also be read as a metaphorical way of complaining about there being "too many cooks in the kitchen."

I have been witness to black women in church kitchens cutting their eyes at one another or arguing about whether or not a dish should be cooked a certain way. But there have been plenty of times when signifying did not imply "ragging on" one another. Instead, it has been an indirect means of "building upon" someone else's culinary craft. This is an illustration of intertexuality, which is by definition a process of repetition and revision.[27] When intertexuality is used, however, the improviser's technique "is to be gauged by the creative (re)placement of these expected or anticipated formulaic phrases and formulaic events, rendered anew in unexpected ways."[28] In the type of culinary play that often takes place in and around church kitchens, it is not difficult to fathom the level of competition that exists among women who belong to various clubs. Having one's standing in the club judged by her culinary talents and skills seems like a ritual of play and jest that can certainly be applied to the notion of signifyin'. Had I wanted to stir up fun controversy among my own informants, I feel certain that asking them to decide who makes the best chicken would have accomplished this task.

This form of play, it should be noted, is not simply the game of individuals. Whole groups often get involved. Women's choirs, usher boards, women's clubs, even men's clubs and various other groups in the church often vie to get into the kitchen. There even exists a gender competition. Who cooked the best meal, the women for Father's Day, or the men for Mother's Day? It is here where some added attention to gender specificity can be applied. There are a number of women executive cooks and professional caterers who offer their catering services to the church. However, the location of the food event generally marks the social territory as male or female terrain. For example, if a fish fry is the event of choice, men are usually the ones organizing the process and quite possibly frying the fish. But women are slicing tomatoes and preparing the coleslaw and other side dishes. Chicken dinners usually belong to women. The rationale here is in the association of fishing as a male activity, a public, outdoor display. "Dressing" a chicken, a task generally performed in or near home, is decidedly "women's work." These gendered strictures might collapse, however, when cooking chicken or other foods is a public display (for example, as chefs, butchers, or short-order cooks or at barbecues). They might also collapse depending upon class, age, and region. Memories of these gendered terrains of difference bear out in the kitchens of my home church.

If there was a major food event taking place, Deacon was going to be there in full regalia from head to toe, which usually entailed a high-styled chef's hat, an executive white-studded-button chef's coat, an apron, the traditional checkered chef's pants, and black shoes. This was always adorned by streams of sweat to attest to the heat in the kitchen and to the amount of work he was doing. This was always the case, despite the army of women who accompanied him in the kitchen. At these events, we could expect the traditional church fare: fried chicken, wax green beans, potato salad, white rolls, iced tea, and pound cake. This was the preferred menu, and Deacon made it clear that he was the "chef," not just another cook. At every major cooking event, you could look up from your plate at the height of the meal to see Deacon standing either behind the long table of food or just inside the kitchen door, seemingly awaiting the moment that he knew would come when praise and approbation would be levied upon his culinary skills.

Volunteering in the church kitchen provided me with poignant memories of gender differentiation. One of the interesting points to note is that it was seldom I heard Deacon issue any compliments to the women who had helped in making these feasts come to fruition. In fact, on more than one occasion I recall him standing over the big black-and-white industrial stove yelling directions at "his helpers" even as sweat dripped off his face near hot chicken grease. Even in the kitchen, he made it clear that it was his domain, and undoubtedly his uniform confirmed this point. Admittedly, my volunteerism was relegated to gofer—putting out desserts, making punch, or performing some other menial task that a teenager could accomplish without getting in the way. Because Deacon was known to be a kind, gentle man, his behavior in the kitchen was always intriguing to me as I watched him fluttering about issuing orders in clipped tones—"get me the butter," "pour some more flour into this bowl," "get the plates ready," "pass that platter over there." Deacon's behavior became slightly more understandable when my family attended a luncheon at his home one summer. In the private domain, it immediately became clear to all of us (almost to the point of embarrassment) that he was not the center of attention in his home kitchen but subject to the chastisement of his wife when he got in her way—and even when he did not. Without resorting to psychological judgments, it seems that when the kitchen was moved into the public sphere of the church, Deacon seized it as an opportunity to command the full respect that his professional culinary skills demanded and that his regalia reinforced.

While this example highlights the gendered dimensions of conflict that can often result around food in the public domain, it also recalls how clothing can be used to signify, just like dining room implements. Similar to Ms. Tilson, who deliberately used crystal and china to bring discomfort to Willie, Deacon in his uniform had the same effect. One of the reasons that this memory is so vivid stems from the constant teasing—by children and adults alike —about the hat worn by Deacon. We signified on him and "called him out" in jest anytime we were out of earshot. Wearing regalia to distinguish himself as a chef was necessary in his mind. However, in doing this, he signified on the women in the church kitchen by reminding them of the fact that, for them, cooking was a necessity and a "hobby." For him, it was a profession!

As emphasized here, culinary signifying comes in many forms. It might have gender dimensions as well as class and/or race dimensions. In some instances, however, it might also have sexual implications. This might certainly be the case when women occupying different positions in the church conflict around issues of food and sexuality. These occasions can be referred to as "food events" because food, though not necessarily the reason for the occasion, might be present during the activity. Certain holidays and celebrations are excellent examples of these cycles. But beyond the holidays, everyone engages in small-scale events on a daily basis. Church-related activities like having a pancake breakfast or luncheon in a church cafeteria have the makings of small-scale events. The importance of recognizing these kinds of interactions as food events is critical to understanding how power and food are interrelated. It is within these kinds of intimate settings that the power dimensions of signifying are almost always present. Turning again to a work of fiction helps to illustrate this dynamic. Ann Allen Shockley's *Say Jesus and Come to Me* offers a short but excellent scene as an example.

Like her predecessors Langston Hughes and Gwendolyn Brooks, Shockley writes of the experiences that surround her. Using people and their lives as her focal point, Shockley finds no act or interaction too insignificant to write about. Shockley draws from social and/or political issues from various historical periods in order to situate her characters. *Say Jesus and Come to Me* is one of Shockley's many works that illustrates black women working to resist oppressions and affect social and political change in and outside the church setting. Though the book was published in the early 1980s, at the beginning of the black feminist period of textual reclamation, Shockley's publication was very short-lived. It is possible that her subject matter—same-gender relationships—has been the cause for this lack of attention.

Through the character of Myrtle Black—a confident, enigmatic, lesbian itinerant preacher—Shockley offers a studied critique of black patriarchy and white feminism. Myrtle Black is a vivacious evangelical speaker who travels by invitation to bring the gospel to lost souls. One of these young souls, singer Travis Lee, falls sway to Myrtle's charms. During the course of the novel, the two of them sacrifice and compromise to assist one another in developing an awareness of their lesbian identities. Simultaneous to this main plot are several subplots. One involves Myrtle joining forces with a team of white women in order to advance a feminist agenda within the city. The second, which conflicts with the first, is Myrtle's desire to contribute to black women's sense of self by marching against social, gender, and racial injustices. Ultimately, and not without strife, the two feminist agendas successfully converge. Through this illustration, Shockley challenges her readers to consider the social institutions and relationships that help to perpetuate latent practices of homophobia, sexism, racism, and intraclass conflict. Shockley's postmodern approach to deconstructing these ideologies is compelling. But more central to this conversation is the lone incident in which chicken factors as a primary variable. This scene is revealing for its insights into the complex interworkings that occur around food and for the ways in which signifying is made manifest as a vehicle for self-definition. As mentioned earlier, there are common perceptions and stereotypes about "the black preacher." Specifically, I am referring to the belief that black preachers have a greater-than-average love for chicks, cash, Cadillacs, and chicken. This tongue-in-cheek characterization certainly is befitting of the fictional Rev. Myrtle Black.

Like her father, the Reverend Elijah Black, Myrtle has to be sharp in her appearance, capture the attention of the audience, and use her charm to save souls in order to "make a living out of the pockets of [the] worshipers."[29] Myrtle feels as if she is constantly competing with her male counterparts. Because of this and the belief that most of them—colleagues or not—endeavor primarily "to take her to bed if given the chance," she "outclasses" them. Myrtle *always* dresses in only the most elegant, expensive, and fashionable robes.

Her ostentatious displays are designed both to signify on the male preachers and to further her sexual chase. This is especially the case "if a woman was around whose interest she wanted to attract." But more than providing her with the means to attract another sexual partner, Myrtle is clear that she competes, on multiple levels, in a masculine domain. Therefore, she is poised not only as a spiritual competitor in her abilities to bring more souls to Jesus but also as a major sexual menace. Myrtle, therefore, was the worst type of threat to her fellow clergy.

Speaking of black lesbians generally, Shockley says, "The independent woman-identified-woman, black lesbian was a threat. Not only was she a threat to the projection of black male macho, but a *sexual* threat too—the utmost danger to the black male's institutionally designated role as 'king of the lovers.'"[30] Who more than the black preacher would feel the sense of sexual and social power as a servant of the "King of Kings and Lord of Lords"? In his "close connection" to God, the pastor embodies the epitome of the King's servant. Why then shouldn't he bestow upon himself the indomitable title of "king" (even if in the diminutive form)? Inasmuch as Myrtle is also a member of this mostly male club, she should be perceived as a king/queen—having all the rights of "king" equally bestowed upon her. This then makes her a "queen of the lovers," using Shockley's rationale. She embodies this image, all the more, if we consider further the outlines of the black preacher joke. Myrtle loves "chicks." She also loves cash. And rounding out the circle, she enjoys the feel of a nice, fine car. Though not a Cadillac, her Buick Riviera serves the same ends in that it denoted "power and affluence, transmitting to people that she was in fact a superior woman who called for respect" (13). Objects such as this complement her sense of self, endowing her with a "supreme[cy] in the sight of herself, [her] public, and Lord" (13). This penchant for fine "high-powered" automobiles again places her firmly within a male-dominated landscape.[31]

The novel describes Myrtle as an alluring, sexy, sensual, beautiful forty-year-old woman who wears pink pantsuits and brushes her tresses until they "glisten." So central is this representation to the telling of the story that Shockley opens the novel with it:

> Myrtle sat as majestic as a black queen in the high, straight-backed throne-like chair in the pulpit of the Hillside Union Church. She made an imposing figure in the red robe with the black braid fringing the collar and sleeves like icicles. Her clerical wardrobe contained gowns for each day's service in a revival week. This was an expensive variation, the way she *looked* was important in getting *herself* across, along with the word of the Lord. . . . Her thick black hair was wrapped in mountainous tiered coils above her head, enhancing the beauty of her rich dark complexion and pointed features. (1)

Later, in a moment of self-appraisal, Myrtle admires her own physical beauty: "She viewed herself in the full-length mirror on the bathroom door, pleased at what she saw. She was in excellent shape. Her body was firm without the bulging stomach or drooping tits of the middle-aged. She didn't intend to let herself get fat and out of shape. Those preachers' wives could set the tempting chicken and dumplings, homemade pies and cakes on the table all they wanted, but she knew how to resist" (12–13).

In these conceptions of beauty, Shockley achieves several ends: one, she issues a challenge to society at large and to the black church in general by debunking the myth of all lesbians as "bull daggers" or "butches." Two, she defies structuralist arguments that state that lifelikeness in a character generally results in cultural stereotypes.[32] At the time of this novel's publication (1982), the perceptions about lesbians as aggressively masculine were still very much recognizable. Consequently, in Myrtle, Shockley counters the perception and points out how black churches (and by extension their communities) are primary purporters of homophobic enmity.[33] Last, by her lifelike depiction of Myrtle, Shockley casts doubt upon the racial stereotypes that sought to directly place the burden of chicken-loving upon black preachers and by extension black people. While Myrtle clearly enjoys the benefits bestowed upon men and women of the cloth, she draws the line when it comes to the perception that all preachers love "good food"—especially chicken.

The scene involving the chicken dinner takes place in Nashville at the home of Rev. Amos Cross, whose church is hosting a revival where Myrtle is to be the guest speaker. Well known for her contralto voice and her "inherent facility for words," Myrtle is an oft-invited speaker for revivals and church engagements. And, as is customary, Myrtle receives a dinner invitation from the pastor and his wife. There is quite a bit to be gleaned from an analysis of this food event. Like many situations involving food, the meal is not a focal point. Though it may initially begin as such, the social and cultural discourses surrounding the meal eventually inform and control the occasion. This is the case with Myrtle and the Crosses. Food, in this situation, is really incidental to Amos Cross having a few moments to intimately meet and get to know his guest preacher. By this meeting, he is able to gauge how the rest of the week will be in her presence. Simultaneously, she too can measure his personality—and does. Given this context, there are a number of circumstances and details that emerge in this account that give rise to an understanding of the "full symbolic range and power of food in American life."[34]

To begin, there is the moment at which Myrtle places a phone call to the Crosses to inform them of her arrival in town. Reverend Cross then checks with Mrs. Cross on the exact time of dinner. The reference to his wife as "Mrs. Cross" prompts Myrtle to mock his formality. She thinks: "*Mrs. Cross indeed! . . . The uppity black imitating whites: 'Mr. Blank will have his dinner at eight,' or 'Mrs. Blank wants the house cleaned'*" (22). This air of formality is furthered by the fact that, when Myrtle arrives, Reverend Cross is formally dressed for dinner despite the intense heat of the house caused by the preparations going on in the kitchen. But this is part of the masquerade that he plays as a southern black minister.[35] Knowingly, Myrtle quickly assesses that "southern black ministers were stifled by the need to maintain an image of formality. Suits worn during the week were a mark of distinction, especially among small town ministers. That was the way people distinguished between high and low" (25). But the moment when the phone conversation had briefly turned to the time of the affair and Myrtle had witnessed the pretentious attitude of her host was the point at which she made a decision about her own behavior. Long before the end of the meal, she knows her sentiments toward her host: "This would be the last [meal] eaten here" (28).

Myrtle perhaps thought of herself as a class above the Cross family. As she approaches the house, she describes it as "rambling, faded brick and stone two-story." The house seems in disrepair with its lopsided gate and porch that juts out like a "swollen lip." The interior, though clean, is filled with mismatched and recycled furniture. Myrtle seems to read these ill trappings of material life as revelations belying the Crosses' attempts at decorum and ritual. The ostentatious display of gentility expressed by Reverend Cross on the phone is contradicted by his true position. He is a man of little financial means with many material burdens, since his family of five seems to exist solely on his salary as a preacher (there is no mention that his wife works outside the home). Yet, despite the condition of the Crosses' furniture — hand-me-downs and in some cases broken-downs — which speaks volumes about levels of affordability, the overall care and appearance portray a sense of elevated propriety. Reverend Cross's status as a preacher and his furnished home (regardless of the condition) is evidence of his achievements. And the fact that Reverend Cross believes in this validation is reinforced by his insistence upon wearing a suit and tie to dinner.

If we turn to a more latent level of meaning and examine specific forms of signifying (mostly between Lucy Cross and Myrtle Black), we can gain a better understanding of how women signify on chicken (and one another) in order to claim their own sense of self. From the moment that the women are introduced to one another, it is clear that there are distinctions between them. Although we are left knowing little of Mrs. Cross's age, we are given the impression that she appears older than her years. The use of basically pejorative descriptors — "dumpy," "matronly," "Sears cotton print dress," premature graying — are in stark contrast to the spry, shapely, sophisticated Myrtle. Even the Cross's oldest daughter, who "looked like her mother in a more attractive way," recognizes this difference, staring openly at Myrtle in "admiration." Reverend Cross fares slightly better in Shockley's description, being short and rotund with a stomach that protrudes over his belt where his black tie rests "like a fallen twig" (26). His face, shaped like "a moon," is "slightly lighter in complexion than his wife['s]." And completing his facial description is the inclusion of "two gold front teeth" (25). But what the Crosses lack in appearance they make up for in respectability — pretensions aside. Embedded in these details are the social elements that conjoin and converge with the actual food to create the environment or setting of the food event. But the social interactions surrounding the food influence what is being eaten (or not) as well as who is eating. Food events are, above all else, an "intertwining of human business."

So it comes as no surprise that a bountiful meal is served, including "two kinds of chicken—fried and stewed with dumplings," sweet potatoes, macaroni and cheese, turnip greens and ham hocks, beets, coleslaw, and "hot-water corn bread"—a cornucopia of southern and "soul" delights for many people, regardless of their status as clergy. But Myrtle is undaunted by this culinary trap. She watches Reverend Cross's "face [light] up" with delight at the array of foods offered, and he queries, "Now-w-w, what part of the chicken do you like best, Reverend Black?" (28). Her quick and ready response of "The leg will be fine" reflects her familiarity with this ritual. Even more insightful is her awareness that if she does not issue a preference, she will be served "the choice piece of meaty breast" (28). Having been in this position numerous times, Myrtle has learned the art of "eating like a sparrow." She takes small quantities of everything, pushes food around on her plate to make it seem as if she is consuming more than she is, and avoids starches completely. With this pretense she maintains her personal appearance. She knows better than to offend the church sisters who were usually more than miffed if "plates weren't filled and emptied with pleasure" (28).

Lucy Cross, as the hostess of this food event, has her own significant role to play in this analysis. First, there is the meal. Like many women of small churches in even smaller towns, Lucy has the role of cooking for her family and any additional guests her husband invites for dinner. This is a customary ritual and therefore accompanied by a certain set of expectations and preparations.[36] First, the grocery shopping has to be completed. Then the food has to be cooked, which is not an easy task with several children afoot— and the text tells us that there is a great deal of food. Two different types of chicken dishes were prepared. Cheese was probably grated for the macaroni and cheese and the cabbage for the coleslaw as well. The turnip greens had to be washed and cleaned before they could be cooked. And last, the sweet potatoes had to be boiled, peeled, and seasoned while the bread was laid down for the yeast to rise in the rolls.

This was a Sunday meal hosted on a Friday. Thus, this disruption in the ordinary commerce of the household would have also placed an extra burden on Mrs. Cross. The living room, for example—usually kept cleaned and reserved only for company—was no doubt given an "extra clean" in order to prepare for their guest's arrival. This point does not go unnoticed by Myrtle, who observes that the "company only room" is "clean and austere." The dining room, which was probably used as an everyday room to accommodate the numbers in the Cross household, would also have been cleaned. With several children in the house, it is doubtful that the white linen cloth that adorns the table during the meal had actually remained clean during the week. And even if it had, it certainly would have been washed again to ensure its cleanliness. The dining room table also has to be set, a task quite possibly delegated to the oldest daughter. Even with all of these preparations, Myrtle notices that "unappealing shadows" hover around the room. This is undoubtedly due to one or two burned-out lightbulbs in the room's chandelier. Inasmuch as Mrs. Cross seems to be meticulous in the arrangement of her home's artifacts, it is probable that this small detail was forgotten.

Attention is called to this minutiae to stress the amount of unseen labor employed in the provisioning of a meal. All of these preparations give rise to the various investments that participants have toward the meal. Consequently, the food event, like other aspects of life, is set against a backdrop of power relations. For example, nowhere in the text is there any mention of Reverend Cross's role in the actual preparation of the meal. Other than responding to the phone call from Myrtle, inquiring about the time of dinner, and having his offer of a ride rebuffed, we are told little of his role in the getting ready process. So, then, reading this event should first be set within the context of how power functions within family and domestic production.

The nature of this power and its function increases the tension between Myrtle and Lucy Cross. The material conditions of the Cross household suggest that she might not work beyond the home. Therefore, as a housewife and preacher's wife, Mrs. Cross is in a very different position than Myrtle when it comes to her subordination within the family economy. Yet, despite her position (or maybe it is because of it), she exerts a fair amount of power within the domestic realm. For example, by Reverend Cross deferring to his wife on the time of dinner, it is clear that she controls that particular portion of the household protocol. Had Reverend Cross given Myrtle a time of arrival without first consulting his wife (as Lester did when he invited Willie to his house for dinner without consulting his mother), then we would know that he held the complete balance of power in the home. As it stands, by asking his wife about these nitty-gritty details, we are given to know that the meal is not within his control. Even when Myrtle arrives, there is a lapse in time before Mrs. Cross announces that dinner is ready. This again reaffirms that she controls what the family eats and when they eat.

Though the actual reasons for the dinner invitation should perhaps be attributed to Reverend Cross—to meet his guest and his "opponent" (all ministers feel some element of competition when another clergyperson enters their pulpit)—the ways in which that invitation plays out is left up to Lucy Cross. In briefly examining Mrs. Cross's responsibility for the meal-taking process, I aim to highlight the power struggles that can ensue during the course of dinner. To begin this part of the discussion, I return to an earlier point about meal taking—the customs and rituals that sometimes go along with eating. As is customary, the visiting minister or guest "blesses" the food and the "hands that prepared it." Myrtle does this by giving a short but elaborate blessing. The next portion of the ritual involves the apportionment of food, which Reverend Cross clearly sees as his "right" and "privilege." He relishes the opportunity to show off his largesse (it is a Sunday meal on Friday) and his wife's cooking. The two rituals of blessing and distributing the food having been completed, the focus now turns to the surreptitious monitoring of eating behavior. There are a couple of things that will easily heighten the ire of the cook when it comes to eating. One is when the food is ready and the guests linger before coming to the table. This is a major food faux pas, suggesting to the cook that the guests are uninterested in the amount of time and energy that went into the preparations of the meal. It is almost as bad, if not worse, as refusing to eat at all.

This brings me to the second point of indignation—accepting and refusing food. The Crosses, probably adhering very closely to custom and certainly being unaware of Myrtle's agenda to control her food intake, expect her to readily embrace the breast. After a hearty "Amen," Reverend Cross turns to Myrtle with "Now-w-w, what part of the chicken do you like best, Reverend Black?" When she selects the chicken leg, there is probably disappointment. Had this been a real-life situation, someone probably would have commented on her selection. Her choice of a chicken leg might even have caused tension during the remainder of the dinner. When there are differences in expectations, relationships can sometimes be strained over the acceptance, refusal, or apportionment of food. Amy Shuman calls this the "rhetoric of portions." Shuman explains that certain rules of conduct, perceptions of social hierarchy, and questions of etiquette most always accompany food distribution. During a meal, food portioning serves as an "act of communication."[37] Myrtle's actions, then, become a signal to Mrs. Cross that she, as the hostess, now has to monitor what her guest is eating. The rejection of food is equal to the rejection of the Cross's hospitality. In not offering the obligatory caveat "I will only take a small piece since I try to watch my weight" or something to this effect, Myrtle has in essence committed food heresy.

Yet, as Shuman and others have pointed out, monitoring people's eating behavior is not simple. When "errors of interpretation" occur in food events and situations of food sharing, they always create dilemmas for everyone involved in the exchange.[38] That is why the relationship between the cook, the host, the hostess, and the guests is very important. Inherent in this observation is an indication of the social distance that might exist between the two sets of individuals. In the example of the men at Craig Field Southeastern Air Training Center, there is a racialized tension that separates the African American cooks (not chefs) and the white field cadets. Mrs. Cross and Myrtle have a similar relationship to one another but from a gendered point of view. There is the obvious domestic disparity. Unlike the Craig Field cooks, who do not eat with the cadets, Mrs. Cross dines with her guest and her family. But, in addition to being the one who prepared the food, she also monitors the behavior of her children and makes sure everyone receives enough food (especially her guest). This is the role she is supposed to play while Myrtle and her husband talk "business." Thus, the private and public spheres collide instead of intersect. Myrtle, devoid of children and thus replete with freedom, is serious and controlled in ways that Mrs. Cross is not and cannot afford to be. On the other hand, Mrs. Cross also has "business." In this setting, her main concern is that of ensuring that her family offers the best hospitality. Here some of the power negotiations are revealed. Etiquette says that when you are offered hospitality at the home of another, you enjoy their graciousness, or at least pretend to do so. Within the social organization of the meal, Myrtle, as the guest and a minister, actually commits sacrilege by first refusing the largest piece of chicken, then hardly eating at all, and last by not acknowledging the tastiness of the meal (regardless of her feelings about it). In not offering the obligatory compliments, she is in effect signifying on the Crosses' food, Mrs. Cross, and the family's overall hospitality.

We know why Myrtle makes a pretense at eating by moving the food around her plate. But under the stealthy gaze of Lucy Cross, her ruse is no doubt uncovered. Myrtle's refusal to suspend her eating regimen speaks volumes about who is in "control" of this food situation. Her dietary preferences, sans the caveat about weight and diet, can be read as, one, the Crosses' food is not good enough, and two, she is above their level of hospitality. Although Myrtle recognizes that it is "an affront to the sisters if plates weren't filled and emptied with pleasure," she does not render any praise upon Mrs. Cross for the meal's offerings (29). Herein lies Myrtle's ultimate act of signifying as well as the most overt display of power exercised during the meal. Withholding praise from the cook or chef after a meal is a major power play. It sends any number of messages to the hostess/host. In this context, her signifying might be construed as a message of class bias. To add further insult, Myrtle has no qualms about not accepting the invitation to stay at the Crosses' home (even though they probably did not have the room and it would have been an encumbrance). The point here is that Myrtle seems to have rejected all of the Crosses' hospitality. They, the Crosses, who had "sacrificed" (as the dutiful propitiators of God that their name implies) to provide a bountiful meal and good southern hospitality, were being rejected by a preacher, and a woman preacher at that.

As a single itinerant woman preacher who exudes sexuality, Myrtle is very different. From her food intake to her personal choices, she does not embody the "traditional" male preacher, and she is definitely not the "traditional" woman. Myrtle is a discomfort to the black Christian establishment made manifest by the Reverend and Mrs. Cross. For example, when Reverend Cross offers to pick her up for dinner, she instantly refuses, not wanting him to know where she is staying. When she travels, her hotel room is home, her private domicile. She wants no intrusions upon her space from men "just dropping in," as she feels they are prone to do (22). Unbeknownst to the Crosses, this is one of the reasons that Myrtle rejects their invitation to stay in their home. All of these rebuffs lead the Crosses to ask, "What kind of woman is independent and free-spirited traveling around like that by herself (even if she is spreading the word of God)?" Much later in the novel they believe they have found an answer to their question when they learn that Myrtle is a lesbian. But I would suggest that Myrtle is a proverbial blues woman, "Preachin' the Blues."

In her study *Blues Legacies and Black Feminism*, Angela Davis discusses the concept of "Preachin' the Blues" as one of Bessie Smith's compositions merging the "spirit of the blues" with the "spirit of religion." [39] Smith, according to Davis, defines the blues as spiritual sermons, rebuking the notion that Christianity is somehow above the discourse of the blues. [40] Myrtle, as a parody of the blues woman, embodies a similar stance in both her sexual attraction and the means by which she acts on this attraction—through her sermons. Her veracity with and "facility for words" are her charm. When her tongue follows the "snakelike path" and she screams, "Say Jesus and come to me!" she is speaking on a spiritual and sexual level to one or more willing church sisters. And Shockley offers a perfect example of call and response when a young woman yells back in "ecstatic" and "convulsive orgasmic agitation," "I'm *com-m-ing*!" (7).

Although I have taken liberties in the analysis of Shockley's novel, and in particular the food-sharing scene, this discussion serves to illustrate how food events are actually snapshots in the greater realm of social life. They are filled with a number of social, cultural, economic, political, and sexual ramifications. Myrtle certainly has the right to behave any way she likes during dinner—no matter how rude. But, among other things, "the rhetoric of portions requires the covert cooperation of all parties to turn situations with limited resources and a priori expectations into the appearance of unqualified generosity and appreciation."[41] Indeed, it is doubtful that Shockley was even aware of how loaded the situation could be beyond the realm of debunking the obvious stereotypes. The food event is situated early enough in the novel so as to address and disregard the notion, strongly held by black people as well as whites, that all preachers love chicken. But the location of this scene at the beginning of the novel also foreshadows Myrtle's struggle to control and manipulate many of her appetites.

Shockley's presentation of another side of black women's lives in the character of Myrtle Black is critical to witnessing different expressions of black women's self-definition in the company of domesticity. Not all black women have contact with chicken from the standpoint of selling, cooking, and eating. Myrtle is a case in point. The acts of signifying that go on in the Cross household, both by Mrs. Cross and Myrtle, speak to the ways in which some black women exercise self-expression and self-empowerment. Contemporary black women come together in church kitchens and other domestic spaces to cook, socialize, or conduct business (where food happens to be involved) and to transcend and transform what is often perceived as commonplace. Recognizing that cooking is generally disdained as "women's work," they use these notions to their advantage when engaging in activities to promote community building and social activism. Yet even in this, women work as cultural agents. Though it is usually unconscious, when they signify on one another and other people, be it through indirect or direct address, they are transmitting cultural values. They are "schooling" their children and sometimes each other in the ways of black folk play. In signifying upon one another's cooking styles, they are living what many African American writers illustrate in their texts. And they are engaging in the "risky pleasure" of "putting their foot up" on somebody, in the same way that somebody has most surely done to them.

These are the stories that need to be told in order to negate the images that have relegated black women's cooking to the space of relative insignificance. But more important than this recovery process, black children need to hear of these stories and understand that their mothers (and fathers) are walking repositories of African American culture. Understanding that signifying does not necessarily involve violence, or the suggestion of violence, to "keep it real" opens up another dimension of understanding one's self in the context of one's own community. Being able to recognize signifying as a trope goes far toward enabling an appreciation of an oral culture and black expressive culture. However, understanding the multiple meanings behind these oral expressions goes even further in that it also reveals how black women are signified on in order to get them to "shut up"—or to silence black women's voices. What emerges then is a competition over who speaks for black women and how this representation reveals itself. In the next two chapters, I consider how black men propose to speak for black women—by signifying on them as females, cultural transmitters, and creative culinary artists. While many men propose to "know" what black women are doing and therefore how to "represent" them, they may in fact be committing something akin to gender malpractice.

II

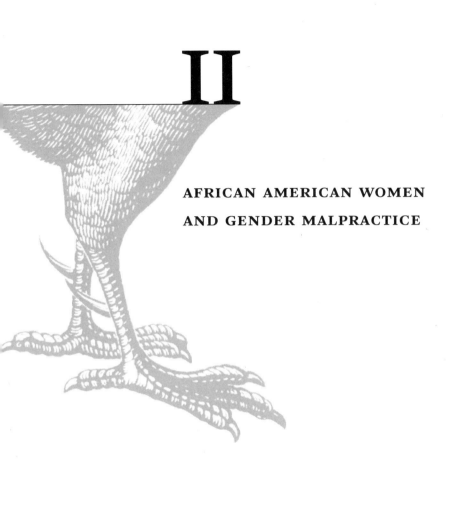

AFRICAN AMERICAN WOMEN
AND GENDER MALPRACTICE

TAKING THE BIG PIECE OF CHICKEN

6

*Janie: You sho loves to tell me whut to do, but Ah can't tell you nothin'
Ah see!*

*Jody: Dat's 'cause you need tellin'. . . . It would be pitiful if Ah didn't.
Somebody got to think for women and chillun and chickens and
cows. Igod, they sho don't think none theirselves.*

*Janie: Sometimes God gits familiar wid us womenfolks too and talks
His inside business. He told me how surprised He was 'bout y'all
turning out so smart after Him makin' yuh different; and how
surprised y'all is goin' tuh be if you ever find out you don't know
half as much 'bout us as you think you do. It's so easy to make
yo'self out God Almighty when you ain't got nothin' tuh strain
against but women and chickens.*

—*Zora Neale Hurston,* Their Eyes Were Watching God

Women signify. Women signify, specify, and play the dozens just as well as any man, given half a chance. In Zora Neale Hurston's *Their Eyes Were Watching God*, Janie eloquently conveys this point. Her response comes on the heels of a conversation between her husband, Joe "Jody" Starks, and two Eatonville men as they discuss the merits of beating a woman. Janie's response is the result of a consciousness that unfolds during the course of the novel. Her consciousness reveals itself when she thrusts herself into the male conversation, something she had never done before. The only response to her statement comes from her husband, who says, "You gettin' too moufy, Janie."[1]

The connections here between women, chicken, and self-consciousness are interesting for what they lend to this discussion. Though black women like Janie are placed in a category with livestock and chickens, Janie says that women "know uh few things" and "thinks sometime too."[2] Most often (though not always), thinking turns to action when black women speak. This part of the discussion primarily concerns itself with two matters: the ways in which those other than black women purport to "know" and "think" for them and how the road to black women's self-discovery can begin when they speak for themselves. These arguments are posed as a part of the ongoing, complex dialogue around the ways in which black women are represented in relation to chicken. When others assume to know black women, gender malpractice and misrepresentation are often not far behind. In looking at several instances where gender malpractice has occurred, I want not only to draw attention to this practice but also to explore its consequences upon black women and black communities as well.

Gender malpractice is a concept that borrows heavily from the work of philosopher Tommy Lott. In *The Invention of Race*, Lott explains that black artists have been charged with cultural malpractice when black dialect or some other form of vernacular has been used in a way that misrepresents black people. In Lott's formulation, this misrepresentation can occur on many levels. He explains, "The material image might include phenomena—such as misspelled or mispronounced words, sambo and mammy caricatures, simianized portrayals or even gorillas themselves—as a sign of the inferiority of black people."[3] When those outside the race display these phenomena, it is relatively easy to levy a charge of racism. The more difficult task of assigning judgments reveals itself when the perpetrators are "in-group" or black, and in some contexts of this discussion, female.[4] In my use of the term "gender malpractice," I am considering instances when black women have been intentionally misrepresented by white people and ambiguously misrepresented by blacks.

But as Lott rightfully points out, there is a lack of agreement over what constitutes misrepresentation. To uncritically embrace the term "misrepresentation" overlooks underlying ideologies that might be at work. When an artist employs what might be perceived as misrepresentations (for example, minstrelsy, folk culture, lyrical poetry using dialect, calling women "bitches" and "hos" in rap music), it is not always clear whether he or she is working from a particular political agenda—"accommodationism, resistance, or both."[5] And if denigration is to be perceived as resistance, how do we reconcile this when it offends our gendered, racialized, and sexualized sensibilities? Deciding that someone has committed gender malpractice does not negate his or her work. Rather, it highlights and showcases his or her artistry to call attention to the complexities inherent in the production of cultural artifacts, particularly those surrounding black people. Because we do not know the underlying intentions behind these acts in most cases, Lott argues that this charge is largely perceptual, in need of justification. This discussion will attempt to do just that: offer justification, or at least a critical examination, of instances where we can read perceived gender malpractice.

Before I discuss gender malpractice by African American men, I first want to illustrate how non-black women can exercise the same practice. In *Idella: Marjorie Rawlings' "Perfect Maid"* is a kind of misrepresentation that may be familiar to some black women who performed domestic service—Idella Parker's recipes were improperly "borrowed." In her memoir, Parker shares a statement made by her employer: "Idella, I thought all you people knew how to pick ducks and chickens."[6] Rawlings's assumption that all black people knew how to pluck ducks and chickens was as commonplace as her assumption (also recounted by Parker) that black people were too stupid to know when they were being talked about or having fun made of them.[7] The combination of these two assumptions might be the reason Rawlings took the liberty to "borrow" some of Parker's recipes for Rawlings's cookbook, *Cross Creek Cookery*.[8]

The cookbook, according to Parker, required "months and months together" in Rawlings's tiny kitchen extracting the recipes from "[Parker's] hands and head." She says: "Many of the recipes in the book were mine, but she only gave me credit for three of them, including 'Idella's biscuits.' There were several others that were mine too, such as the chocolate pie, and of course it was me who did most of the cooking when we were trying the recipes out."[9] In the end, Parker, whose many contributions made the cookbook a reality, received only an autographed copy. But of this she says, "In those days I was grateful for any little crumb that white people let fall, so I kept my thoughts about the cookbook strictly to myself."[10]

In this case, black vernacular language or caricatures do not affect the material image of Parker. But while Parker was supposedly capable of plucking a chicken, she was less knowledgeable when it came to cooking "roasted squab," "chicken croquettes," or "chicken dumplings." Had she known how to cook these delectable dishes, then certainly Rawlings would have included Parker's name alongside these recipes. Though I am speaking facetiously, the point is well-taken that Rawlings's assertions about the recipes in her book seem more than disingenuous. This is particularly interesting in light of the fact that Rawlings indicates that "a few" of the recipes were not hers, nor her mother's, relatives', or friends'. Despite her reluctance to attribute these recipes, Rawlings maintains that desserts like Black Bottom Pie proved so "superlative" that she believes it "unkind not to share them, as they were shared with me." She then goes on to make a curious statement: "There are cooks who guard secret and precious recipes with their lives. This seems to me ungenerous in practitioners of art. Occasionally a cook or housekeeper is unworthy to receive a choice recipe, and I have been known to be vague with such as these."[11] When Rawlings calls those cooks who guard their artful culinary productions "ungenerous" for not sharing their gift, she is seemingly oblivious to the reasons such care would be taken to prevent people like her from pirating these treasures. By her own admission, Rawlings says she would "hang tenderly over the shoulders of Florida backwoods cooks, often sportsmen," watching as they cooked a new dish. Nonetheless, she seems to disregard the idea that people might want credit for the contributions that helped to increase her wealth. Like Rawlings, black women would also have been "vague" in sharing their techniques were they given a choice. However, we know from literature and other discourses about black domestics that these choices were seldom available.

This practice of careless neglect has occurred far too often to enumerate, and much of it has been due to the highly politicized nature of this form of vernacular tradition. Vernacular, as used here, describes a common everyday object like food that is usually associated with the mundane, informal, and intimate. Unlike the forms of vernacular misrepresentation that Lott refers to—transcription, or deliberately misspelling words to represent black dialect—food is more elusive. Mass exchange of foods and food habits that occurred between early Africans, Europeans, and Native Americans has made it more difficult for one group or another to claim the "origins" of a recipe. Food historians Jessica Harris and Karen Hess along with cultural historian Robert Hall and others have been exemplary in explaining the connections between some aspects of African American food culture and various portions of the African continent. However, it is well known that most African retentions or Africanisms were subject to major cultural transformations under the horrific influence of slavery and the transatlantic trade.[12] With these marked transitions came vast amounts of mutual exchange resulting in an amalgamation between and among cultures. This undoubtedly gave way to gender malpractice when some white women began to record southern recipes.

During the course of research for this project, I interviewed a group of culinary scholars. One member of the research group offered this observation about culinary legend Mary Randolph:

> I read the book that you reviewed by [Diane] Spivey and I especially read the chapter on migration and black cooks and then tried very hard to see her sources. And I had no idea that these, for the lack of a better term, blue-haired little old ladies were flouting the southern cuisine in the late 1800s and early 1900s and completely taking away from the African slave who made the meals. . . . I work at a federal period southern plantation so I read eighteenth-century cookbooks continuously—and we learned that Mary Randolph took these British recipes and because of this the African who was making these meals was using these British recipes[, and] all of a sudden they are no longer British, they are southern cuisine. And it's because of that enslaved cook.[13]

The point made by this speaker illustrates the ways in which foods change and evolve over time. However, a closer examination of this speaker's comments brings to light my point—when recipes were adapted to southern tastes and palates, though derivative of another country, they became southern by way of their modifications. These recipes, which were borrowed and modified by African and African American female cooks to include their own creative twists, were readily acculturated into the cuisine of the South. Yet because these foods are not embodied by linguistic variations and are relatively indistinguishable from white (particularly poor white) culinary habits, they have been left out of the cultural forms identified as "distinctly" African American, such as spirituals, sermons, and literature written in dialect.[14] This lack of such a distinguishing feature furthermore made food susceptible to cultural, social, and physical appropriation by white women (and men).[15]

Despite the changes and modifications that occurred to recipes and various culinary delights of the South and other regions where black women were cooking, this facet of African American vernacular contribution has been left unrecorded until recently. It is as if the whole of African American culinary culture is the product of recipes handed down without black women having left a single imprint. This is one of the myriad ways that foods like fried chicken have been claimed and reclaimed as inherently "southern" (coded as white). Diane Spivey has labeled this phenomenon "Whites Only Cuisine," explaining it this way:

> The end of the [Civil] war also signaled the beginning of the redefining of southern white heritage. The "Lost Cause," or southern white elites' efforts to hold on to their old way of life, centered around food. Cooking and cuisine were remade to look uniquely southern. . . . Asserting that the recipes were "southern" made these cookbooks exclusionary, and therefore racist, because the cookbooks and recipes contained therein were heralded as the creations of the elite southern white women. In an attempt to promote southern white culture, therefore, the concept of "southern cooking" started out as "Whites Only Cuisine."[16]

This is not to suggest that we need to uncover the "pure" forms that Africans and African Americans brought to the culinary arts—this is hardly possible. However, what is at issue here is how women like Idella Parker and countless other cooks and housekeepers took recipes that originated in their own minds or in the countries, hands, and minds of others to create their own culinary repertoire. Many of these selections were then spirited away and brought together to create a cookbook, which was then praised as "authentic" southern cuisine.[17]

This is one of the major concerns I have with this type of gender malpractice. Idella Parker shares this concern. In the preface to her book, she remarks several times that she has a story that she has wanted to tell "for a long time." She maintains the veracity of her life story, saying, "I recall things that happened, stories that I have never told anyone, not even my family, until now. I remember every detail of how the house looked then, and what it was like to live out there. I can almost hear Mrs. Rawlings' footsteps on the wooden floors, and my ears listen for her voice or for the little bell she kept by the bedside to ring when I was needed. So enjoy your reading, and believe what I am about to tell you, for all of it is true, about both Marjorie Kinnan Rawlings and me, Idella, 'the perfect maid.'"[18]

Parker's repeated references to the truth speak in part to the audience she knows she might reach with her narrative—friends and relatives of Marjorie Rawlings. Rawlings, author of *The Yearling* and several other writings, was well known throughout Florida and the white literary world. Not wanting to offend any of Rawlings's friends and family members might have been one reason why Parker, in various ways throughout her text, affirms the kindness of her employer. But she also notes, "In other words, she was a human being, with human faults and troubles, and so am I." Placing herself on an equal humanistic footing with Rawlings gives Parker further confidence to assert that Rawlings was "hard to get along with and impossible to reason with at times." But this confidence also carries with it what Janie's voice offers—a sense of self-expression. By finally telling her experience, Parker, in effect, reclaims the stories that were buried in the recipes that she maintains Rawlings took from her. Regardless of how close Parker and Rawlings were said to be, Parker was clear that "[they] were still a black woman and a white woman, and a barrier of race was always there."[19]

The social context of the racial barrier enables a reading of this type of scenario as both gender malpractice and cultural malpractice. In this case, there are no "subversive strategies" being employed so that a reading of this as culinary theft is possible. Holding back a critical reading of black women's stories of culinary pilfering endangers our understanding of this type of women's work. I should add here that black women engage in culinary borrowing all the time. But it is not the same thing. In those instances, absent the context of commodification, one can read it as signifyin' more than taking. Black women have borrowed and revised recipes for centuries. Though not always in jest (sometimes recipes are used to woo and win lovers and partners), this is more an example of reinventing and revising than it is "taking." Most assuredly, somewhere right now a black woman is lamenting and bemoaning how "so-and-so" "stole" her recipe for sweet potato pie or even chicken croquettes. But there is less harm in this exchange than there is in the sort of culinary pirating described here.

One of the many problems inherent in a scenario like Rawlings and Parker's is that the only foods left to describe the essence of black people are "scraps."[20] It is true that black people who were enslaved seldom ate high on the proverbial hog. It is also true that most of what was eaten was culled from various sources—the master's table, gardens, discarded foods, the lesser entrails of hogs. However, these facts do not account for what black people were eating through centuries of their existence in the United States. And yet, this notion is often stereotypically present in mainstream media, advertisements, literature, and film (oftentimes by blacks themselves). Not only has not enough been written about the varieties of other foods and forms that are and have been created by black people, but also little is known by the mass populace about the foods that are consumed by various regions, classes, and ethnicities of black people.[21] So then, if Parker was able to cook a variety of foods, like those contained in *Cross Creek Cookery*, it was necessary for her recipes to be known for reasons that exceeded Parker's personal fulfillment. As it stands now, we are left with a psychological stranglehold that reduces black food consumption to things fried and greasy. This reductionist view makes it difficult not only to accept any variation on this theme but also to see when black women's creative cooking abilities are being exercised.[22]

When a colleague heard about my project, she shared that one of her students had told her about an experience at Wendy's restaurant. According to the student, she and several other black women walked into Wendy's in Carroll County, Maryland, only to have one of the cashiers announce, "Sorry ladies, the chicken won't be ready for another twenty minutes." This account would almost be unbelievable except that the student approached the professor with this troubling narrative. Later, during my guest lecture for the class, the student again shared her story, this time to me. This student recognized that a racist assumption had been made about her eating habits. Because she and her friends are black, the cashier assumed that they had an interest in fried chicken. Not having been there, I cannot verify the statement's context, but certainly the incident frustrated the student enough to talk about it, twice.

In a similar, although comedic, context, Dave Chappelle explains that because a person is black, he or she is assumed to be "genetically predisposed to liking chicken." He elaborates by saying, "Blacks have no say in the matter." In his stand-up routine *Killin' Them Softly*, Chappelle begins the "Fried Chicken" episode with a statement and a question: "A lot of black people can relate to this. Have you ever had something happen that was so racist that you didn't even get mad, . . . you were just like, Goddamn that was racist, that was racist. . . . It was so blatant. . . . You were just like 'wow' like . . . ?" The incident he refers to happened in Mississippi, according to Chappelle. He was there for a performance, after which he ventured out to a restaurant for dinner. While trying to decide what he wanted to eat, the waiter blurted out, "The chicken." Chappelle claims to have been in shock because the thought had crossed his mind. Chappelle says he asked the waiter how he knew that this would be the choice. The waiter looked at him unbelievingly and said (in a mocking white voice), "C'mon buddy, c'monnnn buddy. . . . Everybody knows that as soon as you walked through the Goddamn door you were going to get some chicken. . . . It's no secret down here that blacks and chickens are quite fond of one another." Chappelle says that the situation was like "a fuckin' movie" because he could not believe it actually happened. He says, "I wasn't even mad, I was upset." He finishes the comedy by talking about how he is now shy about eating chicken in public and feigns an incident where he is hurriedly eating in shame. He is spotted by a white person who says, "Look at 'im. He loves it. Just like it said in the encyclopedia. Look how happy he looks." With the exception of the comedic elements of Chappelle's story, it mirrors the one told by the young woman who visited Wendy's.[23]

Hazel Carby helps to contextualize these types of incidents by explaining the role of dominant ideologies and stereotypes. These ideologies function by making one believe that what is experienced and witnessed is a natural, normal process. These kinds of exchanges are not designed to "represent a reality" but rather to function as a "disguise, or mystification, of objective social relations."[24] It seems clear that somewhere along the way, the Wendy's cashier and Dave Chappelle's waiter had heard a story that all black people eat chicken and internalized it as true. But more important, acting on this "truism is unbelievably racist to the black person who encounters it while the perpetrator has no idea (or acts as if they have no idea) that they have just stereotyped the customer."[25]

Television is one of the places where the cashier and waiter might have learned about this kind of racist labeling. According to a group of students interviewed for this project, incidents like those above are not at all surprising. Even though we had been in dialogue long before the incident at Wendy's was revealed to me, the observations of other students disturbingly reinforce this young woman's experience. These students (both men and women) were mostly white with a few Latino and Asian students and no black students. In response to a question asked about the foods believed to be associated with African American culture, several of these students indicated that the media is one of the major vehicles of transmission for many of the perceptions and beliefs that they hold on this and other such subjects. In particular, one student replied: "Black-eyed peas, fried chicken, okra, sweet potato pie, chitterlings, pig's feet, hog maw. This is all from *Friday*. . . . I'd just like to expand on that. It's like I said before; it may have been from the media. But it's not necessarily like a biased view or something like that, because like I said it's from *Friday* and it's Chris Rock and stuff like that."

This student tries to be clear that we can rely upon his viewpoint because everything that he knows about African American foodways comes from the movie *Friday*.[26] The flawed reasoning he offers is particularly interesting and extremely problematic in its implications about representation as well as about critical thinking. Accordingly, the argument of this student, Jon, is that his perceptions are unbiased because he got them from *Friday* and "Chris Rock."[27] That several of these students based their logic on something they had heard or seen in the media should have clued them in to the possible fallacies. Unfortunately, many people rely upon the media, the Internet, and other forms of popular communication to be their primary transmitters of knowledge. Rarely did any of these students say that they had actually engaged in intercultural dialogue with African American people for sustained periods of time. Rather, what several of them did share is that from a solitary comment made by one of their African American peers, or from a solitary experience, they deduced that the foods mentioned above were a regular part of black people's diets.

After one of the other students mentioned that several of these foods were stereotypical, the discussion moved deeper into this realm. One young man argued, "At the same time, there's also truth to every stereotype." What follows are some of the students' replies in response to the question of whether or not African Americans perpetuate stereotypes when they consume some of these foods as part of their cuisine.

Larry: I think so. Like when I was just talking to this one girl about it one time, she was talking about all the food they eat. And . . . she said, "We do eat all these different things." So I mean, it may have just been with her own family, but yeah.

Mike: When I first came here for orientation, they did a little thing about the diversity thing. There was one African American girl. . . . I guess when she first came, her roommate was, like, asking her all these questions, like, "Do you just eat, like, everything" that's on that list [of foods from the initial research question]? And she was, like, "Not at all. Where would you get an idea like that?"

Jeffrey: I did some volunteer work with my old school and fixed up a park in downtown Philly or near downtown Philly. And we would go to my friend's, this kid who was in my class, we would go to his house afterwards, and his mom would make us dinner. And it was a lot of the stereotypical foods. Like a lot of the deep-fried fish, fried chicken. We had french fries, barbecues, and things like that. At the same time I went back there, when she didn't have to make food for twenty people, . . . it was, like, normal. Like it was pasta and maybe some chicken. So it all depends also on, like, the situation. At a big barbecue, maybe it's easier to make that kind of food, where if it's a family gathering . . .

Psyche: You used the word "normal"; say more about that.

Jeffrey: Not necessarily normal, less stereotypical eating.

Some of these students seemed to be engaging in the beginnings of a critical thinking process, while others unequivocally accepted a single comment made by a black person as a hegemonic representation of African American culinary habits. Another set of students offered a different set of responses to the same question:

Micah: Regardless of whether or not it's . . . it stems from truth. The reason it's called a stereotype is because it's been, like, falsely changed or blown out of proportion by groups other than the group that the stereotype is of. And usually it's something negative of the group. It's like the fact that maybe in times of slavery they ate chitterlings because that's all they could get. Now other groups are making it out like it's all they wanted. And it's made into a negative thing when really it was this nonchoice.

Jilly: Oh, you're not doing it. You're not, like, "Let me make sure everyone keeps the stereotype going forever, so I'm still going to eat chicken." But it just shows, like, maybe comedians, a lot of times their acts are . . . from personal experiences, things they know well. So when they depict black stereotypes or even like a Jewish comedian making fun of a Jewish stereotype, they're doing something in that way because it's close to home; it is something you understand. So even if it's a stereotype, it may be true as well.

This discussion is presented here at length in order to illustrate the complexities of the problem. These students make it clear that when an artist uses stereotypes, there are a number of factors that have to be considered. Before turning to a discussion of such artists, I want to further place into context the ways in which stereotypes can be readily accepted and some of the reasons for this discussion's complexities.

In their work on rumor and race in America, folklorists Patricia Turner and Gary Alan Fine consider how rumors can be accepted as "truth claims."[28] Even though rumors are claims based on "unauthenticated, unsecured and unverified information," they will be believed if a certain amount of credibility can be found in them. When information is based on something that could be correct or plausible, it becomes a truth claim with a certain amount of "cultural logic." Turner and Fine explain that these claims might make "cultural sense" (for example, all black people eat fried chicken), although there is no definitive evidence to substantiate them.[29] Consequently, cultural sense claims can be used as a powerful tool in the hands of people who feel that from a social, economic, and political perspective, they have "little or nothing to lose."

An excellent example of how truth claims, cultural logic, and cultural sense operate is found in Turner's extensive research on Church's Fried Chicken. By way of entering into this discussion, I refer to one of the female students who mentioned that she had seen a Church's Fried Chicken commercial that suggested that the restaurant was targeting a black clientele. While the other students mentioned Popeye's and Kentucky Fried Chicken when queried about eating establishments that serve chicken, she included Church's, saying: "Also Church's. I remember Church's. . . . Church's is very southern. I don't know if you guys know it. . . . It's also in the St. Louis and midwest areas." When she described the restaurant's roots as "southern," she may have been referring to the rumors that circulated for years about Church's Fried Chicken and its association with blacks and the Ku Klux Klan.

The general strain of the rumor alleged that the Ku Klux Klan owned Church's. Klan members supposedly tainted their chicken recipe so that when eaten by blacks, the men would become sterilized. This rumor had a particularly devastating impact on the economic success of Church's.[30] The rumor could not be substantiated. But in the minds of many black people, history dictated that it was entirely possible that the Klan could own and operate a chicken eatery named Church's. It was also conceivable that such an establishment could be used to facilitate black cultural genocide. Turner elaborates on several factors that may have contributed to the rumor's circulation and how it gained merit in the black community. These factors included George Church's use of his own last name, descriptive of the institution near and dear to the hearts of many African Americans. Additionally, he offered foods that are familiar to the African American diet—southern fried chicken, okra, corn on the cob, biscuits, gravy, and catfish. Then there was the belief that the restaurants primarily were located in southern states like Alabama and Georgia, which would afford the KKK greater access to black consumers. And last, since the KKK historically has been responsible for many instances of violence and brutality against blacks, it would not be surprising if it used sterilization products in food to try to wipe out the black race. The perception that this type of action is *possible* defines the cultural logic that black people found with this rumor. The claim made cultural sense, even though there was no direct evidence linking the KKK to such action.

The truth claims that derive from the forces of cultural logic and cultural sense fuel the beliefs we hold about ethnic and racial groups in American society. This is what enabled Marjorie Rawlings to assume that all black people knew how to pluck chickens and ducks. It also made cultural sense to her that "her maid" would not mind if she "borrowed" the recipes, especially since they were going to contribute to Rawlings's personal gain. Believing that black people were too unintelligent to know when they were being manipulated, she assumed this practice would go unnoticed or, worse, unquestioned.

But, rumors are not relegated to the thinking of certain ethnic or racial groups, nor are they beholden to one gender or another. People operate within belief systems that are predicated on truth claims, cultural logic, and cultural sense on a daily basis, and much of this information is funneled through television and film. This point was most poignantly made when the young adults shared that their concepts of black people's eating habits were often garnered from films like *Friday*, *The Nutty Professor*, and *Boomerang*.[31] A point germane to many of the comments made by these respondents is that comedians are prone to use chicken and other cultural stereotypes in the telling of their jokes. And the black comedian whose name happened to surface most was Chris Rock. One young student had this to say:

> I think that a lot of black comedians use [the chicken stereotype]. But I think they kind of have to do that because maybe they wouldn't be taken as seriously in the beginning. Like, if you look at Chris Rock in his beginnings, he was really all [about], like, the difference between a black man and a nigger. And now, like, he's moved onto more, like, larger societal

problems. And he could be successful with it because he has name recognition now. Like, Chris Rock, if he can make money, he's going to make fame off of playing the stereotype, he's going to do it. Most people would, despite race or whatever.

Other young people had similar comments. For example, another student said: "I guess I'll elaborate on some comments about people in the media, like how they would perpetuate it. I mean they do [perpetuate these views] on their shows and stuff like that. But then again, that's an act. Chris Rock may not necessarily go home and eat Kentucky Fried Chicken. It's just like the way they are and the way they are on TV. [All black comedians] are perpetuating it. They are all contributing to the stereotypes." In this example, those who "perform" for the media are often very different from those who are either cooking foods at home out of "convenience" (as in frying chicken because there is a large group) or cooking during formal or informal family gatherings.

Several black comedians have been known to joke in their routines about black people's consumption of chicken, Eddie Murphy and Dave Chappelle among them. Interestingly, however, it was Chris Rock more than any other comedian who was named by those interviewed.[32] It also has to do with the way in which Rock has the ability to align himself with the subject position of the viewer, thus appealing to a crossover audience. On the surface, it might seem laudable that Rock has such appeal. However, an examination of his discussion of black women and chicken provides the foundations for what I believe is an ambivalence that leads one to question if Rock is indeed committing gender malpractice or doing something more subversive, like contesting hegemonic representations of black women.

Humor has always had an interesting role in African American culture. As evident by oral narratives dating back to slavery, humorous stories have been told and retold. Many of these jokes and stories involve black folks "outwitting ole' massa" over a chicken or (in the case of Joe, who stole and cooked a turkey [see chapter 2]) other fowl. Black humor has always contained elements of subterfuge, parody, and irony, even when it pertains to mocking blackness. But this humor also has sexist, stereotypical, and exploitive dimensions. These dimensions are certainly found in doing the dozens. Using the stage as their metaphorical "porch" on which to sit or roam while telling stories, doing/playing the dozens, and signifying, black comedians have used their verbal expertise to weigh in on social, political, and cultural issues as well as to tell their own stories.[33]

Rock's humor, then, has an extensive history as a particular form of black expressive culture. In his comedy routines, Rock uses chicken and other "taboo" issues to wage war upon anything with which he finds fault. He is a clever performer, however, in that he relies upon a number of "in-group" techniques to accomplish his goal. He offers black audiences comic relief while simultaneously playing to the white audiences that control the media purse strings. Rock is like a modern-day griot of sorts, bobbing about on the stage, sharing different versions of his comic narrations. The types of narrations that Rock employs are a form of "narrativizing." Geneva Smitherman says that this particular black discursive practice turns "everyday conversational talk" into stories.[34] Rock uses narrativizing to wage social commentary on a variety of issues. But he also uses it to issue verbal play against black women, in particular "Mama."

In his 1999 HBO production *Bigger and Blacker*, Rock critiques the capitalist exploitation by pharmaceutical and insurance companies. He takes to task the medical industry that has no intention of curing AIDS (because it is more profitable not to), white people who feel that they are losing in the competition over resources ("They think they are losing the country; who's winning if ya'll losing?"), and racism ("Everybody is yelling racism"; "Where are the Indians?"). But the scene that accords with this discussion's focus on gender malpractice involves the "*Big Piece of Chicken*" (Rock's emphasis). He couches this vignette around the discourse of fatherhood and how "a real daddy" receives little praise for "making the world a better place." Daddy pays the light bill and the mortgage, provides food, and so on but rarely receives any praise for his "accomplishments." Against the cheers and applause of the men and women of the audience, Rock never acknowledges in this show, though he has done elsewhere, that praise should not be necessary because these tasks are like "landing the plane."[35] In other words, these are some of the roles that accompany parenthood, so why should anyone receive credit? But what Rock really does in this part of the narrative is set up his commentary on chicken and black people—with a new twist. Rather than simply evoke the imagery of black people as chicken lovers, he moves surreptitiously into this presentation by saying, "Nobody gives a fuck about Daddy. Nobody appreciates Daddy. Now Mama got the roughest job, I'm not gonna front. . . ."

By way of illustrating that "nobody appreciates Daddy," he points out that Daddy works hard all day long, fighting against the stress of living in a predominantly white society, and then comes home to more stress because all Daddy gets when he arrives home is extra added grief:

And what does Daddy get for all his work? The *big piece of chicken*. That's all Daddy get is the *big piece of chicken*. That's right. And some women don't want to give up the big piece of chicken. Who the fuck is you to keep the *big piece of chicken*? How dare you keep *the big piece of chicken*. A man can't work for twelve hours and come home to a wing! When I was a kid, my mama [would] lose her mind if one of us ate the *big piece of chicken* by accident. "What the fuck? You ate the *big piece of chicken*. Oh Lawd, no, no, no! Now I got to take some chicken and sew it up. Shit! Give me two wings and a po'k chop. Daddy'll never know the difference." [36]

Rewarding Daddy with the "big piece of chicken" is hardly a novel concept. Many African American women have shared real-life stories of how they and their children, in their less significant familial status, were given the wings, feet, and other extremities to eat. On the other hand, the father or the "men of the house," including at times the boy children, were favored with the more preferable pieces of chicken or food in general. [37]

Rock makes manhood and fatherhood synonymous with the right to have the largest piece of chicken, not simply as a reward but as a given. His point that "a man can't work for twelve hours and come home to a wing" suggests that Daddy, in the formal sector, is working much harder than Mama in her domestic capacities. The last few lines of this particular repertoire represent the contradictions inherent in this depiction. As part of her domestic capacities, Mama now has to make up for the fact that one of her children has eaten the wrong piece of chicken. In his lamentation is perhaps the inadvertent rationale for why Mama gets the most praise — she not only has to prepare the chicken but also has to feed the children. Furthermore, she has to ensure that they do not eat the "wrong" piece of chicken. If they do, Mama then has to "repair" the chicken that the children, either mistakenly or intentionally, have eaten. After all of this, Mama will undoubtedly have to "do a jig" so that Daddy does not recognize her necessary handiwork and then placate him if he does.

What is left unnoticed in all this is that while Mama is not seen in the paid work force, she is nonetheless involved in a system of "work." It is private sphere work, economically undervalued work, and from this example, aesthetically unappreciated work. But even in Rock's formulation, her work must still go unappreciated, because even though Mama has used her culinary ingenuity to take a wing and a pork chop to create a "big piece of chicken," this cannot be acknowledged since it will only make Daddy feel that he gets even less (only a "repaired" big piece of chicken) for all his "hard work." Clearly the parody and humor of this situation are evident. All the same, it is problematic for its ambivalence toward its gender and racial agenda. Even though the audience knows it is a joke, there is uncertainty over whether Mama's work is being praised or ridiculed. Moreover, there are the questions of whether or not Rock is waging some sort of commentary on the stereotype that all black people eat chicken. Or, is he pointing out that there is a great deal of female culinary ingenuity involved in black folks' chicken-eating? A more in-depth examination of this vignette might make my concerns more evident.

Quite possibly, many in the audience see Mama's work as a labor of love that is taken for granted, not needing any particular recognition. In fact, Rock half-heartedly suggests this when he implies that Daddy is the sole bread-winner paying the mortgage, the light bill, and other bills. Soon after, however, he backtracks and says, "Now Mama got the roughest job," and tells the audience not to "front" on this piece of knowledge. But if at some point he intones praise in his description of how Mama takes a wing and a pork chop to create a new piece of chicken for Daddy, by the end of his show he definitively reinstates his initial masculinist stance. To close his performance, Rock very strategically but irritatingly ends with: "Women talk too much. They always want you to be listenin'. Let a man get situated! Let me get my other foot in the door! Let me get somethin' to eat. Let me get somethin' to drink! Let me take a shit! Go in the fuckin' kitchen and get me my *big piece of chicken*!" And it is on this note that Rock ends the show leaving the audience on their feet cheering and gesturing in approval. It is easy to become swept up in the prose and delivery until one considers what has just been said and the sexism inherent in both the rhetoric and the performance of leaving the stage having said all that he had to say on the matter.

Like the students who suggested that Rock was advancing stereotypical notions of black people, others have been critical of his work, maintaining that his politics and his presentations "commodify black stereotypes" through "coon comedy." But little is said about the sexism, as if this can be excused on the grounds that he is a comedian, or that racial issues prevail.[38] But to his detractors, Rock might argue that he is evolving and changing just like the world, commenting that he "hates anyone that embraces ignorance." In Rock's declaration about social ignorance are grounds for considering Wahneema Lubiano's statement that inherent in aspects of African American cultural production are numerous "political difficulties." These cultural sites are ripe for examining the possibilities of opposition, resistance, and subversiveness.[39] Lubiano's point registers here because while I have taken liberties at laying out the problems embedded in Rock's presentation, there is also room to acknowledge the subversiveness it creates.

Rock's comedy, and certainly this routine, offers a catharsis—a relief from the normal stresses of life. It feels good for audiences to laugh at jokes whose content they recognize. This classic syndrome, which Langston Hughes long ago referred to as "laughing to keep from crying," is part of the history of black humor. Many black people watch these performances by black comedians and laugh uproariously, knowing that much being said is sexist, racist, classist, and in some cases pure sacrilege. However, there is something to be said for the performances and the ways in which these comedians (men and women) "talk that talk" and "walk that walk," or otherwise "perform" to make audiences momentarily forget about their plights. As Lubiano goes on to say in her critique of Spike Lee's work, there are different "strategies of representation," and while we as communities of people need to be careful about wholeheartedly accepting any one representation as the "true" voice of the people, we also need to be careful not to engage in the reductionist plan of simply discarding the work because it offends our various levels of subjectivity. Rather, we need to "claim, insist on, African-American subjectivity/subjectivities, but also to elaborate and complicate that subjectivity/those subjectivities by speculating on their varied and fragmented relations to their products—abstract and/or concrete, formalized and/or ephemeral."[40] In other words, we are not perfect critics; sometimes those performances that are morally wrong or politically unsavvy are appealing. To say otherwise would suggest that there is no need to be critical of our own subject position. We, like these comedians, also sometimes engage in the slipperiness of black cultural politics.[41]

While all of this may be true, Rock's need to invoke the "shut up" philosophy when it comes to black women is troubling—both for what it does and for what it does not say. The implication here is that people should be able to see his jokes for what they are—comedies. Rock has a point in that these are jokes and, indeed, excellent demonstrations of the kinds of verbal art that resonate within the black community. However, the underlying foundations of some jokes are "misrepresentations" centering on African American women, work, voice, and self-expression. The meanings behind Rock's work, though plentiful, are too weighted with ambivalence and concerns that affect larger cultural issues.

The art of verbal play has always been a vehicle of self-expression for black men. Black women have also engaged in this banter but have not been recognized as doing so until the work of scholars such as Lawrence Levine, Claudia Mitchell-Kernan, and Geneva Smitherman brought these expressions to light. It is clear that Rock knows his craft. He understands the role of signifying in the black community. He employs it very well in this context. But what he is actually doing even more is playing the dozens. From Rock's references to the fact that Daddy experiences stresses all day from working in a "white world," we can assume that Daddy feels little or no economic power. Consequently, in order to establish his manhood, he needs to assert his authority at home. Therefore, one of the things he needs is the "big piece of chicken" to reaffirm his status in the household. The chicken functions here both metaphorically and literally. The chicken is actually whatever Daddy wants and needs at home. Mama stands in the way of this because she "talks too much."

In his 1997 publication, *Rock This!*, Rock has a section called "I Said, 'Shut Up!'" One joke from the book that mirrors the closing of Rock's HBO routine is called "Yakety Yak, Don't Talk Back." The end of the routine goes like this:

> Men have to know when to listen. Women, on the other hand, have to learn when *not* to talk. (That's not the same as listening.) It's not that men don't want to hear women talk, it's that they should not talk so much *just as soon as we get home.* You ever notice that no man comes home straight from work? A man gets off work; he's got to go somewhere. He's got to drink something. He's got to smoke something. He's got to watch a game.
>
> He's got to hang out with his boys.
>
> *He's got to do something that'll get him mentally prepared for all the talking he's getting ready to hear.*
>
> We put a foot in the door and it's "You ain't gonna believe . . . blah, blah, blah."
>
> We take another step, and it's "So I tol' that bitch . . . yak, yak, yak."
>
> Let a man get situated. We don't need to hear it all right away. Let us get our other foot in the fucking door. Let us get something to drink. Let us get a ham sandwich. Let us take a shit![42]

It is clear that Rock signifies on his own text during the HBO routine. What is interesting to note is that during the HBO performance, however, he substitutes chicken for the ham sandwich. This is probably because he knows that chicken is readily identifiable to black people and therefore will garner more laughs. But, why create the scenario of Mama as a culinary artist, sewing chicken and pork chops? This might have been done to momentarily appeal to the women in the audience. He does something similar in the book. To appeal to the women readers, he says, "Women love to talk. If there was talking in the Olympics, a man wouldn't stand a chance. . . . All a woman needs is to be asked the correct question that will allow her to run her mouth."[43] During the performance of this scenario, you can see audience members laughing and rocking back and forth in their seats in agreement.

The larger problem with this part of the performance (both in the book and on-screen) is that he makes it seem fine for women to be silenced. Though he offers the clarifying caveat that it is only when men arrive home that they want to be left alone, the point is the way in which he gives men verbal permission to silence women. This is more pronounced in the on-screen performance because following his statement "Go in the fuckin' kitchen and get me my *big piece of chicken*!" he leaves the stage. This verbal slaying of black women that occurs in Rock's performance(s) is obviously problematic on multiple levels. In addition to silencing women's actual voices, there is the silencing of black women's creative expression. The chicken scene illustrates this. In an act of gender malpractice, Rock signifies on black women's known (or perceived) abilities to cook fried chicken—even though Rock never specifies whether the chicken is fried or baked, it is assumed—reinforcing his comfort level with the audience. Relying upon the audience's familiarity with foods tradition- ally consumed by most blacks, he launches into his humorous dramatization of Mama's cooking talents. But in the same voice, he discounts Mama's work by not showcasing it. Daddy cannot know that he is not being favored with a bona fide big piece of chicken. This kind of rhetorical play is emblematic of that which regularly occurs in male spaces—spaces wherein women are generally denied the ability to speak. When Rock does not allow Mama's in- genuity to be expressed, he too takes "the bloom off things."[44] He does not allow her story to be told through the chicken. In this context, this is the story of her day, and her troubles, and her battles—equally as fierce as Daddy's.

In his book, Rock tries to offer a caveat to this silencing. Knowing that some of his material will be subjected to closer scrutiny, he asks the reader not to turn him into a "role model." He claims that this is the responsibility of parents, not entertainers or athletes, "people who are popular to young people for a while."[45] Rock also does not want the reader to believe that he beats his wife (one of his routines refers to beating women). He says, "I don't beat women. Why? Because I'm not into that." He clarifies that it is not be- cause he is an entertainer but because "it's just not cool." Delivering this ex- posé, Rock hopes to convince "young people" that he is merely an entertainer, not there to deliver values. But what about the older men and women who leave Rock's performances believing some of the things he says? It is conceivable that some male members leave believing that it is okay to silence women and make her get him his "big piece of chicken." We know this is conceivable because there are people like the student respondents who believe the rhetoric of entertainers like Rock, and not all of them are "young people."

Were Rock a white man who performed the same joke, undoubtedly there would be cries of sexism and racism. So what distinguishes Rock from any other performer? Clearly, race would be the resounding response, and because he is employing age-old black rhetorical traditions, he should be understood. However, what is unclear here is the nature of Rock's agenda, his motivation, and his intentions. Among some white audiences, the racist imagery of black people as voracious chicken lovers is perpetuated—"they know it's true, they saw it on Chris Rock." Among black audiences, Rock's performance is laudatory and celebratory, a point that cannot be overlooked. But inasmuch as we are unsure of Rock's intentions and have evidence of what his performances do, it is possible to levy a charge of gender malpractice.

What Rock's performances, although they are comedy, inherently stress is the danger of men thinking they know what motivates black women or in any way trying to speak for them. When black women speak for themselves and recognize this as an empowering stance, the process of self-discovery and awareness usually begins. How do we read the process of black men speaking and thinking for black women, particularly when they do so in an authoritative voice? One of the things that may happen is that the concerns of black women get totally erased and concealed by the larger issues being conveyed by the speaker. Objects are useful for elucidating this type of obscurity, as shown in the close reading of Rock's "Big Piece of Chicken" routine.

Objects are politicized by the meanings inscribed in their uses and associations historically and contemporarily. This is particularly salient to an object like chicken that is perceived to be generic in its uses among many races and ethnicities of people. The meanings that chicken holds for black people are as diverse as they are. But when chicken is put alongside collard greens, fried fish, macaroni and cheese, peach cobbler, and sweet potato pie, it is usually designated as "soul food." The mention of these foods conjures up feelings of nostalgia and longing for a simpler time. It also calls to mind images of "big mamas" and warm homes where familiar aromas emanate from the kitchens. But there is a less comfortable side to soul food and one that is rarely seen and discussed. That side involves obesity, high blood pressure, and diabetes—serious health issues that specifically affect the black community. But what happens when an artist juxtaposes these issues without addressing the harmful effects of the aforementioned foods? What happens when the lovable Big Mama dies as a result of those foods, and nothing is said or done to transform the eating habits of the remaining family members? These questions are the focus of the discussion of George Tillman Jr. and his motion picture *Soul Food*.

STILL DYING FOR SOME SOUL FOOD?

Soul food is cooking from the heart.
—*Mama Joe, in George Tillman Jr.,* Soul Food

Soul Food . . . *is a phenomenal movie.*
—*Audience member, after viewing* Soul Food

*I'm a black filmmaker—[which] means that there are certain
prescriptions that you're expected to take on board. I'm not particularly
troubled by that because that is par for the course. What I am troubled
by is the Kantian nature in which that prescription is placed on us as a
separate categorical imperative—a black filmmaker has to do this. I
think this is not just wrong because it's absurd, but it's also wrong
because it forecloses questions we need to ask.*
—*John Akomfrah, quoted in bell hooks, "Artistic Integrity"*

In 1997, George Tillman Jr. surprised the box office with *Soul Food*, the story of a middle-class African American family living in Chicago. The Joseph family is threatened with the loss of a forty-year tradition of Sunday dinners after the matriarch of the family dies from complications related to diabetes. At the heart of the film are the lives of "Big Mama," or Mama Joe;[1] daughters Teri, Maxine, and Bird; their respective spouses; and two grandchildren, Ahmad and Kelly. Several other minor characters, including a cousin, an ex-boyfriend, and a preacher, complete the cast. Ten-year-old Ahmad—Maxine and Kenny's son—is the omniscient narrator of the story that is based in large part on Tillman's own life experiences.[2] What Ahmad sees and tells throughout the film are the many perplexities, petty anxieties, and jealousies that often erupt between family members on any given day. What does not get told, especially as it relates to black women's health, however, forms the basis of most of this chapter's discussion. Taking this direction, this chapter expands the focus on black women and chicken by looking at the corpus of foods associated with African American cuisine. The central aim of this chapter is twofold: to consider Tillman's participation in the discussion of gender malpractice, begun in the previous chapter, and to question whether or not he also engages in culinary malpractice by homogenizing (and therefore misrepresenting) the eating practices of African Americans.

There is a "burden of representation" that is placed on African American filmmakers to speak for their communities. This expectation forecloses questions that many artists want to ask. One of Tillman's central questions in this film is, What happens to a family tradition when the matriarch dies? The female head of the family dies of complications related to diabetes, a very serious health issue that plagues many in black communities.[3] As an African American feminist working in the areas of material culture and cultural studies with a particular eye toward food, I am interested in Tillman's question. Seeing the film through these lenses raises a number of questions about Tillman's consideration of women and food in African American life. Close scrutiny of the film suggests that a number of questions be posed: Why did the family matriarch have to die of complications related to diabetes? Once the viewer knows why the family matriarch dies, what can be done in the film to circumvent the same thing happening to other family members? And how can corrective health action taken by family members contribute to the continuation of the Sunday dinner ritual? By considering these questions, I hope to open up the possibility of the ways in which they could have been addressed within the context of the film that Tillman created. In doing this, I hope to encourage more gendered ways of presenting and viewing black women, as well as to encourage black women to think more critically about self-representation. Do not misunderstand; Tillman has attempted to tell a notable story. And therefore it is not my intent to castigate Tillman for the film he did not make. I simply want to consider the implications of uncritically lauding *Soul Food* and to create a dialogue around the ways in which our formulations of black culture and life might be expanded.

Tillman tries to work around the encumbrances of black representation by employing the strategy of telling a story that captures his own family experiences. He makes no claims to confront any social issues. His goal was to simply create a film that entertains, reminds people of the past, and makes them feel good. Though he never speaks openly of a social agenda, black women and food are at the heart of the story. Tillman admits to praising black women and especially grandmothers. He explains that he grew up around six "strong" black women—seven, if you include his grandmother—who were a major influence on this film. In several of his interviews and the commentary he offers about the making of the film, he emphasizes the "strength" of black women as well as the nostalgia of eating foods that made a person feel a sense of "happiness" and a sense of home. He says, "My grandmother was a very strong woman who had a lot of respect for the Sunday dinner tradition." This is why the film revolves around the Sunday meals orchestrated by Mama Joe, the fictional grandmother.

The women in *Soul Food* present contemporary examples of the controlling images that were borne out of white historical formations but still exist in the mind's eye regarding black popular culture.[4] Considering some of these images might better reveal my concerns. Big Mama, played by Irma P. Hall, is the quintessential stereotype of a grandmother whom we all want to know and love. For some, she is reminiscent of "mammy": she is heavyset, dark-skinned, scarf-wearing, and able to cook everything that comes her way—from scratch.[5] She symbolizes the comfort and reassurance with which many moviegoers want to connect. Regardless of whether any of us actually have a heavyset, buxom, dark-skinned woman as our grandmother, the image is comforting. At a time when grandmothers are getting younger and younger because their offspring are having children of their own sooner, and many more black women are taking better care of their health, why is this image of the perceived asexual, large black woman still resonating in our visual imaginations?[6] One reason is that it has aesthetic appeal. It is much more reassuring to consider this image as opposed to any other. As Trudier Harris rightfully notes:

> Large size in black communities frequently brought with it an authority of sorts, and that may well have been an additional factor in forging oneself into the prevailing image. Few skinny women in African American communities are perceived as capable of directing the lives of others. Indeed, smaller women can be made fun of, if not outright rejected. . . . Larger women who had the physical prowess to back up their directives with physical force usually held sway. The affectionate name assigned to grandmothers in this tradition makes clear the force of their size and their power; they are generally called "Big Mama." Of course there are problems in this correlation between size and health, size and authority (some physically larger women may be incapable of commanding anyone, and some small women may be absolute authorities in their household), but the overall pattern nonetheless holds sway.[7]

Many television watchers might recall the character Florida Evans on the 1970s sitcom *Good Times*, both because of her size and because she appeared so often on the show. Now in syndication some twenty-five years later, *Good Times* has introduced her to a new generation. Even more exaggerated in size and character are the distorted images of black women in the films *The Nutty Professor* and *Big Mama's House*. But one would be hard-pressed to recall either of the grandmotherly figures from *The Cosby Show*. In keeping with the definitions provided here, neither Cliff Huxtable's mother, Anna Huxtable (Clarice Taylor), nor Clair Hanks Huxtable's mother, Carrie Hanks (Ethel Ayler), would fit the characterization of "Big Mama" due to their smaller size, their polished image, Ayler's light skin, and their infrequent presence in the kitchen preparing food. It is as if the only black women who can or wish to command a presence must attend to a particular body image and size, use vernacular language, and inhabit the kitchen.

Mama Joe perfectly fits this bill. In her kitchen, she is clearly the conductor of an orchestra of sights, sounds, and smells that reinforce her household dominance. As a culinary composer, she is queen of ensuring that the yellows, oranges, and greens of corn bread, macaroni and cheese, string beans, collard greens, and kale are present. She labors over the chicken and fish sizzling in hot frying pans. The aromatic blends of biscuits, cobblers, cakes, and pies provide southern comfort. All the while she is able to keep everyone and everything around her in check by delving out bits and pieces of "mother wit." Tillman's intention was to show the grandmother's "strength in the kitchen," working in the tradition of "creating something out of scraps." She is, in essence, the epitome of the strong black woman upon whom the gods had miraculously bestowed culinary gifts. Yet, for all of her knowledge and wisdom, she is either unable or unwilling to care for herself. She is, in fact, dying for some soul food.

This depiction is problematic for a number of reasons, including Mama Joe's inner frailty that belies her outer superhuman—or, as Harris calls it, "suprahuman"—strength. The iconic image is conjured up of black women who are able to leap tall buildings in a single bound with merely a spoon in their hands. Mama Joe is actually much more fallible and weak than initially displayed. She is overweight and stricken with diabetes. Unhealthy women, like Mama Joe, are least capable of exerting any real power because they struggle with their own health issues. Perhaps unintentionally this dilemma is embodied by Mama Joe's character. She desires to be everything to everyone, neglecting her own care.

This issue most poignantly emerges in the film while Mama Joe is talking with her grandson Ahmad. As she admonishes him about putting the dishcloth too close to the stove, she burns her arm over an open flame. It is clear that she has not been taking her insulin as instructed because she is unable to feel the pain. Once the burn is revealed, Mama Joe hastily asks for some butter while Teri proclaims in frustration, "You don't need butter, you need ice." When the daughters reprimand her for not taking her medication, Mama Joe replies with superstitious wit, "It's nothing that my herbs, turpentine, or salve can't cure." To this Teri smartly replies, "Except your diabetes." It would seem at this juncture that an educative moment about black women's health is on the horizon. It is not, however, forthcoming, as Tillman's goal was to illustrate what happens to a family when the matriarch dies. Accordingly, the family begins to lose its traditions and sense of place amid arguments over everything from adultery to who enjoys a better lifestyle.

By using the narrative-within-the-narrative mode with the grandson serving as the omniscient narrator, Tillman seems to address the notions of voice and storytelling. But, voice is also at the heart of my concerns about the film. It is significant that Ahmad is the primary storyteller and not Mama Joe or even one of the daughters. Aside from eclipsing the female voices (Ahmad's sister is never heard speaking at all), the issues that Ahmad chooses to present to the viewer are compelling for what they reveal about age and gendered perceptions.

Jealousies and sibling rivalries often arise in one's family. Tensions can revolve around everything from birth order to positions in society. This particularly can be the case when it is perceived that one sibling has a better way of life than another. All of these issues provide a source of familiar anxiety and are therefore readily identifiable throughout *Soul Food*. One scene in the film is particularly poignant: the family is huddled around the hospital bed of Mama Joe, who has slipped into a coma following a procedure to amputate her leg—a complication commonly associated with diabetes. Given the stress of the moment, it is not inconceivable that the sisters would begin arguing. But the argument ensues after Maxine announces that she is preparing to leave the hospital in order to shop for the next day's ritual dinner. Teri raises some concern about the appropriateness of this action given the current circumstances. Perhaps her concern is for her sister, but more than likely it is concern regarding the suitability of the occasion. Rather than maintain focus on this point, though, their squabble veers off into the direction of "she thinks she is better than me" and so on.

There are several reasons that this scene is troubling, not the least of which is that it stands as the nexus of the problem that can emerge when men purport to speak for women. It is clear that the moment in the hospital is a somber one because it is unclear if Mama Joe will live or die. One would think that at this time, the most important concern of the daughters would be pertinent family matters—financial concerns and the like—that will immediately take precedence should their mother cross over. Given this, it might be Maxine's intention to bring a sense of levity to the situation by continuing her family's Sunday dinner ritual. The sisters know all of the work that must ensue between the time they leave the hospital and the next day's dinner hour. Because of the emotional stress and strain of the current situation, it is conceivable that they would relinquish their hold on the usual way of carrying out the forty-year tradition in order to deal with more pressing issues. If the goal of the ritual were to extend fellowship, then a makeshift meal—food from a local carryout with a host of side dishes—would have been more convenient and seemingly fulfilled the same purpose. Concerns with making a grocery list, shopping and putting away groceries, cooking and baking, setting a table, and serving food to continue a ritual is not necessarily inconceivable, but it is a bit unbelievable.[8] And ritual notwithstanding, I am given to wonder why preparing such a labor-intensive dinner would be a priority when the mother of these women lies in a state of unconsciousness.

These depictions support my concerns about the consistent overall lack of depth of the women characters in the film. These are the very issues that lend themselves to a charge of gender malpractice. Unlike Marjorie Rawlings, who pilfered black women's recipes, or Chris Rock, who seeks to silence his women, Tillman seeks to represent women's experiences despite his lack of knowledge. In the *Soul Food*'s DVD commentary, Tillman admits that he, like many men, was unfamiliar with the actual preparation of the food because in his experiences, "men weren't allowed in the kitchen." His absence from the kitchen creates a notable remove from the actual labor involved in the planning and execution of a meal of this size. This might provide more of an understanding as to why food would seem paramount at a time when Mama Joe is in a coma.

Maxine, the middle daughter, portrayed by Vivica A. Fox, is on her way to securing the position held by her mother.[9] She is the only sister who has children (when the film commences, she is about to give birth to baby number three), and she is the only one who can cook.[10] To recall, Maxine is the sibling who suggests shopping for dinner, determined as she is to cook egg pie, collard greens, and macaroni and cheese to fulfill the family's lengthy tradition. Given this characterization, it is only a matter of time in the film before she assumes the role—and all of its consequences.

If Mama Joe is the matriarch who holds the family together, and Maxine is next in line to replace her mother, Teri is the Sapphire who repeatedly emasculates her man.[11] Teri, played by Vanessa Williams, is a successful attorney who shares the same field with her spouse, Miles, but Teri has a different commitment to her career. Miles yearns for a career in the music industry. Teri, not wanting to hear of these plans, rejects her husband and his emotional advances at every turn, grossly foreshadowing the adulterous liaison to come between Miles and Teri's cousin Faith. In addition to being the "frigid bitch" who dismisses her man, she is prone to violence. After witnessing her husband and her cousin having sex, she goes after him with a butcher knife.

Teri's inability to "cook in the bedroom" extends to the kitchen—she is unable or unwilling to nurture her husband with culinary talents and skills. In short, Teri is incapable of being a successful attorney, in love, and caring at the same time.[12]

Besides Mama Joe and Maxine, the other darker-skinned women characters, Bird and Faith, are nothing if not the epitome of the Jezebel image. Bird, newly married to ex-convict Lem (Mekhi Phifer), is rightfully lustful toward her husband. However, she is the ever-present seductress with her myriad hairstyles and nail designs, benefits of owning a beauty salon. These attributes of beauty coupled with her over-heightened desire for uncontrollable sex—even when family matters turn serious—depict her as the Jezebel incarnate. For example, Bird is so alluring that on her wedding day, her ex-boyfriend Simual arrives at the reception to slip a monetary wedding gift into her protruding nuptial cleavage. Later in the film, she thrusts that cleavage upon the same ex-boyfriend as she uses her sex appeal to entice him into assisting her unemployable spouse. That same evening, we see her clad in sexy attire awaiting her husband with candlelight, wine, and deception. Unknowing, he comes home to share the joy of his "newly acquired job."

In an earlier scene, her sexual stimulation is at its height when she and her co-workers arrive home unexpectedly and find her husband coming out of the shower. Surprised by his wife and her friends, he drops his towel. In a serious "marriage moment," he begins to share the woes of how he was fired for lying on his job application about having been to jail. All the while (co-workers present and all), Bird cannot resist staring at her husband's penis, prompting him to yell, "Stop staring at my dick!" But, sex seems to be the extent of Bird's passion; it does not extend into the kitchen. Every time she tries to cook, she either overseasons or overcooks the food. In one instance, she attempts to execute the family's Sunday dinner ritual only to have those who attend find the food to be inedible.

Juxtaposed to the Joseph sisters is cousin Faith, the fair-skinned (not as light-skinned as Teri or as dark-skinned as Bird) former nightclub dancer who, the viewers are told from the moment she arrives on the scene, "is trouble." When Teri confronts Faith, telling her "they don't want no shit from her this time," it is clear that there will be some coming. When Faith encounters Miles on the street minutes before a dance audition, she convinces him to play for her after having been abandoned by her musician with only minutes to spare. The success of this encounter (for both Faith and Miles) leads Faith to suggest a celebration and ultimately sexual intercourse. Over food and drink, the two reminisce about the day's successes. Faith, clad in a skimpy red skirt and black ankle boots (streetwalker attire), is obviously to blame for leading the married Miles to this level of debauchery. During the sex scene, which lasts for minutes, Faith is pinned to the wall in a moment of supposed unrestrained and unbridled passion and ecstasy. In reality, it is little more than a moment of total penetration. Both characters are left feeling "disturbed." But it is the hot, libidinous Faith, with her checkered past and troubling present, who slumps to the floor in an act of shame and repentance, having seduced her cousin's husband in her cousin's house.[13]

The ease with which Tillman follows these traditional formulations of black women's characters is problematic. Though he would certainly argue that he is celebrating black womanhood, closer examination reveals that honoring or acknowledging black women requires more than merely putting them into a movie. It also requires broader consideration of women's lives beyond their roles as cooks, emasculators, sex kittens, and baby-makers.[14] Of course there are women, even siblings, whose lives mirror the melodrama of these depictions. But as art historian Michael Harris argues in another context, "There are not enough affirming images in our environment for these negative images to ever be fully drained, controlled, and mastered."[15] I would not go so far as to deem these illustrations negative as much as I would classify them as limited in the dimensions in which these women can be perceived. I also would not suggest that Tillman intended to "drain, control, or master" the ideological constructions that are used to define black women. His stated desire was to create a film that showed happiness, comfort, and nurturance. But his script stopped short of revealing women in greater capacities. Had he gone a bit further, we might have heard more than the silences that emanated from these women's talking heads.

I have been explaining my charge of Tillman's gender malpractice through the lens of gendered stereotypes. In an effort to "speak back" to these depictions and to challenge an uncritical embracing of this or any other film, I want briefly to turn to the charge of culinary malpractice. If cultural malpractice involves the intentional misrepresentation of black people, and gender malpractice involves instances when black women have been subject to the same, then culinary malpractice simply adds food to the equation. In this discussion, culinary malpractice describes the misrepresentation of African American food and foodways by reducing blacks' culinary repertoire to "scraps" and leftovers. Discussions of African American foodways can take the path of either a pleasant review of the Sunday dinner menu or a gut-wrenching tiptoe through a culinary minefield. As with most situations that are potentially dangerous, the worst thing one can do is to plow ahead without knowing what one is doing. The remainder of this discussion points out several problematic interpretations that Tillman might have avoided as he told the story of an African American family and its food. It further suggests a way of thinking about these aesthetic issues in order to arrive at more emancipatory visions of black womanhood.

Fried chicken, macaroni and cheese, collard greens, corn bread, butter beans, and sweet potato pie are all foods that may make even the most conservative mouths water. This imagery peppered the scenes of *Soul Food* and captivated many of those who viewed the film on the big screen. But unlike many who left the film feeling "*Soul Food* is a phenomenal movie," I was loath to accept Tillman's nostalgic depictions without challenge. For one, my own life circumstances made me question what I had seen; and two, there is a healthy amount of research on African American foodways that invites the viewer to question some of Tillman's representations.

Both my maternal and fraternal grandmothers died of complications related to diabetes and heart disease. And though my maternal grandmother fit the "Big Mama" image in her size, complexion, and nurturance, real-life family stresses coupled with the debilitation of diabetes led her to an early grave. To compound this reality, my father was stricken with the disease when I was a child, leading us to change our family diet. This is not to say that all families respond to the crises of diabetes, hypertension, and obesity in the same ways; clearly this is not the case. Understanding Tillman's caveat (that he wanted to produce neither an overtly social nor political film), I am nonetheless discomforted by the ease with which we accept seeing black women die in order that others might live.[16] Were this not so, there would probably have been a great deal more angst and controversy over the film's depiction of a black woman dying in a way that education and slight modifications could have prevented.

It was these components—education and prevention—that further impeded my ability to wholeheartedly accept the film's premises. Each viewing of the film left me troubled by the number of black women who left the theater believing that their eating habits, however dangerous, had been reaffirmed by the issues of comfort that were constantly reinforced. And here I return to Mama Joe. Her stance in the film is an ambivalent one. She knows that she has an illness but refuses to care for herself. There is never any dialogue in the film, except for Mama Joe's reference to her "herbs, turpentine, or salve," to explain her reluctance to seek medical attention. Is it because she dislikes doctors? Or are we to infer from her reference to the traditional cures that she has complete faith in these medicines? Ironically, though the issue of diabetes is by and large ignored, and Mama Joe says little to explain why she will not take care of herself, she is the one who exercises the most agency—by her refusal.

Other than Mama Joe, who makes a conscious choice not to take any corrective action regarding her disease, none of the other women are ever seen exercising any agency over their health. Most troubling is the lack of response by the younger Joseph women. For all of their knowledge and ways of knowing about the world, why are they unable to convince their mother to care for herself? They are obviously bright young women, so why were none of them scripted to question more forcefully the disease that so unjustly took their mother? The best that they could offer her was the gentle admonishment "You haven't been watching what you eat." How then does this bit of information and Big Mama's resulting death affect the foodways habits of these young women? If one is to believe Tillman's representation of the sisters, it does not affect them at all. They do not exercise or change the ways in which they cook their Sunday dinners or suspend the dinners; in fact, they do not miss a beat at all. The overall absence of any attention to this real-life dilemma completely effaces the serious health repercussions of this illness. Moreover, it disguises the personal (and often political) nature of this type of food preparation and consumption for black women. If the Joseph daughters continued to eat the kinds of foods that were prepared for Sunday dinner on a weekly basis, they too might be victims of this deadly disease. Tillman's lack of regard for this issue amounts to a double silencing of the women in the film. They are both cloaked in a conspiracy of silence about their mother's health (as is Mama Joe) and silenced by the lack of serious character development.

Throughout the film are plenty of modern-day trappings (the hairstyles, clothes, nail designs, music) that show that the Joseph sisters have a modern sense of self. But what are the social and cultural dynamics under which these women live? For example, what does Maxine do as a stay-at-home mom? Presumably she cares for her children, completes housework, and tends to bills and numerous other errands. Is this also when she does the grocery shopping? And prior to Mama Joe's death, did she assume the task of taking her mother to the grocery store to purchase the goods for their elaborate Sunday meals? Or did Mama Joe make her own way to the store, and if so, what was her mode of transportation?[17] These questions go far toward addressing the second point of departure from the romantic portrayals of the food depicted in the film. The foods prepared, displayed, and consumed in the film are clearly borne out of a southern consciousness. The fictional Joseph family, living in Chicago, is from Mississippi. Therefore, the fried chicken, chitlins, collard greens, and other southern foods seen directly reflect their migratory pattern. However, this is not the totality of black food habits. *Soul Food*, by its title, is double-edged. Viewers are led to believe that they are going to learn something about the food and its meanings to the culture out of which it presumably derives and is associated. And for the most part, this is what they get. Tillman follows the description of soul food that can be found in almost any cookbook, where references to it almost always place its culinary origins in slavery and trace these foods through the Great Migration to land at the door of the contemporary moment.[18] But soul food has also become a term of convenience. It has become comfortable simply to use the term to describe everything from food to feelings.[19]

Emotions are to be expected, given that they are directly tied to memory. Recognizably, these viewpoints will be more closely related to lived reality and thus subject to the "uncritical embracing" that Wahneema Lubiano warns about. But, these perspectives are also bound to the problem of quirk and bias. They are "slanted by the teller's choice" and the ways in which the teller shapes the tale. These retellings are basically a "created version" of a time long since past.[20] And here Tillman steps on the proverbial land mine. He does exactly what others have done when defining soul food—he goes to his memory bank. This is not to suggest that Tillman presented the wrong information; quite the contrary. If the above discussion shows anything, it is that Tillman relies upon his memory in the same way that others do. If his point was to illustrate how food is bound to memory, then he succeeded wholeheartedly. If his point with the movie was to show how a family survives after the mother is gone, then he was irresponsible for all the reasons discussed in this chapter. And if he wanted to show how the foods of black people brought families together, then he presented a one-dimensional, static representation.

For the film to have succeeded on this level, most of its action needed to be dedicated to furthering the notion that food is one of the main sources of family get-togethers. To this end, scenes involving the preparation and consumption of food beyond Sunday dinner would have helped to explain why those dinner traditions are important. Outside of the Sunday dinner, wedding, or holiday, there never is a real presence of food in the film. There are always implications that food has been eaten, but consumption tends to occur only at pivotal moments. For example, in one scene at Miles and Teri's house, Miles is putting the finishing touches on what is probably a salad. Showing the viewers the process by which Miles procured the food and prepared a meal for his wife might have done more to advance the argument that he was committed to making his marriage work in a way that Teri was not. Her rejection of the meal would also have reinforced Tillman's view of her as "stern."

Another way Tillman could have illustrated food as the linchpin of the movie would have been to show viewers Mama Joe's vegetable garden. We are not made aware of the fact that a garden exists until the conclusion of the movie when Maxine and her children are removing tomatoes and other vegetables from the bed at the side of the house. This would have illustrated the freshness of foods connected to African American culture. This view also would have been preferred to the comment made by Mama Joe that "soul food" derives from "scraps." Some foods eaten by black people have their origins in the plantation master's leftovers, but not all.

While these points might seem trivial, they are central to the overall presentation of the film's title and, by implication, its argument. Tillman satisfies not only his goal of showing what happens to a family when the matriarch dies but also his desire to participate in the food film genre.[21] Some of these changes might also have quieted my frustrations with black women's lack of voice. As I have emphasized in previous chapters, cooking is an excellent example of cultural work. An illustration of the foods eaten during other times of the week would have done a great deal to advance the argument that on a day-to-day basis, black people have varied diets. If Tillman insisted on the theme of southern food = soul food = scraps, then more needed to be said and done to satisfy the concern that African American foods are always presented as merely "throwaways."

This interpretation goes hand in hand with the strong black woman thesis, and it is time for both of these myths to be dispelled. All black people's diets were not comprised of animals' remains and castoffs any more than all black women were strong or able to cook. Slavery certainly left an indelible stamp upon patterns of African American eating. However, there were free blacks living in and outside of the South. Factors like region, class, religion, health concerns, and taste need to be taken into account. For example, food historian Karen Hess points to African okra stews, gumbos, and rice dishes that characterized much of the foodways of South Carolina, New Orleans, and other areas of the Low Country.[22] On some levels, *Soul Food* really ended up being more about the foods Americans—many blacks included—would like to *think* are eaten on a regular basis, as opposed to what actually forms these dietary patterns.

This discussion began with a statement about artistic responsibility, a hotbed of controversy and contradiction. Understanding this leads to the question of what is representative. Tillman took great pains to communicate that his story was based on personal experience. Yet, how many moviegoers left theaters feeling as if he had identified their families? More than a few, if the published accounts are to be believed. Did Tillman thus have some responsibility to dissect and address multiple perspectives regarding the definition of soul food? As it stands, at least from a food perspective, he commits vernacular misrepresentation. He has simplified the diets of black people. But, for him to have created a film using any other foods would have subjected him, quite possibly, to the wrath of black audience members or moviegoers. Many people in the black community do not know anything other than this culinary representation. So Tillman captures one aspect of black culinary expression—albeit a dominant one—and in doing so appeals to the masses. Along the way, however, he reinforces various ideological assertions. As James Lull says, "Dominant ideological streams must be subsequently reproduced in the activities of our most basic social units—families, workplace networks and friendship groups in the many sites and undertakings of everyday life."[23] Food unquestionably is a part of this dynamic. Hegemony relies upon static (mis)representations and depends upon "subordinated peoples accepting the dominant ideology as 'normal reality or common sense.'"[24] But until most black people begin to realize that what they perceive as soul food does not define the whole of black eating habits, then who and what is being misrepresented is subject to particular subject positions. Did Tillman engage in some aspects of cultural malpractice along with gender and culinary malpractice? In some ways, undeniably, yes. The ways in which he claims to celebrate black womanhood and then silences women's voices are indisputable. And even though the same foods can have different meanings for different groups of people, Tillman makes a conscious choice to present foods that represent only one aspect of black culture and life. This is a decision of aesthetics, just as it was to select certain characters like Irma P. Hall and Vanessa Williams to play the parts of the Big Mama and the Tragic Mulatta.[25]

The dilemma inherent in these kinds of decisions is made all too real as we turn to my final example of gender malpractice. The following discussion is taken from an examination of how chicken operates in the work of a black female artist and of the contradictions and controversy that surround her presentations.

FLYING THE COOP WITH KARA WALKER

Regardless of the actual content of Black women's self-definition, the act of insisting on Black female self-definition validates Black women's power as human subjects.
—*Patricia Hill Collins,* Black Feminist Thought

The silhouette says a lot with very little information, but that's also what the stereotype does.
—*Kara Walker,* Carnegie International 1999/2000

Still, I could perhaps have done a better job of clarifying "what it is I think I am doing anyway." Whether I will it or not, as a black female artist my work is at the nexus of aggravated psychic and social forces as yet mostly uncharted. I could have explained my view, and shown the implications for my work, of the multiple tensions between contemporary art and critical theory, subjectivity and culture, modernism and postmodernism, and, especially for a black female, the problematic of psychoanalysis as a leitmotif through all of these.
—*Lorraine O'Grady, "Olympia's Maid:*
   Reclaiming Black Female Subjectivity"

In Gurinder Chadha's film *What's Cooking?*, four middle-class families in Los Angeles—the Jewish Seeligs, Mexican Avilas, Vietnamese Nguyens, and African American Williamses—compose a narrative about celebrating Thanksgiving. Amidst discussions of making in-laws content and maintaining family traditions, the viewer finds contested culinary ideas. Audrey Williams (Alfre Woodard) has decided to stray from the traditional southern fare in favor of a different menu. Included in Audrey's refined list of ingredients are shiitake mushrooms, which she uses to make Thanksgiving stuffing. Audrey insists upon making the stuffing and rebuffs the invitation from Grace (her mother-in-law) to make macaroni and cheese, a dish favored by Ron, Audrey's husband. Grace protests this change, managing to solicit her grandchild and son's disapproval, and in the end contributes the macaroni and cheese, along with other traditional dishes.

Chadha's film, and this scene in particular, is poignant for what it communicates about food and interpersonal politics. But for the purposes of this chapter, the significance lies in the juxtaposition between the shiitake mushroom stuffing and the macaroni and cheese. In contrast to George Tillman, who in *Soul Food* adheres primarily to one formulation of African American culinary expression, Chadha offers an alternative. On the other hand, the alternative (the shiitake dressing) relies upon its foil, the macaroni and cheese, in order to have its impact. Chadha's decision to combine these foods works precisely because she includes the macaroni and cheese—a familiar cultural marker for many African Americans. When dinner is finally served, the grandmother remarks, "Shiitake mushroom dressing—interesting," offering this comment from a position of contemplation rather than condemnation, illustrating her ability to be open and exposed to something new. Though the dinner preparation was the cause of much tension and strife, it ultimately also served as a site of enlightenment.

The contentions found in this chapter rest on the strength of the kinds of parallels presented by Chadha. She offers more than one way to read and understand African American culinary experiences. Black people are not represented as static but dynamic and capable of experiencing the familiar and the new. Central to the analysis of black representation found here is the work of African American artist Kara Walker. Her work has been a topic of considerable debate and controversy because it raises certain questions about the nature of representation in general and African American representation in particular. Among other animals and imagery, chickens, roosters, and swans factor into Walker's work. In keeping with this trajectory, I concentrate on interpreting only two images out of Walker's entire installations, prints, and drawings: *Keys to the Coop* and *Drumstick*.[1] Both of these works are illustrative of the intricate techniques used by Walker to comment on historical, social, and cultural contexts. Consequently, they are just as good as any of Walker's work on which to locate what Gwendolyn DuBois Shaw describes as "the collective terror of our shared legacies," which can be transcended by using "cultural mythologies."[2] Placing Walker's images in the larger cultural context of this study's focus on black women and chicken further highlights the heterogeneous nature of black women's relationship to the "gospel bird." Yet, more than any other, this chapter illustrates the ambivalent nature of meaning and representation and the ways in which these variables become even more complicated when placed in the historical context of race and racism in America. These two points combined with the numerous questions and emotions evoked by her works make Walker a fitting place with which to end the arguments set forth in this book.

Kara Walker's work has much of its impact because it draws attention to powerful cultural ideas, behaviors, and myths. It is equally compelling for its lack of clarification, making it subject to multiple interpretations. And perhaps more critical, her work is nothing if not thought-provoking, dangerous, and enlightening. Some may know her as the artist who brought new vigor over the last decade to the Victorian-age technique of cut-paper silhouettes.[3] Walker is very deliberate in her choice of this antiquated form because of its ability to reveal and obscure. She is even more purposed in her selection of the images produced in this form. The graceful black shapes—the result of tracing a shadow—are rendered devoid of color and definable features while simultaneously allowing some elements of identity to remain.[4] And although this form was once intimately associated with white middle- and upper-class sensibilities, Walker turns all of that on its head with imagery that is often discomforting. Her life-sized silhouettes engage in everything from fornication, cunnilingus, defecation, murder, and suicide to dancing, singing, and eating. And no one is exempt: man, woman, boy, or girl, white or black, or animal. Compounding the lewd acts on display are the hidden features of the silhouette figures ambiguously playing out or injected into Walker's tense racial melodramas.

What follows is devoted to the consideration of how the images *Keys to the Coop* and *Drumstick* participate in the creation of a provocative paradigm of black women claiming and disavowing relationships to chicken. But there is nothing easy about interpreting Walker's work, and she has purposely made it that way. These pieces are enshrouded in and promote ambivalence, forcing the viewer to assume various subject positions and to question others. But aesthetics and techniques aside—for there is no doubt that her work is visually arresting—the average viewers of Walker's work, the ones who have leisure time to visit the museum, have a really hard time figuring out what Walker is trying to do or say. Her narrations are often open-ended and complex, combining source material from historical romances, the Civil War, slave narratives, and pop fiction. Instead of conveying linear narratives, she leaves viewers to their own devices to fathom the implications. Forcing viewers to suspend easy definitions and understanding, she compels them to either "look or don't look" but challenges, "I'll make it as long as I have to,"[5] inviting them to comment and offer criticism.

Keys to the Coop depicts a young girl running forward with a ring of keys in one hand (figure 8.1). In her other hand she holds a chicken head. Her mouth is open and her tongue is sticking out in anticipation. In tandem with the young girl, the accompanying chicken is running with its head cut off. At first glance, it might seem as if this girl is simply running alongside a chicken. By relying on phenotype, as the image forces the viewer to do, one realizes that this nappy-haired black girl has apparently ripped the head off the chicken and is about to enjoy her catch. Art historians Andrea Barnwell and Kirsten

FIGURE 8.1.

Kara Walker, *Keys to the Coop* (Landfall Press, 1997), linoleum cut, 1169 × 1537 mm. Courtesy The Baltimore Museum of Art: Print & Drawing Society Fund, with proceeds derived from the 1998 Contemporary Print Fair (BMA 1997.154).

Buick lend some agreement to this interpretation: "Walker portrayed her subject as bestial: the girl approaches her prey ferociously; and girl and fowl, although clearly distinct, are nevertheless conjoined by similar restless, animated contours, and analogous poses."[6] This picture tells us as much about the artist as it does about ourselves because what one takes from it depends in large part upon how one reads it. As Stuart Hall observes, "It is as much constructed around what you can't see as what you can."[7] The girl is issuing a sidelong glance, peeking voyeuristically even as she appears in profile. Consequently, we cannot see what she is looking at or what is in front of her, nor can we really know her intentions inasmuch as she does not actually consume the chicken head. The picture stops short of this revelation. But, the "absence" of what the girl does not see (and what we the viewers do not see) is as important as what is shown. So then, both in Walker's skilled hand and in the nature of meaning, we are constantly kept off-balance—kept in a state of "suspended attention" as well as wonder.

Who is this precocious girl with the chicken head? Is it the woman artist Kara Walker who finds herself holding the "keys to the coop"? Is it Kara E. Walker, Negress? Or, is it the "nigger wench"? Finally, is she all of these or none of these, and does it matter? It does seem to be an issue because the girl/woman is in a state of usurpation. She is taking control and not looking back. Barnwell and Buick insist, "She has not only managed to feed herself, but has done so by securing access to the coop, perhaps by a lucky accident, theft, or some other means. Regardless . . . she has succeeded in satisfying her hunger and attaining a measure of control over her life."[8] She has taken control indeed, and yet unless there is a careful, multilayered reading of this work, quite possibly with several resources at hand, a viewer might get stuck on the raw image of the black girl rapaciously hungering for a chicken. What gets lost is a recognition of the ambivalent spirit of the young usurper exercising control that few young women in general, and women of color in particular, are able to express in society. Walker assumes multiple personas, inhabitants of a fictive world like that embodied by the young girl, in order to argue from various subject positions:

Plantation Master!

Up until this point, I had not been thinking of myself or my work in a racialized way.

Plantation Master?

Why, everyone can see I'm a tall young tawny vixen,

a good Negress,

a comely wench,

a coffee-scented, hot black and sweet, dark-ish berry, possessing sweet-ish juice, a topsy-turvy jungle-dancing darky,

a mahogany idol drowning in sweet decadence at the tail-end of Josephine Baker's life,

a cakewalk dark buck strutting to a commercial free Watts riots reenactment

an antsy Anita Hill unaware of the suspicion that whites think smart blacks need better sex

a slave to fashion

an active miscegenationist

the possessor of the secret of joy

a lusty and murderous rage

a scheming, chicken-stealing, hoop-skirt haulin', mistress-balling monster of the American imagination.

Plantation Master. And His obedient concubine to boot.[9]

As one of many personas, Walker fashions herself as the "good Negress." But as a successful young artist, she might also be said to hold "the keys to the coop." She accepts this, though, as one of many subject positions, seeing her role as a black female artist as unfettered: "I wrote my story with and on my own body, and I became the viewer, ravenous for another dramatic twist, an uncanny turn of events, eager to submit to a forbidden passion—UNCHAINED!"[10] The "nigger wench" emerged as an attempt to identify herself as an artist at a time when identity art was in vogue. It was a way for Walker to define herself in contrast to external descriptors. On constructing this persona, Walker explains, "She didn't have a clear identity, but as I pursued literature and cultural studies and essays, reading everything pertaining to black women, this characterization became clear. My favorite reference is in Thomas Dixon's *The Clansmen*. There is a character, the 'tawny vixen,' black mistress to the white statesmen. The description is ambivalent in a way; the message is pretty clear. She is all catlike, trying to influence the powers that be with her wily ways. It's a persistent stereotype, the black woman whose powers overwhelm the 'good' and the 'just' white people."[11] The power of the Negress is in her mischievous, sly, and cunning ways. Her sexuality makes her dangerous even when, or perhaps especially, within the realm of food.

In this context, Walker uses chicken to signify on the notion of the faithful servant. Her etching simply titled *Drumstick* portrays a large, dark-skinned mammy-like figure approaching a Confederate soldier bearing a grossly enlarged chicken drumstick (figure 8.2). Though the reproduction is a bit hard to read, the soldier's flaccid body is clad only in his wide-brimmed slouch hat. Stripped of his clothes, the soldier seems to be helpless, reiterated by the fact that he is either sitting on his haunches or on amputated legs and has sunken eyes and wayward stubble. But for two small additions—the appearance of protruding nipples and a semi-erect penis—the soldier is at the mercy of inertia. In Walker's narrative, the passerby is the kindly, loyal black servant who, with a knowing smile, approaches her charge. All of this takes place amidst the angry gaze of the protruding face emerging from the shadowy background alongside the shack from which the black woman has most likely emerged. The subject of the etching is as much the angry onlooker silhouetted in the background as it is the mammy and the soldier.

Walker's subversive interpretation of the faithful slave signifies on historical narratives like Margaret Mitchell's *Gone with the Wind* and Nina Hill Robinson's *Aunt Dice: The Story of a Faithful Slave*, which detail the lengths to which black slaves would supposedly go in order to appease and please their masters. As repeatedly discussed and described by Walker herself, this is part of her design to evoke stereotypical images from historical novels, folklore, minstrel shows, cartoons, movies, and even modern-day Harlequin romances.[12] The story of Aunt Dice is particularly fitting. Despite her master going off to war and her mistress dying of heartbreak over his long absence, Aunt Dice remains spurred to duty by the thought of her returning master. Day in and out she watches slaves abandon the Riverside Plantation in search of freedom. She is even deserted by her own son, and still she stays on waiting dutifully for Mos' Sam. Though her unwavering fidelity is questioned and challenged, "her stern old eyes did not quail. She knew not the meaning of

FIGURE 8.2. Kara Walker, *Drumstick* (Landfall Press, 1997), etching with white ink, sheet: 305 × 304 mm; plate/image: 164 × 150 mm. Courtesy The Baltimore Museum of Art: Purchased as the gift of Lorraine and Mark Schapiro, Baltimore (BMA 1999.423).

'martyr'; she had never heard of a 'noble Roman'; but her one lesson of faithfulness she had learned well."[13] When her charge returns in the quiet of the evening, she sobs uncontrollably amidst his complaints of being near starvation. But his condition is not to be prolonged, because although she initially tells him there is nothing to eat but "a piece 'o' co'n bread," she later reveals that she had survived on corn husks, saving every available piece of food for the hour of his return. The hour having arrived, with deft hands and springing step she flitted back and forth, from kitchen to dining room, grown young again in her great joy. Her dear old eyes, dim with watching, shone bright through happy tears. And such a repast! Corn pones, brown enough; but such flaky biscuits, such fragrant coffee; and chicken, fried a delicate brown! She did not stop to consider or even conjecture what stint and frugality, under the prevailing prices, brought forth these treasures of coffee, lard, and flour. She poured the coffee, waiting upon her master, watching him, who ate as if all those pent-up years of hunger and starvation were requited in that one meal![14]

Recasting the white, virile, patriarchal soldier as a feminized, debilitated figure appears to strip the soldier's power. But despite the soldier's ineptitude, Walker suggests a "not so fast" interpretation. The semi-erect phallus in the face of the approaching black female servant tells another story altogether. Similar to Robinson's Aunt Dice who fulfills Mos' Sam's hunger for food, the mammy figure walks steadily toward the soldier with the chicken leg designed to do the same. But what of the sexual hunger? The mythical image of mammy as a large, big-breasted, dark-skinned woman, nurturing and kind, is captured in Walker's rendition. She is supposedly asexual, the opposite of Sapphire, Jezebel, or the "negro wench." But, rather than read the erect penis of the soldier as a prelude to rape, the viewer can read the scenario as a "fancy trade"—that is, mammy as in control, trading the chicken leg for sex.[15] Mammy becomes the "negro wench" embodied with the "gross physical aspects of being female, gross from the southern point of view . . . as sensuous, as funky, the part of woman that white southern America was profoundly afraid of."[16]

Evidence from slaves' narratives tell us of the sexual atrocities experienced by black women at the hands of white men. But few tell of other "unspeakables"—sexual violations of black men, women, and children at the hands of white women and same-gender sexual relations between black and white women and men and between black women. Nor do we have a lot of insight into black women who willingly traded sexual favors with white men for special privileges. On these subjects, sociosexual relations are all but unconsidered, and with good reason.[17] These kinds of relationships between black women and white men have long been overshadowed by the gross legacy of black women's sexual abuse at the hands of white men who could rape and kill with impunity. During and after slavery, violence and intimidation was also used to enforce the social and sexual code prohibiting black men and white women from having any contact. Consequently, few black women or men would have written favorably of interracial love affairs for fear of being ostracized and criticized by larger black communities.

The power of these truisms makes any other configuration of love and sexuality generally all but inconceivable. Because black people have been so profoundly affected by racism in all facets of life—and particularly around issues of sexuality—little room has been left available to recognize and/or discuss any deviation from this narrative. As Cheryl Clarke points out, black people have been so vested in arguing against notions of sexual depravity that they have adopted an extreme point of view. Like most Americans, black people have taken a Puritanical stance toward sexual relations. From this vantage point, she argues, "Sex is for procreation, occurs only between men and women, and is only valid within the confines of heterosexual marriage. . . . Black folk have to live with the contradictions of this limited sexual system by repressing or closeting any other sexual/erotic urges, feelings, or desires."[18] Walker, however, exploits such a configuration in the wake of prevailing discourses on slavery by exploding the controlling images that surround black women and redefines the sexual parameters—mammy can and does have sex. In Walker's formulation, this act of trade is part of the "dirty, disgusting, and funky sex associated with Black people" that is more "intriguing and interesting" but is something people prefer not to talk about.[19] Because history offers a limited view of African American sexuality and the readily available trope (white man/black woman rape) does not offer a workable script, Walker has possibly constructed her own narrative combining elements of truth, fantasy, and fiction. In this construct, there is black female empowerment and control intertwined with interracial sexual desire. Perhaps anticipating the kinds of hostilities that would beset her work, Walker includes the angry black face in the background displaying its ardent disapproval.

While we may pretend or think we know Walker's intentions, we cannot, authorial intentions being what they are. Borrowing from these historical discourses, placing them in performative friezes, and then allowing the audience to shape and interpret them at will is part of Walker's genius, but it is also the danger inherent in interpretation. Walker is aware of this problem but is reluctant to resolve it for the viewer, one of the many issues that rankles some of her harshest critics. Resistant to being viewed as either teacher or leader, Walker says, "What I've tried . . . to avoid in my own work, is this overbearing explanation. The images stand on their own, but there's this need . . . to explain, to make sure that everyone understands and, in a way, it's almost sad. . . . It's sad in a way that you have to tell people things that they probably should already know, and tell them cut-and-dry."[20] Walker approaches each viewer as if he or she is fully aware of these discourses in all of their complexities, a perspective that makes her work both enlightening and dangerous.

The images considered here are no different from those discussed in earlier chapters. These two images can be read in terms of what they convey about race, the limited information provided by the captions notwithstanding. Stuart Hall would instruct us to ask, Which of the many meanings in this image does Kara Walker mean for us to privilege? What meaning does she prefer that we take from this image? Roland Barthes argues that the relay—the message imparted by the caption—helps one to better understand and "fix" the meaning.[21] Given Barthes's suggestion on reading images, *Keys to the Coop* is certainly about some element of control. How the young woman acquired the keys—a gift or theft—is another part of this complex story. In *Drumstick*, the direction and guidance seem a bit less clear. Are we simply to focus on the large chicken leg? If so, how are we to read the many meanings associated with this imagery, particularly given that the bearer of the drumstick is dressed in clothing representative of mammy? What commentary is Walker making about race, gender, cultural identity, and food? It is difficult not to read this etching as somehow also carrying a message about sexuality, given that the soldier is naked. Though the image is ambiguous, it seems clear that Walker is signifying on all four variables—race, gender, sexuality, and food—in order to remind us of the fact that mammy, though appearing asexual, was never beyond the reach of any white man, even one who was decrepit or otherwise incapable of caring for himself.[22]

I deliberately provided two totally different readings of Walker's *Drumstick*, one operating outside the prevailing historical discourse on most black women's relationships to white men during the nineteenth century and the other borrowing from the trope of black women's sexual assault, in order to suggest the ways in which Walker wants the viewer to approach her work. The problem, however, is that I am an informed reader of the world, and I had to search far and wide, reckoning with many demons, in order to come away with interpretations that satisfied. The average viewer over the Internet or in the museum probably has less time to indulge and certainly less inclination, lending the work to a series of misinterpretations. These misinterpretations are linked directly to historical stereotypes with modern-day currency, a point that cannot or should not be overlooked. Nor does Walker want viewers to forget this; rather, she wants them to suspend the dichotomies. Thelma Golden says, "These are the slave narratives that were never written. . . . Kara's work takes from fact but also fantasy and throws on its head any notion we might have of good and bad, right and wrong, black and white. There are no clear dichotomies."[23] Nor does there seem to be any real point in offering these romanticized versions of slavery and African American history other than to titillate viewers and entice us to probe the deep recesses of our psyches for the latent repressed sexual urges and desires.

What does seem clear is that in this contemporary era of perceived vanishing racism, Walker uses her art to claim a space for deviating from the accepted paradigmatic narratives of slavery, despite its tendency to place her on the margins. But the margins are an okay place to be, particularly given their place in African American resistance struggles. And Walker is certainly waging a struggle of her own for the belief in heterogeneous black identities. As Marlon Riggs's classic documentary *Black Is, Black Ain't* has illustrated, many are loath to actually accept what that heterogeneity looks like, despite protests to the contrary. With her art, Walker has given viewers a clear and present image in her rejection of "the compulsion to repeat the massive story of slavery."[24] And why should contemporary black artists not have the right to reject that narrative? This perspective has been, after all, sanctioned by some participants of the civil rights movement as one of the tangible benefits of the black political struggle. And more important, rejecting dominant scripts is a hallmark of African American resistance.[25]

Like other artists, Walker questions and challenges the "noble history of Black American resistance" that pervades much of the thinking about American history. In this regard, it has been suggested that Walker is trying to "retrain" her audiences by "blurring common-sense notions" about the worst aspects of slavery and her use of the silhouette. Walker challenges the idea that "slaves were always victims and masters victimizers" while forcing her audience to "confront their half-conscious ideas about the appropriateness of certain 'base' forms of thought and communication within high art and culture."[26] These arguments might be true, but their import is lost on the average viewer who gains access to Walker's work via popular media where the interests of postmodern culture, high and low, conflate, intersect, and collide. In these settings, Walker's melodramas are completely devoid of context—and oftentimes viewed independent of the complete dioramas from which they were extracted. It is one thing to view these images in the confines of modern museums of contemporary art where a certain level of a priori knowledge is expected.[27] It is quite another to encounter one of Walker's pieces floating in cyberspace after conducting a Google search on chicken, thieves, blacks, or some other innocuous terminology. In this age of global mass media, Walker has absolutely no control over misrepresentation and seems as unconcerned about misinterpretation almost as much as she is concerned with her own rights to representation. This is the point that seems contemptible. And therein lies the rub with regard to Walker's work—it seems irresponsible of her to produce such beautiful and important work that has the capacity to demonstrate the transformative possibilities of recontextualizing the fictions of race, gender, class, and sexuality but to choose not to do so because she does not want the burden. Who among us engaged in cultural work does want to accept that burden in its immensity? But if others of us must accept this task by virtue of our chosen professions, then artists should as well, particularly when their work does nothing if not contribute to prevailing stereotypes. But as an artist and an individual, Walker would argue (and has done so), that is not her burden to bear.

The past and present identities of African American people are ever-evolving and being shaped. They are shaped not by some mythic "past" but by mythic pasts. Walker's concern, then, is not how her work might help debunk racial stereotypes; rather, its concern is with the ways in which we produce and reproduce memory and negotiate black American identities. Robert Reid-Pharr makes an interesting point that bears quoting at length. Of Walker's aesthetic, he argues:

> The fact that a people survived the particularly harsh forms of slavery that existed on the American continents suggests both incredible acts of heroism and humanity and a certain amount of acclimatization, a willingness, if you will, to participate in the horror that was all around them. . . . That we look at cut black paper on a presumably white wall should work to remind us that Walker does not wish to impose a patina of historical depth on her art. . . . Walker—and her audiences—have not the full, deep, real history of slavery at our disposal but its image, its thin reflection.

He goes on to admonish readers to remember that none of us has a direct memory of slavery; we rely upon historical artifacts and our interpretation of those articles, an interpretation "that is always filtered through contemporary concerns and prejudices."[28] I am reminded of two episodes that recently occurred that help to crystallize Reid-Pharr's points.

In 2002, director George Tillman Jr. emerged upon the silver screen again with his comedic blockbuster film *Barbershop*, about the fate of a neighborhood institution and the goals and dreams of the heir to the shop. The film ignited a short-lived controversy when Eddie, the cantankerous veteran barber played by Cedric the Entertainer, makes the comment that "black people need to stop lyin'." He goes on to cite incidents involving Rodney King, O. J. Simpson, and Rosa Parks. He also makes reference to Martin Luther King Jr.'s

THE BOONDOCKS   BY AARON McGRUDER

FIGURE 8.3. *The Boondocks.* © 2005 Aaron McGruder; distributed by Universal Press
Syndicate; reprinted with permission; all rights reserved.

acts of infidelity and blatantly dismisses Jesse Jackson with expletives and
profanities. Eddie's comments are met with resounding rebuke from those
within earshot. This chastisement was echoed by many real-life black Americans who saw the film.

The other example is taken from another controversial artist, Aaron Mc-
Gruder, the creator of *The Boondocks.* In 1999, McGruder's work began to appear in major newspapers across America featuring black characters with
razor-sharp wit and keen observations about anything and everything. In the
comic strip seen in figure 8.3, Martin Luther King Jr. is celebrating his birthday by singing and dancing to popular hip-hop songs like 50 Cent's "In Da
Club" and Terror Squad's "Lean Back." Clearly McGruder is having a bit of
fun, but for the sake of those who might argue that the strip is disrespectful, he inserts Huey's voice of wisdom, "No, I don't think that's what Martin
Luther King is doing in heaven right now," to which his younger brother, Riley,
responds, "Yeah, but we really don't know for *sure* . . ." With this strip, Mc-
Gruder, by using the voice of youth and innocence, questions the sanity, on
some level, of upholding the African American icons as sacred without also
seeing them as individuals capable of making mistakes, telling lies, and even
having fun on their birthday. Riley, in typical childlike questioning, begs us
to consider King as a person, with his own quirks and proclivities, even as we
celebrate his legacy.

Artists in this new generation ask some very provocative questions with
their work. For some, they are questions that are best left unasked and even

more unanswered. For others, their questions keep some of us employed in the task of dissecting culture, identity, race, and even food. But there seems to me to be an inherent danger in considering only one side of this very complicated race issue. The danger raises its head in many ways but in particular by a statement made by Walker. In a 1996 interview with Elizabeth Armstrong for the Walker Art Center in Minneapolis, Walker remarks, "I think really the whole problem with racism and its continuing legacy in this country is that we simply *love it*. Who would we be without it, and without the 'struggle'? . . . In its absence, in the middle-class black America I grew up in, I guess I was overcome by the need to feel a certain amount of pain." Several years later she made a similar statement at the Museum of Modern Art during an informal conversation about her work: "I knew that if I was going to make work that had to deal with race issues, they were going to be full of contradictions. Because I always felt that it's really a love affair that we've got going in this country, a love affair with the idea of it [race issues], with the notion of major conflict that needs to be overcome and maybe a fear of what happens when that thing is overcome—And, of course, these issues also translate into [the] very personal: Who am I beyond this skin I'm in?"[29]

While only Kara Walker can answer the question regarding her personal identity, she makes an interesting observation about race relations in American society. If we carefully consider her first question about the struggle, then it seems the point is not that "we" love the struggle but that the struggle will not turn "us" loose. The racisms of the past are still the racisms of today; they are simply manifested in more insidious ways. As Patricia Hill Collins succinctly observes, the new racism of the twenty-first century, with its elements of color blindness, heterosexism, and individuality, has not disappeared but has become almost invisible. Like a plague, the new racism still lingers as evidenced by African Americans and people of African descent who are still overwhelmingly disadvantaged and disenfranchised in today's global economy. And images of African American sexuality and gender continue to persist, albeit in more naturalized, normalized forms. Perhaps the only radical difference, aside from increasing class differences among black communities, is the mode of dissemination traveled by the ideologies of new racism—it is swifter and more broadly defined.[30] For many blacks, visibility in career positions, a few more economic opportunities, a better class status, and generally a better way of life than that of their ancestors signal the end of racial discrimination. Separating themselves along class lines, some blacks see their socioeconomic status, education, and other attainments as insulating them from the problems that confront "others," read those uneducated or poor.

They see the problems surrounding these groups of blacks as the product of their own actions.

Like the young woman discussed in chapter 5 who believes eating chicken at one's office desk is "ghetto," black people in this new generation want nothing to do with any social markers that might identify them as belonging to "that" group of black people. Thus, when confronted by the "struggle," many of these black Americans are wholly ill-equipped to deal with the situation and are bewildered by its presence. Recalling comedian Dave Chappelle's confrontation while purchasing his evening meal should alert us to the fact that racial assumptions do not simply disappear just because we usher in a new millennium. And changing the race and gender of the artist who creates stereotypical images of African Americans and chickens does not change their meaning; head on or off, it is still chicken, and a chicken leg is still a chicken leg, large or small.

Given this reality, Walker's question can be countered with another: Where would we be if we did not know how to recognize "the struggle"? While Walker works through her multiple personas employing "glorified rape fantasies" and the like, many black women are still battling to dismantle the perception that black women's bodies are entry points for white male sexual fantasies. My own experiences as a black woman, an educator, and a scholar tell me that we as a society of people do not use "common sense" when it comes to issues of gender and racialized bodies. Therefore, I am not as sanguine as Walker about "the struggle." It seems that many would rather live without it but are daily confronted by it. In a discussion with radio commentator Tavis Smiley on the subject of the *Barbershop* controversy, columnist Mary Mitchell of the *Chicago Sun Times* makes the point that kids can discern the difference between a joke and reality. If they cannot, then parents need to deal with that issue in the home. When asked by Smiley if black comedians should "air the dirty laundry" of the black community before non-black audiences, Mitchell rejoins that although black people try to keep these issues quiet, there are those who "mispronounce words" or voice "ridiculous ideas" only to have them shouted down. In others words, she says, blackness needs to be explored in its totality as a heterogeneous group of people with non-static identities.[31]

But *Barbershop* does more than simply point to "hoopla" over statements made about African American icons; it illustrates the power of disrupting narratives. If one fictional cantankerous elder can voice an opinion that disrupts nostalgic memories of the past, what can a group of artists do when they try to question larger historical and cultural narratives? And are we pre-

pared for the conflict that ensues when these disruptions begin to destabi-
lize power struggles? We need "the struggle," to know multiple pasts, so that
when the present finally dislodges itself African American people have some
semblance of a script to which to refer. In each of the examples referred to
here—Chadha's food juxtaposition in *What's Cooking?*, Tillman's *Barbershop*,
and McGruder's *The Boondocks*—there is an alternative view and there is the
African American dominant script, macaroni and cheese in the first example
and the voices of rebuke in the latter two. The disruptions sought by all of
these artists, Walker included, do not require the total disavowal of one script
over another. That is, Walker can present her points of view and still have "the
struggle."

With all of the artists discussed in this chapter, the central concern seems
to be figuring out what they are doing and for whom. Many are concerned
with making money, of course, others with exploding the myths of a single
black identity. But regardless of the challenges being made to various "common sense" assumptions around black identities, it does not need to be done
in one fell swoop. It also does not make sense at this point in history to simply
do away with the dominant narrative script(s) of African American history
and culture. Those scripts will always exist and have various meanings to seg-
ments of the population. Instead, strategies can be adopted to incorporate
multiple perspectives on dismantling the power structures that keep various
inequalities in place. It might be wise to first acknowledge the complexities
inherent in dismantling and disavowing rigid historical paradigms and narratives that speak to a mythic African American past. As Homi Bhabha notes,
"[Disavowal] is a non-repressive form of knowledge that allows for the possibility of simultaneously embracing two contradictory beliefs, one official
and one secret, one archaic and one progressive, one that allows the myth
of origins, the other that articulates difference and division."[32] Building on
Bhabha's suggestion, it would be equally advantageous to figure out how to
deal with these scripts and then create equally productive paradigms without acting as if the slate is blank.

Like every artist, Kara Walker brings to this discussion a distinct version of
an African American experience. It is shaped in no small part by her own personal history. As a young adult in the 1980s, Walker was witness to feathered
hair, turned-up collars, and jeri curls. Interracial dating and its related trau-
mas were all the rage, accepted but far from recognized as the pathway to
racial equality. The historical setting surrounding Walker's rise in the world
of high arts coincided with the era of Reaganomics. The cultural landscape of
the 1980s and 1990s was littered with moments of reactionary rhetoric from

the NAACP and feminist groups, and the Anita Hill and Clarence Thomas hearings brought racial and class-based strife to the fore along with the sexual troubles of Michael Jackson and the memorable O. J. Simpson debacle. Add to this the backlash against rap music from the Reverend Calvin Butts and C. Delores Tucker and the controversies surrounding the work of Robert Mapplethorpe and others, and one can have an understanding of the black cultural politics that inform Walker's works. Walker speaks of this stage in her life as one of pain: "I was spending a lot of time hanging around with [whites] who had absolutely no respect for me as a human being." Of these "people," she says she "worshipped them," describing one traumatizing experience that occurred while she was dating interracially.[33] During a conversation with Tommy Lott, she alluded to having left Atlanta when she "discovered . . . that possessing a black body through which history and fiction coexist was the stuff performances are made of, and I performed a number of parts in a series of vignettes too sordid to relate here to you, my dear audience."[34] Leaving Atlanta with a BFA from Atlanta College of Art, she later took her MFA from the Rhode Island School of Design in 1994. By 1997, she was the recipient of the coveted MacArthur Award, and in 2002 Walker was the U.S. representative to the 2002 São Paolo Bienal in Brazil. Her work has been exhibited at some of the finest museums in the world, but through it all Walker has had to confront the politics of her art and her ever-evolving subject positions maintaining her agency as a black female artist. Her work, like that of others in this generation—my generation—encodes on many levels the dilemmas and growths that come with such a rapid rise to fame.

African American representation in the age of global capitalism and new technologies is on the mind of many cultural critics and has been since the late 1980s. It should come as no surprise then that questions would be raised about Walker being catapulted to some of the highest rungs of the art world ladder. Although cast off as "sour grapes," Betye Saar's piercing questions concerning the white arts establishment—one of the largest bodies to purchase Walker's works early in her career—should not go ignored.[35] Saar is quoted as having raised an ever-important question of the art community: "How do young persons just a few years out of school get a show at a major museum? The whole arts establishment picked up their work and put it at the head of the class. This is the danger, not the artists themselves. This is like closet racism. It relieves the art establishment of the responsibility to show other artists. Here we are at the end of the millennium seeing work that is very sexist and derogatory."[36] Saar's question more than reflects a generational rift, as some have proposed; it conveys the complex, multifarious concerns inherent in cultural production in general and black cultural production especially. But these are age-old concerns, not new by any means. Anytime artists deviate from the collective narrative past of African American history, they can expect to be embraced by the wider society and in return probably to receive some form of backlash from black communities.

I return to the film *Barbershop* to illustrate further this point. In the aftermath of the film's release, Jesse Jackson and Al Sharpton tried to get controversial portions of the film removed prior to its release on video. Most of the news reports surrounding this incident pointed not only to the generational divide but also to the belief that many young people simply have no knowledge, understanding, or recollection of freedom struggles.[37] While that argument is certainly part of the issue, it is far from capturing the amazing complexity of these recent "cultural moves." As Herman Gray remarks:

> I propose that the response [to Kara Walker's work] might be understood culturally and politically as a *move* by those offended to otherwise contest, excise, and even repress the historical legacy of black debasement. . . . Because popular representation and memory constitute the highly charged and unstable terrain on which Walker and members of her generation have elected to disarticulate and rearticulate claims for black expressive culture, they expose the complicity and possibly even a liberatory role for popular culture and representation in black cultural politics.[38]

This "move" to which Gray refers is, as he notes, "highly charged and unstable terrain" because, on the one hand, there are artists of this generation who are living in an age of fluid cultural identity. There is no fixed notion of blackness. Actually, there never was, but this generation more than perhaps any other contests any elements of rigidity. Therefore, many of these artists "push the envelope" on what they deem appropriate to criticize and otherwise articulate through their art—"truth" being one aspect. Through her art, Walker questions to some extent exactly how much we know (or care to admit) about the horrors of slavery. In *Barbershop*, Eddie questions why African Americans will not tell "the truth" about Rosa Parks refusing to give up her seat on the bus. He makes the point that other blacks also refused, but Rosa Parks got attention because she was the secretary for the NAACP.[39] Despite the truthfulness of this statement, many of the younger clients and barbers shout down the outspoken Eddie, remarking that his comments were "disrespectful" or had "crossed the line."

Walker is not the first black female artist to grapple with "crossing the line," and she certainly will not be the last. She joins a long list populated by other black women artists like Zora Neale Hurston, Dorothy West, and Alice Walker, to name a few, who have often been used "*against* the cultural, communal, collective mass" from which they came to convey the more nuanced message that while they are better than their own, they are not quite as good as the white masters.[40] These conflicting messages have caused so much internal confusion and pain that many artists turned inward toward black communities where jokes, music, and art could be used in the community as vindication and catharsis. Black people used in-group joking, signifyin', the dozens, and other forms of cultural expression to inform a shared set of experiences. The real differences among and between black people were seriously masked to the point where what emerged and circulated in the public sphere was an unmediated definition of blackness. The promotion of this undisturbed concept has been not only embraced but also encouraged by American popular culture, according to Herman Gray. And black people who have desired to make good with white corporate establishments have committed various acts of "cultural malpractice" by rendering vernacular misrepresentations in order to satisfy popular culture desires (read white). This is a contentious point laid bare by the political ideologies underlying issues of representation among members of black communities.[41] "Bitches" and "hos" have become commonplace and acceptable as castoffs of black youth vernacular expression, and black lives have become tabloid material. Black bodies are used to titillate and stimulate, as evidenced by the motion picture industry bestowing its highest honors upon Halle Berry for her role in *Monster's Ball* and Denzel Washington for his role in *Training Day*. Once again, what the white arts establishment has regarded as premium, many have seen as less than virtuous.

Whether we choose to respond to Walker's work or find it wholly offensive, consideration must be given to the fact that she and other artists of this generation are forcing us to question our collective pasts while they look forward to an even more ambiguous future. Part of the growth that accompanies such a project is recognizing how politics and control circumscribe images and representations. During the last several years, Walker has clearly come to this realization, admitting, "I don't have much control anymore. In fact, I'm losing control lately and I'm trying to get it back. Initially, I thought this situation was just the perfect sort of irony, the perfect 'what goes around comes around' situation. I mean, of course my work's going to go to a rich, white collector and I'm going to be, you know, the typical black artist—getting corrupted by the man, then becoming dependent. But really the only thing that bothers me is when collectors are so proud of owning something that they show it indiscriminately."[42] At the heart of this comment by Walker is one of the cruxes of the representation dilemma. When people release their art—be it a recipe, a joke, music, or visual images—they no longer have control over its use. Countless black women have learned this lesson.

From the standpoint of both this chapter and the overall argument of this project, Walker is exercising the same type of self-definition that I credit to other black women. She is controversial but simultaneously carves out a path of independence, self-actualization, and self-discovery through her art. In this way she is, as Patricia Hill Collins notes, participating in "the act of insisting on Black female self-definition [that] validates Black women's power as human subjects," even as she takes a path divergent from the collective narrative past of African American history, culture, and identity. If I see a space in which to release Walker from the charge of gender malpractice it is here, as the female artist at work. However, that artistic brilliance is called into question when it comes to what she is conveying. My personal subject positions do not allow me to recognize her individuality at the expense of virtually ignoring the ways in which her work contributes to important social discourses and issues that still pejoratively and disproportionately affect African American people as a whole. For this reason, this chapter has been a difficult one to write. The complexities surrounding this discussion exceed Walker and her art. Rather, they span corporate politics, race and sexual politics, poverty, imagery, and a host of other critical variables.

There are no easy solutions to the paradoxes considered in this analysis. The answer cannot be to refrain from exhibiting such imagery in whatever form or fashion that artists choose. Neither can it be that artists disregard the ways in which their work contributes to contemporary discussions of cultural politics and new technologies of racism. The past has not ceased to exist, and contemporary versions of age-old stereotypes did not emerge yesterday. The meanings they held yesterday, however, may not be exactly the same, but they are equally potent. In this context, there are no easy answers to the question of how to use food imagery when it is circumscribed by racism, old or new. How this is to be done is a disturbing question that rarely begins with policing the work of the artist. Rather, what is clear from these discussions is that reading food (and its intersection with gender, race, and class) as an essential critical text does not solve the problem but contributes to the project of strategizing the demise of racist discourse that dominates popular perceptions of blacks and chicken.

FROM TRAIN DEPOTS TO COUNTRY BUFFETS

My mother usually visits us every couple of months. On one of these occasions, upon entering the car, she remarked, "I'm so hungry I don't know what to do." I asked her what she had in mind for dinner. Her reply was, "You know, let's go to my favorite place." "What place?" I asked. "That soul food place near where you live." After a moment of mumbling and puzzling over what she was talking about, I realized she was referring to a restaurant called the Old Country Buffet. Having established that, we set out for that destination. I never realized that this was a place she favored. Yes, I knew that we often ate there, but I had not made the connection. The buffet boasts of "home-cooked foods," and my mother's words affirmed this because when I asked her why she liked the food, she said, "It's down home."

Though it's "down home" cooking, there is one food my mother tends to shy away from—chicken. My niece, on the other hand, chews chicken bones just like her grandmother does when eating home-cooked chicken. In fact, this is where she learned how to do it properly without choking. And while her mother, my sister, does not chew chicken bones, we rely upon her to always ask the same question when planning a family gathering—"Who's bringing the wing *dings*?"—with emphasis for some reason on the "dings."

The point of these reflections is not simply to share my family's eating habits. Certainly, since I have been working on this project I have been told more "chicken stories" and have had more memories shared than I could ever manage in a lifetime. But I am glad of this. I am glad because it means that this project and my work have people thinking about what food means in their lives and in the lives of people around them. I probably would not have thought twice about my mother's desire for the Old Country Buffet any more than I would have noticed that my niece sucks chicken bones or that my sister has to have "wing dings" if not for this book. What is revealed in the larger narrative of these women's and this girl's desire for (or avoidance of) certain kinds of chicken is how they see themselves in relationship to food.

For this reason alone, this project had to be completed. These stories had to be told for all of the African Americans who share their chicken stories and for all of the women whose lives have been defined by cooking over hot stoves for families, churches, and even strangers. What I have tried to do with this project is to promote the understanding of black women's lives as cultural work, particularly that part of their lives that may have involved chicken. More than knowing what black women ate or now eat, I wanted to know what those foods mean to them. But even beyond that, I wanted to know the variety of ways in which chicken has played a part in their lives. Throughout the course of this book, I have shared various stories and testimonies—from the old Negro woman who verbally sparred with Ned to the entrepreneurs in Gordonsville, Virginia, the signifyin' sistas of black churches, the black professional who disdains chicken-eating in the workplace, and the artistry of Kara Walker. Ultimately, these narratives teach us that for black women, chicken can be about more than what other people think it is or should be in their lives. It is about how they define it for themselves. Black women are more than "chicken vendors"; they are all metaphorical "waiter carriers"— that is, they define themselves and the relationship of chicken in their lives in ways palatable to them.

When I began this project, I found myself looking at these relationships from the standpoint of how narratives about chicken have been loaded with racist and stereotypical associations. That is the way I was introduced to this subject. As mentioned in the introduction, I heard a commercial for KFC. This was the defining moment for refining my work within the genre of African American foodways. But several drafts later, it dawned on me that I still was not telling the story that I believed needed to be told. By looking at this discussion through a preformulated, one-dimensional lens—stereotypes— the larger picture was being overlooked. It was then that I went to the study and began again.

I began the revision process with the women's voices in chapter 4 and then worked outward to the other chapters. Only then did I understand the importance of self-definition, self-actualization, and self-discovery to the study of African American women and chicken. When I went back and listened to Ida Long, I understood why she cooked chicken and tamale dinners in a way that I do not believe I had before, and I understood why Ida needed to jog to stay alive! When I went back, I could finally see that much of what those black churchwomen were doing—in most all capacities—was signifyin' on one another, on their recipes and the chicken. And finally when I went back to the center of this study and worked outward, I realized why Bella Winston, her mother, and the women who preceded them insisted that they be called "waiter carriers." The emergence of empowerment, self-definition, and ingenuity as essential themes could not be denied.

These women—real-life and fictional—affirmed my need to conduct this study. At first I insisted upon needing to figure out how black women saw themselves in relationship to larger society—how black women saw themselves in spite of stereotypes that persist in popular culture. While this is a necessary aspect that emerges from the process of self-definition, it is not the only facet. And I knew this because I kept asking myself, "Why are black women important to this project?" Because I was focusing on material culture and racist iconography, I consulted folklorist Patricia Turner. Using the voices of black women in the church, I shared my arguments with womanist religion scholars Cheryl Townsend Gilkes and Kelly Brown-Douglass. Everywhere I went, I asked this question and received various responses, all of which were useful in one way or another. But had I listened early on, I would have found the answer in two places—in my aunt's response and in Gordonsville, Virginia.

While visiting my aunts in rural Virginia, they asked me about my project and how it was going. I felt the familiar twang of apprehension in my stomach as I tried to figure out the best way to share that I was working on a project about black people and chicken stereotypes. After I explained it the best I could, I asked them what they thought. I vividly recall one of my aunts, with her back to me while washing dishes, responding, "We need something like that. There are not enough stories out there about what black people eat and what that means to them. Uh-hum, we need something like that. Especially on black women." And then she went on to tell me about a number of other studies we need relating to black people and food. It was an ordinary statement, really, and one I had heard aspects of before. But the point was this: an ordinary, everyday black woman had confirmed this study. She said to me, this work you are doing—as mundane as it may be—is important work *to me*. It was important to her life. I should have known then that this study could not be just another academic exercise; it had to mean something to the women about whom I was writing. For that to happen, I had to start with their stories and their experiences, not what others have said about them.

That is what happened in the "eleventh hour" of working on this project. While initially finishing one of the final chapters, I rummaged through an old folder and came across another "chicken article." A fellow foodways scholar had passed this one on to me a year ago, at which time I had glanced at it and stuffed it in the folder. However, on this day, I took a break from gazing at the computer screen long enough to notice that the women in the article's photograph had on nineteenth-century clothing. I immediately read the article in full. The headline stated "Fried-Chicken Contest Is Nod to Town's Past," announcing the second annual fried-chicken festival in Gordonsville. But this was not of interest to me. The more provocative part of this story was that the festival was celebrating black women who were considered the "first female entrepreneurs in Orange County, Virginia."[1] These women, I have come to know, called themselves "waiter carriers." This discovery was immediately affirming. It gave credence to the arguments that black people have been using chicken for centuries for more than food. It further confirmed that black women were at the center of these narratives but also that there was more to these women's lives than simply being "chicken vendors," which is how newspaper articles continue to refer to them. Not only were these enterprising women, but they had families, owned land, and built material lives for themselves using chicken and other foodstuffs. There are other women who complete this composite, but for various reasons their voices are being left until the next book project. For example, there is Julia Brown, who lived in Corinth, Mississippi. Brown and her daughter Lizzie "played a main part in leading their fellow ex-slaves into one of Corinth's greatest outbursts of business activity and ownership." Mother and daughter sold fried chicken and "fruit-pie lunches" to the traveling public.[2]

These stories are not anomalies. There are numerous women like the waiter carriers of Gordonsville and Julia Brown and her daughter Lizzie. There are others waiting to have stories told about their use of chicken to contribute to their personal and community economies. The challenge is both in finding these stories and in convincing black people (not just black women) that these stories are worthy of being told, because many older black people are still ashamed to verbalize their affinity for chicken, especially in public. Surely this is understandable, given the racial and cultural politics surrounding this relationship. But as the late Barbara Christian wisely noted, "One of the best ways of maintaining a system of oppression has to do with the psychological control of people."[3] Some black people have been so affected by this kind of imagery that they alter their lives to avoid public consumption of fried chicken.

Then there is the other group—those who know so little about African American culture and history that they perpetuate these stereotypes in the name of "keepin' it real." The problem is not the innovative styles of hip-hop crew Nappy Roots, with their album *Watermelon, Chicken and Gritz*, nor is it necessarily the "bad nigga" image of Trick Daddy eating chicken for his video single "I'm a Thug." Though both play into a variety of stereotypes, albeit in subversive ways, this is not the primary concern. The problem is the generations of people with no real knowledge of African American history. They cannot understand how, in the words of African American novelist J. California Cooper, "the future has a past." Devoid of this knowledge, they are ill-equipped to identify modern-day versions of berating images, or worse, they could not care less. They live as if they are in a cultural vacuum, and many of them are. The reality of this scenario is frightening for its implications. We need only to look around us today and see the results of this paucity of these narrative pasts.

In February 2002, a Giant Food Store supermarket in Pennsylvania displayed a sign indicating that fried chicken would be on sale to honor Black History Month observances. After a customer complained, the sign was removed, prompting the corporate office to issue an apology.[4] What is sad and nonsensical about this situation is that the young manager who had developed the sign could not understand the problem. Even after his supervisor tried to explain the implications of his wordage, he still was in the dark. Perhaps. I am not sure how many young people of the last several generations know of the chicken stereotypes. Furthermore, my research tells me that even if they had heard the story, they might have had the same reaction as that manager, race, gender, and ethnicity differences aside. One black columnist, writing about this issue, called it a "lack of intercultural dialogue" in this country.[5] And he is correct. But it is more than that. Who is telling young black people about African American history, culture, and life? More important, how are they to know about the struggles that, despite what we would like to believe, still exist to some degree today? Where are the African American cultural transmitters who insist upon certain traditions so that their children are grounded in the past and see a connection to the future? As painful as it may be, we need to make sure today's generation knows the connotations of "the eye-rolling, slow-talking, chicken-bone-sucking black"[6] and how it has been an enduring figure in white racist propaganda—even unto today, albeit less insidiously.

For all of the research, knowledge, and history we have on African American culture, there is still much more to be done so that we do not rehash static narratives of "the African American past." Rather, we question and probe the past in ways that enable us to appreciate it while pushing the envelope into the future. We have to understand the fundamentals of how race, class, gender, power, and oppression continue to surround and encircle black lives so we will understand how to dismantle the structures that keep them illiterate, impoverished, and disenfranchised. Exploring the connections of African American cultural history and everyday life (involving foodways) will perhaps help to "keep it real" and deepen this understanding.

As delineated here, food has the capacity to "break things down" to a level where most people can understand and connect with it. That is part of its power. The hope is that by inserting black women's voices into the current discourse on material culture studies, foodways, black women's studies, and women's work, I may connect with a black woman or man who still has shame about consuming chicken in public because of particular childhood experiences or because they have painful memories of racist iconography. Perhaps this study will give the black professional a bit more pride so that she is not ashamed of eating chicken at the workplace (if this is her desire). In any event, the goal is to be as transformative as those foremothers who worked at train depots, building their literal and metaphorical houses out of chicken legs.

NOTES

INTRODUCTION

1. This study recognizes the problematics of using the terms "black" and "African American" interchangeably. However, one point of contention brought out by this study is the essentialist notion of blackness based on physiological attributes. Skin tone and color as well as other obvious physical characteristics have been used to render a person black regardless of his or her geographical origins. Consequently, stereotypes associated with chicken and "black" people get assigned indiscriminately. This point drives home the oversimplified rationales of blackness as opposed to seeing race as politically and culturally constructed. See S. Hall's "New Ethnicities," 443.

2. Though by no means exhaustive, Doris Witt includes a nice summary of food in African American literature. See *Black Hunger*, 7–14.

3. Here, I am referring to the range of foods indicated by African American female informants throughout the course of researching this project. Non-black informants similarly named these foods as those they perceived black people to consume. These foods include fried chicken, candied yams, lima beans, greens, macaroni and cheese, succotash, watermelon, corn bread, fried fish, and so on.

4. Black women have historically had a formidable, albeit often silenced, presence in social institutions such as the community and black churches. Consequently, the church has been a relative "safe space" where chicken has been used as a source for food, income, sacred rituals, and ceremonies, connecting to cultural tradition and heritage. The women who agreed to participate in this study are a part of this legacy and are now living throughout the Washington, D.C., metropolitan area and southern Virginia. For more on black churches, women, and chicken, see Dodson and Gilkes, "There's Nothing Like Church Food." On black women's work in the church and related activities, see Higgenbotham, *Righteous Discontent*; and Gilkes, "'If It Wasn't for the Women.'"

5. Selecting respondents from one's social network may be beneficial, but there is the potential for bias. Linda Williamson Nelson discusses the implications of researchers conducting interviews in their own communities. Using a variety of informants helped guard against assuming that they would have no problem sharing information or that their responses would confirm a priori ideas. Nelson, "Hands in the Chit'lins," 184. Focus groups were also conducted among other populations of people, including employees of a nonprofit organization, professional food organizations, and traditional-aged undergraduate students at a historically black university and majority white universities.

6. There is an existing body of scholarship that could be considered "classics" in food

studies. Among them are Douglas, "Deciphering a Meal"; Anderson, "Scholarship on Contemporary American Folk Foodways"; Brown and Mussell, *Ethnic and Regional Foodways*; Camp, *American Foodways*; Levenstein, *Revolution at the Table*; Root and deRochement, *Eating in America*; and Don Yoder, "Historical Sources for American Foodways Research." None of these early works includes discussions on African American food patterns in detail if at all.

7. Within the extensive body of historical literature on slavery and early African American diets, extensive focus on food includes Hilliard, *Hogmeat and Hoecake*, 37–69; and Taylor, *Eating, Drinking, and Visiting*, 83–91. For early studies that complicated African American consumption, see Genovese, *Roll, Jordan, Roll*, 540–49 and 599–612. Several early studies were produced in sociology examining the food habits of rural people, which often mentioned black people. But the work of anthropologist Tony Whitehead bears mentioning for his work on African Americans beyond the era of slavery; see his "In Search of Soul Food and Meaning."

8. The literature on African American foodways housed in archaeology is plentiful, but two authors especially emphasize the roles of African American women: Yentsch, *Chesapeake Family*, "Hot, Nourishing, and Culturally Potent," and "Gudgeons, Mullet, and Proud Pigs"; and Singleton, *Archaeology of Slavery*. Other useful studies include Deetz, *In Small Things Forgotten*; Joyner, *Down by the Riverside*; Singleton, *Archaeology of Slavery and Plantation Life*; McKee, "Food Supply and Plantation Social Order"; Ferguson, *Uncommon Ground*; and Warner, "Ham Hocks." For a related discussion pertaining to Caribbean blacks, see Pulsipher, "They Have Saturdays and Sundays to Feed Themselves." Tony Whitehead's early article "In Search of Soul Food and Meaning" is one of the few that looks beyond slavery.

9. Jessica Harris's work should be noted for the brief introductory histories she includes in her cookbooks. See, for example, *Iron Pots and Wooden Spoons* and *The Welcome Table*. Howard Paige's *Aspects of African American Foodways* provides a nice overview of African American cookery and is useful for its illustrative content and bibliography. Diane M. Spivey's book-length study on foods of the African Diaspora, *The Peppers, Cracklings, and Knots of Wool Cookbook*, offers an in-depth historical analysis. But for an extensive chronological bibliography of cookbooks from the African Diaspora, especially those contributed by African Americans, see Witt, *Black Hunger*, 221–28.

10. Tracy Poe has added to our understanding of food in Chicago in "The Origins of Soul Food in Black Urban Identity." See also Poe's dissertation, "Food, Culture, and Entrepreneurship." In literature there is the work of Zafar, "The Signifying Dish"; Toombs, "Confluence of Food and Identity"; Titus, "Groaning Tables and Spit in the Kettles"; and Witt, *Black Hunger*, "In Search of Our Mother's Cookbooks," and "What Ever Happened to Aunt Jemima?"

11. Interestingly, in 2004 another incident occurred involving Martin Luther King Jr.'s birthday. Northwestern University reportedly offered a special buffet in King's honor. The buffet included collard greens, corn bread, and fried chicken, among

other foods. Although at least one student protested, the university maintained that the cafeteria staff, many of whom are black, set the menu and probably saw this gesture as laudatory. For more on this subject, see Jacobson, "Short Subjects." Incidents of this nature occur often and are frequently unreported, attesting to the spurious nature of this subject even in the current historical moment.

12. In *Black Hunger*, 3–7, Witt provides a satisfying discussion of the Tiger Woods incident from the standpoint of race, nationality, and culture. Coverage by the popular press was extensive. See Harry Blauvelt, "Zoeller Says His Comments about Woods Made 'in Jest.'"

13. KFC's full-blown animated Colonel advertising campaign debuted in September 1998. This year was declared "Year of the Customer" and was credited with delivering a major "sales surge." According to the Tricon Global Restaurants, Inc., Web site, "the animated Colonel certainly broke through," showing awareness of KFC "up 45 percent." Tricon, which houses KFC, Pizza Hut, and Taco Bell franchises, is also the exclusive "quick-service restaurant sponsor" of the NCAA. See <http://www.triconglobal.com>.

14. *Black Enterprise* carried the cover story of how the hip-hop community had taken Wall Street by storm. As a global commodity, hip-hop has forced businesses to stand up and take notice of the billions of dollars it generates. Consequently, marketing strategies need to change in order to better peddle products to African American youth consumers. In a related discussion, the feature indicates commercials that have either been labeled "hits" or gotten "dissed" by black communities. The article mentions the same or a similar KFC ad that describes the Colonel as "rapping" and "doing the cabbage patch," a dance that had lost its popularity in black communities years before the ad. Accordingly, "some found the animated elderly southern white man, who strutted amid chants of 'Go Colonel, Go Colonel' somewhat offensive." For more on this discussion, see A. Hughes, "Hip-Hop Economy," 75. KFC continues to have problems with its advertising that concern black people even outside the United States. See Matthews, "Advertising." Eric Lott does an excellent job of complicating this kind of minstrelsy, arguing that the "commodification of the dispossessed" goes beyond white people borrowing black cultural materials. Instead, this process involves complex issues of racial desire even as whites "try on" blackness. See E. Lott, *Love and Theft*.

15. Cooper, *Voice from the South*, 31.

16. Collins discusses the meanings of "self-definition" and "self-valuation" as one of three key themes in understanding black feminist thought. She argues that while no single platform exists, black women, by virtue of some shared "commonalities of perception" and, I may add, experiences, have a common standpoint. Collins has been heavily criticized for her use of the term "unique standpoint" and rightfully so. However, her argument is tangible here, not as reductionist or essentialist, but for her application and delineation of themes related to gender, race, power, and stereotypes. See "Learning from the Outsider Within."

17. Paynter and McGuire, *Archaeology of Inequality*, 1.

18. Ibid.

19. Gates, *Signifying Monkey*, xxvi. Similar to Gates's definition of signifying, the word is used in this book to suggest times when someone is being "told off" or criticized in a subtle way. Although the "g" is used when discussing the concept, the letter is removed when spoken in the vernacular, as in "stop signifyin'."

20. I have made clear all along that this discussion focuses on the lives of black women. Yet, this could not take place without being aware of the ways that chicken affected and continues to affect the lives of all black people in one way or another.

21. Lott's account of cultural malpractice employs a more complex view of this assertion involving nineteenth- and twentieth-century black intellectuals and artists like Paul Laurence Dunbar. See T. Lott, "Black Vernacular Representation," 84–110.

CHAPTER ONE

1. Longstreet's *Georgia Scenes* employs the voices of two genteel narrators: Lyman Hall, who tells the tales of the men and therefore relays this incident, and Abraham Baldwin, who recounts the stories mostly involving women. Among other things, Longstreet was a historian of Georgian life during the early years of the Republic. With *Georgia Scenes* he sought to capture elements of the cultural milieu for readers of the future. He was quite dismayed, however, that his book was received with more humor than he had anticipated. Rachels, *Georgia Scenes Completed*, xlvii.

2. Longstreet, *Georgia Scenes*, 47–48.

3. Hawkers and street peddlers have been active in American society almost since its beginnings. Most accounts refer to young white men who peddled everything from clocks and beaver pelts to food. African Americans, like itinerant travelers, used this as an opportunity for economic advancement, albeit limited. Unless they were freed men and women, they most likely peddled locally. Richardson Wright, *Hawkers and Walkers in Early America*, 17–41; Burke, "Rolling Carts and Songs of Plenty."

4. Most of the Africans who arrived during the colonial period were disembarked along the eastern seaboard stretching from New England to South Carolina. Archaeological and historical research involving African Americans and their interactions with chicken in the marketplace can be found among records taken from these geographic areas. Understandably, this is a relatively problematic approach from a historian's point of view. However, this chapter is intended simply as an introduction to a larger cultural argument and not as a comprehensive overview of slavery. For an insightful critique of this approach, see Berlin, *Generations of Captivity*, wherein scholars are taken to task for engaging in a telescopic approach to historical inquiry.

5. There seems to be no one definitive source on this matter. And while conversations continue to ensue regarding the origins of the domestic chicken, the generally held view refers to it being a descendant of eastern India and Java. It is thought that

chickens were domesticated in 1400 B.C. This is partly because images of fowl can be found in the art of most every country, especially Egypt, Greece, and Rome. There is an unresolved debate in the extensive literature on chicken as to whether or not chickens preceded Columbus to the Americas. The sources listed here offer numerous perspectives: Aldrovandi, *Aldrovandi on Chickens*; De Reaumur, *Art of Hatching*; Toussaint-Samat, *History of Food*; Smith and Daniel, *Chicken Book*; A. Smith, *Oxford Encyclopedia of Food and Drink in America*; A. Davidson, *Oxford Companion to Food*; Katz and Weaver, *Encyclopedia of Food and Culture*; Kiple and Ornelas, *Cambridge World History of Food*; West and Zhou, "Did Chickens Go North?"; Gay and Gay, *Encyclopedia of North American Eating and Drinking*; Mariani, *Dictionary of American Food and Drink*. Not surprisingly, many poultry histories begin their discussions in the mid-nineteenth century rather than engage the question of origins. The James M. Gwin Poultry Collection at the National Agricultural Library in Beltsville, Maryland, is invaluable.

6. Because of their abundance, turkeys were undervalued and often could be had in the market for very little. In their study on the history and management of wild turkeys, Henry Mosby and Charles Handley make the point that contrary to popular belief, many Native Americans did not encourage the consumption of certain wild animals, turkey among them. These wild birds were more valued for ceremonial and adornment uses. See Mosby and Handley, *Wild Turkey in Virginia*, 9; and Baird, *History of North American Birds*. On American markets, see Kulikoff, "Households and Markets."

7. Streeter, *Papers*, 38. Numerous accounts by early European settlers exist to document the prevalence of wild fowl and domesticated poultry. Many of these early records were used to advertise and promote the benefits of the New World. Among those records wherein the presence of fowl is detailed are L. Wright, *Newes from the New-World*, 15; and Gray and Thompson, *History of Agriculture*, 19–20.

8. Byrd, *Secret Diary of William Byrd*, 480–91; C. Andrews, *Colonial Folkways*, 99–104. A Carter relative, Robert Beverly wrote *The History and Present State of Virginia*, which is considered the first extensive analysis on that state's social and political climate. Included in this discussion is a chapter on "Wild Fowl, and Hunted Game," 153–58.

9. Bolzius, "Johann Martin Bolzius Answers a Questionnaire," 251.

10. Even though Carter's plantations were among the wealthiest, he rarely mentioned poultry in his inventories. Elizabeth B. Pryor sums it up when she explains that even though travelers' accounts indicate the extreme presence of poultry at most plantation houses and farms, few planters mention the possession of chickens, turkeys, and geese. This is not surprising, however, since eighteenth-century chickens, in particular barnyard fowl, were so abundant that their value was underestimated and considered less of a luxury than beef, sheep, hogs, and horses. See Pryor, *Colonial Poultry Husbandry*, 8. For one perspective on African American husbandry in early American society, see Kulikoff, "Origins of Afro-American Society," 243.

11. The guinea fowl is spread throughout Africa, south of the Sahara. It is said to take

its name from the Guinea Coast, from where these birds were taken. They tend to flourish near people so as to have access to food and water but are wandering birds, seldom remaining in one place for long. Bement, *American Poulterer's Companion*, 226–29; Appleby, Mench, and Hughes, *Poultry Behavior and Welfare*, 11–12; Yentsch, *Chesapeake Family*, 196–215.

12. The literature on the internal and external trade of Africans is extensive and complex. And because that topic is outside the scope of this project, it will not be elaborated upon here. Among the numerous sources on this topic are Curtin, *Atlantic Slave Trade*; Inikori and Engerman, *Atlantic Slave Trade*; Eltis, Behrendt, Richardson, and Klein, *Trans-Atlantic Slave Trade* and "Volume and Structure of the Transatlantic Slave Trade"; and Walsh, "Chesapeake Slave Trade." A comprehensive overview can be found in Heuman and Walvin, *Slavery Reader*.

13. Scholars have noted the ways in which West African women employed their skills in trading foodstuffs in pre- and postcolonial Africa. Among these are Clark, *Onions Are My Husband*; House-Midamba and Ekechi, *African Market Women*; Sudarkasa, *Where Women Work*; Steady, *Black Woman Cross-Culturally*; J. Walker, "Trade and Markets"; Osirim, "State of Women"; and Yentsch, "Hot, Nourishing, and Culturally Potent." Nigerian author Buchi Emecheta in her fictional character Nnu Ego from *The Joys of Motherhood* provides a twentieth-century example. While her husband is away fighting in World War II, Nnu Ego struggles to feed her children. When possible, she sets up a display outside her home to sell cigarettes, matches, and kerosene. Her oldest child tends to the goods until there is a customer, then she is summoned to complete the sale. See *Joys of Motherhood*, chap. 9.

14. Considerable attention, for example, has been devoted to Mary and Anthony Johnson, an African couple who were brought to the Virginia colony sometime in the early seventeenth century. They were able to eventually secure their freedom, become landowners, and obtain a measure of wealth virtually unobtainable a generation later. For more on the Johnsons and other freed blacks who owned considerable livestock that was said to have been legally obtained, see Breen and Innes, *"Myne Owne Ground,"* 7–18, 81–83; K. Brown, *Good Wives*, 108–13; Woods, *Black Majority*, 30–31, 119–25; P. Morgan, *Slave Counterpoint*, 17–21; and L. Bennett, *Shaping of Black America*, 14–16, 24–27.

15. Archaeologist Lorena Walsh underscores this point in her work on Carter's Grove, a Virginia slave community. She explains that slaves parceled their small plot of land in such a way as to probably have a poultry yard. In addition to acquiring livestock, they also obtained household goods. See *From Calabar to Carter's Grove*, 171–203. In a personal conversation, another archaeologist, Joanne Bowen, said a substantial amount of work has been completed indicating "a continual presence" of chicken in and around slaves' sites. This suggests the consumption of chicken by slaves "at least if not more than in white sites." Other archaeologists who address African American food consumption in some way include Yentsch, "Hot, Nourishing, and Culturally Potent" and "Gudgeons, Mullet, and Proud Pigs"; McKee, "Food

Supply and Plantation Social Order"; Deetz, *In Small Things Forgotten*; Ferguson, *Uncommon Ground*; and Singleton, *Archaeology of Slavery*. For a related discussion pertaining to foodways of Caribbean blacks, see Pulsipher, "They Have Saturdays and Sundays to Feed Themselves"; and Heuman and Walvin, "Slave Economy and Material Culture," in *Slavery Reader*.

16. Berlin and Morgan, *Slaves' Economy*; McDonald, *Economy and Material Culture of Slaves*; P. Morgan, *Slave Counterpoint*, 318–76; Yentsch, *Chesapeake Family*, 239–55. For at least one nineteenth-century slave's account of participation in this economy, see Ball, *Fifty Years in Chains*, 203–32.

17. P. Morgan, *Slave Counterpoint*, 358–76; Yentsch, *Chesapeake Family*, 239–55; McDonald, *Economy and Material Culture of Slaves*. Along the Windward Islands it has been noted, however, that in addition to providing the slaves with more provisions, the increase encouraged slaves to remain loyal to the property and the planter. Marshall, "Provision Ground and Plantation Labour," 471. As previously stated, not all slaves were allowed to benefit from this kind of economic activity. The presence of flexible schedules was the case in the Tidewater areas of Virginia, the Low Country of Georgia and the Carolinas, and the slave provinces of the Caribbean like Jamaica and Montserrat where a task system was employed. See also Pulsipher, "They Have Saturdays and Sundays to Feed Themselves"; and Mintz, *Sweetness and Power*, 53–71, and *Tasting Food, Tasting Freedom*, 35–49.

18. Letter to Battaile Muse from James Mercer, Battaile Muse Papers, April 3, 1779, Duke University. Philip Morgan, who devotes a fair amount of attention to this element of the slave economy, argues that when it came to trading chickens, blacks seemed to dominate the market. Accepting this as true, it must be acknowledged, however, that this is still very much a small-scale phenomenon. Because more blacks at this time would have been responsible for the care of such birds, seeing women, and most likely children, in this capacity would not have been necessarily surprising. It simply might mean that those slaves were given more privileges than others. P. Morgan, *Slave Counterpoint*, 358–72.

19. Greene, *Diary of Colonel Landon Carter*, 2:1095. P. Morgan details the extent to which slaves raised, bartered, traded, and sold chickens and other poultry. He also makes the very important point that many Chesapeake slaves were able to engage in all areas of petty trade except tobacco. Planters like Thomas Jefferson believed that there had to be a way of "drawing a line" between one another's property. P. Morgan, *Slave Counterpoint*, 359–61.

20. Though it is uncertain who is referred to by the word "servants" mentioned in the earlier laws, by the end of the seventeenth century, slaves and "Negroes" are mentioned directly. Hening, *Statutes at Large*, 1:274 (1642); 1:412 (1655).

21. Pleasants, *Archives of Maryland*, 49:495.

22. Cooper and McCord, *Statutes at Large of South Carolina*, 3:487–88.

23. Former eighteenth-century slave Charity Duchess Quamino became a legendary pastry chef in Newport, Rhode Island. Also in Rhode Island, Emanuel and Mary Ber-

noon opened an oyster and ale house, supposedly started from Mary's bootlegging business. L. Bennett, *Shaping of Black America*, 288; Hine and Thompson, *Shining Thread of Hope*, 21–22; J. Walker, *History of Black Business*, 42; Spivey, *Peppers, Cracklings, and Knots of Wool Cookbook*, 227–28; and Schenone, *Thousand Years over a Hot Stove*, 69–71. Shane White explains that while most free blacks in New York performed domestic service and a variety of other skilled work, there was a noticeable presence of activity in the oyster and general vending trades. White, " 'We Dwell in Safety,' " 456, 459; R. Roberts, *House Servant's Directory*.

24. Fraunces Tavern received the federal registry designation, but it came too late to be included in B. Savage's *African American Historic Places*. For more on Fraunces and the folklore surrounding his daughter, see the children's book by J. Griffin, *Phoebe the Spy*; D. Freeman, *George Washington*, 199; Horner, "Sam Fraunces"; and Haskin, "Samuel Fraunces."

25. "Ministers of the South."

26. Gomez, *Exchanging our Country Marks*, 25, 27.

27. Agricultural manuals of the late eighteenth century encouraged farmers to include chickens among their livestock. But at this time, poultry husbandry was very lax, and the business of poultry trading was for the most part quite informal. Farmers took little inventory of their birds and were unconcerned about their care and breeding. Several factors, including food spoilage, disease, breeding, starvation, wandering, theft, and other issues, were of major concern for colonial inhabitants and prevented large-scale export. Unlike Britain and Europe, where cockfighting and importing and exporting exotic birds were in full swing, America had not yet developed formally the chicken and egg trade. In the colonial era, women and slaves were left in charge of these birds, which largely remained a cottage industry of selling small-scale surpluses at the market. For a detailed discussion of these issues in the seventeenth century, see Pryor, *Colonial Poultry Husbandry*, 8–34.

28. Bakhtin, *Rabelais and His World*, 7. Russian literary theorist Mikhail Bakhtin introduced the concept of carnival to describe the European medieval world and its ritualized festivities as spaces of cultural equality. Carnival is a place where hierarchical barriers are dissolved, people are unified, and the sacred and profane intersect. For a different perspective on carnival celebrations in North American ethnic communities, see Gutiérrez and Fabre, *Feasts and Celebrations*.

29. Bakhtin, *Rabelais and His World*, 94.

30. Ibid., 90–91.

31. In his discussion of "play" in *Georgia Scenes*, Ahmed Nimeiri makes the point that in the original publication of the text (1835), Longstreet was identified on the title page as "a Native Georgian." Nimeiri suggests but stops short of actually asserting that Ned and Longstreet are one and the same. Ned's character, more than any other in the book, best expresses Longstreet's "conservatism," and his peculiarities exist to "mask his closeness to his creator." "Play in Augustus Baldwin Longstreet's *Georgia Scenes*," 51 n. 4.

32. Longstreet, *Georgia Scenes*, 41.

33. Nimeiri quickly addresses and dismisses Jessica Wegmann's argument about the intersection of humor, sexism, and racism in *Georgia Scenes*. He believes that Wegmann has overexaggerated the importance of these issues. And where these concerns exist, the stories are "redeemed" by their wit and humor as well as by what they reveal "of the creative potential in the individual and the possibility of human community." In this argument Nimeiri completely overlooks the inherent existence of power in elements of play. Nimeiri, "Play in Augustus Baldwin Longstreet's *Georgia Scenes*," 44–46. For more on Wegmann's argument, see "'Playing in the Dark.'"

34. Jessica Wegmann makes the very convincing argument that most critics of *Georgia Scenes* overlook or ignore the overt racism and sexism that lurk in the shadows of the stories in favor of focusing on the humor and comedic aspects. She argues that throughout the tales, Longstreet infuses theories of paternalism and religiosity to sanction slavery, which is more evident in other writings by the author. "'Playing in the Dark,'" 13–14. To a greater or lesser degree, other Longstreet scholars, including Kimball King (*Augustus Baldwin Longstreet*, 84) and John Donald Wade (*Augustus Baldwin Longstreet*, 182), support this argument.

35. Isaac, "Ethnographic Method in History," 47.

36. Quoted in Olwell, "'Loose, Idle, and Disorderly,'" 101. See also Yentsch, *Chesapeake Family*, 242–43; and P. Morgan, *Slave Counterpoint*, 368–72.

37. Olwell, "'Loose, Idle, and Disorderly,'" 102.

38. McDonnell, "Money Knows No Master," 34–35.

39. Lichtenstein, "'That Disposition to Theft.'"

40. Ball, *Fifty Years in Chains*, 194.

41. F. Jones, *Days of Bondage*, 6.

42. Learning and Spicer, *Grants, Concessions, and Original Constitutions*, 357.

43. Cooper and McCord, *Statutes at Large of South Carolina*, vol. 3, ch. 670; York County (Virginia) Records, Order Book no. 4, 1774–84, p. 85.

44. Fithian, who would often forego dinner because of bad weather, must have been impressed by this display because food details are scarcely mentioned in his diary. His inclusion of this fact is probably more indicative of Fithian's desire to illustrate Robert Carter's ability to supply commodities and other foodstuffs to neighbors and friends as much as anything else. *Journal and Letters of Philip Vickers Fithian*, 42.

45. Quoted in Lebsock, *Free Women of Petersburg*, 93, 281 n. 13. In fact, free blacks were often accused of associating with slaves on equal terms not only to corrupt them by encouraging their escape but also to influence them to engage in uprisings and other serious crimes. One need only recall Nat Turner's influence over countless numbers of slaves in Southampton County, Virginia, in 1831, or Denmark Vesey's attempt in 1822, to know this was true.

46. A. C. Cole, "The Whipping Post," Works Progress Administration of Virginia, "Historical Inventory: Nottoway, April 10, 1936," Library of Virginia, Richmond.

47. Burton, *Memories of Childhood's Slavery Days*, 4.

48. In support of life's necessities as a motivation for taking great risks, Philip Schwarz writes in "Crime" that food and clothing were the primary articles stolen by slaves. For a complete account of the incident described by Ball, see *Fifty Years in Chains*, 109–21.

49. Washington, *Up From Slavery*, 31.

50. Lichtenstein, "'That Disposition to Theft,'" 415.

51. Ball, *Fifty Years in Chains*, ix–xi.

52. Douglass, *My Bondage and My Freedom*, 189 (original emphasis).

53. Stroyer's story sounds remarkably like one described in Charles Ball's narrative. See Stroyer, *Sketches of My Life*, 33; and Ball, *Fifty Years in Chains*, 109–21.

54. Perdue, Barden, and Phillips, *Weevils in the Wheat*, 116.

55. Rawick, *American Slaves*, 2:116–19.

56. J. Roberts, *From Trickster to Badman*, 33. Lawrence Levine also establishes connections between the African American trickster and the acquisition of food. See "The Slave as Trickster" in *Black Culture*, 121–33.

57. "Important Decision [about Negro Cookshops]." W. Sherman Savage makes the point that in contrast to the South, where slaves were deprived of a voice in court proceedings, those in the West were able to testify on their own behalf. See W. Savage, "Slavery in the West," 21.

58. Bremer was said to be disappointed with America, particularly with the institution of slavery, despite the often favorable impressions she reported regarding the living conditions of some slaves. *Homes of the New World*, 1:294–97.

59. Olmstead, *Journey in the Back Country*, 54.

60. As John T. Edge notes in his compendium on chicken as one of America's long-standing icons, Gordonsville is among many places that witnessed this kind of entrepreneurial activity. He notes the story of Julia Brown of Corinth, Mississippi, and residents of Philadelphia. There are several tales of women throughout Virginia and probably many more at other crossroads towns throughout the United States. *Fried Chicken*, 97–103. There is a wonderful 1860 etching by Sir Henry Wentworth Acland of a black woman, head tilted back, large tray in hand, bearing rolls and chicken legs in a Richmond, Virginia, train station. See Yentsch, *Chesapeake Family*, 243; and Schenone, *Thousand Years over a Hot Stove*, 70. LuAnn Jones has written an excellent account of poultry's role in the lives of southern farmwomen in *Mama Learned Us to Work*.

61. "Waiter Carrier," B7. Although I was unsuccessful in interviewing any of the direct descendants of the waiter carriers, John T. Edge managed an interview with Pete Avery, a descendant of vendor Elsie Swift, prior to his death. See *Fried Chicken*, 99–101.

62. "Waiter Carrier," B7. For information on Hattie Edwards, see Loving, "Fried Chicken, Ham." Phone interviews conducted with two members of the Orange County African American Historical Association—Rebecca Coleman and Gloria

Gilmore—confirmed that most of what was known about the legacy of these women can be gleaned from the two articles on Winston and Edwards. Coleman and Gilmore answered what they could about the black communities of Gordonsville but shared that most of the history of the waiter carriers died along with family members. Gilmore confirmed that "Hattie's Inn" was located on Cobb Street, an area still inhabited primarily by blacks. She also said that "Ms. Hattie" sold sodas, candies, cakes, and pies. She, however, was not allowed to frequent the establishment because her parents believed it was a "hangout" for adults.

63. During her interview, Winston was asked to confirm or deny a legend that a salesman, who was a regular customer of the women, carved his initials into a chicken leg bone. The customer claimed a few weeks later that he was eating another leg of chicken and noticed his initials were also on that bone. Of course, this scenario could not have happened, but the salesman seemed to be implying that initials were being carved into bones to exaggerate the sales and reputation of the vendors. "Waiter Carrier," B7.

64. Loving, "Fried Chicken," 2.

65. The 1910 and 1920 censuses provide answers to some of these questions. For example, there was at least one other woman who indicated "chicken vendor" as her occupation and others who listed "snack vendor." Still others appear to have owned homes, and many were widowed or single. Edge, *Fried Chicken*, provides information from Peter Avery on how the chicken was prepared, but many more critical questions remain unanswered.

66. Local politics has also played a role in making an ironic statement. The plaque rests at the Exchange Hotel, a site used as a Confederate hospital during the Civil War. According to sources in the county, this placement was a source of contention and contestation by board members of the museum. However, the advantages to tourism were stressed and placement ultimately granted. Tourism also played a role in initially getting the plaque. The dedication was held during the second annual "Fried Chicken Festival," a celebration that has caused ire among some townspeople. A few who recall the periods of racial propaganda are resistant to having these women's lives "reduced" to simply "chicken vendors"—the terminology often used on literature advertising the women (though they are celebrated as entrepreneurs). The extent to which black residents were involved in the initial planning of this festival also remains a question. And lastly, racial discord still prevails. Some white residents were unhappy about the recognition given to the waiter carriers. Nonetheless, memories of African American female entrepreneurship in Gordonsville now share a home with a museum dedicated to a pivotal decisive battle of the Civil War.

67. Hodder, "Interpretation of Documents," 343.

68. As previously discussed, one of these meanings was theft. Bella Winston reminds us, however, that whites stole as well. One newspaper article about the waiter carriers details a story of an "unSouthern gesture" carried out by a harried white male

passenger. Apparently, the passenger snatched an entire platter of food from one of the carriers just as the train was pulling out of the station. The townspeople were outraged until the thief, obviously out of regret, disembarked at the next station and sent a ten-dollar bill back to cover the cost of the food and the platter. Evans, "Chicken Legs and the Hotel," 22.

CHAPTER TWO

1. Shortly after the publication of *Roots*, it was found that several passages had been copied from Harold Courlander's *The African*.
2. Eric Lott explains that in the early nineteenth century, the term "coon" referred to a white rural person or an opportunist. It was not until the 1820s that the word began to take on racial connotations associated with a blackface minstrel character. But even then the stereotype was not necessarily widespread. Modern racist parlance, Lott argues, is the product of late-nineteenth-century popular culture images that identified blacks with the face and mannerisms of raccoons. Marlon Riggs's documentary *Ethnic Notions* offers a compelling look at this character and its evolution in American popular culture and the social politics of the post-Reconstruction era. *Ethnic Notions*, directed by Marlon Riggs; E. Lott, *Love and Theft*, 23, and "Coon."
3. It is very likely that Chicken George is wholly fictional. Some African American men may indeed have been cock handlers, but very little has been written to suggest this to a degree of certainty. In some small way this lack of information might be related to the fact that cockfighting is ancient to most every country—Asia, India, Europe—besides Africa. Charles Ball mentions a cockfight attended by the sons of a slave owner, but there is no other direct reference. *Fifty Years in Chains*, 61. Page Smith and Charles Daniel mention two men known as "Uncle Billy Rodgers" and "Uncle Pete" and suggest that Uncle Billy "was probably a black man." They do not speculate upon the race of Uncle Pete, nor do they indicate what led to their conclusions about race. They later refer to a man named "Nigger Jackson," but again do not indicate a source. Smith and Daniel, *Chicken Book*, 103. Despite this lack of historical information, there is some sporadic evidence that blacks at least attended, even if they did not train for, cockfights.
4. Haley, *Roots*, 479. All subsequent page numbers from this work are given in the text.
5. Haley describes hackfighting as an event where poor whites and blacks—slave and free—could make small wagers ranging from twenty-five cents to as much as twenty dollars (513). It is not clear whether Haley made up this definition to distinguish this type of gambling from that of the wealthy who would wager heavily with tobacco, property, and money. This arena was also where men could flaunt their manliness, the size of one's estate notwithstanding, and free blacks as well as the Irish were readily welcomed in some parts of the United States. See K. Brown, *Good Wives*, 278; and Smith and Daniel, *Chicken Book*, 105. Cockfighting among the wealthy is seldom mentioned in studies of Virginia gentry. However, it is made clear that George Washington, Abraham Lincoln, and Andrew Jackson were heavily

involved in the sport. Landon Carter, Robert Beverly, and especially William Byrd were among the heaviest gamblers when it came to cards, dice, and horse racing. Breen, "Horses and Gentleman," 248; Isaac, *Transformation of Virginia*; Gorn, "'Gouge and Bite.'"

6. Berlin, *Slaves without Masters*, 187, 189.

7. Geertz's work marks a turning point in cockfighting scholarship. It is the essay from which most all other writing on this subject derives. That being said, Geertz interpreted the cockfight exclusively in terms of Balinese culture. Nonetheless, the connection between "maleness" or male virility and cockfighting is evident in most every other culture. See Geertz, "Deep Play," 6. Ondina Fachel Leal is in the minority when she contends that equating cocks to penises is an "oversimplification specific to English-speaking people." She maintains that among the Portuguese or Spanish-speaking people, this homonym does not exist. See "The Gaucho Cockfight in Porto Alegre, Brazil," 213. Leal's essay is among those compiled in Alan Dundes' *The Cockfight*. In it are several perspectives—some descriptive, others interpretive—and most all of them compare cocks to penises or see maleness as evident in dress, language, and behavior. See, for example, essays by Wollan (esp. 83); Cook (esp. 237); and Dundes. See also Smith and Daniel, *Chicken Book*, 51–55; and Cobb, "Chickenfighting."

8. Smith and Daniel, *Chicken Book*, 55. Folklorist and quilt researcher Gladys-Marie Fry comments that the sun and the resurrection (symbolized by the chicken) were consistently used, although disguised, in the quilting patterns made by slaves. These elements were masked primarily when quilters were forced to work within a Euro-American tradition. Animals and elements of African cosmology like the sun were frequent motifs of slave quilters. See *Stitched from the Soul*, 7.

9. "Not 'All Quiet along the Lines.'"

10. J. Jones makes this argument in *Labor of Love*, 58.

11. Quoted in L. Bennett, *Shaping of Black America*, 201.

12. For a fuller discussion of the ways in which popular images are historically situated in politics, see Kenneth W. Goings's excellent analysis in *Mammy and Uncle Mose*. E. Lott, *Love and Theft*, points to the effects of black expressive culture (particularly music, dance, and humor) upon the psyches of the northern white working class. In the process of imitating blacks and their expressions, white males seized control over the troubling figure of black sexuality and black maleness as a whole.

13. Mercer, "Reading Racial Fetishism," 184.

14. Barbara Fields argues that ideologies are the necessary language through which people understand their day-to-day reality. By default, then, ideologies must "be constantly created and verified in social life; if it is not it dies." The argument of Eric Hobsbawn, that in moments of intense and "rapid [societal] transformation" new traditions are invented to replace old ones, thereby establishing necessary continuities with the past, is also relevant for this discussion. Both of these observations can be found quoted in Goings, *Mammy and Uncle Mose*, 7–8.

15. Douglass, "A Tribute to the Negro."

16. Du Bois quoted in Gates, "Black Person in Art," 3.

17. E. Lott, *Love and Theft*, 134.

18. Goings, *Mammy and Uncle Mose*, 44. Lott, *Love and Theft*, 131–35, offers a compelling discussion of the "dandy" as the image relates to issues of minstrelsy, abolition, and class. Bogle, *Toms, Coons, Mulattoes, Mammies, and Bucks*, 7–9, also provides a succinct context for the coon image, putting the image in dialogue not only with the pickanniny, tragic mulatto, and mammy but also within the coon genre itself to comprise the triumvirate of Rastus, Stepin Fetchit, and Uncle Remus. To further make this connection, Bogle points to some of the chicken films of this genre: *How Rastus Got His Turkey* (c. 1910) and *Rastus and Chicken* and *Chicken Thief*, both of which appeared in the early twentieth century.

19. I rely here on Barthes's semiotic method of analysis found in "Rhetoric of the Image." His essays on "Steak and Chips" as well as "Ornamental Crockery" are equally instructive. See Barthes, *Mythologies*, 62–64 and 78–80.

20. Bhabha references Fanon's use of the notion "epidermal schema" as well as the discussion of common knowledge in "Other Question," 376. See also Fanon, *Black Skin*, 112.

21. For a compressed view of the therapeutic ethos of the nineteenth century, see Lears, "From Salvation to Self-Realization." For a more extensive examination of this topic, see Lears, *No Place of Grace*. Essentially, he argues that with the increasing industrial transformations of the nineteenth century, political wagers and other political factors influenced the changes in the market economy. These changes fostered an increased sense of fragmentation and a loss of the autonomous self (the "self-made man"); people felt their lives spiraling out of control. Religiosity was being questioned, resulting in a loss of moral stability, while all around them was the injunction to produce more goods and commodities. This sense of "over-pressure" or "anxious anxiety," as Lears terms it, actually led some people to take to their beds with "nervous prostration."

22. One of the signature texts on trade cards in America is Robert Jay's *The Trade Card in Nineteenth-Century America*. For a more racialized gendered interpretation, see Mehaffy, "Advertising Race/Raceing Advertising"; and McClintock, "Soft Soaping Empire."

23. Sontag, "Image World," 82.

24. In contrast to free blacks like Frederick Douglass who could choose how they wanted to be captured in still life and thus perceived by their audience, newly freed blacks and even many slaves were subject to the white photographer's gaze. This gaze was extended to include those beyond America's shores because many of the captions written on the front of the stereographs were translated into additional languages. For a brief discussion of this phenomenon and an interpretation of Douglass as subject of the camera, see Wells, "Visual History." For additional analy-

sis on African Americans in early photographs, see Willis, *Picturing Us*; and Natanson, "From Sophie's Ally to the White House" and *Black Image in the New Deal*.

25. See the same illustration but with a different form and caption in Lemons, "Black
Stereotypes," 112.

26. Grant McCracken's discussion is a good one on the ways in which consumer goods
helped to preserve hopes and ideals during the Victorian era. "Evocative Power of
Things," 104.

27. Ibid., 110.

28. Here the linguistic message serves in the capacity of a "relay," which is a snatch
of dialogue that really advances the action of the image. Barthes, "Rhetoric of the
Image," 38.

29. Many of these photographs were used as forms of entertainment. They were often
displayed in people's homes, collected, mailed, or given as gifts. I obtained the
stereographs used in this book from the on-line auctioneer eBay where they are a
part of the Black Americana genre. These images were commercially produced for
the entertainment and amusement of whites almost a century ago, but today they
are advertised as if for much the same purpose. Advertisements for various artifacts reflecting crude, debasing, and otherwise destructive imagery are considered
"adorable" and "cute." The description for the postcard featuring a chicken pulling
on a little boy's penis read, "You are bidding on an *adorable* postcard featuring
a chicken confronting a little black boy!" Another advertisement declared, "THE
FUNNIEST NEGRO PRINT YET! CURIOUS?" (original emphasis). The irony here is
that these images and their accompanying selling points are problematic precisely
because they are believed to be, and in some instances are marketed as, cute. One
auctioneer offered a disclaimer indicating, "Thankfully, these are from a bygone
era and represent the mores of a culture that existed nearly a century ago." While
this is true, the prevalence of the previous types of commercial announcements
should leave us wondering if we are as far removed from that "bygone era" as we
would like to believe. In 2001, eBay banned the sale of Nazi and other hate-related
material from its site, but no mention was made of it curbing the ways in which
these materials are advertised.

30. Baldwin, "On the Verso." A number of postcards in my personal collection are blank
because of their use as memorabilia. Others were purchased specifically for the
information contained on the verso. In some instances the messages are clearly
derogatory; other messages reflect that they are personally representative or were
used merely as a tool of communication.

31. Dunbar collaborated with musician and composer Will Marion Cook to write "Who
Dat Say Chicken in Dis Crowd." The two wrote all of the songs and the libretto in
one ten-hour session. The protest waged by Cook's mother is a direct reflection
upon the quandary in which Dunbar found himself and which plagued him until
his death. A lot has been written on the complexity of Dunbar's works; among them

are Candela, "'We Wear the Mask,'" 60–61; Gates, *Signifying Monkey*, 176–77; and D. Turner, "Paul Laurence Dunbar."

32. Goings, *Mammy and Uncle Mose*, 20.

33. Johnson, *Along This Way*, 152–53.

34. Taking Gayle's interpretation of Dunbar's reactions as true, one can believe that Dunbar was unhappy over the performance of his songs. This lends itself to the possibility that Dunbar was concerned over the *ways* that the songs were interpreted. James Dorman also provides a thorough discussion on the "coon song" phenomenon but does not offer any discussion of irony or opposition in "Shaping the Popular Image of Post-Reconstruction American Blacks."

35. In his biographical sketch of Dunbar, Gayle says that Dunbar "despaired" over his contributions to *Clorindy*, vowing never again to write such lyrics. See *Oak and Ivy*, 88. This might account for Darwin Turner's remarks that Dunbar was intolerant of behaviors he deemed silly and ignorant. "Paul Laurence Dunbar," 13. Several other black artists and musicians would later be embarrassed by the contributions they made toward perpetuating the coon image. Ernest Hogan's song "All Coons Look Alike to Me" is said to be the reason why the genre has its nickname. It is claimed that on his deathbed, he lamented having ever written the song. Morgan and Barlow, *From Cakewalk to Concert Halls*, 86.

36. For example, Marva Griffin Carter considers Dunbar's "A Negro Love Song" as something of an ethnographic poem. Carter argues that embedded in the song and its call-and-response rhythms are oppositional phrases, which assisted Cook and Dunbar in achieving their goal of "removing the minstrel mask." She applies this analysis to many of Dunbar's lyrics and several future collaborations between the two artists, but she stops short at considering how "Who Dat Say Chicken in Dis Crowd" operates within the same oppositional mode. See "Removing the 'Minstrel Mask.'"

37. Quoted in Carter, "Removing the 'Minstrel Mask,'" 207.

38. Countless scholars have written about lynching as a major form of social control during the late nineteenth century and well into the twentieth. It has been considered one of three major catalysts for African Americans leaving the South in droves. Although lynching was most often attributed to white female rape, Ida B. Wells-Barnett and other anti-lynching advocates demonstrated that the threat was more political and economic than anything else. Wells-Barnett, *On Lynchings*.

39. Dunbar, *The Heart of Happy Hollow*, mentioned in D. Turner, "Paul Laurence Dunbar," 12. Dunbar also wrote the poem "The Haunted Oak" in which a tree despairs over the lynching that has occurred upon it.

40. Carter argues that both Cook and Dunbar were making this attempt in the creation of *Clorindy* as well as several of their other musical collaborations.

41. D. Turner, "Paul Laurence Dunbar," 3, 7.

42. Cunningham, *Paul Laurence Dunbar and His Song*, 144, wages this argument around these and other lines extracted from Dunbar's poem "We Wear the Mask."

43. Dunbar was born in Ohio to parents who had been slaves. But Dunbar had no real experience with the life of the enslaved man or woman from the deep South or the mid-South.

44. Gayle, *Oak and Ivy*, 144.

45. Carter, "Removing the 'Minstrel Mask,'" 209.

46. Ibid., 208–9. For a more detailed discussion of the song's origins, see Cunningham, *Paul Laurence Dunbar and His Song*. Also see Southern, *Readings in Black American Music*, 217–23.

47. "Pork Chops and Chicken."

48. Kytle, *Willie Mae*, 121.

49. Annie Mullins, interview by author, April 1996.

50. This fondness for Thomas Dorsey was registered in "Colored Gentlemen of Philadelphia." In his landmark study, *The Philadelphia Negro*, 119, Du Bois discusses not only Dorsey but also his predecessors, Henry Jones and Henry Minton, who comprised the triumvirate band of caterers. Cookshops and other illegal food stops are frequently mentioned in the black newspapers of Richmond, Virginia, especially when they were raided. Juliet Walker discusses caterers and cookshops in *History of Black Business*, 83–126.

51. I was initially made aware of The Coon Chicken Inn from Goings's *Mammy and Uncle Mose*. Information about the restaurant can be found at <http://members.aol.com/mlgcci/mlgcci.htm>, which claims to have been established by Graham's grandchildren, who remain anonymous. In addition to offering a racial disclaimer for the presence of the Web site, the other primary purposes are to explain the history of the restaurant and to caution buyers of CCI memorabilia against purchasing expensive replicas. In an e-mail correspondence in August 2001 with one of the grandsons (Scott), I was informed that Graham's memoirs provide the primary source of information for the site. However, there is no mention in the memoirs of the logo's origins. Another site exists, <http://www.coonchickeninn.com>, but primarily for informational purposes.

52. Roy Hawkins, interview by author, August 1, 2001.

53. Ibid.

54. My uncle, a longtime short-order cook, also gave me this advice, saying that a customer never knows what the cook (or waiter for that matter) will do to their food. A former Sunday school teacher, Mr. A——, shared the story of how once he was harassed by a customer when working at a "dive" in New Jersey. The man ordered a chicken sandwich. In those days, a good sandwich consisted of a piece of fried chicken between two slices of white bread. As the story goes, the chicken looked nice and fried on the outside, at which Mr. A—— said, "Have you ever bitten into a piece of half-cooked chicken?" Clearly, that was enough to turn my own attention away from fried chicken for a long time. For more about Roy Hawkins's experience, see Foster, "Black Pioneers Blazed Their Own Utah Trails."

55. Hawkins interview.

56. Ibid.

57. Ibid.

58. The photographs and captions referred to are a part of the Farm Security Administration/Office of War Information Photograph Collection housed at the Library of Congress, Division of Prints and Photographs. Individual images are identified in the notes by call number. Geertz, "'Thick Description,'" 3–30.

59. The notion that objects have a cultural biography tends to relate to the history of its ownership and how it passes from hand to hand. This approach asks about the status of an object as it moves from place to place and person to person. Examining these sociological contexts enables a better reading of how people relate to objects and how those objects carry various meanings depending upon their contexts. See Appadurai, *Social Life of Things*, 4–5, and Kopytoff, "Cultural Biography of Things," 64–94. Barbara G. Carson also provides a perspective on this method in her article "Interpreting History through Objects," 132.

60. Parren, "Job Ahead," 398; "Food for Defense Poster," 1941, Farm Security Administration/Office of War Information Photograph Collection, available at <http://lcweb2.loc.gov/cgi-bin/query/D?fsaall:6:./temp/~ammem_AXKZ::> (USF345-007702-ZA-A).

61. Turkeys and chickens were the only foods not rationed during World War II, so the war was, to some extent, beneficial to the poultry industry. Because the Eastern Shore of Maryland and Virginia (Delmarva area) dominated the commercial broiler industry at this time, the federal government, through the War Food Administration, placed a freeze on the chicken supply from other vendors. The government had sole access to the chickens from this region. With the close of the war, however, in 1946, the government essentially dealt wrongly with those in the Delmarva area because they abruptly canceled their contracts for chickens. This, coupled with a greater demand for beef in the postwar era, effected a severe economic blow. Gordy, "Broilers," 390–91; Nybroten, *Consumer Preferences for Poultry Meat*, 5; Sawyer, *Agribusiness Poultry Industry*.

62. U.S. Department of Agriculture pamphlet, image no. BN11007X, National Archives and Records Administration, Still Pictures Division, Federal Works Agency, Office of Information.

63. The FSA photographs are part of the most well known but highly underutilized collections (with the exception of a few popular photos). Its images depict the living and social conditions of Americans in suburban, urban, and rural areas during the Depression and World War II. Rexford Tugwell initiated this massive collection in order to document loans to farmers provided by the Resettlement Administration of the U.S. Department of Agriculture. He appointed Roy Stryker to direct the project. Photographers like Dorothea Lange, Walker Evans, Marion Post Wolcott, and Gordon Parks were major contributors. Quite a bit has been written on the photographs, including the finding aide *America, 1935–1946*; Fleischhauer and

Brannan, *Documenting America, 1935–1943*; and Collier and Collier, *Visual Anthropology*.

64. Richard Doud, "Interview with John Collier."

65. Ibid.

66. In his interview, Collier says that he availed himself of the suggestion made by cataloger Paul Vanderbilt to put his photographs together to form a complete experience. Organized by LOT number or call number, the photographs are designed to stay together in order to convey a particular interpretation conceived by the photographer. When one considers the sequence of photographs that makes up this story, LC-USF34-080259 to LC-USF34-080361, it is entirely possible to believe that this was Collier's intention.

67. Collier, Craig Field Cook (LC-USF34-080317-E).

68. The image of the heavyset, bandanna-wearing black woman with a spatula or some other cooking implement overwhelmingly dominated southern literature and advertisements (see chap. 3 of this study). Venerable classics like Harriet Beecher Stowe's *Uncle Tom's Cabin* and Margaret Mitchell's *Gone with the Wind* feature black women as this kind of illustrative cook.

69. Collier, Craig Field Cook (LC-USF34-080311-D). This caption leads me to question the sequence of these events. Based on this statement, these preparations were made in a single day. However, the ways in which the photographs are numbered suggests that these events must have occurred over a longer period of time. For example, in one photograph a cook is loading up with FSA chickens. In the previous photograph, a cook is cleaning and preparing the chicken to be floured. It is conceivable that some of the photographs were numbered incorrectly. There are enough, in fact, to alter slightly the narrative.

70. Titus, "Groaning Tables and Spit in the Kettles," 15. There are excellent examples of how food is a marker of social segregation, including the incidents at the Woolworth's lunch counter in Greensboro, North Carolina. For more information about this topic, see Yeingst and Bunch, "Curating the Recent Past."

71. The photos taken by Jack Delano affirm that there were some African American FSA farmers. Of those he photographed in Woodville, Georgia (Greene County), none are shown actually preparing their goods for sale. Most of these photographs show the farmers waiting for an FSA meeting to begin. Delano, "At a Meeting of Negro FSA Borrowers" (Farm Security Administration/Office of War Information Photograph Collection, LC-USF34-044163-D to LC-USF34-044200-D).

72. Richard Allen Burns makes this point in his brief article "Foodways in the Military." He recalls the reservations that he had about joining the U.S. Marine Corps only to learn that he had been assigned the "rather effeminate job" of field cook. Like Burns in 1969, there were some white men assigned to the mess hall in the 1940s at Craig Field. Some of these men can be seen in Collier's photographs but not to the extent that the African American cooks are featured. See Burns, "Foodways in

the Military," 22; Collier, "Private Sykes, Assistant Mess Sergeant" (see figure 2.21); and Dickson, *Chow*.

CHAPTER THREE

1. The image of the asexual, overweight, bandanna-clad black woman was as frequent as the hypersexual black woman. Studies that have examined Aunt Jemima from a feminist point of view have overlooked the extent to which the kinds of foods that are produced speak volumes about gender division of labor, dominant ideologies about black people and food, and food and power. A notable exception to this observation is Manring, *Slave in a Box*, 131–35.

2. Chickens had to be eaten right away because there was little means of refrigeration other than an icehouse or access to a well or a stream. Salt was expensive and not a ready option. Hume, *Food*, 10–26.

3. J. Bennett, *Poultry Book*, 14–15. Although treatises attested to the serious nature of poultry breeding, hatching, and raising, a lot of fun was had. Caleb N. Bement, for example, wrote *The American Poultry Book* under the pseudonym Micajah R. Cock. After his first book was positively received, he revealed his true identity in *American Poulterer's Companion*. George P. Burnham, another poultry man, wrote a fanciful account of the craze in *The History of Hen Fever*. More contemporary sources include, among others, Hanke, Skinner, and Florea, *American Poultry History*; Smith and Daniel, *Chicken Book*, 207; and Gordon, "Chicken Story."

4. J. Bennett, *Poultry Book*, 13. Continued use of the phrase "semi-luxury" might be attributed to historians like Sam Hilliard, who uses it in his seminal food study but provides no context or reference for his statement. *Hogmeat and Hoecake*, 46. Other scholars have repeated the phrase, usually referring to Hilliard. See, for example, S. Smith, "Food for Thought," 210. McMahon puts forth a similar contradictory argument in "Comfortable Subsistence," 34–35. Moreover, data can be found to contradict these experiences. In particular are Sitton, *Harder Than Hardscrabble*; Adams, *Transformation of Rural Life*; L. Jones, *Mama Learned Us to Work*; L. Jones, Oral History of Southern Agriculture at the National Museum of American History, Smithsonian Institution, Washington, D.C.; and the primary sources found in the James M. Gwin Poultry Collection and the American Poultry Historical Society Collection, both at the National Agricultural Library, Beltsville, Maryland.

5. Jaspar, "Marketing," 360–63. The broiler industry as it is known today is said to have started in Ocean View, Delaware, by Wilmer Steele in the 1920s. Even though it was still in its infancy, in the 1930s over half the total number of broilers in the United States produced commercially were raised on the Eastern Shore of Maryland, Virginia, and particularly Delaware, which badly needed the new enterprise. The late 1940s witnessed an almost complete overhaul of the poultry industry with most references to chicken and poultry meaning the modern broiler, not farm-raised chicken. By 1952 commercial broilers became the primary source of farm

income. Gordy, "Broilers," 377; Termohlen, Kinghorne, Warren, and Radabaugh, "Economic Survey of the Commercial Broiler Industry," 3.

6. In a personal e-mail (February 23, 2005), Gregory Martin, Penn State Cooperative Extension, offered a similar explanation for the sale of surplus chicken and eggs.

7. Evans, *Extension Work among Negroes*, 11–12. Black farmers who could afford chickens likely had a small crop because they were inexpensive to care for and they could roost anywhere and eat offal or other remains. Black farm agents were first appointed in 1905 in cooperation with Tuskegee Institute to teach farmers how to cultivate and maintain crops and livestock. Thomas Monroe Campbell, African American field agent for the extension service, offers a firsthand account in *The Movable School Goes to the Negro Farmer*. Both LuAnn Jones and Carmen Harris point out in their studies of home extension agents that with instruction came reform and regulation. African American women created roadside markets in the wake of limitation and regulation. L. Jones, *Mama Learned Us to Work*, 62–67. Harris offers similar perspectives in her extensive survey of African American extension agents in South Carolina in " 'A Ray of Hope for Liberation.' " In personal correspondence in May 2005, Harris also shared information on Charles "Chicken" Davis, considered the first black poultry man and extension poultry specialist.

8. Hamilton and McGee, *Economic and Social Status*, 21–24. Black farmer discussion groups were held to address pertinent issues like food, clothing, shelter, and education for the children. One subject that emerged as a topic of discussion was poultry raising, a testament to its importance in the lives of African American farmers in the 1930s. Chambers, *Minutes*, 19.

9. All informants' names have been changed at their request. Ruby Baker, interview by author, March 24, 1996.

10. Ibid.

11. Logan, *Motherwit*, 7, 6.

12. Rice, *He Included Me*, 17. All subsequent page numbers from this work are given in the text.

13. Angela Y. Davis makes the observation that music provides a window for us to see how the condition of slavery made black women and men beholden to one another in order to survive. However, with the abolition of slavery, a different kind of individualism was forged that the blues exemplifies and allows for. Other cultural artifacts such as food provide a similar window in that while some black women chose to share foods as part of their cultural and community work, others privileged their families, which were equally important to community survival. A. Davis, *Blues Legacy and Black Feminism*, 3–5.

14. Strother, "Virginia Illustrated," 176–77.

15. For works detailing stereotypes in aspects of African American material culture, see Joyner, "Soul Food"; and Lemons, "Black Stereotypes." On the ways African Americans and other darker races of people have been portrayed beyond the West,

see Pieterse, *White on Black*. For an overview on African American memorabilia and its production and consumption, see Buster, *Art and History of Black Memorabilia*; Goings, *Mammy and Uncle Mose*; and P. Turner, *Ceramic Uncles and Celluloid Mammies*. Deborah Willis's work illustrates the ways black people have created and portrayed themselves in photography, while Michael Harris's stunning array of imagery informs our understanding of African American experiences through visual representations. See Willis, *Picturing Us*, and Willis-Kennedy, *Reflections in Black*; and M. Harris, *Colored Pictures*.

16. It was not uncommon for African Americans to value greatly the accolades they received from white people. Verbal affirmations, just like objects, that were handed down from employers to domestics went far toward giving some black people a sense of importance and validation.

17. This particular Wesson oil and Snowdrift ad was also found in the December 1924 issue of *Good Housekeeping*, but it was limited to one page. In *Ladies' Home Journal*, this ad covered two pages, with most of the first page bearing the image of Sarah, Sarah's attempt to explain how she uses the oil in a painful parody of southern dialect, and Mrs. Clark's statement of proof. Page 2 of the layout is dedicated primarily to further trying to persuade its mostly middle-class white readership to try this new cooking oil. In her book *Inarticulate Longings*, Jennifer Scanlon offers a concise analysis of African American women in the advertisements of *Ladies' Home Journal* and a thorough cultural history of the magazine. For a viewpoint on African American magazines, see Rooks, *Ladies' Pages*.

18. Bobo, *Black Feminist Cultural Criticism*, xvii.

19. Collins, *Black Feminist Thought*, 106–7.

20. Counihan, "Female Identity," 52.

21. Richard Wright, *12 Million Black Voices*, 110, 114. Discarded fruits and vegetables not only served as ingredients for meals but also served for fruit pies and other delicacies—often sold to those who initially discarded them. In her family memoir, Kathryn Morgan mentions how her grandmother would scour the garbage of restaurants and well-to-do whites, picking out spotted fruit that had been thrown away. She would remove the spots and make preserves and then sell them. She also purchased rag barrels and made quilts to sell. See K. Morgan, *Children of Strangers*, 22–23.

22. W. E. B. Du Bois and Augustus Granville Dill included this comment in their multi-state social study, *Morals and Manners among Negro Americans*, conducted for Atlanta University on the state of "Negro Problems."

23. Historian Deborah Gray White explains that middle-class black clubwomen were often "their own best argument" in reflecting the goals of race and black female advancement. See *Too Heavy a Load*, 88; and Nieves, "'We Gave Our Hearts and Lives to It.'" On black working-class people as a social problem, refer to Locke, *The New Negro*.

24. C. Brown, "Negro and the Social Graces." In "Beating the Biscuits in Appalachia,"

Elizabeth Engelhardt provides an interesting analysis of white middle-class reformers and their perspectives on corn bread as opposed to biscuits.

25. Most of Brown's biographers have noted that it is impossible to discuss the full light of her educational achievements without intertwining a discussion of her adult life and the formation and development of Palmer Memorial Institute. However, that discussion is outside the scope of this project, which seeks primarily to home in on Brown's emphasis on social graces and etiquette and the importance of those standards to etiquette within the black community. For more information on Brown's life and accomplishments at Palmer Memorial Institute and within the black community, see two full-length biographies: Wadelington and Knapp, *Charlotte Hawkins Brown and Palmer Memorial Institute*; and Marteena, *The Lengthening Shadow of a Woman*. In addition to entries in dictionaries and encyclopedias on Brown, see Hunter, "'The Correct Thing'"; and Smith and West, "Charlotte Hawkins Brown."

26. Even as they rallied for social reforms—better living and working conditions— organizations like the National Urban League joined forces with white citizens in voicing their concerns about the impact of African American migrants on the northern landscape. For examples, see "National Urban League Discusses Migration Question" in the *Cleveland Advocate* and a flier distributed to migrants by the Urban League, "Which? For Me!," in Spencer Crew's exhibition catalog *Field to Factory*, 41.

27. Various precursors to Brown's guide may have provided guidance and inspiration: R. Roberts's *The House Servant's Directory*; E. Woods, *Negro in Etiquette*; and Green, *National Capital Code of Etiquette*. Though hardly any attention is given in detail to the prescriptive principles of decorum for social affairs, Willard Gatewood provides an excellent discussion overall of African American gentility in *Aristocrats of Color*. See in particular "Genteel Performance," 182–209. Gatewood also discusses several newspapers and weeklies that provided prescriptives for proper decorum. These include the *Sentinel (N.J.)*, *Detroit Plaindealer*, *Washington Bee*, *Half Century Magazine*, *New York Age*, and, of course, the *Chicago Defender* and the *Baltimore Afro-American*. Noliwe Rooks's *Ladies' Pages* examines early African American publications to illustrate how these magazines informed and helped to shape the domestic lives of women.

28. At least one scholar believes that Brown went to "ridiculous lengths" to advance her thoughts on ladyhood. Her motives were labeled "superficial" for their focus on grooming, diction, and courtesy. Mealtime manners could probably also be added to this list. See Giddings, *When and Where I Enter*, 178.

29. Brown, *Correct Thing to Do*, 47. All subsequent page numbers from this work are given in the text.

30. "Program for Married Ladies Afternoon Club of Xenia, Ohio," and "Dinner Program Honoring Robert H. Terrell."

31. Hine, "Rape and the Inner Lives of Black Women."

32. Gretchen Lemke-Santangelo discusses this problem in her study on African American migrants to the East Bay community of San Francisco. See *Abiding Courage*, 133.

33. Ibid.

34. On this point, Tracy Poe has suggested that columnists like Mrs. F. Fletcher and Dr. A. Wilberforce Williams urged African American women to prepare foods fashionable in white women's magazines, abstaining from the foods familiar to them. While Poe makes a valid point in referring to the numerous European dishes found in the various columns, she says little to account for the recipes that also include foods like turnip greens, spinach, and other fresh vegetables. Even though the recipes do not call for the use of fatback, bacon, and other greasy meats, they do exist, albeit in a more urbanized fashion. See Poe, "Origins of Soul Food," 9.

35. Nannie Helen Burroughs Papers, "Annual Fellowship Dinner," box 114.

36. In a letter to the *Chicago Defender*, Dr. M. A. Majors chastises porters (and by default, black people) who poke fun and humiliate other blacks. He admonishes blacks to stop allowing themselves to be the "butt" of a joke. Rather than standing together, helping one another to reach their aspirations, he complains, often members of the race refuse to defend their own people, preferring to cater overzealously to whites. See Majors, "Big-Headed, Noisy Porter and Waiter Great Race Evil," 23.

37. *Women's Era*, 7. Pauline Hopkins wonderfully illustrates how food is used both to raise money and to foster friendly competition among women. A rivalry between two groups of women from different social classes takes place at the church fair. At the center of the squabble is a southern delight from the Old Dominion. Hopkins says, "The knowing ones could trace the odor of [the] rare and tempting dainty—the opossum!" See the novel *Contending Forces*, 212.

38. For more on Burroughs, see Harley, "Nannie Helen Burroughs"; and Higginbotham, *Righteous Discontent*, especially 211–29.

39. See Dr. A. Wilberforce Williams's "Talks on Preventive Measures, First Aid Remedies, Hygienics and Sanitation" and Mrs. F. Fletcher's "The Housekeeper" columns in the *Chicago Defender*.

40. See the September 6, 13, and 27 "Recipes—Economical and Easy to Prepare" columns in the *Baltimore Afro-American*.

41. Advertisement for "Criterion Café."

42. James Borchert makes this observation in connection with alley dwellers in Washington, D.C., in *Alley Life in Washington*, 178–79.

43. The story of Lillian Harris ("Pig Foot Mary") chronicles the life of a heavyset black woman who travels to New York and sets up for business on a Sixtieth Street sidewalk. There, using a baby carriage as a food stand, she sells chitlins, corn, hog maw, and pig's feet. From this enterprise, she amasses quite a fortune and is able to make hefty investments in Harlem real estate. See D. Lewis, *When Harlem Was in Vogue*, 109–10.

44. Advertisement, "Elite, No. 2 Opens Thursday, January 28, Palatial Cape." Marya Mc-

Quirter has begun work on the African American consumption of Chinese food and the intersecting relationships between the two groups; see "Stirrings."

45. "Observer Finds Conditions Far Unsatisfactory."

46. Barbara Christian argues that African American women's fiction reflects the tensions between sexism and racism in American society. The negation of stereotypical imagery takes it toll in terms of self-expression and self-empowerment in that black women novelists struggled to represent "the totality of [a black female] self." See *Black Feminist Criticism*, 172.

47. Hopkins, *Contending Forces*, 103.

48. Though Langston Hughes has titled his character Jesse B. Semple, he is often known by the lone moniker "Simple." For this reason, subsequent references to the character will refer to him as Simple. Hughes, "Bones, Bombs, Chicken Necks," in *Best of Simple*, 199. All subsequent page numbers from this work are given in the text.

49. For more on this illustration, see Williams-Forson, "'Suckin' the Chicken Bone Dry,'" 169, where my mother recalls memories of cracking chicken bones in order to suck the marrow, which, according to her, held the most flavor.

50. This argument was deftly made and illustrated in Richard Wright's *12 Million Black Voices*, but Farah Jasmine Griffin, *Who Set You Flowin'?*, expounds on the notion that migrant men, poor and black, were caught in complex webs of adjustment once they reached the urban landscape. Motivated by confusion, fear, and a lack of understanding, they were dominated and exploited as both economic and racial subjects. I suggest that in light of the types of etiquette prescriptions mentioned here, they were also dominated as cultural subjects.

51. Davies, "Introduction—Migratory Subjectivities," 21.

52. In "Learning from the Outsider Within," Collins describes black women as finding themselves in a tangle of "cross-cutting relationships" when they seek refuge from the external forces that objectify by turning inward to the black community. Oftentimes, however, the internal community is equally as guilty of perpetuating the same ideologies. From their liminal position as the "outsider within," black women often have to confront these controlling images.

53. In separate contexts, Collins and Mary Helen Washington refer to this phenomenon as "the assimilated woman." These women reject connections to other black women and all the while jockey for special treatment. For more on this, see Collins, *Black Feminist Thought*, 84.

54. Mae King is referring primarily to situations of black women's sexual exploitation and representation vis-à-vis white America. However, the notion of black women having a particular "place" that is almost always lower in caste and certainly oppressive when it comes to sexual, social, and economic relations is relevant here. M. King, "Politics of Sexual Stereotypes," 19.

55. Dorothy West, *Living Is Easy*. All page numbers from this work are given in the text.

56. The novel's title is taken from Dubose Heyward's lullaby "Summertime," a libretto

in George Gershwin's *Porgy and Bess*. Having had a role in the play, West was most familiar with the meaning of the piece. However, the double entendre employed here suggests that the living is easy in the North while simultaneously reflecting the idyllicism of the South. Clearly, neither of these interpretations is wholly adequate, as both history and the novel reveal. This ambiguous tone, however, supports the satiric nature of West's novel and African American middle-class life in the North.

57. Rodgers, "Dorothy West's *The Living is Easy*," 169.

58. Christian, *Black Feminist Criticism*, 76. Also, Washington, *Invented Lives*, xv–xxxi, 387–405, and "Gwendolyn Brooks."

59. Chicken appears in several places throughout Brooks's work, shifting in importance and symbolism depending upon her contexts. It is used to describe how a mother feels when her heart has been broken ("wrung like a chicken neck") and becomes part of a loving meal (always chicken and noodles or chicken and rice). In Brooks's Pulitzer Prize–winning poetry collection, *Annie Allen*, "Sunday Chicken" remarks on the life of a young girl and her struggle to express her creativity. In the same-titled poem, Annie Allen likens herself to the sacrificial Sunday chicken.

60. Brooks, *Report from Part One*, 193.

61. Brooks, *Maud Martha*, 294. All subsequent page numbers from this work are given in the text.

62. Ibid., 295. In the early 1950s, chicken consumption had increased about ten pounds per person since before World War II. After beef and pork, chicken was considered the best buy, fresh more than frozen, with more being eaten in the summer than winter, consumed more on the weekends than the weekdays. Appearance, taste (too much chicken eaten during the war), and price factored into reasons why housewives would opt out of purchasing chicken. Smith and Hoecker, *Retail Merchandising and Consumer Acceptance of Eggs and Poultry*, 25; also see H. Smith's 1950 survey of consumers in three northeastern cities—Baltimore, New York City, and Trenton, New Jersey—in *Consumer Preferences and Buying Habits for Chicken*, 21–22. A West Virginia study conducted in 1950 revealed that families with lower incomes, age being a factor, had a higher preference for either roasting or stewing but lower interest in frying. Black homemakers in low-income areas indicated less interest in frying but overall had a greater desire for this method of cooking than did the white homemakers. The data suggest that the favored way of cooking was influenced by the market price of chicken suitable for different ways of cooking. Nybroten, *Consumer Preferences for Poultry Meat*, 10–11.

63. In her autobiography, *Report from Part One*, Brooks states that rituals were a major part of her family's cohesiveness and that they were always carried out: "Certain things were done. Certain things were not done. We did not put Christmas trees outdoors. We did not open Christmas presents on Christmas Eve" (40).

64. Christian, *Black Feminist Criticism*, 176.

65. Richard Wright, *12 Million Black Voices*, 106.

66. Brooks, *Blacks*, "Kitchenette Building," 20.

CHAPTER FOUR

1. Conversations around black expressive culture tend to forget that food is part of the genre. Consider, for example, the introduction to Andrews, Foster, and Harris, *Oxford Companion to African American Literature*, xiii. In *Stylin'*, a critical examination of African American culture, Shane White and Graham White also overlook food.

2. This account is quoted at greater length in J. Jones, *Labor of Love*, 49.

3. I should acknowledge here that this practice may not necessarily reflect the experiences of all black people. Given its historical connections and foundations, this tradition may primarily be carried out among those who have working-class and middle-class backgrounds and hail from southern regions or, quite possibly, rural areas within those areas. On the other hand, it can be argued that knowledge of this practice transcends these regional and class variables inasmuch as the majority of black people living during the pre–civil rights era were subject to limitations placed on their ability to travel within U.S. society. Today, variations of this custom are still carried out under the influence of regional and racial cultural traditions as well as those pertaining to class and family.

4. Bernice Reeder was one of many black women who provided narratives for Elizabeth Clark-Lewis's study on African American women and who traveled to Washington, D.C., to perform domestic work in *Living In, Living Out*.

5. Clark-Lewis, *Living In, Living Out*, 65.

6. Angelou, *I Know Why the Caged Bird Sings*, 3–4. I am grateful to my colleague Mary Bendel-Simso, who reminded me of this very poignant example.

7. So vital is chicken to the African American travel experience that it has earned a place in the Smithsonian Institution's National Museum of American History exhibit *Field to Factory: Afro-American Migration, 1915–1940*. In the exhibition, a young girl is posed sleeping in an upright position on a train. On the seat across from her is a pail that possibly contains her food and other personal travel items. Although the exhibit does not indicate that this young traveler has chicken in her pail, the exhibition catalog elaborates on these more pertinent details. The catalog explains that because of Jim Crow laws, African Americans "purchased quick meals during stops or brought their food in a basket or cardboard box." See Crew, *Field to Factory*, 30.

8. The legend of the "chicken bone express" is all but hidden from written sources. Many older African Americans interviewed for this project indicated that they had heard of the anecdote, but few could point to a particular source. What was repeatedly disclosed, however, is that many black people still pack boxed lunches today when they travel—regardless of the distance—because eating chicken and riding has become a part of the African American travel experience. For a brief mention of this subject, see Valentine, "Road to Freedom."

9. In tracing black women's journeys toward definition of self through African American women's literature, Christian notes that black women's movement through

space, time, class, and economics did not appear in earnest until the early 1980s. Noting that prior to this period, black women were restricted from traveling because of race and gender, fiction of the last two decades finds black women moving about in various ways in order to find self-fulfillment and empowerment.

10. Morrison, *Sula*, 19.

11. I am borrowing here from Farah Griffin, *Who Set You Flowin'?*, who discusses the sexualized body of the black woman as an exotic and grotesque other (155).

12. Morrison, *Sula*, 24.

13. I would be surprised if Morrison intentionally ignored a discussion of food, given its place in several of her other novels.

14. Darden and Darden, *Spoonbread and Strawberry Wine*, 290–91.

15. Ibid.

16. Denkler, "Sustaining Identity," 146.

17. The *Negro Motorist Green Book* was a guide or pamphlet issued by the U.S. Travel Bureau that contained a list of designations (bars, service stations, lodgings) that were amenable to African American patrons. See Denkler, "Sustaining Identity," 145–46.

18. African American literature and popular culture are filled with images of women who work as prostitutes and pimps. But there are other types of work that straddle the lines of legality. There is Mrs. Hedges, the undercover madam, in Ann Petry's *The Street* (1946), and Eve, who runs a boardinghouse and rents only to single women, in Gloria Naylor's *Bailey's Cafe* (1992). Walter Moseley's Iula has a makeshift diner created from cinder blocks and abandoned trailers in *Always Outnumbered, Always Outgunned* (1999). And who can forget the life led by Shug Avery in Alice Walker's *The Color Purple* (1982), or the bootleggers and gamblers rampant throughout blaxploitation films, in which Pam Grier plays a significant part?

19. B. Campbell, *Your Blues Ain't Like Mine*, 34. All subsequent page numbers from this work are given in the text.

20. Cousin Louis's attire sounds like a zoot suit, clothing worn by African American and Latino men during the mid-1940s as an expression of culture and defiance. For more on zoot-suiters, see Kelley, *Race Rebels*, 161–82; and White and White, *Stylin'*, 248–62.

21. Juke joints have been written about extensively as havens of African American cultural expression in several scholarly discussions, including Kelley, *Race Rebels*, 46–47; White and White, *Stylin'*, 164; Hazzard-Gordon, *Jookin'*, 63–94; and Hunter, *To 'Joy My Freedom*, 171. Harley employs the term "jill" joint to designate a female host in her article "'Working for Nothing but a Living,'" 54. D. Lewis briefly explains the purposes behind rent parties and buffet flats in *When Harlem Was in Vogue*, 107–8.

22. When I first read the novel ten years ago, it seemed odd that Ida sold tamales. I have since come to learn that tamales are almost as common as catfish in the Delta region. Joe St. Columbia, owner of Pasquale's Tamales in Helena, Arkansas, discussed the creolization of southern cuisine at the 1999 Southern Foodways Symposium. He detailed his Italian family's first exposure to tamales and the recipes they

exchanged with Mexican migrant workers. Since this encounter, they have adapted and modified the recipe and now sell them on-line at <http://pasqualetamale.com/index.htm>. In a related paper, "Hot Tamales from the Mississippi Delta," prepared for the June 2000 conference "Grits and Greens and Everything in Between," John T. Edge shared St. Columbia's account. Also see Edge's cookbook *A Gracious Plenty*, 162. Brett Williams offers another insightful perspective on the importance of tamales to Tejano culture in her article "Why Migrant Women Feed Their Husbands Tamales."

23. Carby, "It Jus Be's Dat Way Sometime," 12.

24. Angela Y. Davis talks about the ways in which blues women enabled numbers of black women to aesthetically associate themselves with travel. This analysis borrows Davis's claim but does not presuppose the same representations found in Ma Rainey or Bessie Smith. Rather, in applying it to Ida, a fictional character, I suggest that she conceivably represents many black women who were encouraged by real traveling blues women of the 1940s and 1950s. See A. Davis, *Blues Legacies and Black Feminism*, 66–91.

25. Carby, "It Jus Be's Dat Way Sometime," 16.

26. William's statement on the "naturalness" of chicken might also be interpreted in relationship to the occasion of death. During funeral events, African Americans generally provide foods like chicken, potato salad, and macaroni and cheese—the foods that are considered familiar and comforting. For more on African American funeral rituals and practices, see Karla F. C. Holloway's folkloristic study *Passed On*.

27. All informants were given pseudonyms.

28. Other novelists like Sam Greenlee and Barbara Neely also remind the reader of the "greasy bag" (even if Neely's Blanche eats a chicken sandwich with lettuce and tomato and garlic mayonnaise) that accompanies some African American travelers from force of habit. See Greenlee, *Spook Who Sat by the Door*, 125; and Neely, *Blanche among the Talented Tenth*, 11.

29. Whitehead, "Festive Occasions." Also discussed in Whitehead and Williams-Forson, "African American Foodways."

30. While this rationale is applicable to this discussion because many African Americans tend to travel with chicken lunches, it certainly is not relegated only to black culture. This argument would be one of many to explain why there generally tends to be a congregation gathered in kitchens and other major food areas during planned and impromptu gatherings.

31. This dilemma is very common for those who have chosen vegetarianism or veganism. As vegetarian "outsiders" in a slowly changing carnivorous society, vegetarians usually provide their own food. The same concept applies to this scenario. There are inherent dangers to this philosophy that can be co-opted by those wanting to justify majority/minority issues. The argument here, however, is directly centered on food and what happens when cultural beliefs change around food. In some settings, it is entirely appropriate to expect that one's dietary habits have changed. In

situations such as the one in this example, attending to different eating patterns was not possible for the tour director (nor should it have been expected). Therefore, the responsibility to adapt to the menu was mine. For this reason, one passenger, who was aware that chicken was being provided, brought along a fish sandwich.

32. All informants were given pseudonyms.

33. For many African American people, the change in times and eating habits has ushered in the removal of certain rituals. Many, like myself, might still engage in the process of food preparation prior to a trip, but for some who no longer eat chicken, a part of the travel act is excluded.

34. Little was placed on trial while serving an initial sentence for a charge of larceny and breaking and entering. So important was the trial to women's and civil rights groups that it became a cause célèbre requiring several changes in venue and a heavily guarded courtroom. Major fund-raising efforts involving the Southern Poverty Law Center, the Black Panthers Party, and numerous grassroots organizations took place to secure defense money. Charges were reduced to manslaughter after various pieces of evidence verified Little's story and her testimony was substantiated by a lie detector test. Citing overall lack of evidence, a jury acquitted Little. This case set a precedent for rape victims who wanted to argue self-defense. It also set in motion numerous investigations of women being abused in North Carolina jails. For more complete details on this story, see Wayne King's coverage for the *New York Times*.

CHAPTER FIVE

1. Hurston, *Dust Tracks on a Road*, 57 (original emphasis).

2. Geneva Smitherman discusses the rapper as a postmodern griot in her article " 'The Chain Remain the Same,' " 4. Smitherman refers to speed and lyricism when talking about rappers "coming wit' it." My analysis borrows this notion to refer both to cooking chicken and to the verbal play involved in the competition that sometimes surrounds it.

3. Storms, "Church to Have Soul Food Benefit."

4. At one point in my research for this project, I came across a sign that said "Barbecue Chicken Dinners." I immediately ran home to get my camera in hopes of photographing and talking with some of the parishioners. When I arrived at the church, they seemed a little uncertain about my presence. I purchased a dinner and then left, taking a few pictures of the signs outside the edifice. When I recounted this experience to a friend, she said, "Silly girl, you should have known it wasn't black; it [the sign] said barbecue. Black folk up this way don't have no barbecue chicken dinners." Personal exchange, Philipia Hillman, August 2001.

5. Dodson and Gilkes, "There's Nothing Like Church Food," 523.

6. Mary C. Beaudry, Lauren J. Cook, and Stephen A. Mrozowski argue that the use of objects and their symbolism in the process of constructing cultural identity is more than anything else "a public act of mediation between self and other." They suggest

that through an analysis of material items, one can begin to understand the ways in which individuals use objects important to self-expression and self-definition in the construction of identity. They go on to conclude that individuals and members of a subculture create their identity by using an object or sign that allows a person to "make his self manifest." This process, they suggest, generally occurs through leisure or during off-work hours. This analysis does not suggest that black women's church work, including cooking, is leisure or anything less than work. To the contrary, it is important social work; however, for the purposes of this discussion, social activities in the church are considered an addition to the formal production of labor. See Beaudry, Cook, and Mrozowski, "Artifacts and Active Voices," 154.

7. Gates, *Signifying Monkey*, 64.

8. Major, *Dictionary of Afro-American Slang*, 104, and *Juba to Jive*, 138, 416.

9. Abrahams, *Talking Black*, 51; and LeFever, "'Playing the Dozens,'" 73.

10. Levine, *Black Culture*, 354–55.

11. Mitchell-Kernan, "Signifying," 313.

12. In today's parlance, to refer to someone as "ghetto" means that they are trifling or "triflin'," as it is said among members of the black community.

13. Gates, *Signifying Monkey*, 81 (original emphasis).

14. Mitchell-Kernan, "Signifying," 314.

15. Davis is cited in Kelley, *Race Rebels*, 39.

16. Naylor, *Linden Hills*, 50. All subsequent page numbers from this work are given in the text.

17. J. White, *Soul Food*, 248.

18. Dodson and Gilkes, "There's Nothing Like Church Food," 520.

19. Though he did not necessarily coin this term, Charles Camp in his extensive discussion of such occurrences reflects that he noticed the awkwardness of using the phrase "food event" to describe these occasions. However, he also notes that until a collective name can be identified for such gatherings, we are left with this blasé piece of terminology. See Camp, *American Foodways*, 55.

20. Simonsen, *You May Plow Here*, 78–79.

21. M. Hughes, "Soul, Black Women, and Food," 277.

22. I am grateful to Philipia Hillman for providing me with this observation from Rev. Dr. G. Martin Young, "Hold On Help Is on the Way."

23. The conversation about sexuality and the church brings to mind discourse about the Catholic Church and the upsurge in revelations about sexual molestations that have taken place for years. While those are pertinent, the goal here is to link some of the encounters in black churches to metaphors of cooking. Issues of theological conservativism regarding women's sexual and reproductive freedom and homosexuality yield what Kelly Brown-Douglas calls "unhealthy expressions" of sexuality in the black community and, by default, its churches. Major contributors to this climate of sexual oppression within black churches include internalized racism and sexism, the historical treatment of African American sexuality by American society,

and a reluctance to talk about sexuality issues in general. For a good dialogue regarding African American women, sexuality, and spirituality, see the panel discussion moderated by Marcia L. Dyson, "Can You Love God and Sex?"

24. The issues plaguing black Baptist churches are no different from any other. One needs only to be reminded of the situation involving Rev. Henry Lyons, former president of the National Baptist Convention, U.S.A., who was convicted on multiple counts of fraud and tax evasion. At the center of that debacle was a long-term relationship with another woman. The point here is not to ridicule Lyons as much as to point to the culture of patriarchal hypocrisy within the black church community. Even as Lyons resigned his post as president, he received a vote of confidence from the predominantly male body of constituents at the convention.

25. J. White, *Soul Food*, 222.

26. Mitchell-Kernan, "Signifying," 318.

27. Gates, *Signifying Monkey*, 60.

28. Ibid.

29. Shockley, *Say Jesus and Come to Me*, 11. All subsequent page numbers from this work are given in the text.

30. Shockley, "Black Lesbian," 135.

31. The perception/reality of the black preacher's fondness for fancy cars, fancy women, and lots of cash is an everlasting conundrum, given that they are representative servants of Jesus Christ, who clearly issued the instructions in Mark 6:8–9 (NIV): "Take nothing for the journey except a staff—no bread, no bag, no money in your belts. Wear sandals but not an extra tunic." There is a noted difference between having basic necessities and excess (depending upon who supplies the definition), a point of contention between me and those unfamiliar with growing up in a clerical household. Preachers are often one of the least compensated; perhaps this is why Shockley has her protagonist place an emphasis on charming the worshipers out of their pockets/pocketbooks.

32. As a librarian, critic, and editor, Shockley was undoubtedly aware of literary conventions that suggest "showing" a character over "telling," the latter being a "violation of artistry." Yet by employing this method, Shockley achieves several goals, including demystifying and debunking racial, gender, and cultural stereotypes. See Abrams, *Glossary of Literary Terms*, 23–24.

33. Shockley, "Black Lesbian," 134.

34. Camp, "Food Event," 55.

35. Stuart Hall makes this point as well when he says, "But the fact is that greater and greater numbers of people (men and women)—with however little money—play the game of using things to signify who they are." See Morley and Chen, *Stuart Hall*, 235.

36. Recall the process of chicken preparation by Sara Brooks's mother, as she would work for weeks in anticipation of the preacher's arrival. While Mrs. Cross would not

have had to endure all of the labor-intensive parts of this process, she nonetheless certainly performed the other necessary tasks for preparing such a weighty meal.

37. This is exemplified also when a host serves a very expensive meal (lobster, prime rib, etc.) and the guests select huge portions rather than choose portion sizes equal to others'. Choices and selections—unless one informs the cook in advance—can lead to a strained dinner environment. Refer to Shuman's delightful and insightful article "Rhetoric of Portions" for further reading on the rules of food apportionment, 72.

38. Ibid., 76–77.

39. A. Davis, *Blues Legacies and Black Feminism*, 129.

40. Ibid., 130.

41. Shuman, "Rhetoric of Portions," 80.

CHAPTER SIX

1. Hurston, *Their Eyes Were Watching God*, 75.

2. Ibid., 71.

3. T. Lott, "Black Vernacular Representation," 85.

4. In his discussion, Lott uses the example of Ted Danson donning blackface in his 1993 roast of Whoopi Goldberg. Several black people in attendance were deeply offended, feeling that the skit was a vicious objectification of black people. They continued to hold Danson accountable despite being informed that Goldberg collaborated on the performance. Lott also makes the point that generally black people do not ridicule their own—Richard Pryor, Redd Foxx, Chris Rock—when they use racist humor in their performances, but they tend to always take to task white performers who employ a similar tactic. This incident, wherein Goldberg was also held accountable, reflects a break with that practice. T. Lott, "Black Vernacular Representation," 84–85.

5. Ibid., 85.

6. Parker and Keating, *Idella*, 71.

7. Parker's memoir contains a fabulous photograph of several white people, Rawlings included, crowded in Rawlings's living room at Cross Creek. The dinner guests, one of whom was a state senator, appear to be listening intently as she and several unidentified black men and women entertain the guests with singing and other forms of "amusement," 81.

8. Ibid.

9. Ibid., 69. On this point, Parker is accurate. There are three recipes attributed to her: luncheon muffins, biscuits, and a cheese soufflé. Several of the other recipes, including the chocolate pie, appear to have no origin.

10. Ibid.

11. Rawlings, *Cross Creek Cookery*, 3.

12. Jessica Harris has written that foods like sesame seeds (benne) are a "corruption"

of sesame (bene), a term used among the Wolof people of the Senegambia region. She makes similar connections with foods like okra and fritters. Karen Hess also references fritters of ground black-eyed peas as having their affiliations with West African cookery. Robert Hall's contribution echoes Harris's and Hess's, including a discussion of the malegueta pepper. For more, refer to J. Harris, *Welcome Table*, especially the appendices, 245–67; Hess, *Carolina Rice Kitchen*, 132; and R. Hall, "Savoring Africa in the New World."

13. Interview with member of the Culinary Historians of Washington, D.C., November 2000.

14. Lott indicates that dialect distinguishes these three cultural forms as distinctly African American in "Black Vernacular Representation," 100.

15. Mary Randolph was the owner of several boardinghouses and the author of the heralded southern cookbook *The Virginia Housewife*, which contains one of the first recipes for fried chicken. Randolph's recipe book also includes a range of foods, from those considered foreign (gazpacho) to those considered exotic for the time period (broccoli and mushrooms). In his cookbook *Around the American Table*, food writer Michael Krondl indicates that a great deal of English influence is present in Randolph's cookbook by her inclusion of herbs, wines, and spices to roast and cook meats. For more on this subject, refer to Krondl, "Founding Mothers," 55.

16. Spivey, *Peppers, Cracklings, and Knots of Wool Cookbook*, 263.

17. Clearly African Americans are not the only racial group to experience this type of culinary exchange. See chap. 4 of this study where I mention Brett Williams's work on tamales and its importance to Tejano women.

18. Parker and Keating, *Idella*, xi.

19. Ibid., ix, 128.

20. Vertamae Grosvenor argues this point very succinctly, describing how it makes her "madder than a wet hen" to hear such assertions. See Shange, foreword, xiii.

21. By ethnicities, I mean to include the ever-present globalization of black communities, which reflects the mixing of cultures within the United States and around the world.

22. Though a variety of cookbooks has been released within the last decade, and a few prior to this time, the majority of people still consider hog's entrails, collard greens, and sweet potato pie to compose the whole of black culinary repertoires. Among other notable chefs, an exception is and always has been Edna Lewis.

23. Chappelle, *Killin' Them Softly*.

24. Carby, *Reconstructing Womanhood*, 22.

25. I once entered a grocery store and purchased some steamed shrimp. When my order was ready, the young clerk came from behind the counter to hand me my order and then whispered that they also had some ham hocks on sale that day. I looked at him bewildered and then asked what would make him believe that I wanted anything related to a pig when I had just ordered shrimp. He smiled and said, "Have a good day." This incident, though very slight, has remained with me

until this day. I am not certain if he was simply being nice and offered this sale item to every customer (although I doubt this, not having seen him approach other customers) or if it was my full figure and race that prompted him to make such a suggestion.

26. *Friday* is a cult film starring singer Ice Cube and actor Chris Tucker. The basic story line is about two young, unemployed black men who spend the entire day dodging their nemesis, skirting authority figures, and having a good time.

27. All students have been given pseudonyms.

28. Turner and Fine, *Whispers on the Color Line*, 18.

29. In chap. 7 of Turner and Fine's *Whispers on the Color Line*, they offer examples of some truth claims or statements that have been taken as true, even though little or no evidence was available to support them. Among these examples are the cases of Tawana Brawley and Susan Smith, wherein men opposite their races were fingered as the perpetrators in their attacks. Though later it was proven that there were fallacies to both claims, the incidents were initially accepted as true by the wider American public because they made cultural sense.

30. Patricia Turner has written extensively on rumor in black communities. For these discussions, refer to "Church's Fried Chicken and the Klan," "Ambivalent Patrons," and *I Heard It through the Grapevine*, 84–92; and Turner and Fine, *Whispers on the Color Line*, 86–89.

31. On the other hand, my research conducted at the historically black college and university yielded that students saw chicken as a central object of negation on late-night cartoon reruns.

32. Certainly, some of this might have to do with these students having access to more of television's viewing privileges, including HBO, a venue geared most directly to the socioeconomic audiences from which they emerged. Dave Chappelle also offers interesting insight on why Rock might have been on the minds of these informants. In a 2005 interview with *Time* magazine, Chappelle is cited as having explained that many black people believe in the "HNIC—the Head Negro in Charge" syndrome. This is the notion that in the United States—because of racism, generally—there can be only one black person on top in any field at any one particular time. In the field of comedy at that time, Rock was being favored, so Chappelle was unable to share the limelight. Farley and Robinson, "Dave Speaks," 68.

33. The porch is a central site for storytelling in African American culture, held and recognized as a space for men who "tell tall tales." Zora Neale Hurston's *Their Eyes Were Watching God* enables the character Janie to disturb this tradition. Janie tells her best friend, Phoeby, all about her life while sitting on the steps of the back porch "with the lamps all filled and the chimneys cleaned." Trudier Harris's *The Power of the Porch* is another useful reference for understanding the role of the porch in African American culture.

34. Smitherman, "'The Chain Remain the Same,'" 12.

35. In another context, Rock castigates fathers for expecting such praise for these every-

day tasks. That Rock would not invoke the same rhetoric in this instance is interesting in that it calls into question the recycling of material for social or entertainment value geared toward specific audiences.

36. Rock, *Bigger and Blacker*.

37. Sara Brooks talks about this division of food by gender in her narrative account.
Simonsen, *You May Plow Here*, 78–79. This is not at all a strictly African American
custom. Buchi Emecheta speaks of similar food practices and divisions of labor in
Joys of Motherhood, 104–5. A former colleague and friend shared a similar experience about growing up in Grenada. She said that it was not until she was much older
that she realized other pieces of chicken existed besides the neck, liver, and gizzard.

38. Driver, "Mirth of a Nation."

39. Lubiano, "But Compared to What?" 254.

40. Ibid., 268.

41. A conversation with Tammy Sanders put this discussion into perspective. Her suggestion that Rock employs a kind of "slipperiness" has complicated my thinking
about cultural production, entertainment, and race.

42. Rock, *Rock This!*, 169 (original emphasis).

43. Ibid., 168.

44. In Hurston's *Their Eyes Were Watching God*, this space is the front porch of the store
owned by Jody, Janie's second husband. When the signifying rituals would begin
at the store, Janie was forced to go inside. She could not participate in the games
and was disallowed this form—and ultimately any form—of real self-expression. In
one instance she says that her husband's attempts to silence her "took the bloom
off things" (43).

45. Rock, *Rock This!*, 238.

CHAPTER SEVEN

1. Trudier Harris makes the point that the spelling of the mother/grandmother's
name (J-o-e) "reinforces her role in the family as husband, father, 'masculine' pro-
vider." This argument can be found in Harris-Lopez, "Ugly Legacies," 198.

2. From an artistic point of view, I understand what Tillman is trying to do. But, as
I hope this analysis will illustrate, the dynamics inherent in having a male child
tell about women's thoughts, feelings, and ideas is problematic. On some levels, it
reduces women's complex personalities to a childlike state, capable of being interpreted even by a boy. It is interesting and significant to this argument that Ahmad's
young sister is not the narrator. In fact, she is virtually voiceless, maybe saying one
or two words throughout the entire film.

3. According to the American Diabetes Association, in the past thirty years, the rate
of the disease has tripled in the black community to where it now has reached epi-
demic proportions. Approximately 2.8 million (13 percent) of all African American
people are afflicted, and one in four African American women over age fifty-five has
the disease. Because at least one-third of those afflicted are unaware of its pres-

ence, the ADA has begun an "African American Program" to raise awareness and to educate more people about prevention. One of the initiatives within this program is called "Diabetes Sunday" wherein pastors or other designees are asked to share information with the congregation about the seriousness of the disease. See <http://www.diabetes.org/main/community/outreach/african_americans>.

4. I agree with Jacqueline Bobo, who argues that representations of black women as Sapphires, matriarchs, and Jezebels no longer carry the weight that they once did. Though this may be true, there is still a need for vigilance lest these constructions that have shrouded black women's characters and constantly reinforced the ideological workings of patriarchy return in greater force. *Black Feminist Cultural Criticism*, 199. I take, perhaps, the more obvious approach to the film—analyzing the women, who are the main characters. In "Ugly Legacies," however, Harris-Lopez takes a different approach. Although she also remarks upon the redundant representations of African American women, she identifies familiar stereotypes of black men and their sexual appetites, 199–202.

5. Similar heavyset, dark-skinned, bandanna-clad women were played by Claudia McNeil as Mama Lena Younger in Lorraine Hansberry's *A Raisin in the Sun* and Esther Rolle as Florida Evans in television's *Good Times*. More contemporary images leave little to the imagination in the way of character definition. These women are curiously ambiguous. As Cheryl Townsend Gilkes explains, the black community has mixed emotions about heavyset women. On the one hand, they are highly respected (especially when older). On the other hand, they are often ridiculed as "culturally deviant" for not complying with European standards of beauty. See Gilkes, "The 'Loves' and 'Troubles' of African American Women's Bodies," 234; and Bass, "On Being a Fat Black Girl."

6. The phenomenon of Oprah's Boot Camp notwithstanding, every year *Essence* magazine publishes pages of black women who do not resemble this image but are instead in charge of their weight and health. These women range in age from the early sixties to late nineties, in some cases. Moreover, the Black Women's Health Project and countless other organizations seek to educate black women about healthy living.

7. T. Harris, *Saints, Sinners, and Saviors*, 9.

8. My assertion always presents a point of contention when discussed with audiences who saw the film. Participants usually try to remind me that the film's goal is to illustrate how a family maintains rituals when the mother/grandmother dies. This point is well taken, but I have found that these respondents generally do not consider some of the film's more subtle points, like misrepresenting all the work that preparing these kinds of meals would entail. As a result, I tend to agree with the comments of several informants for this project who revealed that they have ceased cooking big Sunday dinners, and particularly frying chicken and fish on a regular basis, because it is simply too cumbersome. How much more readily might the sisters in this film have suspended this style of cookery given that their mother's life

hangs in the balance? Interestingly, the participants who most often favored going forth with the dinner are male.

9. This observation is underscored by the fact that Maxine's Uncle Pete, the all-but-invisible black male elder who hides in his room for days on end, emerges only after Mama Joe dies, and then it is to provide Maxine with her marching orders on taking Mama Joe's place in the household.

10. The one time that Bird (the youngest sister) attempts to cook a meal, it is a disaster. Teri is seen only twice in the kitchen, fulfilling some innocuous role. In addition to being able to bear children and cook, Maxine is also the one who dispenses motherly wisdom throughout the film. This is shown in the opening scene when Bird is disturbed about an ex-girlfriend who appears at her wedding, and is shown again later when Maxine assuages Bird's hurt feelings (caused by Teri) and when she shares her wit and wisdom upon finding out that Bird is pregnant.

11. A Sapphire is a pervasive stereotype of an African American woman who is overly aggressive, domineering, and emasculating. The characterization came into existence with the 1920s radio show *Amos 'n' Andy*, in which Sapphire Stevens would berate her husband regularly. For further reference, see Andrews, Foster, and Harris, *Oxford Companion to African American Literature*, 644.

12. According to Tillman, this role was written with Vanessa Williams in mind. She is supposed to be "mad with the world," and this image comes across viscerally. Making her cold and stern is supposed to imply that she does not see the forest for the trees in her life because she is so consumed with something other than what is before her. This would be one of the reasons that "everything she loses, she loves." Again, this is not to imply that the Teri character is not exemplary of some black women, but there are too many indicators that thrust her into a characterization borne directly out of distorted historical formulations.

13. Trudier Harris-Lopez rightfully describes this scene as primitive and jungle-like. The scene implies that in Miles, "you can take the man out of the jungle but you cannot take the jungle out of the man." "Ugly Legacies," 199–200.

14. I have been attempting to discuss the lack of gendered sense in the film. A point of departure to this observation, and one carefully disguised as concern for women, comes when Maxine and Kenny are engaged in an intimate moment just after the birth of their last child. In his DVD commentary, Tillman says that "he tried to impart some things" during the film. By having one of the brothers-in-law arrive to disrupt the scene, Tillman says he conveys the fact that women are supposed to wait six weeks after giving birth before engaging in sex. He then goes on to add, "Most guys would go back to it if they could." Initially, this point might seem to be mindful of women's well-being. At a second glance, it is directly related to issues of men and sex. Once again, women are rendered as objects, subject to satisfying men by cooking and making babies.

15. Quoted in K. Dalton, "Past Is Prologue," 20.

16. Like Barbara Christian, Patricia Hill Collins, and others, hooks makes the disturb-

ing observation that "unenlightened" blacks and other nonwhite groups have been conditioned by society to accept negative portrayals. Sadly, she says, black people are disappointed when they do not see characters fulfilling familiar stereotypes. "Artistic Integrity," 75.

17. On some level, the cable series that is a follow-up to the film helps to answer some of these questions, implying that it could not all be said in the movie.

18. A notable exception to this is Witt's analysis of the period from the standpoint of its relationship to masculinity and issues of "filth" vis-à-vis pork products (chitlins, hog maws, and so on). See the chapter in *Black Hunger*, " 'Eating Chitterlings Is Like Going Slumming,' " 79–101. Soul food was important on the highly intellectualized level to which Witt advances it, but this analysis advances an argument that accords with my informants' descriptions of soul food.

19. A generic search on any of the popular Internet search engines will yield definitions of the term ranging from foods associated with African American vernacular to articles found in *Better Homes and Gardens* to the advertisements for Quaker Oats oatmeal as "soul food"—good for the heart and soul. This leads me to believe that now more than ever, Witt's observation that any discussion of soul food needs to be situated within the particular intraracial contexts is particularly salient. And yet, to situate this discussion within those contexts would silence the voices of those who are at the center of the cultural practice described by the array of competing discourses over soul food. See Witt, *Black Hunger*.

20. Fabre and O'Meally, *History and Memory in African-American Culture*, 5.

21. In the film commentary, Tillman states that he patterned *Soul Food* after another commonly known food film, *Big Night*. Although no formal definition exists for this genre, the definition (and cinematic portrayal) that tends to be most accepted is one in which the food drives the action of the narrative. A valuable contribution to this genre is Anne Bower's essay collection *Reel Food*. The discussions involve movies that have food as the central focus alongside those wherein foods merely appear (albeit importantly) in the films.

22. Though this study addresses chicken specifically, the impact that regional variations have had upon African American foodways cannot be ignored. Karen Hess's *The Carolina Rice Kitchen* is instructive for its contribution to these variations. Also valuable are the Rice Museum of Georgetown, South Carolina (see <http://www .ego.net/us/sc/myr/rice/>); Charles Joyner's *Down by the Riverside*; Philip Morgan's *Slave Counterpoint*; and Peter Woods's *Black Majority*.

23. James Lull is quoted in hooks, "Artistic Integrity," 75.

24. Ibid.

25. bell hooks, "Artistic Integrity," 73, talks about ethical dimensions to aesthetic choices, using as an example the decision to cast a black man in the role of a thief. T. Harris-Lopez also raises this argument in "Ugly Legacies," 214, arguing that movies like *Soul Food* are "modern links in chains" that bind African Americans to "the almighty American dollar." And the only way that African Americans can take

hold of even the smallest part of the prize is to accept and participate in denigration and ridicule.

CHAPTER EIGHT

1. This chapter takes a very narrow view by focusing on only two images from Walker's oeuvre because to do otherwise is beyond the scope of this research. Although much has already been written on the total output of this artist, the aim here is to concentrate on the variegated dilemmas posed by her work within the context of the larger discussion of this text.

2. Gwendolyn DuBois Shaw offers one of the best comprehensive discussions of Kara Walker's work from the perspective of an art historian. Her analysis points out the inspiration for many of Walker's pieces, locating them in African and African American visual culture. See *Seeing the Unspeakable*, 6.

3. I first learned of Walker's art in 2000 when informed about an exhibition on newly acquired African American art at the Baltimore Museum of Art (BMA). Walker's work was displayed once again at the BMA along with that of Robert Colescott, Michael Ray Charles, Renee Cox, and Carrie Mae Weems, among others. They were part of the exhibition called *Looking Forward/Looking Black*. By this time, Walker's art had been described in every conceivable way, ranging from "lewd, provocative —and beautiful" to "shocking and appalling" and even "painful to view." She has been compared to other black artists who are perceived to have "sold their souls to the white art audience." J. Dalton, "Kara Walker."

4. Shaw offers a nice explanation of Walker's employment of this craft in *Seeing the Unspeakable*, 20–26.

5. Kara Walker quoted in Sheets, "Cut It Out!," 127.

6. Barnwell and Buick, "Portfolio of Works by African American Artists," 83.

7. S. Hall, *Representation*, 59.

8. Barnwell and Buick, "Portfolio of Works by African American Artists," 83.

9. T. Lott, "Kara Walker Speaks," 70.

10. Ibid., 71. Another character of Walker's imagination is Missus K. E. B. Walker, who is described as the key to freeing the Freudian superego that women are made to repress. Shaw, *Seeing the Unspeakable*, 52.

11. Golden, "Kara Walker," 44–45; Dixon, "A Negress Speaks Out," 13.

12. Almost any interview or serious discussion of Walker's work refers to the performative aspects of her work that has its basis in a fantasy slave plantation world. The impetus for these fantasies, according to Walker, is nineteenth-century literature, film, and other popular culture media. On the importance of the antebellum period to Walker, see Golden, "Kara Walker."

13. Robinson, *Aunt Dice*, 80. The image of the black female domestic is a perennial one. As discussed throughout this book, black women have typically been associated with all aspects of the foodways process. This analysis could have easily been sus-

tained, for example, by a discussion of "Old Dinah" in Stowe's *Uncle Tom's Cabin*, 270–77.

14. Robinson, *Aunt Dice*, 82.

15. Deborah Gray White refers to the "fancy trade" as the sale of light-skinned black women for the primary purpose of concubinage or prostitution. Although some dark-skinned women were generally excluded from this practice, there was no guarantee of protection because of skin tone. Black women in general were assumed to be willing prostitutes. See White, *Ar'n't I a Woman?*, 37–38.

16. Barbara Christian, *Black Feminist Criticism*, 2, argues convincingly that the ideal southern woman would have us deny these elements of mammy's existence in order to render her harmless, perpetually enslaved, a pillar of security for all the fears and concerns harbored by white society.

17. Other than the real-life stories of Sally Hemings and Thomas Jefferson or Harriet Jacobs's *Incidents in the Life of a Slave Girl*, among a few others, narratives documenting interracial love stories are scarce. For fictional accounts of interracial liaisons, see William Wells Brown, *Clotel* (1853); Nella Larsen, *Passing* (1929); Lillian Smith, *Strange Fruit* (1944); Andrea Lee, *Sarah Phillips* (1984); and Shirley Anne Williams, *Dessa Rose* (1986), among others.

18. Clarke, "Failure to Transform," 192.

19. C. West, *Race Matters*, 83.

20. Walker makes this point in reference to the work of Jacob Lawrence as well as to her own during an informal conversation at the Modern Museum of American Art. See <http://www.moma.org/onlineprojects/conversations/kw_f.html>.

21. S. Hall, *Representation*, 228–29; Barthes, "Rhetoric of the Image," 38.

22. Walker's *Drumstick* might be said to signify to some degree upon Francis W. Edmonds's *Devotion*, particularly because the black cook in *Devotion* is foregrounded as the primary subject of the painting, even as she serves as the caretaker of an elderly infirm man sitting slumped in a bedroom chair. The positioning of the man and his infirmities put me in mind of *Drumstick*. Yet in contrast to the spry, able-bodied, smiling servant of Walker's imagination, the female servant in *Devotion* is herself elderly but nonetheless takes care to provide her charge with a steaming bowl of hot soup. See O'Leary, *At Beck and Call*, 147–48, and plate 6.

23. Golden quoted in Sheets, "Cut It Out!," 126.

24. In her article on Williams's *Dessa Rose*, African American literary critic Deborah McDowell asks why there exists a compulsion by black authors to dwell upon the story of slavery in contemporary African American novels. See "Negotiating between Tenses," 144.

25. Walker explains that following one round of criticism, her artist father responded to the article by defending his daughter's right to use the imagery, saying that he and his generation had fought hard for this freedom. Hannaham, "Pea, Ball, Bounce," 119.

26. Reid-Pharr, "Black Girl Lost," 28, offers one of the most insightful, compelling discussions of Walker's work, but on this point I must disagree.

27. What is more disconcerting, however, is that when reading reviews of her work by art historians, the explanations and interpretations that they offer seem perfectly plausible. Their abilities to link her work to historical imagery, novels, events, and so on suggest that the rest of us are idiots for walking away with "no clue" or with explanations that are far removed from Walker's intentions.

28. Reid-Pharr, "Black Girl Lost," 33. Reid-Pharr's points are well taken, though they speak to complicated dilemmas. There were times when I struggled with whether to acknowledge outright that some blacks stole chickens. They did so not because they were hungry or were being tricksters; they did so because they wanted to and because those individuals were, in effect, thieves. But how does one acknowledge that point in black America and not be labeled a traitor to the race, or have the lone admission cast aspersions on the entire race?

29. Armstrong, "Kara Walker Interviewed by Liz Armstrong," 107; Museum of Modern Art, "Conversations with Contemporary Artists, Kara Walker."

30. Collins, *Black Sexual Politics*, 1–52.

31. Experience and research suggest that Mitchell's first point is not quite accurate. Many kids of this generation do not know the difference, and many parents are not, unfortunately, telling them different because they too are unaware. See Smiley, "Barbershop Controversy."

32. Bhabha, "Other Question," 376.

33. Hannaham, "Pea, Ball, Bounce."

34. T. Lott, "Kara Walker Speaks," 70.

35. In May 2005, Walker reportedly sold at auction her five-part silhouette piece *The Battle of Atlanta: Being the Narrative of a Negress in the Flames of Desire—A Reconstruction*. The piece was said to have an estimated value of $150,000 to $200,000, but it sold for $300,000. This broke her previous auction record, which was in the $50,000 range. Walker's piece was among those that broke their own records, but in the Sotheby's press release of the event, no mention was made of the sale, it being overshadowed by pieces from Versace and Andy Warhol, both of which sold for millions. Art Market Watch, "$68 Million at Sotheby's Contemporary."

36. During the summer of 1997, Betye Saar mounted a letter-writing campaign against the exhibition of Walker's work and Walker's receiving the MacArthur Award. Citing the promotion of Walker's negative images as her impetus, Saar tried to make people aware of the potential dangers inherent in Walker's presentations. See the account of the controversy and Saar's comments in Juliette Bowles, "Extreme Times."

37. As one who has taught courses on the civil rights movement, I can attest to this fact but would argue that this lack of awareness is not relegated only to a younger generation. Many people are unaware of the intricacies of slavery, stereotypes as-

sociated with African Americans, or any facet of the civil rights struggle. A. King, "*Barbershop* Controversy."

38. Gray, *Cultural Moves*, 8.

39. This "truth" is that months before Parks's arrest, several others had been arrested for refusing to give up their seats on the bus. The concern, however, was that none of the others were community leaders, nor were they middle-class black women (a point often submerged as well). More than being a wearied, tired soul on the day of her arrest, Parks was part of the larger system of organization set up to defeat segregation in the South at that time. On the day Parks was arrested, the leadership of the Dexter Avenue Baptist Church systematically went about putting the boycott into motion. Kohl, "Rosa Parks and the Montgomery Bus Boycott"; Armstrong, Edwards, Roberson, and Williams, *Teaching the American Civil Rights Movement*.

40. See Greg Tate's comment in "Discussion," 269.

41. A visual example of this practice appeared as the premise for Spike Lee's *Bamboozled*, which was a broadside attack on minstrelsy and the HBO movie *Dancing in September*, which aired in February 2001. *Dancing in September*, which was written, produced, and directed by Reggie Rock Bythewood, creator of television's *A Different World*, depicts a television sitcom writer's desire to produce a new African American TV series. The writer, played by Nicole Ari Parker (who incidentally plays Teri on Showtime's series *Soul Food*), develops a hit show, but when the network decides to expand the audience to include white viewers, the ratings for the show fall. In order to increase ratings, Tomasina Crawford (Parker's character) and her boyfriend, network executive George Washington (played by Isaiah Washington), begin hitching the characters and the show with a series of stereotypes to make it funnier. One scene involves a restaurant where the star of the show and his mother argue and begin hitting one another with chicken bones. As one article puts it, there is "neck rolling, Ebonics and even a new-millennium update on Jimmy Walker's 'Good Time' mantra, 'Dyn-o-mite!'" See Denene Millner, "Envisioning a Better Black TV."

42. Hannaham, "Pea, Ball, Bounce," 117.

EPILOGUE

1. Coronado, "Fried-Chicken Contest."

2. This information was shared by John T. Edge. Also see Edge's *Fried Chicken*, 98.

3. Barbara Christian makes this insightful comment on black memorabilia in Marlon Riggs's *Ethnic Notions*.

4. "Monday Morning."

5. Pitts, "Black History Is No Game of Chicken."

6. Ibid.

BIBLIOGRAPHY

Manuscript Collections
Beltsville, Maryland
   National Agricultural Library, Rare Book Collection
     American Poultry Historical Society Collection
     James M. Gwin Poultry Collection
Charlottesville, Virginia
   University of Virginia Library, Special Collections
     Jackson Davis Collection of the African-American Educational Photographs
     The Holsinger Studio Collection
     The Albert and Shirley Small Special Collections Library
College Park, Maryland
   National Archives and Records Administration, Still Pictures Division
     Bureau of Agricultural Economics, 1876–1959, Record Group 83-G
     Committee of the Legislative Branch, Record Group 148-MS
     Extension Service, Record Group 33
     Federal Works Agency, Office of Information, Record Group 162
     U.S. Department of Agriculture, Record Group 16-G
     U.S. Department of Labor, Women's Bureau, Record Group 86-G
     Works Progress Administration, Record Group 69-N
Durham, North Carolina
   Duke University, Rare Book, Manuscript, and Special Collections Library
     Battaile Muse Papers
Richmond, Virginia
   Library of Virginia
   Virginia Historical Society
     Bagby Family Papers
     Wallace Davenport Family Papers
     Marie E. Bowery Delaney Family Papers
     Jubal Anderson Early Family Papers
     Foster Studio Collection
     Records of Upper Goose Creek Baptist Church
     Vertical File—Exchange Hotel and Civil War Museum
     Vertical File—Gordonsville, Virginia
     Dora Waldrop Family Papers
     Wynne Family Papers
Washington, D.C.
   Division of Prints and Photographs, Library of Congress

Farm Security Administration/Office of War Information
Photograph Collection
Manuscript Division, Library of Congress
Nannie Helen Burroughs Papers
Smithsonian Institution, National Museum of American History, Archives Center
Oral History of Southern Agriculture
Warsaw Collection
York County, Virginia
Records, Order Book no. 4, 1774–84

Microform Collections
Hampton, Virginia
Hampton University Newspaper Clippings File

Government Documents
Chambers, C. L. *Minutes, Regional Conference for Negro District Agents, Petersburg, Virginia*. Petersburg, Va.: United States Department of Agriculture, Extension Service, 1937.
Evans, J. A. *Extension Work among Negroes Conducted by Negro Agents, 1923*. United States Department of Agriculture. Department Circular 355. Washington, D.C.: Government Printing Office, 1925.
Hamilton, A. B., and C. K. McGee. *The Economic and Social Status of Rural Negro Families in Maryland*. Bulletin X-4. College Park: University of Maryland, Agricultural Experiment Station and Extension Service, 1948.
Nybroten, Norman. *Consumer Preferences for Poultry Meat*. Bulletin 389. Morgantown: West Virginia University, Agricultural Experiment Station, 1956.
Smith, Harold D. *Consumer Preferences and Buying Habits for Chicken*. Bulletin X-5. College Park: University of Maryland, Agricultural Experiment Station and Extension Service, 1951.
Smith, Harold D., and Harold Hoecker. *Retail Merchandising and Consumer Acceptance of Eggs and Poultry*. Bulletin X-6. College Park: University of Maryland, Agricultural Experiment Station and Extension Service, 1951.
Termohlen, William D., J. Kinghorne, E. L. Warren, and J. H. Radabaugh. "An Economic Survey of the Commercial Broiler Industry." USDA, Agricultural Adjustment Poultry Section. Division of Marketing and Marketing Agreements. Washington, D.C., 1936.

Other Sources
Abrahams, Roger. *Talking Black*. Rawley, Mass.: Newbury House, 1976.
Abrams, M. H. *A Glossary of Literary Terms*. 5th ed. Fort Worth, Tex.: Holt, Rinehart and Winston, 1999.

Adams, Jane. *The Transformation of Rural Life: Southern Illinois, 1890–1990*. Chapel Hill: University of North Carolina Press, 1994.

Advertisement. "Criterion Café." *Washington Sun*, July 23, 1915, 2.

Advertisement. "Elite, No. 2 Opens Thursday, January 28, Palatial Cape." *Chicago Defender*, January 23, 1915.

Ajayi, J. Ade, and Michael Crowder. *History of West Africa*. New York: Columbia University Press, 1972.

Aldrovandi, Ulisse. *Aldrovandi on Chickens: The Ornithology of Ulisse Aldrovandi (1600)*. Vol. 2, bk. 14. Translated by R. L. Lind. Norman: University of Oklahoma Press, 1963.

America, 1935–1946. Cambridge, Eng.: Chadwyck-Healey Ltd., 1980. Microfiche.

Anderson, Jay. "Scholarship on Contemporary American Folk Foodways." *Ethnologia Europaea* 5 (1971): 56–63.

Andrews, Charles. *Colonial Folkways: A Chronicle of American Life in the Reign of the Georges*. New Haven: Yale University Press, 1919.

Andrews, William, Frances Smith Foster, and Trudier Harris, eds. *The Oxford Companion to African American Literature*. New York: Oxford University Press, 1997.

Angelou, Maya. *I Know Why the Caged Bird Sings*. New York: Bantam Books, 1969.

Appadurai, Arjun, ed. *The Social Life of Things*. Cambridge: Cambridge University Press, 1988.

Appleby, Michael, Joy Mench, and Barry Hughes. *Poultry Behavior and Welfare*. Edinburgh, U.K.: Roslin Institute, 2004.

Armstrong, Elizabeth. "Kara Walker Interviewed by Liz Armstrong 7/23/96." In *No Place (Like Home)*, exhibition catalog, edited by Elizabeth Armstrong et al., 104–15. Minneapolis: Walker Art Center, 1997.

Armstrong, Julie B., Susan H. Edwards, Houston R. Roberson, and Rhonda Y. Williams, eds. *Teaching the Civil Rights Movement*. New York: Routledge, 2002.

Arnoldi, Mary Jo, Christraud M. Geary, and Kris L. Hardin, eds. *African Material Culture*. Bloomington: Indiana University Press, 1996.

Art Market Watch. "$68 Million at Sotheby's Contemporary." *Artnews.com*, May 13, 2005. <http://www.artnet.com/Magazine/news/artmarketwatch2/art marketwatch5-11-05.asp> (June 15, 2005).

Associated Press. "Kentucky Fried Chicken Redesigns for New Image." *Marketing News*, March 18, 1991.

Baird, Spencer Fullerton. *A History of North American Birds*. Boston: Little, Brown, 1875.

Bakhtin, Mikhail. *Problems of Dostoevsky's Poetics*. Edited and translated by Caryl Emerson. Theory and History of Literature, 8. Minneapolis: University of Minnesota Press, 1984.

———. *Rabelais and His World*. Translated by Hélène Iswolsky. Bloomington: Midland-Indiana University Press, 1984.

Baldwin, Brooke. "On the Verso: Postcard Messages as a Key to Popular Prejudices." *Journal of Popular Culture* 22.3 (Winter 1988): 15–28.

Ball, Charles. *Fifty Years in Chains, or, The Life of an American Slave*. 1858. New York: Dover Publications, 1970.

Barbot, Jean. *Barbot on Guinea: The Writings of Jean Barbot on West Africa, 1678–1712*. London: Hakluyt Society, 1992.

Barnwell, Andrea, and Kirsten Buick. "A Portfolio of Works by African American Artists Continuing the Dialogue." In *Creating Their Own Image: The History of African-American Women Artists*, edited by Lisa E. Farrington, 45–83. Boston: Oxford University Press, 2005.

Barthes, Roland. *Mythologies*. Translated by Annette Lavers. New York: Hill and Wang, 1972.

———. "Rhetoric of the Image." In *Visual Culture: The Reader*, edited by Jessica Evans and Stuart Hall, 33–40. London: Sage Publications, 2001.

Bass, Margaret K. "On Being a Fat Black Girl in a Fat-Hating Culture." In *Recovering the Black Female Body*, edited by Michael Bennett and Vanessa D. Dickerson, 219–30. New Brunswick, N.J.: Rutgers University Press, 2000.

Beaudry, Mary C., Lauren J. Cook, and Stephen A. Mrozowski. "Artifacts and Active Voices: Material Culture as Social Discourse." In *The Archaeology of Inequality*, edited by Robert Paynter and Randall H. McGuire, 150–91. Oxford: Basil Blackwell, 1991.

Belasco, Warren J. *Appetite for Change: How the Counterculture Took on the Food Industry, 1966–1988*. New York: Pantheon, 1989.

Bement, Caleb N. *American Poulterer's Companion: A Practical Treatise on the Breeding, Rearing, and General Management of Various Species of Domestic Poultry*. New York: Harper and Brothers, 1856.

Bennett, John C. *Poultry Book: A Treatise on Breeding and General Management of Domestic Fowls; with Numerous Original Descriptions and Portraits from Life*. Boston: Phillips, Sampson and Company, 1850.

Bennett, LeRone. *The Shaping of Black America*. Chicago: Johnson Publishing Company, 1975.

Beoku-Betts, Josephine. "We Got Our Way of Cooking Things: Women, Food, and Preservation of Cultural Identity among the Gullah." *Gender and Society* 9.5 (October 1995): 535–56.

Berlin, Ira. *Generations of Captivity: A History of African-American Slaves*. Cambridge: The Belknap Press of Harvard University Press, 2003.

———. *Slaves without Masters: The Free Negro in the Antebellum South*. New York: Pantheon Books, 1975.

Berlin, Ira, and Philip Morgan, eds. *Slaves' Economy: Independent Production by Slaves in the Americas*. London: Frank Cass, 1991.

Beverly, Robert. *The History and Present State of Virginia*. Edited by Louis B. Wright.

Chapel Hill: Published for the Institute of Early American History and Culture at Williamsburg, Va., by the University of North Carolina Press, 1947.

Bhabha, Homi. "The Other Question: The Stereotype and Colonial Discourse." In *Visual Culture: The Reader*, edited by Jessica Evans and Stuart Hall, 370–78. London: Sage Publications, 2001.

Billings, Warren M. "The Cases of Fernando and Elizabeth Key: A Note on the Status of Blacks in Seventeenth-Century Virginia." *William and Mary Quarterly*, 3rd ser., 30.3 (July 1973): 467–74.

Birch, Thomas. "Zip Coon." New York: Atwill's Music Saloon, 1834. Uncle Tom's Cabin and American Culture: Multi-media Archive, Digital Media Center, University of Virginia, Charlottesville. <http://jefferson.village.virginia.edu/utc/minstrel/zipcoon.html> (April 20, 2002).

Birmingham, Stephen. *Certain People: America's Black Elite*. Boston: Little, Brown, and Company, 1977.

Birth of a Nation. Directed by D. W. Griffith, 1915. Produced by Lillian Gish. Image Entertainment, 2002.

Blake, John W. *European Beginnings in West Africa, 1454–1578*. London: Longmans, Green, and Company, 1937.

Blassingame, John. *The Slave Community: Plantation Life in the Antebellum South*. New York: Oxford University Press, 1979.

Blauvelt, Harry. "Zoeller Says His Comments about Woods Made 'in Jest.'" *USA Today*, April 22, 1997, 1C.

Blench, Roger M., and Kevin MacDonald. *The Origins and Development of African Livestock: Archeology, Genetics, Linguistics, and Ethnography*. London: University College of London, 2000.

Bloom, Harold, ed. *Modern Critical Views: Gwendolyn Brooks*. Philadelphia: Chelsea House Publishers, 2000.

Bobo, Jacqueline. *Black Feminist Cultural Criticism*. Malden, Mass.: Blackwell Publishers, 2001.

———. *Black Women as Cultural Readers*. New York: Columbia University Press, 1995.

———. "Sifting through the Controversy: Reading the *Color Purple*." *Callaloo* 39 (Spring 1989): 332–42.

———. "'The Subject Is Money': Reconsidering the Black Film Audience as a Theoretical Paradigm." *Black American Literature Forum* 25.2 (Summer 1991): 421–32.

Bogle, Donald. *Toms, Coons, Mulattoes, Mammies, and Bucks*. 4th ed. New York: Continuum, 2001.

Bogus, Sdiane A. "The 'Queen B.' Figure in Black Literature." In *Lesbian Texts and Contexts: Radical Revisions*, edited by Karla Jay and Joanne Glasgow, 275–79. New York: New York University Press, 1990.

Bolles, A. Lynn. "Flying the Love Bird and Other Tourist Jobs in Jamaica: Women

Workers in Negril." In *Sister Circle: Black Women and Work*, edited by Sharon Harley and the Black Women and Work Collective, 29–47. New Brunswick, N.J.: Rutgers University Press, 2002.

Bolzius, Johann Martin. "Johann Martin Bolzius Answers a Questionnaire on Carolina and Georgia: Part II." *William and Mary Quarterly* 15 (April 1958): 228–52.

———. "Reliable Answer to Some Submitted Questions Concerning the Land Carolina." *William and Mary Quarterly* 14 (April 1957): 223–61.

Borchert, James. *Alley Life in Washington*. Urbana: University of Illinois Press, 1982.

Borden, Anne. "Heroic 'Hussies' and 'Brilliant Queers': Genderracial Resistance in the Works of Langston Hughes." *African American Review* 28.3 (Autumn 1994): 333–45.

Bower, Anne, ed. *Reel Food: Essays on Food and Film*. New York: Routledge, 2004.

Bowles, John P. "Blinded by the White: Art and History at the Limits of Whiteness." *Art Journal* 60.4 (Winter 2001): 39–43.

Bowles, Juliette. "Extreme Times Call for Extreme Heroes." *International Review of African American Art* 14.3 (1997): 3–16.

———. "Stereotypes Subverted: The Debate Continues." *International Review of African American Art* 15.2 (1998): 44–51.

Boynton, Charles B. 1867. "A Duty Which the Colored People Owe to Themselves. A Sermon Delivered at Metzerott Hall, Washington, DC." In *African American Perspectives, 1818–1907*. <http://memory.loc.gov/ammem/aap/aaphome.html> (August 14, 1996).

Breen, Thomas. "Horses and Gentleman: The Cultural Significance of Gambling among the Gentry of Virginia." *William and Mary Quarterly*, 3rd ser., 34.2 (April 1977): 239–57.

Breen, Thomas, and Stephen Innes. *"Myne Owne Ground": Race and Freedom on Virginia's Eastern Shore, 1640–1676*. New York: Oxford University Press, 1980.

Bremer, Fredrika. *The Homes of the New World: Impressions of America*. 2 vols. Translated by Mary Howitt. New York: Harper and Brothers, 1853.

Brewer, James H. "Negro Property Owners in Seventeenth-Century Virginia." *William and Mary Quarterly*, 3rd ser., 12.4 (October 1955): 575–80.

Bridenbaugh, Carl. *Cities in Revolt: Urban Life in America, 1743–1776*. New York: Alfred Knopf, 1955.

Brooks, Gwendolyn. *Blacks*. Chicago: Third World Press, 1992.

———. *Maud Martha*. In *Blacks*, 141–322. Chicago: Third World Press, 1992.

———. *Report from Part One*. Chicago: Broadside Press, 1972.

Brooks, Sara. *You May Plow Here: The Narrative of Sara Brooks*. New York: W. W. Norton, 1986.

Brown, Charlotte Hawkins. *The Correct Thing to Do—To Say—To Wear*. 1940. New York: G. K. Hall and Company, 1995.

———. "The Negro and the Social Graces." Radio address, March 10, 1940. Washington, D.C.: Moorland-Spingarn Research Center, Howard University.

Brown, Elsa Barkley. "To Catch the Vision of Freedom: Reconstructing Southern Black Women's Political History, 1865–1880." In *African American Women and the Vote, 1837–1965*, edited by Bettye Collier-Thomas et al., 66–99. Amherst: University of Massachusetts Press, 1997.

Brown, Gillian. "Getting in the Kitchen with Dinah: Domestic Politics in *Uncle Tom's Cabin*." *American Quarterly* 36 (Fall 1984): 503–23.

Brown, Kathleen. *Good Wives, Nasty Wenches, and Anxious Patriarchs*. Chapel Hill: Published for the Omohundro Institute of Early American History and Culture at Williamsburg, Va., by the University of North Carolina Press, 1996.

Brown, Linda Keller, and Kay Mussell, eds. *Ethnic and Regional Foodways in the United States: The Performance of Group Identity*. Knoxville: University of Tennessee Press, 1984.

Brown, Stephen, Lorna Stevens, and Pauline Maclaran. "I Can't Believe It's Not Bakhtin: Literary Theory, Postmodern Advertising, and the Gender Agenda." *Journal of Advertising* 28.1 (Spring 1999): 11–25.

Brown-Douglas, Kelly. *Sexuality and the Black Church: A Womanist Perspective*. New York: Orbis Books, 1999.

Bugos, Glenn E. "Intellectual Property Protection in the American Chicken-Breeding Industry." *Business History Review* 66.1 (Spring 1992): 127–70.

Burke, Padriac. "Rolling Carts and Songs of Plenty: The Urban Food Vendor." *Journal of American Culture* 2.3 (Fall 1979): 480–87.

Burnham, George P. *The History of Hen Fever*. New York: George P. Burnham, 1855.

Burns, Richard Allen. "Foodways in the Military." *Digest: An Interdisciplinary Study of Food and Foodways* 18 (1998): 21–26.

Burton, Annie. *Memories of Childhood's Slavery Days*. Boston: Ross Publishing Company, 1909. Edited by Natalia Smith. In *Documenting the American South: The Southern Experience in Nineteenth-Century America*. Chapel Hill: Academic Affairs Library, University of North Carolina, 1996. <http://docsouth.unc.edu/burton .html> (January 2, 2002).

Buster, Larry V. *The Art and History of Black Memorabilia*. New York: Clarkson Potter, 2000.

Byrd, William. *The Secret Diary of William Byrd of Westover, 1709–1712*. Edited by Louis Wright and Marion Tinling. Richmond, Va.: Dietz Press, 1941.

Cà da Mosto, Alvise. *The Voyages of Cadamosto and Other Documents on Western Africa in the Second Half of the Fifteenth Century*. London: Hakluyt Society, 1937.

Cameron, Dan. "Kara Walker: Rubbing History the Wrong Way." *On Paper* 10 (September–October 1997): 11–14.

Camp, Charles. *American Foodways: What, When, Why, and How We Eat in America*. Little Rock: August House, 1989.

———. "Food in American Culture: A Bibliographic Essay." *Journal of American Culture* 2 (1979): 559–70.

Campbell, Bebe Moore. *Your Blues Ain't Like Mine*. New York: Ballantine Books, 1992.

Campbell, Jane. "An Interview with Bebe Moore Campbell." *Callaloo* 22.4 (1999): 954–72.

Campbell, Thomas Monroe. *The Movable School Goes to the Negro Farmer*. Tuskegee: Tuskegee Institute Press, 1936.

Candela, Gregory. "'We Wear the Mask': Irony in Dunbar's *The Sport of the Gods*." *American Literature* 48.1 (March 1976): 60–72.

Carby, Hazel. "Encoding White Resentment: Grand Canyon—A Narrative for Our Times." In *Race, Identity, and Representation in Education*, edited by Cameron McCarthy and Warren Critchlow, 236–47. New York: Routledge, 1993.

———. "It Jus Be's Dat Way Sometime: The Sexual Politics of Women's Blues." *Radical America* 20.4 (June–July 1986): 9–22.

———. "Policing the Black Woman's Body in an Urban Context." *Critical Inquiry* 18.4 (Summer 1992): 738–55.

———. *Reconstructing Womanhood: The Emergence of the Afro-American Woman Novelist*. New York: Oxford University Press, 1987.

Carey, Brycchan. *British Abolitionism and the Rhetoric of Sensibility: Writing, Sentiment, and Slavery, 1760–1807*. New York: Palgrave, 2005.

Carr, Lois Green, and Lorena Walsh. "The Standard of Living in the Colonial Chesapeake." *William and Mary Quarterly*, 3rd ser., 45.1 (January 1988): 135–59.

Carretta, Vincent. "Olaudah Equiano or Gustavus Vassa? New Light on an Eighteenth-Century Question of Identity." *Slavery and Abolition* 20 (1999): 96–105.

Carroll, Michael P. "The Logic of Anglo-American Meals." *Journal of American Culture* 5 (Fall 1982): 36–45.

Carson, Barbara G. "Interpreting History through Objects." *Journal of Museum Education* 10.3 (1985): 129–33.

Carson, Cary. "Doing History with Material Culture." In *Material Culture and the Study of American Life*, edited by Ian M. G. Quimby, 41–64. New York: W. W. Norton and Company, 1978.

Carson, Jane. *Colonial Virginians at Play*. Williamsburg: University Press of Virginia, 1965.

Carter, Marva Griffin. "Removing the 'Minstrel Mask' in the Musicals of Will Marion Cook." *Musical Quarterly* 84.2 (Summer 2000): 206–20.

Cary, Phoebe. "The Chicken's Mistake." *Christian Recorder*, February 2, 1867.

Caughey, John. "Introduction: What Is Life History and How Do You Do It?" In *Negotiating Cultures and Identities: A Life History Approach*. Lincoln: University of Nebraska Press, forthcoming.

Chappelle, Dave. *Killin' Them Softly*. Platinum Comedy Series, Ventura Distribution, 2003.

"Chicken Thieves About." *Petersburg Press*, December 10, 1859, 1.

Chimezie, Amuzie. "The Dozens: An African-Heritage Theory." *Journal of Black Studies* 6.4 (June 1976): 401–20.

Christian, Barbara. *Black Feminist Criticism: Perspectives on Black Women Writers*. New York: Pergamon, 1985.

Clark, Gracia. *Onions Are My Husband: Survival and Accumulation by West African Market Women*. Chicago: University of Chicago Press, 1994.

Clarke, Cheryl. "The Failure to Transform: Homophobia in the Black Community." In *Homegirls: A Black Feminist Anthology*, edited by Barbara Smith, 190–201. New Brunswick, N.J.: Rutgers University Press, 2000.

Clark-Lewis, Elizabeth. *Living In, Living Out: African American Domestics in Washington, D.C., 1910–1940*. Washington, D.C.: Smithsonian Institution Press, 1994.

Cobb, Russell. "Chickenfighting for the Soul of the Heartland." *Text, Practice, Performance* 4 (2003): 69–83.

Cohen, Lizbeth. "The Class Experience of Mass Consumption." In *The Power of Culture*, edited by Richard W. Fox and T. J. Jackson Lears, 135–60. Chicago: University of Chicago Press, 1993.

Collier, John, Jr., and Malcolm Collier. *Visual Anthropology: Photography as a Research Method*. Albuquerque: University of New Mexico Press, 1986.

Collier-Thomas, Bettye, and James Turner. "Race, Class and Color: The African American Discourse on Identity." *Journal of American Ethnic History* 14.1 (Fall 1994): 5–31.

Collins, Patricia Hill. *Black Feminist Thought: Knowledge, Consciousness, and the Politics of Empowerment*. New York: Routledge, 1991.

———. *Black Sexual Politics: African Americans, Gender, and the New Racism*. New York: Routledge, 2004.

———. "Learning from the Outsider Within: The Sociological Significance of Black Feminist Thought." *Social Problems* 33.6 (1986): 514–32.

"Colored Gentlemen of Philadelphia: Thomas Dorsey." *Christian Recorder*, November 4, 1865.

Cook, H. B. Kimberly. "Cockfighting on the Venezuelan Island of Margarita: A Ritualized Form of Male Aggression." In *The Cockfight*, edited by Alan Dundes, 232–40. Madison: University of Wisconsin Press, 1994.

Cooper, Anna Julia. *A Voice from the South*. 1892. New York: Oxford University Press, 1988.

Cooper, Thomas, and David J. McCord, eds. *The Statutes at Large of South Carolina*. 10 vols. Columbia: A. S. Johnston, 1836–41.

Corliss, Richard. Review of *Soul Food*, directed by George Tillman Jr. *Time*, October 13, 1997, 88.

Coronado, Kristin. "Fried-Chicken Contest Is Nod to Town's Past." *Richmond Times-Dispatch*, June 14, 2001, D26.

Counihan, Carole M. "Female Identity, Food, and Power in Contemporary Florence." *Anthropological Quarterly* 61.2 (1988): 51–61.

Crew, Spencer. *Field to Factory: Afro-American Migration, 1915–1940*. Washington, D.C.: Smithsonian Institution, 1987.

Crew, Spencer, and John Fleckner. "Archival Sources for Business History at the National Museum of American History." *Business History Review* (Autumn 1986): 474–86.

Cunningham, Virginia. *Paul Laurence Dunbar and His Song*. New York: Biblo and Tannen, 1969.

Curtin, Phillip. *The Atlantic Slave Trade: A Census*. Madison: University of Wisconsin Press, 1969.

Dalleo, Peter T. " 'Thrifty and Intelligent, Moral and Religious': Wilmington's Free African American Community as Portrayed in the *Blue Hen's Chicken*." *Delaware History* 28.1 (1998): 39–70.

Dalton, Jennifer. "Kara Walker." *Review*, November 15, 1998. <http://www.reviewNew York.com/current/98_99/nov_15/review3.html> (March 20, 2001).

Dalton, Karen. "The Past Is Prologue but Is the Parody and Pastiche Progress? A Conversation [with Michael Harris and Lowery Sims]." *International Review of African American Art* 14.3 (1997): 17–29.

Dandridge, Rita B. "Gathering Places: A Selected Bibliography of Ann Allen Shockley." *Black American Literature Forum* 21.1–2 (Spring–Summer 1987): 133–46.

Darden, Norma Jean, and Carole Darden. *Spoonbread and Strawberry Wine*. New York: Doubleday, 1994.

Davidson, Alan. *The Oxford Companion to Food*. New York: Oxford University Press, 1999.

Davidson, Basil. *The African Slave Trade*. Boston: Little, Brown, and Company, 1961.
———. *A History of West Africa, 1000–1800*. London: Longman, 1977.

Davies, Carole Boyce. "Migratory Subjectivities: Black Women's Writing and the Re-Negotiation of Identities." In *Black Women, Writing, and Identity: Migrations of the Subject*, 1–37. London: Routledge, 1994.

Davis, Angela Y. *Blues Legacies and Black Feminism*. New York: Pantheon, 1998.
———. "Reflections on the Black Woman's Role in the Community of Slaves." *Black Scholar* (November–December 1981): 2–15.
———. *Women, Race, and Class*. New York: Random House, 1981.

Davis, Karen. "Thinking Like a Chicken: Farm Animals and the Feminine Connection." In *Animals and Women: Feminist Theoretical Explorations*, edited by Carol Adams and Josephine Donovan, 192–212. Durham, N.C.: Duke University Press, 1995.

Deetz, James. *In Small Things Forgotten*. New York: Anchor Books, 1996.

DeKnight, Freda. *A Date with a Dish: A Cookbook of American Negro Recipes*. New York: Hermitage Press, 1948.
———. "A Date with a Dish—Pheasant." *Ebony*, November 1949.

Denkler, Ann. "Sustaining Identity, Recapturing Heritage: Exploring Issues of Public

History, Tourism, and Race in a Southern Rural Town." Ph.D. diss., University of Maryland at College Park, 2001.

De Reaumur, M. *The Art of Hatching and Bringing Up Domestic Fowls of all Kinds at Any Time of the Year.* 8 vols. London: C. Davis, 1750.

Diawara, Manthia. *Black American Cinema.* New York: Routledge, 1993.

Dickson, Paul. *Chow: A Cook's Tour of Military Food.* New York: New American Library, 1978.

Dill, Bonnie Thornton. "Making Your Job Good Yourself: Domestic Service and the Construction of Personal Dignity." In *Women and the Politics of Empowerment*, edited by Ann Bookman and Sandra Morgen, 33–52. Philadelphia: Temple University Press, 1988.

"Dining with the Fraternal Association." *Christian Recorder*, June 25, 1864.

"Dinner Program Honoring Robert H. Terrell." *The African American Experience in Ohio, 1850–1920.* George A. Myers Papers [MIC00092], Library of Congress American Memory Historical Collections for the National Digital Library, July 23, 2001.

"Discovering a [Confection] Den." *Richmond Daily Dispatch*, August 31, 1853.

"Dishes That Are Tasty and Wholesome: Traditional Thanksgiving Dinner Tastes Best." *Baltimore Afro-American*, November 22, 1930.

Dixon, Annette. "A Negress Speaks Out." In *Kara Walker: Pictures from Another Time*, edited by Kara Walker et al., 11–25. Ann Arbor: University of Michigan Museum of Art, 2002.

Dixon, Thomas. *The Clansman: An Historical Romance of the Ku Klux Klan (The Novel as American Social History).* 1905. Lexington: University of Kentucky Press, 1970.

Dodson, Jualynne E., and Cheryl Townsend Gilkes. "There's Nothing Like Church Food: Food and the U.S. Afro-Christian Tradition; Re-Membering Community and Feeding the Embodied S/spirit(s)." *Journal of the American Academy of Religion* 63.3 (1995): 519–39.

"Domestic Science Class Cooks for School Board." *Chicago Defender*, March 6, 1915.

Donkin, R. A. *Meleagrides: An Historical and Ethnogeographical Study of the Guinea Fowl.* Cambridge: Antiquity Publications, 1993.

Dorman, James. "Shaping the Popular Image of Post-Reconstruction American Blacks: The 'Coon Song' Phenomenon of the Gilded Age." *American Quarterly* 40 (December 1988): 450–71.

Doud, Richard. "Interview with John Collier." Archives of American Art's New Deal and the Arts Project, Archives of American Art, Smithsonian Institution, January 18, 1965. <http://artarchives.si.edu/oralhist/collie65.htm> (June 8, 2005).

Douglas, Mary. "Deciphering a Meal." In *Myth, Symbol, and Culture*, edited by Clifford Geertz, 61–81. New York: W. W. Norton, 1971.

Douglass, Frederick. *My Bondage and My Freedom.* Reprint. Urbana: University of Illinois Press, 1987.

———. "A Tribute to the Negro." *North Star*, April 7, 1849.

Dow, George Francis. *Slave Ships and Slaving*. New York: Dover Publications, 1970.

Driver, Justin. "The Mirth of a Nation: Black Comedy's Reactionary Hipness." *New Republic* (June 2001): 29–35.

Dubin, Steven C. "Symbolic Slavery: Black Representations in Popular Culture." *Social Problems* 34.2 (April 1987): 122–41.

Du Bois, W. E. B. "Industrial Education—Will It Solve the Negro Problem?" *Colored American Magazine* (1904): 333–39.

———. *The Philadelphia Negro*. 1899. Philadelphia: University of Pennsylvania Press, 1996.

———. *The Souls of Black Folk*. In *Three Negro Classics*, 207–390. New York: Avon Books, 1965.

Du Bois, W. E. B., and Augustus Granville Dill. *Morals and Manners among Negro Americans: Report of a Social Study Made by Atlanta University*. 1913. Edited by Apex Data Services, Inc., Joby Topper, and Jill Kuhn Sexton. In *Documenting the American South: The Southern Experience in Nineteenth-Century America*. Chapel Hill: Academic Affairs Library, University of North Carolina, 2001. <http://docsouth.unc.edu/church/morals/dubois.html> (March 13, 2001).

Dunbar, Paul Laurence, and Will Marion Cook. "Who Dat Say Chicken in Dis Crowd." Chicago: M. Witmark and Sons, 1898. Dayton, Ohio: Paul Laurence Dunbar Digital Collection, Paul Laurence Dunbar Library, Wright State University, 1992. <http://www.libraries.wright.edu/special/dunbar/whodat.html> (August 7, 2001).

Dundes, Alan, ed. "The Gallus as Phallus." In *The Cockfight*, 241–81. Madison: University of Wisconsin Press, 1994.

Dvorak, Petula. "Racist Flier Prompts Frank Forum." *Times-Picayune*, February 21, 1997.

Dyson, Marcia L. "Can You Love God and Sex? African American Women on Sexuality and Spirituality." *Essence*, February 1999, 55–59, 100.

Edge, John T. *Fried Chicken: An American Story*. New York: Putnam Publishing Group, 2004.

———. *A Gracious Plenty: Recipes and Recollections from the American South*. New York: G. P. Putnam's Sons, an Ellen Rolfes Book, for the Center for the Study of Southern Culture at the University of Mississippi, 1999.

———. "Hot Tamales from the Mississippi Delta: A Culinary Conundrum." Paper delivered at the "Grits and Greens and Everything in Between" Conference, Chicago, Ill., June 2000.

Editorial Notes. "Burnham's History of Hen Fever." *Putnam's Monthly Magazine of American Literature, Science and Art* 5.29 (May 1855): 549–50.

Edwards, Paul K. *The Southern Negro as a Consumer*. New York: Prentice Hall, 1932.

Ellison, Ralph. *The Invisible Man*. Reprint. New York: Modern Library, 1992.

Eltis, David, Stephen D. Behrendt, David Richardson, and Herbert S. Klein. *The Trans-Atlantic Slave Trade: A Database on CD-ROM*. Cambridge: Cambridge University Press, 1999.

―――. "The Volume and Structure of the Transatlantic Slave Trade: A Reassessment." *William and Mary Quarterly*, 3rd ser., 58.1 (January 2001): 17–47.

Emecheta, Buchi. *The Joys of Motherhood*. New York: George Braziller, 1979.

Emerson, Caryl. *First Hundred Years of Mikhail Bakhtin*. Princeton, N.J.: Princeton University Press, 1997.

Engelhardt, Elizabeth S. D. "Beating the Biscuits in Appalachia: Race, Class, and Gender Politics of Women Baking Bread." In *Cooking Lessons: The Politics of Gender and Food*, edited by Sherrie Inness, 151–68. Lanham, Md.: Rowman and Littlefield, 2001.

Equiano, Olaudah. *The Interesting Narrative of the Life of Olaudah Equiano Written by Himself*. Edited by Robert J. Allison. Boston: Bedford Books, 1995.

Ethnic Notions. Directed by Marlon Riggs. California Newsreel, 1987.

Evans, Larry. "Chicken Legs and the Hotel." *Free-Lance Star*, September 13, 1976, 22–24.

"Everywoman." *Cleveland Plain Dealer*, October 21, 1997, 3E.

Fabre, Genevieve, and Robert O'Meally. *History and Memory in African-American Culture*. New York: Oxford University Press, 1994.

Fanon, Frantz. *Black Skin, White Masks*. New York: Grove Press, 1967.

Farley, John Christopher, and Simon Robinson. "Dave Speaks." *Time*, May 23, 2005, 68.

Ferguson, Leland. *Uncommon Ground: Archaeology and Early African America, 1650–1800*. Washington: Smithsonian Institution Press, 1992.

Ferreira, Patricia. "The Triple Duty of a Black Woman Filmmaker: An Interview with Carmen Coustaut." *African American Review* 27.3 (Fall 1993): 433–43.

Fishkin, Shelley Fisher. "Interrogating 'Whiteness,' Complicating 'Blackness': Remapping American Culture." *American Quarterly* 47 (September 1995): 428–66.

Fithian, Philip Vickers. *Journal and Letters of Philip Vickers Fithian, 1773–1774*. Edited by Hunter Dickinson Farish. Williamsburg, Va.: Colonial Williamsburg, 1943.

Fleischhauer, Carl, and Beverly W. Brannan, eds. *Documenting America, 1935–1943*. Berkeley: University of California Press, 1988.

Fletcher, F. "The Housekeeper—Marketing for Hot Cross Buns." *Chicago Defender*, March 27, 1915.

―――. "The Housekeeper—Marketing for Vegetables." *Chicago Defender*, April 24, 1915.

―――. "The Housekeeper—White Bread/Whole-Wheat Bread." *Chicago Defender*, March 6, 1915.

Flynn, Richard. "'The Kindergarten of New Consciousness': Gwendolyn Brooks and the Social Construction of Childhood." *African American Review* 34.3 (Fall 2000): 483–500.

Foster, Shawn. "Black Pioneers Blazed Their Own Trails." *Salt Lake City Tribune*, February 15, 1998, A1.

Francia, Luis H. "Feeding Frenzy—Aphrodite: A Memoir of the Senses." Review of *If I*

Can Cook, You Know God Can, by Ntozake Shange. *Village Voice* 43.5 (April 1998): 123–27.

Freeman, Carla. "Reinventing Higglering across Transatlantic Zones: Barbadian Women Juggle the Triple Shift." In *Daughters of Caliban: Caribbean Women in the Twentieth Century*, edited by Consuelo López Springfield, 68–95. Bloomington: Indiana University Press, 1997.

Freeman, Douglas. *George Washington: A Biography*. New York: Charles Scribner Sons, 1952.

Friday. Directed by F. Gary Gray. New Line Cinema, 1999.

Fry, Gladys-Marie. *Stitched from the Soul: Slave Quilts from the Ante-Bellum South*. New York: Dutton Studio Books, Museum of American Folk Art, 1990.

Gardiner, Michael. "Ecology and Carnival: Traces of a 'Green' Social Theory in the Writings of Mikhail Bakhtin." *Theory and Society* 22 (1993): 765–812.

Gates, Henry Louis. "The Black Person in Art: How Should S/he Be Portrayed, Part I." *Black American Literature Forum* 21.1–2 (Spring–Summer 1987): 3–24.

———. "The Black Person in Art: How Should S/he Be Portrayed, Part II." *Black American Literature Forum* 21.3 (Fall 1987): 317–32.

———. "Introduction: Criticism in De Jungle." *Black American Literature Forum* 15.4 (Winter 1981): 123–27.

———. *The Signifying Monkey*. New York: Oxford University Press, 1988.

———. "The Trope of a New Negro and the Reconstruction of the Image of the Black." *Representations* 24 (Autumn 1988): 129–55.

Gatewood, Willard. *Aristocrats of Color: The Black Elite, 1880–1920*. Bloomington: Indiana University Press, 1990.

Gay, Kathlyn, and Martin K. Gay, eds. *Encyclopedia of North American Eating and Drinking*. New York: ABC-CLIO, 1996.

Gayle, Addison. *Oak and Ivy*. New York: Doubleday, 1971.

Geertz, Clifford. "Deep Play: Notes on the Balinese Cockfight." *Daedalus: Journal of the American Academy of Arts and Sciences* 101.1 (Winter 1972): 1–37.

———. " 'Thick Description': Toward an Interpretative Theory of Culture." In *The Interpretation of Cultures*, 3–32. New York: Basic Books, 1973.

Genovese, Eugene. *Roll, Jordan, Roll: The World the Slaves Made*. New York: Vintage Books, 1976.

Giddings, Paula. *When and Where I Enter*. New York: William Morrow, 1984.

Gilkes, Cheryl Townsend. " 'If It Wasn't for the Women . . . ': African American Women, Community Work, and Social Change." In *Women of Color in U.S. Society*, edited by Maxine Baca Zinn and Bonnie Thornton Dill, 229–46. Philadelphia: Temple University Press, 1994.

———. "The 'Loves' and 'Troubles' of African American Women's Bodies." In *A Troubling in My Soul: Womanist Perspectives on Evil and Suffering*, edited by Emilie M. Townes, 232–49. New York: Orbis Books, 1993.

———. "The Roles of Church and Community Mothers: Ambivalent American

Sexism or Fragmented African Familyhood?" *Journal of Feminist Studies in Religion* 2.1 (Spring 1986): 41–59.

Gilliam, Angela. "The Brazilian Mulata: Images in the Global Economy." *Race and Class* 40.1 (1998): 57–69.

Goffman, Erving. *The Presentation of Self in Everyday Life.* Woodstock, N.Y.: Overlook Press, 1973.

Goings, Kenneth W. *Mammy and Uncle Mose: Black Collectibles and American Stereotyping.* Bloomington: Indiana University Press, 1994.

Golden, Thelma. "Introduction [to] Oral Mores: A Postbellum Shadow Play: A Project for *Artforum* by Kara E. Walker." *Artforum* 35 (September 1996): 92–93.

———. "Kara Walker: A Dialogue." In *Kara Walker: Pictures from Another Time*, edited by Kara Walker et al., 43–49. Ann Arbor: University of Michigan Museum of Art, 2002.

Goldsmith, Peter. "A Woman's Place Is in the Church: Black Pentecostalism on the Georgia Coast." *Journal of Religious Thought* 32 (1975): 53–69.

Gomez, Michael. *Exchanging Our Country Marks: The Transformation of African Identities in the Colonial and Antebellum South.* Chapel Hill: University of North Carolina Press, 1998.

Gordon, John Steele. "The Chicken Story: The History of the U.S. Poultry Industry." *American Heritage* 47.5 (September 1996): 52–64.

Gordy, Frank. "Broilers." In *American Poultry History 1823–1973*, edited by Oscar Hanke, John Skinner, and James Florea, 390–95. Lafayette, Ind.: American Poultry Historical Society, 1974.

Gorn, Elliott. "'Gouge and Bite, Pull Hair and Scratch': The Social Significance of Fighting in the Southern Backcountry." *American Historical Review* 90 (February–December 1985): 18–43.

Gottdiener, M. "Hegemony and Mass Culture: A Semiotic Approach." *American Journal of Sociology* 90.5 (1985): 979.

Gray, Herman. *Cultural Moves: African Americans and the Politics of Representation.* Berkeley: University of California Press, 2005.

———. "Cultural Politics as Outrage(ous)." *Black Renaissance/Renaissance Noire* 3.1 (Winter 2000): 92–101.

Gray, Louis Cecil, and Esther Thompson. *History of Agriculture in the Southern United States to 1860.* Gloucester, Mass.: Peter Smith, 1958.

Green, Edward S. *National Capital Code of Etiquette.* Washington, D.C.: A. Jenkins Company, 1920.

Greene, Jack P., ed. *The Diary of Colonel Landon Carter of Sabine Hall, 1752–1778.* 2 vols. Charlottesville, Va.: Published for the Virginia Historical Society by the University of Virginia Press, 1965.

Greenlee, Sam. *The Spook Who Sat by the Door.* New Jersey: Richard Baron Books, 1969.

Gregory, Dick. *Nigger: An Autobiography.* New York: Pocket Books, 1964.

Griffin, Farah Jasmine. "Safe Spaces and Other Places: Navigating the Urban Landscape." In *Who Set You Flowin'? The African-American Migration Narrative*, 100–141. New York: Oxford University Press, 1995.

———. "Textual Healing: Claiming Black Women's Bodies, the Erotic and Resistance in Contemporary Novels of Slavery." *Callaloo* 19.2 (1996): 519–36.

Griffin, Judith Berry. *Phoebe the Spy [Phoebe and the General]*. New York: Scholastic Paperbacks, 1992.

Gutiérrez, Ramón, and Geneviève Fabre, eds. *Feasts and Celebrations in North American Ethnic Communities*. Albuquerque: University of New Mexico Press, 1995.

Haley, Alex. *Roots*. New York: Dell, 1977.

Hall, Robert. "Savoring Africa in the New World." In *Seeds of Change*, edited by Herman Viola and Carolyn Margolis, 161–73. Washington, D.C.: Smithsonian Institution Press, 1991.

Hall, Stuart. "New Ethnicities." In *Stuart Hall: Critical Dialogues in Cultural Studies*, edited by David Morley and Kuan-Hsing Chen. London: Routledge, 1996.

———, ed. *Representation: Cultural Representations and Signifying Practices*. London: Sage Publications, 1997.

Hanke, Oscar August, John Skinner, and James Florea. *American Poultry History, 1823–1973*. Lafayette, Ind.: American Poultry Historical Society, 1974.

Hannaham, James. "Pea, Ball, Bounce: Interview with Kara Walker." *Interview* (November 1998): 114–19.

Hansen, Karen V. " 'No Kisses Is Like Yours': An Erotic Friendship between Two African-American Women during the Mid-Nineteenth Century." *Gender and History* 7.2 (August 1995): 153–82.

Harley, Sharon. "Beyond the Classroom: The Organizational Lives of Black Female Educators in the District of Columbia, 1890–1930." *Journal of Negro Education* 51.3 (Summer 1982): 254–65.

———. "Nannie Helen Burroughs: 'The Black Goddess of Liberty.' " *Journal of Negro History* 81.3 (December 1996): 62–71.

———. " 'Working for Nothing but a Living': Black Women in the Underground Economy." In *Sister Circle: Black Women and Work*, edited by Sharon Harley and the Black Women and Work Collective, 48–66. New Brunswick, N.J.: Rutgers University Press, 2002.

Harris, Carmen. " 'A Ray of Hope for Liberation': Blacks in the South Carolina Extension Service, 1915–1970." Ph.D. diss., Michigan State University, 2002.

Harris, Ellen W., and Alvin Nowverl. "What's Happening to Soul Food? Regional and Income Differences in the African American Diet." *Ecology of Food and Nutrition* 38 (1999): 587–603.

Harris, Jessica B. *The Africa Cookbook*. New York: Simon and Schuster, 1998.

———. *Iron Pots and Wooden Spoons: Africa's Gift to New World Cooking*. New York: Athenaeum, 1989.

———. *Sky Juice and Flying Fish: Traditional Caribbean Cooking*. New York: Simon and Schuster, 1991.

———. *The Welcome Table: African American Heritage Cooking*. New York: Simon and Schuster, 1995.

Harris, Michael D. *Colored Pictures: Race and Visual Representation*. Chapel Hill: University of North Carolina Press, 2003.

Harris, Trudier. "From Exile to Asylum: Religion and Community in the Writings of Contemporary Black Women." In *Women's Writing in Exile*, edited by Mary Lynn Broe and Angela Ingram, 152–69. Chapel Hill: University of North Carolina Press, 1989.

———. *From Mammies to Militants: Domestics in Black American Literature*. Philadelphia: Temple University Press, 1982.

———. *The Power of the Porch: The Storyteller's Craft in Zora Neale Hurston, Gloria Naylor, and Randall Kenan*. Athens: University of Georgia Press, 1997.

———. *Saints, Sinners, and Saviors*. New York: Palgrave, 2001.

Harris-Lopez, Trudier. "Ugly Legacies of the Harlem Renaissance and Earlier: *Soul Food* and New Negroes." In *South of Tradition: Essays on African American Literature*, 196–216. Athens: University of Georgia Press, 2002.

Harrison Church, R. J. *West Africa: A Study of the Environment and Man's Use of It*. London: Longmen, 1957.

Haskin, Frederic J. "Samuel Fraunces." *Washington Evening Star*, August 11, 1916, 10.

Hayden, Dolores. *The Power of Place*. Cambridge: MIT Press, 1996.

Hazzard-Gordon, Katrina. *Jookin': The Rise of Social Dance Formations in African American Culture*. Philadelphia: Temple University Press, 1990.

Hening, William W., ed. *The Statutes at Large; Being a Collection of all the Laws of Virginia, from the First Session of the Legislature in the Year 1619*. 13 vols. Richmond, 1799–1823. Reprint. Charlottesville: University of Virginia Press, 1969.

Hess, Karen. *The Carolina Rice Kitchen: The African Connection*. Columbia: South Carolina University Press, 1992.

Heuman, Gad, and James Walvin, eds. *The Slavery Reader*. New York: Routledge, 2003.

Hicks, David. "Blood and Feathers: Masculine Identity in East Timorese Cockfighting." *World and I* 16.1 (January 2001): 194–97.

Higginbotham, Evelyn Brooks. "African-American Women's History and the Metalanguage of Race." *Signs* 17.2 (1992): 3–24.

———. *Righteous Discontent: The Women's Movement in the Black Baptist Church, 1880–1920*. Cambridge: Harvard University Press, 1993.

Hilliard, Sam. *Hogmeat and Hoecake: Food Supply in the Old South, 1840–1860*. Carbondale: Southern Illinois University Press, 1972.

Hine, Darlene Clark. "Rape and the Inner Lives of Black Women in the Middle West: Preliminary Thoughts on the Culture of Dissemblance." *Signs* 14.4 (1989): 912–20.

Hine, Darlene Clark, and Kathleen Thompson. *A Shining Thread of Hope: The History of Black Women in America*. New York: Broadway, 1998.

Hobsbawm, Eric, and Terence Ranger, eds. *The Invention of Tradition*. Cambridge: Cambridge University Press, 1992.

Hobson, Katherine. "Memories for Sale: Pitching New Products with Old Icons." *ABCNews.com*. <http://www.abcnews.go.com/sections/business/DailyNews/nostalgiasells990725.html> (February 2, 2000).

Hodder, Ian. "The Interpretation of Documents and Material Culture." In *Handbook of Qualitative Research*, edited by Norman Denzin and Yvonna S. Lincoln, 343–402. Thousand Oaks, Calif.: Sage Publications, 1994.

Holloway, Karla F. C. *Passed On: African American Mourning Stories, a Memorial*. Durham, N.C.: Duke University Press, 2002.

———. "Revision and (Re)membrance: A Theory of Literary Structures in Literature by African American Women Writers." *Black American Literature Forum* 24.4 (Winter 1990): 617–31.

hooks, bell. "Artistic Integrity: Race and Accountability." In *Reel to Reel: Race, Sex and Class at the Movies*, 69–76. New York: Routledge, 1996.

———. *Art on My Mind: Visual Politics*. New York: New Press, 1995.

———. "The Chitlin Circuit on Black Community." In *Yearning: Race, Gender, and Cultural Politics*, 33–40. Boston: South End Press, 1990.

———. "Postmodern Blackness." In *A Postmodern Reader*, edited by Joseph Natoli and Linda Hutcheon, 510–18. Albany: State University of New York Press, 1993.

Hopkins, Pauline. *Contending Forces*. 1900. New York: Oxford University Press, 1988.

Horner, William, Jr. "Sam Fraunces." *Philadelphia Bulletin*, February 22, 1934, C8.

House-Midamba, Bessie, and Felix K. Ekechi, eds. *African Market Women and Economic Power*. Westport, Conn.: Greenwood Publishing Group, 1995.

"How to Make Chicken Croquettes." *Chicago Defender*, March 31, 1923.

Hughes, Alan. "Hip-Hop Economy." *Black Enterprise*, May 2002, 70–75.

Hughes, Langston. *The Best of Simple*. New York: Hill and Wang, 1989.

Hughes, Marvalene. "Soul, Black Women, and Food." In *Food and Culture: A Reader*, edited by Carole Counihan and Penny Van Esterik, 272–81. New York: Routledge, 1997.

Hume, Audrey Noël. *Food*. Colonial Williamsburg Archaeological Series, 9. Williamsburg, Va.: Colonial Williamsburg Foundation, 1978.

Hunter, Tera. "'The Correct Thing': Charlotte Hawkins Brown and the Palmer Institute." *Southern Exposure* 11.5 (September–October 1983): 37–43.

———. *To 'Joy My Freedom: Southern Black Women's Lives and Labors after the Civil War*. Cambridge: Harvard University Press, 1997.

Hurston, Zora Neale. *Dust Tracks on a Road: An Autobiography*. 1942. New York: Harper Perennial, 1996.

———. *Their Eyes Were Watching God*. 1937. Urbana: University of Illinois Press, 1978.

"Important Decision [about Negro Cookshops]." *Richmond Daily Dispatch*, March 9, 1853.

Inikori, Joseph E., and Stanley Engerman, eds. *The Atlantic Slave Trade*. Durham, N.C.: Duke University Press, 1992.

Isaac, Rhys. "Ethnographic Method in History: An Action Approach." In *Material Life in America, 1600–1860*, edited by Robert Blair St. George, 39–61. Boston: Northeastern University Press, 1988.

———. *The Transformation of Virginia, 1740–1790*. Chapel Hill: University of North Carolina Press for the Institute of Early American History and Culture, 1982.

Jacobson, Jennifer. "Short Subjects: Food for Thought." *Chronicle of Higher Education*, February 4, 2004, 6.

Jaspar, A. William. "Marketing." In *American Poultry History, 1823–1973*, edited by Oscar August Hanke, John Skinner, and James Florea, 306–69. Madison, Wisc.: American Poultry Historical Society, 1974.

Jay, Robert. *The Trade Card in Nineteenth-Century America*. Columbia: University of Missouri Press, 1987.

Jerome, Julia. "Advice to Girls — 'Proper Food Will Ward Off Colds,' 'Rice — Some of Its Uses,' 'Sweet Potatoes Better Than White,' 'Household Hints.'" *Baltimore Afro-American*, January 3, 1931, 17.

Jewell, K. Sue. *From Mammy to Miss America and Beyond: Cultural Images and the Shaping of U.S. Policy*. New York: Routledge, 1993.

Jimoh, A. Yemisi. "Double Consciousness, Modernism, and Womanist Themes in Gwendolyn Brooks' 'The Anniad.'" *MELUS* 23.3 (Fall 1998): 167–86.

Johnson, James Weldon. *Along This Way: The Autobiography of James Weldon Johnson*. New York: Penguin, 1968.

Jones, Friday. *Days of Bondage: Autobiography of Friday Jones, Being a Brief Narrative of His Trials and Tribulations in Slavery*. Washington, D.C.: Commercial Publishing Company, 1883. Edited by Chris Hill. In *Documenting the American South: The Southern Experience in Nineteenth-Century America*. Chapel Hill: Academic Affairs Library, University of North Carolina, 1999. <http://docsouth.unc.edu/neh/fjones/jones.html> (January 5, 2002).

Jones, Jacqueline. *Labor of Love, Labor of Sorrow: Black Women, Work, and the Family from Slavery to the Present*. New York: Basic Books, 1985.

Jones, LuAnn. *Mama Learned Us to Work: Farm Women in the New South*. Chapel Hill: University of North Carolina Press, 2002.

Jones, Rosalind Ann, and Peter Stallybrass. "Introduction: Fashion, Fetishism, and Memory in Early Modern England and Europe." In *Renaissance Clothing and the Materials of Memory*, edited by Rosalind Ann Jones and Peter Stallybrass, 1–14. Cambridge: Cambridge University Press, 2000.

Joyner, Charles. *Down by the Riverside: A South Carolina Slave Community*. Urbana: University of Illinois Press, 1984.

———. "Soul Food and the Sambo Stereotype: Foodlore from the Slave Narrative Collection." *Keystone Folklore Quarterly* (Winter 1971): 171–77.

Kane, Eugene. "Movie's Message Really Hits the Spot." Review of *Soul Food*, directed
by George Tillman Jr. *Milwaukee Journal Sentinel*, October 5, 1997, 3.

Katz, Solomon, and William Woys Weaver, eds. *The Encyclopedia of Food and Culture*.
New York: Charles Scribner Sons, 2002.

Kelley, Robin D. G. *Race Rebels*. New York: Free Press, 1994.

Kent, George. "A Complicated Universe." In *A Life of Gwendolyn Brooks*, 103–16.
Lexington: University of Kentucky Press, 1990.

King, Anthony. "*Barbershop* Controversy: Black Heroes Ought to Be Free of Barbs."
Atlanta Journal-Constitution, October 10, 2002, 19A.

King, Kimball. *Augustus Baldwin Longstreet*. Boston: Twayne, 1984.

King, Mae C. "The Politics of Sexual Stereotypes." *Black Scholar*, March–April 1973,
12–23.

King, Wayne. "Joanne Little." *New York Times*, July 15 and August 2, 1975.

Kiple, Kenneth F., and Kriemhild Conee Ornelas, eds. *The Cambridge World History of
Food*. Vol. 1. Cambridge: Cambridge University Press, 2000.

Kohl, Herbert. "Rosa Parks and the Montgomery Bus Boycott." In *Civil Rights since
1787*, edited by Jonathan Birnbaum and Clarence Taylor, 443–57. New York: New
York University Press, 2000.

Kopytoff, Igor. "The Cultural Biography of Things: Commodification as Process." In
The Social Life of Things, edited by Arjun Appadurai, 64–95. Cambridge:
Cambridge University Press, 1988.

Krondl, Michael. "Founding Mothers." In *Around the American Table*, 55–86.
Holbrook, Mass.: Adams Publishing and The New York Public Library, 1995.

Kulikoff, Allan. "Households and Markets: Toward a New Synthesis of American
Agrarian History." *William and Mary Quarterly*, 3rd ser., 50.2 (April 1993): 342–55.

————. "The Origins of Afro-American Society in Tidewater Maryland and Virginia,
1700 to 1790." *William and Mary Quarterly*, 3rd ser., 35.2 (April 1978): 226–59.

Kupenda, Angela Mae. "For White Women: Your Blues Ain't Like Mine, but We Hide
All Our Faces and Cry: Literary Illumination for White and Black Sister/Friends,
Based on Bebe Moore Campbell's Novel, *Your Blues Ain't Like Mine*." *Boston College
Third World Law Journal* (2001): 67–106. <http://www.bc.edu/bc_org/avp/law/
lwsch/journals/bctwj/22_1/02_TXT.htm> (October 8, 2002).

Kytle, Elizabeth. *Willie Mae*. Athens: University of Georgia Press, 1993.

Leal, Ondina Fachel. "The Gaucho Cockfight in Porto Alegre, Brazil." In *The
Cockfight*, edited by Alan Dundes, 208–31. Madison: University of Wisconsin
Press, 1994.

Learning, Aaron, and Jacob Spicer. *Grants, Concessions, and Original Constitutions of
the Province of New Jersey*. 1881. Somerville, N.J.: Honeyman, Library Resources,
1970.

Lears, T. J. Jackson. "From Salvation to Self-Realization." In *Culture of Consumption*,
edited by Richard Wrightman Fox and T. J. Jackson Lears, 1–38. New York:
Pantheon, 1983.

————. "Making Fun of Popular Culture." *American Historical Review* 97.5 (December 1992): 1417–26.

————. *No Place of Grace: Antimodernism and the Transformation of American Culture 1880–1920*. New York: Pantheon Books, 1981.

Lebsock, Suzanne. *The Free Women of Petersburg*. New York: W. W. Norton, 1976.

LeFever, Harry. "'Playing the Dozens': A Mechanism of Social Control." *Phylon* 42.1 (1981): 73–85.

Lemke-Santangelo, Gretchen. *Abiding Courage: African American Migrant Women and the East Bay Community*. Chapel Hill: University of North Carolina Press, 1996.

Lemons, J. Stanley. "Black Stereotypes as Reflected in Popular Culture, 1880–1920." *American Quarterly* 29 (Spring 1977): 102–16.

"Letter to the Editor from Detroit." *Christian Recorder*, March 21, 1863.

"Letter to the Editor from Elder Warren." *Christian Recorder*, October 27, 1866.

"Letter to the Editor from Xenia, Ohio." *Christian Recorder*, June 3, 1865.

Levenstein, Harvey. *Revolution at the Table*. New York: Oxford University Press, 1988.

Levine, Lawrence. *Black Culture, Black Consciousness*. New York: Oxford University Press, 1977.

Lewis, David Levering. *When Harlem Was in Vogue*. New York: Oxford University Press, 1981.

Lewis, Edna. *The Taste of Country Cooking*. New York: Alfred Knopf, 1976.

Lichtenstein, Alex. "'That Disposition to Theft, with Which They Have Been Branded': Moral Economy, Slave Management, and the Law." *Journal of Social History* 21 (1989): 413–40.

Light, Ivan, and Carolyn Rosenstein. *Race, Ethnicity, and Entrepreneurship in Urban America*. New York: Aldine de Gruyter, 1995.

Locke, Alain. *The New Negro*. 1925. New York: Athenaeum, 1968.

Logan, Onnie Lee (as told to Katherine Clark). *Motherwit, an Alabama Midwife's Story*. New York: Dutton, 1989.

Longstreet, Augustus Baldwin. *Georgia Scenes: Characters, Incidents, &c. in the First Half Century of the Republic*. 1835. Southern Classics Series. Nashville: Sanders, 1992.

Lott, Eric. "Coon." In *The Oxford Companion to African American Literature*, edited by William Andrews, Frances Smith Foster, and Trudier Harris, 172–73. New York: Oxford University Press, 1997.

————. *Love and Theft: Blackface Minstrelsy and the American Working Class*. New York: Oxford University Press, 1993.

Lott, Tommy. "Black Vernacular Representation and Cultural Malpractice." In *The Invention of Race: Black Culture and the Politics of Representation*, 85–110. Malden, Mass.: Blackwell Publishers, 1999.

————. "Kara Walker Speaks: A Public Conversation on Racism, Art, and Politics." *Black Renaissance/Renaissance Noire* 3.1 (Winter 2000): 69–91.

Loving, Boyce. "Fried Chicken, Ham Once Made Gordonsville Station Famous." *Charlottesville Daily Progress*, November 18, 1955, 2.

Lubiano, Wahneema. "But Compared to What? Reading Realism, Representation, and Essentialism in *School Daze*, *Do the Right Thing*, and the Spike Lee Discourse." *Black American Literature Forum* 25.2 (Summer 1991): 253–82.

MacClancy, Jeremy. *Consuming Culture: Why You Eat What You Eat*. New York: Henry Holt and Company, 1993.

Major, Clarence. *Dictionary of Afro-American Slang*. New York: International Publisher, 1970.

————. *Juba to Jive: Dictionary of African-American Slang*. New York: Penguin Books, 1994.

Majors, D. A. "Big-Headed, Noisy Porter and Waiter Great Race Evil." *Chicago Defender*, January 23, 1915.

Mannix, Daniel P. *Black Cargoes: A History of the Atlantic Slave Trade, 1518–1865*. New York: Viking Press, 1962.

Manring, M. M. *Slave in a Box: The Strange Career of Aunt Jemima*. Charlottesville: University of Virginia Press, 1998.

Mariani, John F., ed. *Dictionary of American Food and Drink*. New Haven: Ticknor and Fields, 1983.

"Marketing—Fruits, Vegetables, Eggs, Poultry, and Butter Continues High." *Richmond Daily Dispatch*, October 7, 1853.

Marshall, Woodville K. "Provision Ground and Plantation Labour in Four Windward Islands: Competition for Resources During Slavery." In *The Slavery Reader*, edited by Gad Heuman and James Walvin, 470–85. London: Routledge, 2003.

Marteena, Constance. *The Lengthening Shadow of a Woman: A Biography of Charlotte Hawkins Brown*. Hicksville, N.Y.: Exposition Press, 1977.

Maslin, Janet. "Fried Chicken with Soul Sees a Family Through." Review of *Soul Food*, directed by George Tillman Jr. *New York Times*, September 26, 1997, E10.

Matthews, Robert Guy. "Advertising: KFC 'Soul' Ad Poses Global Issue." *Wall Street Journal*, January 27, 2005, B6.

McClintock, Anne. "Soft Soaping Empire: Commodity Racism and Imperial Advertising." In *Travellers' Tales: Narratives of Homes and Displacement*, edited by George Robertson, 131–54. London: Routledge, 1994.

McCracken, Grant. "The Evocative Power of Things." In *Culture and Consumption*, 104–17. Bloomington: Indiana University Press, 1990.

McDonald, Roderick A. *The Economy and Material Culture of Slaves: Goods and Chattels on the Sugar Plantations of Jamaica and Louisiana*. Baton Rouge: Louisiana State University Press, 1993.

McDonnell, Lawrence T. "Money Knows No Master: Market Relations and the American Slave Community." In *Developing Dixie: Modernization in a Traditional Society*, edited by Winfred B. Moore Jr., Joseph F. Tripp, and Lyon G. Tyler Jr., 31–44. Westport, Conn.: Greenwood Press, 1988.

McDowell, Deborah. "Negotiating between Tenses: Witnessing Slavery after Freedom—*Dessa Rose*." In *Slavery and the Literary Imagination*, edited by Deborah McDowell and Arnold Rampersad, 144–63. Baltimore: Johns Hopkins University Press, 1989.

McKee, Larry. "Food Supply and Plantation Social Order: An Archaeological Perspective." In *"I, Too, Am America": Archaeological Studies of African-American Life*, edited by Theresa Singleton, 218–39. Charlottesville: University Press of Virginia, 1999.

McMahon, Sarah F. "A Comfortable Subsistence: The Changing Composition of Diet in Rural New England, 1620–1840." *William and Mary Quarterly* 42.1 (January 1985): 26–65.

McQuirter, Marya. "Stirrings: African Americans, Chinese Americans, and Chinese Food in the Early 20th Century." Paper delivered at the annual meeting of the Organization of American Historians, Washington, D.C., April 11–14, 2002.

Mehaffy, Marilyn M. "Advertising Race/Raceing Advertising: The Feminine Consumer (-Nation), 1876–1900." *Signs* 23.1 (1997): 130–74.

Melhem, M. H. "Maud Martha, Bronzeville Boys and Girls." In *Gwendolyn Brooks: Poetry and the Heroic Voice*, 81–95. Lexington: University of Kentucky Press, 1987.

Mercer, Kobena. "Reading Racial Fetishism." In *Welcome to the Jungle*, edited by Kobena Mercer, 173–85. London: Routledge, 1994.

Millner, Denene. "Envisioning a Better Black TV." *New York Daily News*, February 1, 2001, 41.

———. "Health Food for the Soul." Review of *Soul Food*, directed by George Tillman Jr. *Buffalo News*, October 18, 1997, C9.

"Ministers of the South." *Christian Recorder*, February 23, 1867.

Mintz, Sydney. *Sweetness and Power: The Place of Sugar in Modern History*. New York: Penguin Books, 1995.

———. *Tasting Food, Tasting Freedom: Excursions into Eating, Culture, and the Past*. Boston: Beacon Press, 1996.

Mitchell-Kernan, Claudia. "Signifying." In *Mother Wit from the Laughing Barrel: Readings in the Interpretation of Afro-American Folklore*, edited by Alan Dundes, 310–28. Englewood Cliffs: Prentice-Hall, 1973.

"Monday Morning—One Promotional Poster. Two Companies. Lots of Confusion." *Washington Post*, February 11, 2002, E1.

Moore, Stacy Gibbons. "'Established and Well Cultivated': Afro-American Foodways in Early Virginia." *Virginia Cavalcade* 39 (1989): 70–83.

Morgan, Edmund. *American Slavery, American Freedom: The Ordeal of Virginia*. New York: W. W. Norton, 1975.

Morgan, Jo-Ann. "Mammy the Huckster: Selling the Old South for the New Century." *American Art* 9 (Spring 1995): 97–109.

Morgan, Kathryn. *Children of Strangers: The Stories of a Black Family*. Philadelphia: Temple University Press, 1980.

Morgan, Philip D. "The Ownership of Property by Slaves in the Mid-Nineteenth-Century Low Country." *Journal of Southern History* 39.3 (August 1983): 399–420.

———. *Slave Counterpoint: Black Culture in the Eighteenth-Century Chesapeake and Lowcountry*. Chapel Hill: Published for the Omohundro Institute of Early American History and Culture at Williamsburg, Va., by the University of North Carolina Press, 1998.

Morgan, Thomas, and William Barlow. *From Cakewalk to Concert Halls*. Washington, D.C.: Elliot and Clark Publishers, 1992.

Morgen, Sandra, and Ann Bookman. "Rethinking Women and Politics: An Introductory Essay." In *Women and the Politics of Empowerment*, edited by Ann Bookman and Sandra Morgen, 3–29. Philadelphia: Temple University Press, 1988.

Morley, David, and Kuan-Hsing Chen, eds. *Stuart Hall: Critical Dialogues in Cultural Studies*. London: Routledge, 1996.

Morrison, Toni. *Sula*. New York: Penguin Books, 1973.

Morton, Patricia. *Disfigured Images: The Historical Assault on Afro-American Women*. New York: Greenwood Press, 1991.

Mosby, Henry S., and Charles O. Handley. *The Wild Turkey in Virginia: Its Status, Life History, and Management*. Richmond: Pittman-Robertson Projects, 1943.

Moseley, Walter. *Always Outnumbered, Always Outgunned*. New York: W. W. Norton, 1999.

Mullins, Paul. "An Archaeology of Race and Consumption: African-American Bottled Good Consumption in Annapolis, Maryland, 1850–1930." *Maryland Archeology* 32.1 (March 1996): 1–10.

———. *Race and Affluence: An Archaeology of African America and Consumer Culture*. New York: Plenum Publishers, 1999.

Museum of Modern Art. "Conversations with Contemporary Artists, Kara Walker." 1999. <http://www.moma.org/onlineprojects/conversations/kw_f.html> (July 20, 2004).

"Nannie Helen Burroughs Papers." *Quarterly Journal of the Library of Congress* 34.4 (October 1977): 356–60.

Natanson, Nicholas. *The Black Image in the New Deal*. Knoxville: University of Tennessee Press, 1992.

———. "From Sophie's Ally to the White House: Rediscovering the Visions of Pioneering Black Government Photographers." *Prologue: Quarterly of the National Archives and Records Administration* 29.2 (Summer 1997): 141–48.

"National Urban League Discusses Migration Question." *Cleveland Advocate*, December 19, 1916.

Naylor, Gloria. *Bailey's Cafe*. New York: Harcourt, Brace and Jovanovich, 1992.

———. *Linden Hills*. New York: Penguin Books, 1985.

Neely, Barbara. *Blanche among the Talented Tenth*. New York: St. Martin's Press, 1994.

"Negro Eating Houses." *Richmond Daily Dispatch*, May 7, 1853.

Negro Motorist Green Book. New York: Victor H. Green and Company, 1948.

Nelson, Linda Williamson. "Hands in the Chit'lins: Notes on Native Anthropological Research among African American Women." In *Unrelated Kin: Race and Gender in Women's Personal Narratives*, edited by Gwendolyn Etter-Lewis and Michelle Foster, 183–99. New York: Routledge, 1996.

Newhall, Beaumont. *History of Photography, from 1839 to the Present.* New York: Museum of Modern Art, 1982.

Nieves, Angel David. "'We Gave Our Hearts and Lives to It': African American Women Reformers, Industrial Education, and the Monuments of Nation-Building in the Post-Reconstruction South, 1877–1938." Ph.D. diss., Cornell University, 2001.

Nimeiri, Ahmed. "Play in Augustus Baldwin Longstreet's Georgia Scenes." *Southern Literary Journal* 33.2 (Spring 2001): 44–61.

Northrup, David. *Atlantic Slave Trade.* Lexington, Mass.: D. C. Heath, 1994.

"Not 'All Quiet along the Lines.'" *New York Herald*, June 12, 1864.

The Nutty Professor. Directed by Tom Shadyac. Universal, 1996.

"Observer Finds Conditions Far Unsatisfactory: Restaurants, Barber Shops and Taxicabs All Try to Put Something Over." *Chicago Defender*, April 7, 1923.

O'Grady, Lorraine. "Olympia's Maid: Reclaiming Black Female Subjectivity." In *Art, Activism, and Oppositionality: Essays from AfterImage*, edited by Grant H. Kester, 268–86. Durham, N.C.: Duke University Press, 1998.

O'Leary, Elizabeth L. *At Beck and Call: The Representations of Domestic Servants in Nineteenth-Century American Painting.* Washington, D.C.: Smithsonian Institution Press, 1996.

Olmstead, Frederick Law. *A Journey in the Back Country.* 1860. Williamstown, Mass.: Corner House Publishers, 1972.

Olwell, Robert. "'Loose, Idle, and Disorderly': Slave Women in the Eighteenth-Century Charleston Marketplace." In *More Than Chattel: Black Women and Slavery in the Americas*, edited by David Barry Gaspar and Darlene Clark Hine, 97–110. Bloomington: Indiana University Press, 1996.

Omalade, Barbara. *The Rising Song of African American Women.* New York: Routledge, 1994.

O'Malley, Michael. "Specie and Species: Race and the Money Question in Nineteenth-Century America." *American Historical Review* (April 1994): 369–95.

Omi, Michael. "In Living Color: Race and American Culture." In *Signs of Life in the USA: Readings on Popular Culture for Writers*, edited by Sonia Maasik and Jack Solomon, 491–503. Boston: Bedford Books, 1997.

Osirim, Mary J. "The State of Women in the Third World: The Informal Sector and Development in Africa and the Caribbean." *Social Development Issues* 12.2–3 (1992): 74–87.

———. "We Toil All the Livelong Day: Women in the English Speaking Caribbean." In *Daughters of Caliban: Caribbean Women in the Twentieth Century*, edited by Consuelo López Springfield, 41–67. Bloomington: Indiana University Press, 1997.

Ottley, Roi, and William J. Weatherby. "Pig Foot Mary." In *The Negro in New York: An Informal Social History*, 187–88. New York: New York Public Library, 1967.

Paige, Howard. *Aspects of African American Foodways*. Southfield, Mich.: Aspects Publishing Company, 1999.

Parker, Emma. "'Apple Pie' Ideology and the Politics of Appetite in the Novels of Morrison." *Contemporary Literature* 39.4 (Winter 1998): 614–43.

Parker, Idella, and Marjorie Keating. *Idella: Marjorie Rawlings' "Perfect Maid."* Gainesville: University Press of Florida, 1992.

Parren, Thomas. "The Job Ahead." *Survey Graphic* 30.7 (July 1941): 396–98.

Passariello, Phyllis. "Anomalies, Analogies, and Sacred Profanities: Mary Douglas on Food and Culture, 1957–1989." *Food and Foodways* 4.1 (1990): 53–71.

Patton, June O. "Moonlight and Magnolias in Southern Education: The Black Mammy Memorial Institute." *Journal of Negro History* 65.2 (1980): 149–55.

Paynter, Robert, and Randall H. McGuire, eds. *The Archaeology of Inequality*. Oxford: Basil Blackwell, 1991.

Perdue, Charles L., Jr., Thomas E. Barden, and Robert K. Phillips, eds. *Weevils in the Wheat*. Charlottesville: University Press of Virginia, 1976.

Petry, Ann. *The Street*. 1946. New York: Pyramid Books, 1961.

Pieterse, Jan N. *White on Black: Images of Africa and Blacks in Western Popular Culture*. New Haven: Yale University Press, 1992.

Pilgrim, David, curator. *Virtual Jim Crow Museum of Racist Memorabilia*. 1999. <http://www.ferris.edu/news/jimcrow/> (May 8, 2001).

Pillsbury, Richard. *No Foreign Food: The American Diet in Time and Place*. Boulder: Westview Press, 1998.

Pitts, Leonard. "Black History Is No Game of Chicken." *Denver Post*, February 12, 2002, C7.

Pleasants, J. Hall, ed. *Archives of Maryland: Proceedings of the Provincial Court, 1663–1666*. Vol. 49. Baltimore: Maryland Historical Society, 1932.

Poe, Tracy. "Food, Culture, and Entrepreneurship: Strategies and Symbols of Ethnic Identity in Chicago, 1900–1965." Ph.D. diss., Harvard University, 1999.

———. "The Origins of Soul Food in Black Urban Identity: Chicago, 1915–1947." *American Studies International* 37.1 (February 1999): 4–33.

"Pork Chops and Chicken." *Union* 13.8 (February 22, 1919). In *The African American Experience in Ohio, 1850–1920*. Library of Congress American Memory Historical Collections for the National Digital Library.

"Poultry Literature." *Living Age* 30.373 (July 12, 1851): 49–55.

Preston, Beth. "The Functions of Things: A Philosophical Perspective on Material Culture." In *Matter, Materiality, and Modern Culture*, edited by Paul M. Graves-Brown, 22–49. London: Routledge, 2001.

"Program for Married Ladies Afternoon Club of Xenia, Ohio." In *The African American Experience in Ohio, 1850–1920*. Charles Young Collection (LC 83-1), Library of

Congress American Memory Historical Collections for the National Digital
Library.

Pryor, Elizabeth B. *Colonial Poultry Husbandry around the Chesapeake Bay*. Accokeek,
Md.: National Colonial Farm, 1983.

Puckrein, Gary. "Beyond Soul Food—African American Chefs Were Known as Epicure
and Elegant, Skilled Cooks a Hundred Years Ago." *American Visions* 13.4 (August–
September 1998): 39–40.

Pulsipher, Lydia Mihelic. "They Have Saturdays and Sundays to Feed Themselves:
Slave Gardens in the Caribbean." *Expedition* 32.1 (1990): 24–33.

Rachels, David, ed. *Augustus Baldwin Longstreet's Georgia Scenes Completed:
A Scholarly Text*. Athens: University of Georgia Press, 1998.

Rawick, George, ed. *The American Slaves: A Composite Autobiography*. Series 2,
vols. 2–10. Westport, Conn.: Greenwood Press, 1977.

Rawlings, Marjorie Kinnan. *Cross Creek Cookery*. 1942. New York: Fireside Press, 1996.

"Recipes—Economical and Easy to Prepare: Bottle Your Own Fruits and Berries,
Peach Nectar, Baked Onions in Tomato Sauce, 'Etiquette.'" *Baltimore Afro-
American*, September 27, 1930.

"Recipes—Economical and Easy to Prepare: Corn Fritters and Ham en Casserole."
Baltimore Afro-American, September 13, 1930.

"Recipes—Economical and Easy to Prepare: Cucumber Recipes, 'Better Biscuits,'
Swiss Steak, and Stuffed Egg Plant." *Baltimore Afro-American*, September 6, 1930.

Reid, E. Shelley. "Beyond Morrison and Walker: Looking Good and Looking Forward
in Contemporary Black Women's Stories." *African American Review* 34.2 (2000):
313–28.

Reid-Pharr, Robert F. "Black Girl Lost." In *Kara Walker: Pictures from Another Time*,
edited by Kara Walker, Thelma Golden, Robert Reid-Pharr, Annette Dixon, and the
University of Michigan Museum of Art, 27–41. Ann Arbor: University of Michigan
Museum of Art, 2002.

Rice, Sarah. *He Included Me: The Autobiography of Sara Rice*. Edited by Louise
Westling. Athens: University of Georgia Press, 1989.

Ritson, Christopher, Leslie Gofton, and John McKenzie, eds. *The Food Consumer*. New
York: John Wiley and Sons, 1986.

Roberts, John. *From Trickster to Badman: The Black Folk Hero in Slavery and Freedom*.
Philadelphia: University of Pennsylvania Press, 1989.

Roberts, Robert. *The House Servant's Directory*. 1827. New York: M. E. Sharpe, 1998.

Robinson, Nina Hill. *Aunt Dice: The Story of a Faithful Slave*. Nashville: M. E. Church,
South, 1897. Edited by Bethany Ronnberg and Natalia Smith. In *Documenting the
American South: The Southern Experience in Nineteenth-Century America*. Chapel
Hill: Academic Affairs Library, University of North Carolina, 1999. <http://
docsouth.unc.edu/robinsonn/robinson.html> (January 5, 2002).

Rock, Chris. *Bigger and Blacker*. HBO Studios, 1999.

————. *Rock This!* New York: Hyperion, 1997.

Rodgers, Lawrence. "Dorothy West's *The Living Is Easy* and the Ideal of Southern Folk Community." *African American Review* 26.1 (1992): 161–72.

Rodman, Margaret C. "Empowering Place: Multilocality and Multivocality." *American Anthropologist* 94 (1992): 640–56.

Romine, Scott. "Negotiating Community in Augustus Baldwin Longstreet's Georgia Scenes." *Style* 30.1 (Spring 1996): 1–27.

Rooks, Noliwe. *Ladies' Pages: African American Women's Magazines and the Culture That Made Them.* New Brunswick, N.J.: Rutgers University Press, 2004.

Root, Waverly, and Richard deRochement. *Eating in America.* New York: William Morrow, 1976.

Roseberry, William. "Balinese Cockfights and the Seduction of Anthropology." *Social Research* 49 (1982): 1013–28.

Salley, Alexander S., Jr., ed. *Narratives of Early Carolina, 1650–1708.* New York: Charles Scribner's Sons, 1911.

Samford, Patricia. "The Archaeology of African-American Slavery and Material Culture." *William and Mary Quarterly*, 3rd ser., 53.1 (January 1996): 87–114.

Savage, Beth, ed. *African American Historic Places.* Washington, D.C.: National Park Service for the National Trust for Historic Preservation, The Preservation Press, 1994.

Savage, W. Sherman. "Slavery in the West." In *African American Frontier*, edited by Monroe L. Billington and Roger Hardaway, 7–23. Boulder: University of Colorado Press, 1998.

Sawyer, Gordon. *The Agribusiness Poultry Industry: The History of Its Development.* New York: Exposition Press, 1971.

Scanlon, Jennifer. *Inarticulate Longings: The "Ladies' Home Journal," Gender, and the Promises of Consumer Culture.* New York: Routledge, 1995.

Schenone, Laura. *A Thousand Years over a Hot Stove.* New York: W. W. Norton, 2003.

Schlereth, Thomas. "Material Culture Studies in America, 1876–1976." In *Material Culture Studies in America*, 1–75. Nashville: American Association for State and Local History, 1982.

Schulman, Norma. "The House That Black Built: Television Stand-Up Comedy as Minor Discourse." *Journal of Popular Film and Television* 22.3 (Fall 1994): 108–15.

Schwarz, Philip. "Crime." In *Dictionary of Afro-American Slavery*, edited by Randall Miller and John David Smith, 158–63. Westport, Conn.: Greenwood Press, 1988.

————. "Slaves and Crime: A Problem of Evidence." In *Twice Condemned: Slaves and the Criminal Laws of Virginia, 1705–1865*, 35–58. Baton Rouge: Louisiana State University Press, 1988.

Shange, Ntozake. Foreword. In *If I Can Cook, You Know God Can*, xi–xiv. New York: HarperCollins, 1998.

Shaw, Gwendolyn DuBois. "Final Cut." *Parkett* 59 (2000): 129–32.

————. *Seeing the Unspeakable.* Durham, N.C.: Duke University Press, 2004.

Shaw, Harry. "Maud Martha." In *Gwendolyn Brooks*, 164–75. Boston: G. K. Hall, Twayne, 1980.

Sheets, Hilarie. "Cut It Out! Kara Walker Plays Havoc with Racial Stereotypes." *ARTNews* (April 2002): 126–29.

Shockley, Ann Allen. "The Black Lesbian in American Literature: An Overview." *Conditions* (1979): 133–42.

———. *Say Jesus and Come to Me*. New York: Avon, 1982.

———. "Soon There Will Be None." *African American Review* 28.3 (August 1994): 441–46.

Shuman, Amy. "The Rhetoric of Portions." In *Foodways and Eating Habits*, edited by Michael Owens Jones, B. Guililano, and R. Krell, 72–80. Los Angeles: California Folklore Society, 1981.

Singleton, Theresa, ed. *The Archaeology of Slavery and Plantation Life*. Florida: Academic Press, 1985.

———. *"I, Too, Am America": Studies in African American Archaeology*. Charlottesville: University of Virginia Press, 1994.

Sitton, Thad. *Harder Than Hardscrabble: Oral Recollections of the Farming Life from the Edge of the Texas Hill Country*. Austin: University of Texas Press, 2003.

Smart-Grosvenor, Vertamae. *Vibration Cooking, or The Travel Notes of a GeeChee Girl*. Garden City, N.Y.: Doubleday, 1970.

Smiley, Tavis. "Barbershop Controversy." *Tavis Smiley Show*, September 26, 2002.

Smith, Andrew, ed. *The Oxford Encyclopedia of Food and Drink in America*. New York: Oxford University Press, 2004.

Smith, Barbara. "African American Lesbian and Gay History: An Exploration." In *The Truth That Never Hurts: Writings on Race, Gender, Freedom*. 1998. <http://www.hsph.harvard.edu/grhf/WoC/sexualities/smith.html> (January 15, 2002).

Smith, Page, and Charles Daniel. *The Chicken Book*. San Francisco: North Point Press, 1982.

Smith, Sandra, and Earle H. West. "Charlotte Hawkins Brown." *Journal of Negro Education* 51.3 (1982): 191–206.

Smith, Stephen. "Food for Thought: Comestible Communication and Contemporary Southern Culture." In *American Material Culture*, edited by Edith Mayo, 208–17. Bowling Green, Ohio: Bowling Green State University Press, 1984.

Smitherman, Geneva. "'The Chain Remain the Same': Communicative Practices in the Hip Hop Nation." *Journal of Black Studies* 28.1 (September 1997): 3–25.

Sobel, Mechel. *The World They Made Together: Black and White Values in Eighteenth-Century Virginia*. Princeton, N.J.: Princeton University Press, 1987.

Soderbergh, Peter A. "Bibliographical Essay: The Negro in Juvenile Series Books, 1899–1930." *Journal of Negro History* 58.2 (April 1973): 179–86.

Sontag, Susan. "The Image World." In *Visual Culture: The Reader*, edited by Jessica Evans and Stuart Hall, 80–94. London: Sage Publications, 2001.

Soul Food. Directed by George Tillman Jr. 20th Century Fox, 1997.

Southern, Eileen, ed. *Readings in Black American Music*. New York: W. W. Norton, 1971.

Spivey, Diane M. *The Peppers, Cracklings, and Knots of Wool Cookbook: The Global Migration of African Cuisine*. New York: State University of New York Press, 1999.

Stamp, Kenneth. *The Peculiar Institution: Slavery in the Antebellum South*. New York: Vintage Books, 1989.

St. Columbia, Joe. "Pasquale's Tamales: A Portrait of Ethnic Assimilation." Paper delivered at the Southern Foodways Symposium, Oxford, Miss., October 1999.

Steady, Filomina Chase. *The Black Woman Cross-Culturally*. Cambridge, Mass.: Schenkman Publishing Company, 1981.

St. George, Robert Blair. *Material Life in America, 1600–1800*. Boston: Northeastern University Press, 1982.

Storms, Jill. "Church to Have Soul Food Benefit." *Hartford Courant*, November 16, 1986, B1.

Stowe, Harriet Beecher. *Uncle Tom's Cabin*. Reprint. New York: Signet Books, 1966.

Streeter, Sebastian, ed. *Papers Relating to the Early History of Maryland*. Freeport, N.Y.: Books for Libraries Press, 1972.

Strother, David Hunter [Porte Crayon]. "Virginia Illustrated: Adventures of Porte Crayon and His Cousins." *Harper's New Monthly Magazine*, January 1856, 176–82.

Stroyer, Jacob. *Sketches of My Life in the South. Part I. 1849–1908*. Salem: Salem Press, 1879. Edited by Lee Ann Morawski and Natalia Smith. In *Documenting the American South: The Southern Experience in Nineteenth-Century America*. Chapel Hill: Academic Affairs Library, University of North Carolina, 2001. <http://docsouth.unc.edu/neh/stroyer/stroyer.html> (January 10, 2002).

Sudarkasa, Niara. *Where Women Work: A Study of Yoruba Women in the Marketplace and in the Home*. Ann Arbor: University of Michigan Press, 1973.

Tanner, Bonnie. *The Entrepreneurial Characteristics of Farm Women*. New York: Garland Publishing, 1999.

Tate, Greg. "Discussion—The Production of Black Popular Culture." In *Black Popular Culture: A Project by Michelle Wallace*, edited by Gina Dent, 264–78. Seattle: Bay Press, 1992.

Taylor, Joe Gray. *Eating, Drinking, and Visiting in the South: An Informal History*. Baton Rouge: Louisiana State University Press, 1982.

Thaggert, Miriam. "Divided Images: Black Female Spectatorship and John Stahl's *Imitation of Life*." *African American Review* 32.3 (Autumn 1998): 481–91.

Thompson, Deborah. "Blackface, Rape, and Beyond: Rehearsing Interracial Dialogue in *Sally's Rape*." *Theatre Journal* 48.2 (May 1996): 123–39.

Titus, Mary. "Groaning Tables and Spit in the Kettles: Food and Race in the Nineteenth-Century South." *Southern Quarterly* 20.2–3 (1992): 13–21.

Tokarev, S. A. "Toward a Methodology for Ethnographic Study of Material Culture." In *American Material Culture and Folklife: A Prologue and Dialogue*, edited by Simon Bronner, 77–89. Ann Arbor: UMI Research Press, 1992.

Toombs, Charles P. "The Confluence of Food and Identity in Gloria Naylor's *Linden Hills*: 'What We Eat Is Who We Is.'" *CLA Journal* 37.1 (1993): 1–18.

Toussaint-Samat, Maguelonne. *History of Food*. Cambridge, Mass.: Blackwell, 1994.

"Travelers' Aid Is Helpful at Stations and Docks—Migrants from South." *Baltimore Afro-American*, November 22, 1930.

Turner, Darwin. "Paul Laurence Dunbar: The Rejected Symbol." *Journal of Negro History* 52.1 (January 1967): 1–13.

Turner, Patricia. "Ambivalent Patrons: The Role of Rumor and Contemporary Legend in African American Consumer Decisions." *Journal of American Folklore* 105 (Fall 1992): 424–41.

———. *Ceramic Uncles and Celluloid Mammies: Black Images and Their Influence on Culture*. New York: Anchor Books, 1994.

———. "Church's Fried Chicken and the Klan: A Rhetorical Analysis of Rumor in the Black Community." *Western Folklore* 46 (1987): 294–306.

———. *I Heard It through the Grapevine: Rumor in African American Culture*. Berkeley: University of California Press, 1993.

Turner, Patricia, and Gary Alan Fine. *Whispers on the Color Line: Rumor and Race in America*. Berkeley: University of California Press, 2001.

Unger, Miles. "Contested Histories." *Art New England* 19.4 (June–July 1998): 29.

"University Tea Room—Special Easter Menu." *Chicago Defender*, March 3, 1928.

Valentine, Valca. "The Road to Freedom: Price Davis' Journey Leads to New York . . . and Back Again." *Charlotte Observer*, December 9, 1989.

Villarosa, Linda, ed. *Body and Soul: The Black Women's Guide to Physical Health and Emotional Well-Being*. New York: Harper Perennial, 1994.

Wade, John Donald. *Augustus Baldwin Longstreet*. Athens: University of Georgia Press, 1969.

Wadelington, Charles, and Richard Knapp. *Charlotte Hawkins Brown and Palmer Memorial Institute*. Chapel Hill: University of North Carolina Press, 1999.

"Waiter Carrier Recalls the 'Fried Chicken' Days." *Orange County (Va.) Review*, July 9, 1970, B7–B8.

Walker, Alice. *The Color Purple*. New York: Pocket Books, 1982.

———. *In Search of Our Mothers' Gardens*. San Diego: Harvest/HBJ Book, 1983.

Walker, Hamza. "Nigger Lover, or Will There Be Any Black People in Utopia?" *Parkett* 59 (2000): 152–65.

Walker, Juliet K. *The History of Black Business in America*. New York: Twayne Publishers, 1998.

———. "Racism, Slavery, and Free Enterprise: Black Entrepreneurship in the United States before the Civil War." *Business History Review* 60 (Autumn 1986): 343–82.

———. "Trade and Markets in Precolonial West and West Central Africa: The Cultural Foundations of the African American Business Tradition." In *A Different Vision: African American Economic Thoughts*, edited by Thomas Boston, 206–52. New York: Routledge, 1996.

Walker, Kara. "Kara Walker's Response." *International Review of African American Art* 15.2–3 (1998): 48–49.

Wallis, Brian. "Black Bodies, White Science: The Slave Daguerreotypes of Louis Agassiz." *American Art* 9 (Summer 1995): 38–61.

Walsh, Lorena. "The Chesapeake Slave Trade: Regional Patterns, African Origins, and Some Implications." *William and Mary Quarterly*, 3rd ser., 58.1 (January 2001): 138–65.

———. *From Calabar to Carter's Grove: The History of a Virginia Slave Community.* Charlottesville: University Press of Virginia, 1997.

Walsh, Lorena, Ann Smart Martin, and Joanne Bowen. *Provisioning Early American Towns: The Chesapeake—A Multidisciplinary Case Study.* Williamsburg, Va.: Colonial Williamsburg Foundation, 1997.

Warner, Mark. "Ham Hocks: Examining the Role of Food in African American Identity." *Archaeology* (November–December 2001): 48–52.

Washington, Booker T. *Up from Slavery.* In *Three Negro Classics*, 23–206. New York: Avon Books, 1965.

Washington, Mary Helen. "Gwendolyn Brooks." In *Black-Eyed Susans and Midnight Birds: Stories by and about Black Women*, edited by Mary Helen Washington, 111–14. New York: Anchor Books, 1990.

———. *Invented Lives: Narratives of Black Women, 1860–1960.* New York: Anchor Books, 1987.

———. "Teaching *Black-Eyed Susans*: An Approach to the Study of Black Women Writers." In *But Some of Us Are Brave*, edited by Gloria T. Hull, Patricia Bell Scott, and Barbara Smith, 208–17. Old Westbury, N.Y.: Feminist Press, 1982.

Weems, Robert, Jr. *Desegregating the Dollar: African American Consumerism in the Twentieth Century.* New York: New York University Press, 1998.

Wegmann, Jessica. "'Playing in the Dark' with Longstreet's *Georgia Scenes*: Critical Reception and Reader Response to Treatments of Race and Gender." *Southern Literary Journal* 30.1 (Fall 1997): 13–26.

Welling, William. *Collector's Guide to Nineteenth-Century Photographs.* New York: Macmillan, 1975.

Wells, Donna M. "Visual History and African American Families of the Nineteenth-Century." *Negro History Bulletin* 59.4 (October–December 1996): 19–22.

Wells-Barnett, Ida B. *On Lynchings: Southern Horrors, A Red Record, Mob Rule in New Orleans.* 1900. Salem, N.H.: Ayer Company York, 1991.

West, B., and B. X. Zhou. "Did Chickens Go North? New Evidence for Domestication." *Journal of Archaeological Science* 15 (1988): 515–33.

West, Cornel. *Race Matters.* Boston: Beacon Press, 1993.

West, Dorothy. *The Living Is Easy.* 1948. New York: Feminist Press, 1982.

White, Deborah Gray. *Ar'n't I a Woman? Female Slaves in the Plantation South.* New York: W. W. Norton, 1985.

———. *Too Heavy a Load: Black Women in Defense of Themselves, 1894–1994*. New York: W. W. Norton, 1999.

White, Joyce. *Soul Food: Recipes and Reflections from African American Churches*. New York: HarperCollins, 1998.

White, Shane. "'We Dwell in Safety and Pursue Our Honest Callings': Free Blacks in New York City, 1783–1810." *Journal of American History* 75.2 (September 1988): 445–70.

White, Shane, and Graham White. *Stylin': African American Expressive Culture*. Ithaca: Cornell University Press, 1998.

Whitehead, Tony L. "Festive Occasions and Network Dynamics in a Southern Community." Unpublished manuscript, 1988.

———. "In Search of Soul Food and Meaning: Culture, Food, and Health." In *African Americans in the South: Issues of Race, Class, and Gender*, edited by Hans A. Baer and Yvonne Jones, 94–110. Athens: University of Georgia Press, 1992.

———. "Sociocultural Dynamics and Food Habits in a Southern Community." In *Food in the Social Order: Studies of Food and Festivities in Three American Communities*, edited by Mary Douglas, 97–142. New York: Russell Sage Foundation, 1984.

Whitehead, Tony, and Psyche Williams-Forson. "African American Foodways." In *The Encyclopedia of Food and Culture*, edited by Solomon Katz and William Woys Weaver, 425–37. New York: Charles Scribner Sons, 2002.

Williams, A. Wilberforce. "Talks on Preventive Measures, First Aid Remedies, Hygienics, and Sanitation: Eating and Exercise." *Chicago Defender*, July 3, 1919.

———. "Talks on Preventive Measures, First Aid Remedies, Hygienics, and Sanitation: The Proper Foods." *Chicago Defender*, July 5, 1919.

Williams, Brett. "Why Migrant Women Feed Their Husbands Tamales: Foodways as a Basis for a Revisionist View of Tejano Family Life." In *Ethnic and Regional Foodways in the United States*, edited by Linder Keller Brown and Kay Mussell, 113–27. Knoxville: University of Tennessee Press, 1984.

Williams, Susan. *Savory Suppers and Fashionable Feasts: Dining in Victorian America*. Knoxville: University of Tennessee Press, 1996.

Williams-Forson, Psyche. "Suckin' the Chicken Bone Dry: African American Women, History and Food Culture." In *Cooking Lessons: The Politics of Gender and Food*, edited by Sherrie Inness, 200–214. Lanham, Md.: Rowman and Littlefield, 2001.

Willis, Deborah, ed. *Picturing Us: Africana American Identity in Photography*. New York: New York Press, 1994.

Willis-Kennedy, Deborah. *Reflections in Black: A History of Black Photographers, 1840 to the Present*. New York: W. W. Norton, 2000.

Willis-Thomas, Deborah. *Black Photographers, 1840–1940: An Illustrated Bio-bibliography*. New York: Garland Publishers, 1985.

Witt, Doris. *Black Hunger: Soul Food and America*. New York: Oxford University Press, 1999.

———. "In Search of Our Mother's Cookbooks: Gathering African-American Culinary Traditions." *IRIS: A Journal about Women* (Spring–Summer 1991): 22–27.

———. "Soul Food: Where the Chitterling Hits the (Primal) Pan." In *Eating Culture*, edited by Ron Scapp and Brian Seitz, 258–87. Albany: State University of New York Press, 1998.

———. "What Ever Happened to Aunt Jemima? Black Women and Food in American Culture." Ph.D. diss., University of Virginia, 1995.

Wollan, Laurin A., Jr. "Questions from a Study of Cockfighting." In *The Cockfight*, edited by Alan Dundes, 81–93. Madison: University of Wisconsin Press, 1994.

Wollenberg, Skip. "KFC Creates Animated Colonel for New Ads." *Naples Daily News*, September 8, 1998. <http://www.naplesnews.com/today/business/kfc.htm> (February 5, 2000).

Women's Era 2.10 (February 1896): 7:

Woods, E. M. *The Negro in Etiquette: A Novelty.* St. Louis: Baxon and Skinner, 1899.

Woods, Peter. *Black Majority.* New York: W. W. Norton, 1974.

Woods-Brown, Letitia. *Free Negroes in Washington, D.C., 1790–1846.* New York: Oxford University Press, 1972.

Worth, Alexi. "Black and White and Kara Walker." *Art New England* (December 1995–January 1996): 26–27.

Wright, Louis B. *Newes from the New-World.* San Marino, Calif.: Huntington Library, 1946.

Wright, Richard. *12 Million Black Voices.* New York: Thunder's Mouth Press, 1941.

Wright, Richardson. *Hawkers and Walkers in Early America.* Philadelphia: J. B. Lippincott Company, 1927.

Yeingst, William, and Lonnie Bunch. "Curating the Recent Past: The Woolworth Lunch Counter, Greensboro, North Carolina." In *Exhibiting Dilemmas: Issues of Representation at the Smithsonian*, edited by Amy Henderson and Adrienne Kaeppler, 143–56. Washington, D.C.: Smithsonian Institution Press, 1997.

Yentsch, Anne E. *A Chesapeake Family and Their Slaves: A Study in Historical Archaeology.* Cambridge: Cambridge University Press, 1994.

———. "Gudgeons, Mullet, and Proud Pigs: Historicity, Black Fishing, and Southern Myth." In *The Art and Mystery of Historical Archaeology*, edited by Mary Beaudry and Anne Yentsch, 283–314. Boca Raton: CRC Press, 1992.

———. "Hot, Nourishing, and Culturally Potent: The Transfer of West African Cooking Traditions to the Chesapeake." *Sage* 9.2 (Summer 1995): 15–29.

Yoder, Don. "Historical Sources for American Foodways Research and Plans for an American Foodways Archive." *Pennsylvania Folklife* 20 (Spring 1971): 16–29.

Zafar, Rafia. "The Signifying Dish: Autobiography and History in Two Black Women's Cookbooks." *Feminist Studies* 25.2 (1999): 449–509.

Bhabha, Homi, 214

Big Mama's House (film), 188

Birth of a Nation (film), 48

Black churches: black women's role in, 3, 225 (n. 4); chicken associated with, 126, 136, 144; and travel, 127; and food events, 144–46, 148–51, 154–61; and patriarchal hypocrisy, 146, 256 (n. 24); and stereotypes of preachers, 152, 153, 154, 256 (n. 31)

Black churchwomen: and signifying, 8, 135, 137, 141, 148–49, 220; and African American food traditions, 97–98; and self-definition, 134; and competition, 135, 136, 146, 148–49, 248 (n. 37), 254 (n. 2); and class issues, 140–41; and inviting preacher for dinner, 144–46, 148, 154–56, 160; and sexuality and spirituality, 146, 148, 151, 160, 255–56 (n. 23)

Black Codes, 47

Black communities: tensions within, 80, 97, 98, 101–2, 103, 104, 248 (n. 36); agricultural extension service in, 82, 245 (n. 7); and food sharing, 83–85, 122, 159, 160, 245 (n. 13); and cooking as menial labor, 114; and retaliatory power of, 121, 122; ethnicities of, 171, 258 (n. 21); and in-group joking, 217; and diabetes, 260–61 (n. 3)

Black dandy: and class issues, 50–51, 238 (n. 18)

Black expressive culture, 109, 178, 216, 217, 237 (n. 12), 251 (n. 1), 252 (n. 21)

Black farmers, 82–84, 245 (nn. 7, 8)

Black feminist consciousness: and African American food traditions, 1, 4, 80, 105, 187; and black people/chicken relationship, 5; and African American literature, 151–52; and self-definition, 227 (n. 16)

Black identity: and African American

cookbooks, 3–4; in Reconstruction era, 46–47; and stereotyped visual and material images, 46–47, 57; and migration, 98; problematizing of, 101; shared identities, 131; and black women's cookery, 133; and black churches, 136–37; and Walker, 203–4, 210, 218; heterogeneous nature of, 209, 213, 214, 216; and popular culture, 217; and blackness, 217, 225 (n. 1)

Black men: stereotypical images of, 5, 37, 38, 39, 43–44, 47, 48–49; and popular culture, 7; as threat to race relations, 7, 37, 43; agency of, 29, 102; and railroad employment, 32; and Zip Coon image, 38, 42, 50–51; financial success of, 41; employment in Reconstruction era, 46; as sexual predators, 48, 55; and cooking chicken as demasculation, 79, 243 (n. 72); and etiquette, 100–101, 249 (n. 50); and cooking skills, 137; and playing the dozens, 137; signifying on black women, 148, 162, 183; and representations of black women, 162, 177, 178–84, 190–91, 193, 260 (n. 2), 261–62 (n. 8), 262 (n. 14); and self-expression, 181

Black minstrelsy, 5, 59, 61, 62, 64–65, 227 (n. 14), 236 (n. 2), 240 (n. 36), 267 (n. 41)

Black people/chicken relationship: and agency, 2; and stereotyped visual and material images, 2, 5, 20, 38, 44, 48–50, 53–55, 95, 220, 223; and blacks as chicken lovers, 2, 35, 53, 62, 171–72, 184; and black women's agency, 2, 37, 38; and advertising, 5; and class issues, 7, 14, 50; history of, 14; and power, 14, 37, 50, 53–54, 142; and racial discourse, 14, 79; and marketplace, 14–15, 21, 228 (nn. 3, 4); and accusations of thievery, 26–27; and Civil War reporting, 44; and black man as sexual predator, 48–49; and Dunbar, 59–62, 64; and West, 70–71; and fried chicken in southern cuisine, 77; and gender and cooking chicken, 79; continuity of, 128; and representation of black women, 165; and racism, 171, 218, 220, 223

Black press, 98–99

Black reformers, 80, 93, 94, 97, 98, 102–3, 111

Black women: chicken's role in lives of, 1–2, 79; and African American cookbooks, 3–4; role in food production, 4; black migrant women, 7, 9; health of, 8, 184–85, 186, 187, 188, 189–90, 194–95, 261 (n. 6); and marketplace, 14, 20, 21–24; exploitation during slavery, 43; in Reconstruction era, 45–46; working-class black women, 80, 81, 85, 93, 96, 98, 99, 103, 110, 113; upper-class black women, 80, 109; middle-class black women, 81, 94, 96, 133; and chicken raising, 82–83; heterogeneity of, 85; complexity of, 87; black women's work, 88, 91, 96, 109; and acts of dissembling, 95; objectification of, 104; sexual lives of, 104, 124; and cross-cutting relationships, 104, 249 (n. 52); devaluation of, 104, 249 (n. 54); and travel constraints, 114–17, 124–25, 251–52 (n. 9); and vicarious travel, 125–26; black men's representations of, 162, 177, 178–84, 190–91, 193, 260 (n. 2), 261–62 (n. 8), 262 (n. 14); others knowing and thinking for, 165; and self-representation, 187; and claiming/disavowing relationship with chicken, 201; and assimilated woman, 249 (n. 53). *See also* Black churchwomen; Images of black women; Self-definition

Black women's agency: and relationship with chicken, 2, 37, 38; and cooking skills, 6; and marketplace, 23–24; and victimization, 29; and black women's work, 90–91; and resistance to white male power, 120; and health, 194–95

Black women's voices: and self-expression, 2; and African American food traditions, 4, 224; eclipse of, 8, 190; and images of black women, 86; and signifying, 162; and self-discovery, 165; silencing of, 183–84, 191, 197, 198

Blues, 103, 123, 124, 125, 133, 160

Boardinghouses, 19

Bobo, Jacqueline, 91, 261 (n. 4)

Bogle, Donald, 238 (n. 18)

Bolzius, Johann Martin, 15

Boomerang (film), 176

Boondocks, The (comic strip), 211, 214

Bowen, Joanne, 230 (n. 15)

Braudel, Fernand, 24

Bremer, Frederika, 31, 234 (n. 58)

Brooks, Gwendolyn, 100, 110–12, 151, 250 (nn. 59, 63)

Brooks, Sara, 144–45, 146, 256 (n. 36), 260 (n. 37)

Brown, Charlotte Hawkins, 93, 94–95, 97, 98, 102, 104, 109, 111, 247 (nn. 25, 28)

Brown, James, 124

Brown, Julia, 222, 234 (n. 60)

Brown, Lizzie, 222

Brown-Douglas, Kelly, 221, 255 (n. 23)

Buick, Kirsten, 201–2

Burnham, George P., 244 (n. 3)

Burns, Richard Allen, 243 (n. 72)

Burroughs, Nannie Helen, 93, 96–97, 98

Burton, Annie, 27–28

Burwell, Carter, 17

Butts, Calvin, 215

Byrd, William, 15, 237 (n. 5)

Bythewood, Reggie Rock, 267 (n. 41)

and marketplace, 20–21; challenging of, 69

self-definition, 134; and playing the dozens, 137; and signifying, 141; and servings of chicken, 178–80, 260 (n. 37)

Gender malpractice: and hegemonic cultures, 8; and misrepresentations, 8, 165, 181; and black men's representations of black women, 162, 177, 178–84, 190–91, 193, 260 (n. 2), 261–62 (n. 8), 262 (n. 14); and whites' appropriation of African American food traditions, 170; and Walker's imagery, 218

Georgia Scenes (Longstreet), 13–14, 21–23, 228 (n. 1), 232 (n. 31), 233 (nn. 33, 34)

Ghetto as adjective: definition of, 138, 139, 255 (n. 12); and class issues, 140, 143, 213

Gilkes, Cheryl Townsend, 144, 221, 261 (n. 5)

Gilmore, Gloria, 234–35 (n. 62)

Goldberg, Whoopi, 257 (n. 4)

Golden, Thelma, 208

Gomez, Michael, 19

Good Times (TV show), 188, 261 (n. 5)

Gordonsville, Virginia, 31–35, 234 (n. 60), 235 (n. 66)

Government: and blacks' political involvement, 47–48

Graham, Maxon Lester, 66, 70, 241 (n. 51)

Grandy, Charles, 30

Gray, Herman, 216, 217

Greenlee, Sam, 253 (n. 28)

Griffin, Farah Jasmine, 249 (n. 50)

Griffith, D. W., 48

Grosvenor, Vertamae, 258 (n. 20)

Guinea fowl, 16, 229–30 (n. 11)

Hackfighting, 40, 236–37 (n. 5)

Haley, Alex, 38, 39–44, 50, 236 (nn. 3, 5)

Hall, Irma P., 188, 198

Hall, Robert, 168, 258 (n. 12)

Hall, Stuart, 202, 208, 256 (n. 35)

Handley, Charles, 229 (n. 6)

Harlem Renaissance, 100

Harris, Carmen, 245 (n. 7)

Harris, Jessica, 168, 257–58 (n. 12)

Harris, Lillian, 248 (n. 43)

Harris, Trudier, 188, 189, 260 (n. 1)

Harris-Lopez, Trudier, 216 (n. 4), 262 (n. 13), 263–64 (n. 25)

Hattie's Inn, 32, 234–35 (n. 62)

"Haunted Oak, The" (Dunbar), 62, 240 (n. 39)

Hawkins, Roy, 66–71

Health regulations, 34

Heart disease, 194

Hermmans, Martha, 148

Hess, Karen, 168, 197, 258 (n. 12), 263 (n. 22)

Heyward, Dubose, 249–50 (n. 56)

Hill, Anita, 215

Hilliard, Sam, 244 (n. 4)

Hine, Darlene Clark, 95

Hip-hop community, 5, 227 (n. 14)

Hobsbawn, Eric, 237 (n. 14)

Hodder, Ian, 35

Hogan, Ernest, 59, 240 (n. 35)

Homophobia, 152, 154

hooks, bell, 262–63 (n. 16), 263 (n. 25)

Hopkins, Pauline, 3, 100, 248 (n. 37)

Hughes, Langston, 100–101, 151, 181, 249 (n. 48); and Jesse B. Semple/Simple, 100–105

Hughes, Marvalene H., 146

Hunter, Alberta, 124

Hurston, Zora Neale, 6–7, 135, 165–66, 213, 217, 259 (n. 33), 260 (n. 44)

I Know Why the Caged Bird Sings (Angelou), 115–16

Images of black women: and cooking skills, 2, 77, 79, 80, 86, 87–89, 108, 110, 189, 244 (n. 1); and mammy figure, 7, 80, 86, 89, 108–9, 110, 188–89, 204,

Naylor, Gloria, 142–44

Neely, Barbara, 253 (n. 28)

"Negro Love Song, A" (Dunbar and Cook), 64

Negro Motorist Green Book, 119, 252 (n. 17)

"Negro song" genre, 59

Nelson, Linda Williamson, 225 (n. 5)

"New Negro" era, 59, 98

Nimeiri, Ahmed, 22–23, 232 (n. 31), 233 (n. 33)

Nutty Professor, The (film), 176, 188

Objects: manipulated in power relations, 6, 35, 37, 49; cultural biography of, 72, 242 (n. 59); as social signs, 141–42; and signifying, 142–43, 256 (n. 35); and meanings, 184–85; and cultural identity, 254–55 (n. 6)

Olmstead, Frederick Law, 31

Olwell, Robert, 24

Oral traditions, 3, 80, 135

Outsider/in group status, 129, 253–54 (n. 31)

Palmer Memorial Institute (PMI), 94, 247 (n. 25)

Parker, Idella, 166–67, 169, 170, 171, 257 (nn. 7, 9)

Parks, Rosa, 210, 216, 267 (n. 39)

Parren, Thomas, 72

Paynter, Robert, 6

Phifer, Mekhi, 192

Photography: staging of, 54, 55, 238–39 (n. 24); and stereotyped images, 54–55; as entertainment, 56, 239 (n. 29); and black photographers, 57; motivations for posing for, 57–58

Plantation life: plantation kitchens, 2; and slaves' responsibility for chickens, 16, 17, 31, 232 (n. 27); and planters' attribution of slaves' thievery, 25, 29;

and economic exchange, 25–26; and black women cooking chicken, 77

Play, 22–23, 232 (n. 31)

Plessy v. Ferguson, 61

Poe, Tracy, 248 (n. 34)

Popeye's, 128, 175

Popular culture: and stereotyped visual and material images, 2, 55, 56, 65, 78; and malignment of black men, 7; and Reconstruction era, 35; Dunbar's response to, 59; and symbolic language of food, 92; and cooking, 110; and images of black women, 111; and black identity, 217; and black women in underground economy, 252 (n. 18). *See also* Film; Media

Porches, 177, 259 (n. 33)

Post, Emily, 94, 104

Poultry industry, 72, 81, 82, 242 (n. 61), 244 (n. 3), 244–45 (n. 5)

Powell, John, 27

Power: chicken as tool of, 2; heterogeneous nature of, 6, 86; and signifying, 6–7, 148, 151; black women's exercise of, 7, 21, 23–24; and black people/chicken relationship, 14, 37, 50, 53–54, 142; and blacks as primary chicken merchants, 20, 21; and play, 23, 233 (n. 33); and blacks' theft of food, 28; and photographic images, 54, 55; and food as politics, 69; and self-definition, 91–92; of food, 101, 151, 154, 158, 159–60

Power delineations, 2, 8

Power relations: objects manipulated in, 6, 35, 37, 49; and resistance, 6, 91, 120; relative nature of, 23–24, 78; black men as threat to, 37; in Reconstruction era, 47; and food traditions, 104; destabilization of, 119–22; and food events, 157

Progressive Era, 65, 80

Pryor, Elizabeth B., 229 (n. 10)
Pryor, Richard, 257 (n. 4)
Public/private self, 141–42

Quaid, Randy, 5
Quamino, Charity Duchess, 231–32
  (n. 23)
Quilting patterns, 237 (n. 8)

Race fetishism, 56
Race relations: black men as threat to,
  7, 37, 43; and Longstreet, 13–14; and
  marketplace, 18, 20, 21, 23, 24; and
  capitalism, 24–25; and thievery, 25, 29,
  235–36 (n. 68); separateness between
  races, 41, 159; and cockfighting, 42;
  in Reconstruction era, 47; and racial
  intolerance, 58–59; and racial tension,
  61; and self-definition, 91; and African American literature, 119–23; and
  gender malpractice, 170; and Walker,
  212
Racial discourse, 14, 79
Racial prejudice, 94
Racism: and stereotyped visual and
  material images, 2, 37; and cultural
  malpractice, 8; of Black Codes, 47;
  commodities of, 55, 56–57; and Dunbar, 62, 64–65; and Coon Chicken
  Inn, 69; and travel, 132; and eating
  chicken at work, 141, 213; latent practices of, 152; and misrepresentations,
  166; of cookbooks, 169; and black
  people/chicken relationship, 171, 218,
  220, 223; and blacks as chicken lovers,
  171–72, 184; and Rock, 184; historical
  context of, 200; and sexuality, 207, 213;
  and class issues, 212–13; and Walker,
  212, 213, 215; of Longstreet's *Georgia
  Scenes*, 233 (nn. 33, 34)
Rainey, Ma, 124
Randolph, Mary, 168, 258 (n. 15)

Rappers, 135, 254 (n. 2)
Rawlings, Marjorie, 166–68, 170, 171, 176,
  191
Reconstruction era: and popular culture, 35; representations of blacks
  in, 35, 37, 38–40, 44–45, 47, 48; and
  antiblack sentiments, 39; and economic freedom/independence, 45–46;
  black identity in, 46–47; and national
  identity, 51
Reeder, Bernice, 115, 251 (n. 4)
Reid-Pharr, Robert, 210, 266 (nn. 26, 28)
Rent parties, 123–24
Representations: in African American
  cookbooks, 4; and black women's
  self-definition, 6; of blacks in Reconstruction era, 35, 37, 38–40, 44–45, 47,
  48; of waiter carriers, 35, 235 (n. 66);
  and black reformers, 80, 93, 111; black
  men's representation of black women,
  162, 177, 178–84, 190–91, 193, 260
  (n. 2), 261–62 (n. 8), 262 (n. 14); and
  black women's relation to chicken,
  165; in media, 172–73, 177, 188–89, 261
  (n. 5); encumbrances of, 187; ambivalent nature of, 200; dilemma of, 217–
  18. *See also* Images of black women;
  Misrepresentations; Stereotyped
  visual and material images
Resistance: chicken as tool of, 2; and
  power relations, 6, 91, 120; and
  marketplace, 23–24; and stereotyped
  images, 57; and Dunbar, 60, 61, 62, 64,
  240 (n. 36); and travel, 117, 132; and
  black churchwomen, 151; and misrepresentations, 166; and rejecting
  dominant scripts, 209
Restaurants, 19, 66–72, 99, 118–19, 241
  (n. 51)
Rice, Sarah, 85, 101
Riggs, Marlon, 209, 236 (n. 2)
Roberts, John, 30

Robinson, Nina Hill, 204–6

Rock, Chris, 173, 176–84, 191, 257 (n. 4), 259 (n. 32), 259–60 (n. 35), 260 (n. 41)

Rodgers, Lawrence, 107

Rolle, Esther, 261 (n. 5)

Roots (Haley), 38, 39–44, 50, 236 (nn. 3, 5)

Rumors, 175–76

Saar, Betye, 215–16, 266 (n. 36)

Sanders, Tammy, 260 (n. 41)

Savage, W. Sherman, 234 (n. 57)

Say Jesus and Come to Me (Shockley), 151–61

Scanlon, Jennifer, 246 (n. 17)

Schwarz, Philip, 234 (n. 48)

Segregation: food as marker of, 78, 243 (n. 70); and travel, 115, 116–17, 118, 127, 130, 132, 251 (n. 7)

Self-definition: and food traditions, 2–3, 91, 96, 100, 103, 105, 108, 110, 111, 113, 225 (n. 3); complexities of, 6; and class issues, 7, 103–4, 107–8; and gender malpractice, 8; and images of black women, 91–92, 100, 108, 221; and self-valuation, 96, 108; and migration, 96, 128; and travel, 128, 134; and signifying, 152, 155, 162; and cooking skills, 161; and Walker, 218; importance of, 220–21; and black feminist consciousness, 227 (n. 16); and identity construction, 255 (n. 6)

Self-denigration, 8

Self-expression: chicken as tool of, 2, 80; and black churchwomen, 8, 136; and class issues, 80–81; and images of black women, 86, 92; and black men, 181; and verbal play, 181–82; and signifying, 260 (n. 44)

Self-valuation: and self-definition, 96, 108; and food traditions, 110; and travel, 132

Sexism: and Shockley's *Say Jesus and*

Come to Me, 152; and Rock, 180, 181, 184; and Longstreet's *Georgia Scenes*, 233 (nn. 33, 34)

Sexual politics: and cockfighting, 42–44

Sharecropping, 58

Sharpton, Al, 216

Shaw, Gwendolyn DuBois, 200, 264 (n. 2)

Shockley, Ann Allen, 151–61, 256 (nn. 31, 32)

Shoe-box lunches, 1, 113, 116, 118, 125–26, 131, 251 (n. 8), 253 (n. 24)

Shuman, Amy, 158, 257 (n. 37)

Shurz, Carl, 47

Signifiers: and stereotyped images, 51, 53–54, 55; and advertising, 87–90; ambiguity of, 90–91; food as signifier of civility and respectability, 98; clothing as, 150–51, 152, 153

Signifying: and power, 6–7, 148, 151; and black churchwomen, 8, 135, 137, 141, 148–49, 220; and oral traditions, 135; and meanings, 137, 138, 139; definition of, 137–38, 228 (n. 19); and troping, 138–39, 162; and class issues, 140, 141, 142–43, 160; and African American literature, 142–44, 151–60, 165–66; culinary signifying, 151; and self-definition, 152, 155, 162; and hospitality, 159; and cultural work, 161–62; and recipes, 170; and black comedians, 177; role of, 182; and shared experiences, 217; and self-expression, 260 (n. 44)

Simpson, O. J., 210, 215

Sketches of My Life (Stroyer), 30

Slave narratives, 3, 25, 28–29, 206

Slaves and slavery: and black people/chicken relationship, 14–15; slaves' responsibility for chicken, 16, 17, 31, 232 (n. 27); and slaves' experience with marketplace, 16–24, 230 (nn. 13, 15), 231 (nn. 17, 18, 19); and capitalism,

24–25; thievery of, 25–29; and accusations of thievery, 26–27; and Haley, 38; free blacks' association with slaves, 41, 233 (n. 45); economic impact of ending, 47; and black women cooking chicken, 77; and African American food traditions, 196, 197; and Walker, 204–5, 207, 208–9, 210, 216, 264 (n. 12); and African American literature, 265 (n. 24)

Slave trade, 16, 230 (n. 12)

Smiley, Tavis, 213

Smith, Bessie, 124, 160

Smith, Clara, 124

Smith, Page, 236 (n. 3)

Smitherman, Geneva, 178, 182, 254 (n. 2)

Soul Food (film): images of black women in, 8, 186, 187–88, 189, 190–92, 195, 261 (n. 4), 261–62 (n. 8), 262 (nn. 9, 10); and African American food traditions, 185, 186, 193–98, 199, 200, 263 (n. 21)

Specifying, 135

Spivey, Diane, 168, 169

Spoonbread and Strawberry Wine (Darden and Darden), 118

Steele, Wilmer, 244 (n. 5)

Stereotyped visual and material images: and black people/chicken relationship, 2, 5, 20, 38, 44, 48–50, 53–55, 95, 220, 223; of black men, 5, 37, 38, 39, 43–44, 47, 48–49; and KFC advertising, 5, 227 (n. 13); and chicken stealing, 45, 47, 49, 53–56; and black identity, 46–47, 57; of black women, 47, 77, 80, 86, 191, 193, 243 (n. 68), 244 (n. 1), 262 (n. 11); social ideologies embedded in, 49, 51, 53, 55–57, 237 (n. 14), 239 (n. 30); and blacks in compromised positions, 56–57; and symbolic slavery of Old South imagery, 58–59; and Dunbar, 62; and Coon Chicken Inn, 70–71; and eating chicken at work,

141, 213; and preachers, 152, 153, 154, 256 (n. 31); of African American food traditions, 171–77, 184–85, 196, 258 (n. 22), 258–59 (n. 25), 263 (n. 19); and Walker, 204, 210, 264 (n. 12); meanings of, 218

Stowe, Harriet Beecher, 243 (n. 68)

Stroyer, Jacob, 30

Subsistence economy, 81, 82

Sula (Morrison), 116–18

Survivalisms, 37

Swift, Elsie, 234 (n. 61)

Swift, Laura, 1

Tamales, 123, 220, 252–53 (n. 22), 258 (n. 17)

Taylor, Clarice, 188

Taylor, Frances, 1

Terrell, Robert H., 95

Their Eyes Were Watching God (Hurston), 165–66, 259 (n. 33), 260 (n. 44)

Therapeutic ethos, 53, 55, 238 (n. 21)

Thievery: as disposition of blacks, 25, 26; and race relations, 25, 29, 235–36 (n. 68); motivations for, 26, 27–29, 234 (n. 48); and victimization, 29; anecdotes of, 29–31; and whites' participation with blacks, 30–31; stereotyped images of, 57; meanings associated with, 235–36 (n. 68); of whites, 235–36 (n. 68). *See also* Chicken stealing

Thomas, Clarence, 215

Till, Emmett, 120

Tillman, George, Jr., 8, 185, 186–87, 189–91, 193–200, 210, 214, 260 (n. 2), 262 (nn. 12, 14), 263 (n. 21)

Train: and Gordonsville, Virginia, 1, 32, 86; and segregation, 115, 116–17; and African American literature, 120; and black women's vicarious travel, 125–26; and shoe-box lunches, 125–26, 131. *See also* Travel

RR

ML

8/06